Praise for Steven Levingston's

Little Demon in the City of Light

"Levingston has unearthed a whopper of a story, and lovingly crafted a dense, lyrical yarn that hits the true-crime trifecta of setting, story and so-what. Such books remind us that times may change, but the human animal does not." —*The New York Times*

"A terrific story well told." —*The Seattle Times*

"Readers are well-served by [Levingston's] reimagining of this amazing true story." —*Minneapolis Star Tribune*

"Levingston's smartly chipper prose and fine attention to detail . . . add an entertaining and authentic sensibility to this re-creation of a culture, a crime, and the first time an accused murderer had put forward a hypnotism defense." —*Booklist*

"Lovingly constructed. . . . Immerses the reader in a period whose newfound obsessions—science and pseudoscience of the mind, criminal forensics, mass media, the macabre, and fame—have a seminal connection to our own time." —*Publishers Weekly*

"A well-constructed, informative work by a talented author." —*Kirkus Reviews*

Steven Levingston

Little Demon in the City of Light

A veteran journalist who has worked in Beijing, Hong Kong, and Paris, along with assignments in New York, Chicago, and Washington, Steven Levingston is the nonfiction book editor of *The Washington Post*. He lives in Bethesda, Maryland, with his wife and two children.

Also by Steven Levingston

The Whiz Kid of Wall Street's Investment Guide: How I Returned 34 Percent on My Portfolio, and You Can, Too (with Matt Seto)

Historic Ships of San Francisco

Little Demon
in the City of Light

A TRUE STORY of MURDER
in BELLE ÉPOQUE PARIS

Steven Levingston

ANCHOR BOOKS
A Division of Random House LLC
New York

FIRST ANCHOR BOOKS EDITION, MARCH 2015

The Library of Congress has cataloged the Doubleday edition as follows:
Levingston, Steven.
Little demon in the city of light: a true story of murder and mesmerism
in Belle Époque Paris / Steven Levingston. — First edition.
p. cm.
Includes bibliographical references.
1. Murder—France—Paris—Case studies.   2. Gouffé, Toussaint-Augustin,
1840–1889.   3. Eyraud, Michel, 1843–1891.   4. Bompard, Gabrielle, 1868–1920.
5. Paris (France)—Social life and customs—19th century.
I. Title.
HV6535.F8P364 2014   64.152'3092—dc23   2013020525

Anchor Books Trade Paperback ISBN: 978-0-307-95030-7
eBook ISBN: 978-0-385-53604-2

Book design by Maria Carella
Author photograph © Suzanne Allard Levingston

www.anchorbooks.com

Printed in the United States of America
10 9 8 7 6 5 4 3 2 1

FOR SUZANNE, KATIE, AND BEN

Little Demon in the City of Light

Prologue

The experiments were chilling. In one, a woman was hypnotized and ordered to shoot a local government official. When handed a gun, she walked directly up to him and pulled the trigger, firing a blank she imagined was a real bullet. After the official—playing along—fell to the floor, she stood calmly over him hallucinating that he was dying in a pool of blood. Under interrogation she admitted to the crime with utter indifference, parroting what the hypnotist-researcher had planted in her head: that she simply didn't like the man. In another experiment, a hypnotized woman was told to dissolve a white powder she believed was arsenic in a glass of water and offer it to a man nearby. If anyone were to ask, she was to say the glass contained sugar water. She did exactly as she was told, and the man quaffed the tainted drink. After she was brought out of her trance, she dutifully followed the hypnotist's final command: She told her interrogator that she didn't remember a thing; she hadn't given a drink to anyone. Most disturbing, she couldn't name anyone who had directed her to do anything.

In the late nineteenth century, doctors, scientists, and professors were desperate to answer an alarming question: Could a person be persuaded under hypnosis to commit a terrible crime, even murder? At risk was the very foundation of law and order. If researchers discovered that hypnotic crime was possible, then who was safe? Thievery, assault, arson, and murder—secretly directed by evil hypnotists—became nightmarish possibilities. And what if a madman launched an army of hypnotized automatons on a presidential palace? Revolution was not out of the question.

In the Paris of the 1880s, the setting for our tale, hypnosis was in its heyday. Doctors had corralled its mysterious powers to treat a range of complaints. In medical clinics, doctors softly encouraged their patients: "Look at me. Think of nothing but sleep . . . sleep. Your lids are closing. Your arms feel heavy. You are going to sleep . . . sleep . . . sleep." While concentrating on the doctor's voice, the patient stared at a bright light, or gazed into his eyes, or watched his hands pass several times in front of her face until she drifted off. When she left the clinic, she was free of back pain, or menstrual cramps, or chronic headaches.

Hypnotism was an ornament of the city's daily life. Society ladies, demonstrating that they were au courant, hosted hypnotism salons. Amateurs learned the techniques and threw their friends into trances. Traveling hypnotists wowed audiences with astonishing stage shows. The famous traveling hypnotist Professor Donato put his bejeweled assistant through the human-plank trick, in which she would lie between two chairs stiff as a board, defying gravity. He hypnotized audience volunteers and had them disrobe to their under-clothing and dance in imaginary ponds and bite into potatoes that they believed were apples. Europeans delighted in the cures and the endless amusement. But the excitement was tinged with fear. No one really knew how powerful hypnosis was, and whether or not it could lend itself to nefarious uses. Courts already had ruled on a few instances of hypnosis-assisted rape. In one notorious case in 1879, a dentist in Rouen was sentenced to ten years in prison for having sex with a twenty-year-old patient he had hypnotized in the dental chair. No court, however, had yet seen a case in which an accused murderer blamed a hypnotist for his crime. That was about to change.

The belle époque, stretching from 1871 to the start of World War I in 1914, is remembered for its pleasures and eccentricities, but it was also a time of magnificent ambition and spectacle and unrelenting dread. The Eiffel Tower went up on the Champ de Mars in 1889, at the time the tallest man-made structure in the world, and served as the centerpiece of the Paris International Exposition, then the larg-est world's fair in history. Paris was a stage, and its inhabitants were actors, dressed for show and behaving outrageously. There was the theatrical star Sarah Bernhardt, who kept a pet tiger and slept with a coffin at the foot of her bed. There were the throngs who strolled past the recently dead at the Paris morgue as if viewing a museum exhibit; the French had a weakness for the macabre, which Sigmund Freud, a young, cocaine-dependent medical student discovered as he explored the city. At night, bizarre indulgences awaited in the music and dance halls: At the Folies-Bergère there was a boxing match between a man and a kangaroo, and at the Moulin Rouge a sidesplitting act by a vaudevillian in a red silk coat and white butterfly tie, who sang "Au clair de la lune" through his anus.

Although the period before World War I was an era of champagne bubbles, men in top hats and monocles, and carefree strolls along the boulevards, it was not the golden age people wished to remember years after the carnage. As the historian Barbara Tuchman put it, "It was not a time exclusively of confidence, innocence, comfort, stability, security and peace. Our misconception lies in assuming that doubt and fear, ferment, protest, violence and hate were not equally present."

Hypnotism reflected not only the era's giddiness but also the unease. France's Republican government was fragile, anarchist rage was brewing, syphilis mercilessly attacked the well-born and the underclass alike. Newspapers sensationalized the bloodiest crimes; in some neighborhoods, people went to bed worrying that teenage thugs would slash their throats while they slept. Parisians looked upon the present with uncertainty and gazed toward the new century with a fear that their glorious nation was sliding into degeneracy. Crime under hypnosis added to French anxieties about the fragility of modern life. But just how serious a danger it posed was a matter of intense debate.

A battle raged between two opposing camps, one based in Paris, the other some two hundred and forty miles east in the city of Nancy. Comforting assurances came from the world's foremost neurologist, Dr. Jean-Martin Charcot, and his disciples at the Salpêtrière Hospital in the thirteenth arrondissement. The forbidding Charcot, described as "half-Dante, half-Napoleon," had a smooth beardless face, deep-set dark eyes, and long hair combed back over his head. He asserted that the outcries over hypnotic crime were exaggerated: An individual in a trance could not be coerced into abandoning her moral resolve and led into deviant behavior. Charcot's research revealed that there were limits to what a hypnotized person would do—dancing like a silly drunk was one thing, murder quite another.

Charcot had bestowed upon hypnotism a new respectability, rescuing it from the scientific hinterlands. Most scientists had denied legitimacy to hypnotism for a hundred years after the early practitioner Dr. Franz Anton Mesmer destroyed its credibility with his wild claims of medical success. Mesmer was a brilliant eccentric who dressed in a lilac silk coat and believed that a universal magnetic fluid flowed through everything, pulling on the tides, on human blood, on the nerves, and that he could heal suffering by controlling the magnetic currents inside his patients. His powerful personality attracted a passionate following; and his influence was so profound that hypnosis is still sometimes called mesmerism. His claims of curing epilepsy, paralysis, and even blindness were ultimately insupportable, however, and he died alone in disrepute, his only companion being his pet canary which, according to rumor, had been trained to drop lumps of sugar into his coffee.

Only a scientist of unassailable credentials could have healed the wounds Mesmer inflicted on hypnotism, and now Charcot's doctrines on the science of hypnosis were accepted as dogma throughout Europe. But on the question of hypnotic crime, he faced a challenge. Professors at the University of Nancy were undaunted by his authority or by the sovereignty of Paris. Among their ranks was the leading expert on hypnotic crime, a professor of law named Jules Liégeois who had poured his findings into a seminal book on the subject in 1884. His conclusions left no doubt about where he stood. A hypnotized individual, in Liégeois's view, lost her faculties of reason, judgment, morality, and will and became "the plaything of a fixed idea," in essence, an automaton acting at the whim of the hypnotist. In such a state, she would carry out a criminal suggestion unhesitatingly and then forget who had placed the notion in her head. The hypnotic subject in Liégeois's scenario is no more culpable than a pistol or knife; the responsible party is the hypnotist who used this human weapon to carry out his evil deed. "All conscience has disappeared in a hypnotized subject who has been forced to commit a criminal act," Liégeois asserted. "Only he who has given the suggestion is guilty, and only he should be pursued and punished."

The battle between the Paris and Nancy camps might have remained just an academic debate if it weren't for a petite twenty-one-year-old with gray-blue eyes and an adventurous spirit. Gabrielle Bompard was a troubled young woman from a wealthy family in Lille who ran away to Paris in 1888. She was neglected at home: Her mother had died when Gabrielle was five; soon afterward her father sent her away to relatives and convents and boarding school. By the time she returned home at age eighteen, she was a volatile, independent-minded teenager in love with fashion and eager for the spotlight. She was similar to her mother, whom she'd barely known and who was described as "subject to brusque and incomprehensible changes in character."

Gabrielle also was an astounding hypnotic subject. When Professor Donato brought his show to Lille, she sneaked away from home and volunteered to go onstage. She also had a secret lover who had learned the hypnotist's techniques and kept her in a near-perpetual trance. The more she was hypnotized, the easier she fell under the powers. Dr. Sacreste, the Bompard family doctor, had discovered Gabrielle's special skill one day in the winter of 1887 when he came to look after an ailing housekeeper. When conversation around the dinner table turned to the popularity of hypnosis, Gabrielle's father, Pierre, challenged the doctor to try it out on his children. Gabrielle's younger brother resisted; he just laughed at the doctor's hocus-pocus, refusing to succumb to the powers.

But Gabrielle was another story entirely. She fell directly into a trance, deeply and fully, with a submissiveness that was startling to behold. She was, Sacreste later recalled, the most extraordinary hypnotic subject he had ever encountered. To test the depth of her spell, the doctor handed her a glass of water and told her it was champagne. No sooner had she taken a few sips than she showed "all the symptoms of drunkenness," he said. On a subsequent visit, he hypnotized her again before removing a wart. "I put her to sleep and suggested to her that she wouldn't feel a thing," he said. During the procedure she showed no sign of pain. The doctor was convinced that her trance was sincere. "It was impossible," he concluded, "to believe she was simulating."

Pierre Bompard was won over to the miracle of hypnosis and asked Sacreste if he couldn't tame Gabrielle's obstreperous personality in a few sessions. Sacreste tried but his efforts were fruitless. Conditions deteriorated at home for Gabrielle, and she begged her lover to rescue her but he would not take her in. Finally she ran off to Paris with her lover's warning fresh in mind. "You have a temperament," he told her, "that finds pleasure in a labyrinth of intrigue. Be careful—because you will be a victim again and again."

Within a year of her arrival Gabrielle took part in a horrific crime, and she became the heroine of a grand Parisian diversion, the darling of the cheap, mass-circulation newspapers. Hers was a tale perfectly rendered for the real-life stage of the belle epoque: an outlandish murder, an amusing and clever gumshoe, a worldwide hunt for the killers, a series of dead ends, and then a remarkable turn of events, aided by a breakthrough in forensic science and capped by a courtroom drama that riveted the nation—and the world. None of it would have taken place had this young bourgeois woman from Lille not been remarkably susceptible to the influence of hypnosis—had she not been, as they say of people easily induced, like "clay in the hands of a potter."

Here, finally, was a real-world test for the competing theories of murder under hypnosis. Gabrielle's case brought the top academics into the courtroom for a showdown over their jealously guarded beliefs. The law professor Liégeois argued on behalf of the defense: that Gabrielle was a hypnotic puppet who acted against her will and therefore was without responsibility. The state brought in experts aligned with the great neurologist Charcot to argue that hypnotism was not to blame; the fault, they contended, lay with the young woman herself: She was an amoral killer, and must answer for her crime with an early-morning march to the guillotine. This courtroom confrontation represented the first time an accused murderer had put forward a hypnotism defense. The outcome of Gabrielle's case could set a legal precedent and influence crime and justice for years to come.

It was a long journey to the courtroom. When *Le Figaro* first reported in July 1889 that a wealthy gentleman, a widower with a slight limp and an unquenchable libido, had vanished, his absence was just another curious incident in the messy life of Paris. There was no inkling that a year and a half later this small mystery would attract the world's attention as a sensational hypnotic crime and turn Gabrielle into the prototype of a celebrity killer.

Her case spilled far beyond its French borders, as she and her accomplice fled Paris for New York, Vancouver, and San Francisco.

Gabrielle filled headlines across the United States as Americans avidly followed the detectives' chase and later the trial, amused by the spectacle but also uneasy about her hypnotism plea. If the French courts ruled in Gabrielle's favor, then murderers across the world would have a cunning new strategy for escaping justice.

Chapter 1

In Paris in 1889, even murder was a form of theater. And what Michel Eyraud had in mind was a brilliant bit of staging: a sexual farce full of suspense and melodrama and then a tragic denouement. Eyraud had a cockeyed sense of himself. In his invented world he fancied himself a romantic, a flaneur at his ease strolling along the boulevards, a raconteur idling at Maxim's, a ladies' man, a conjurer who glided like the devil between the light and the dark. And pushed to the edge, he could kill with style.

He and his mistress had acquired all the props they needed for the evening's performance. They'd been to London and bought some rope, a pulley, a silk *cordelière* for use as a noose, and a trunk so big it could hold a human. They'd rented an apartment under an alias on a quiet side street near the *grands boulevards,* taking rooms on the ground floor so no one below could hear the thud of a body hitting the floor.

Gabrielle was a skilled seamstress, a craft she learned during her years in the convents, and for two nights she had sat by the window stitching two pieces of burlap together to form a human-size bag. He was the show's director and set designer. On this Friday evening, July 26, he climbed onto a chair in the sitting-room alcove, with his mistress spotting him, and hammered the pulley into a crossbeam; he ran the rope up through the pulley and down again to the floor. He installed a curtain across the alcove and placed a wood chair next to the dangling rope. Here was his hiding spot, where he was to lie in wait. He pushed a chaise longue next to the alcove, then scurried about creating a romantic atmosphere for the killing. He lowered the gas jets, lit candles, and arranged cognac and biscuits on a silver tray.

And again he instructed his actress in her scene, how to speak her lines, how to slide the red silk *cordelière* off her dressing gown and secretly turn it into a noose. Gabrielle was the star of this show, a petite twenty-one-year-old, the sexual bait tossed before a genial man of wealth. She had been on her own in Paris for a year—about a hundred and forty miles from her home in Lille—and now she was desperate and broken, a near-hysterical runaway, a femme fatale, lethal to her lovers.

———

A short distance away, on boulevard Montmartre, Toussaint-Augustin Gouffé sat with three friends on the terrace of Café Véron sipping absinthe. His silk hat was impeccably shined, his beard was well-groomed, and his shirt bore his monogram. Gouffé was a bailiff, who, in France, was not the stolid uniformed officer known to sit in American courtrooms but a professional of a higher order: a business figure who handled legal matters and was somewhat comparable to an attorney. The man looked rich, satisfied, and untouchable.

But he had his vulnerabilities: A careful eye watching him on the street might detect his slight limp, and a casual ear did not miss his high-pitched voice and minor lisp. Lifting his glass to his lips, he revealed manicured fingernails and on his pinkie was a treasure that marked him as a target for murder: a gold ring with a sapphire mounted in a halo of diamonds.

Outside on the boulevard the world of Paris circulated: dandies and wits, mesdames in plumed hats, messieurs in white gloves, demi-mondaines in heavy face paint and feather boas. Across from Café Véron was the stone-arch entrance to the Musée Grévin, the famed wax museum. Inside stood molded kings and queens in breathtaking three-dimensional realism. Down the block, at the Théâtre des Variétés, the comic opera *La Fille à Cacolet* was on the boards. Earlier in the year, high society had flocked to the premier of *L'Affaire Édouard,* the latest work by the playwright Georges Feydeau, who was establishing himself as the master of stage farce.

On this Friday, the rain had pelted off and on, muddying the thoroughfare but not intimidating the giant Percherons thundering along, drawing the double-decker Impériale omnibuses. On the boulevard, as one historian fondly recalled, there was a "bedlam of noise . . . a cacophony of hoofbeats, whirling wheels, rattling pushcarts, cries of hawkers and the occasional neigh of an impatient horse."

Paris was an urban carnival, bold in its amusements: music halls, café concerts, rickety roller coasters. A guidebook promised, "Paris is the only corner of the world where pleasure is a social necessity, a normal state." Tourists expected a bacchanal, flooding in to escape rigid Germany, stuffy Britain, puritan America. To the outside world Paris floated on a champagne bubble. "It is we," declared a French journalist, "who have infected the world with gaiety, this brightness."

But the dark also beckoned: Paris swayed between delight and doom. Since the Prussians humiliated France on the battlefield in 1870, capturing Louis-Napoléon, annexing Alsace-Lorraine, and precipitating a bloody civil rebellion, the country had slept fitfully, tossing and turning over a grim question: Was French glory a thing of the past? The indignity of defeat lingered. The scars were written on the drunks in the alleyways, the blank-eyed syphilitics in the insanity wards, and the anxious faces of the politicians. The Third Republic teetered perennially on the edge of collapse.

The gaiety of Paris, this brightness, could suddenly go dark, as could the electric lights just beginning to glimmer across the city. And no one was immune—not presidents, generals, famous authors, or the rich. Though he looked untouchable, Gouffé was as exposed to the dangerous uncertainties as the next man. He too was dancing on a volcano. And like his countrymen, all he could do before stumbling into the abyss was to raise a glass and laugh with friends, in the spirit of the Montparnasse poet who cried: "People must make merry before dying."

As Gouffé dug into his meal—pasta with carrots and green beans—one of his companions, a newspaperman, enlivened the table with a tale of his experiences among the anarchists. Although the anarchists were feared for their bold ultimatums—vowing to deliver "the bomb that cleanses" and "the knife that purifies"—so far they were waging mostly a war of words. Their ranks were growing, but the waves of deadly bombings were still on the horizon. The early warnings came in published manifestos and in promises to slit the throats of government ministers. Gouffé and his dinner companions might nod somberly at the threat but were confident they themselves stood at a safe remove.

After dinner, Gouffé's friends invited him for a stroll around the International Exposition, the massive world's fair sprawling along the Champ de Mars, the quai d'Orsay, and the Trocadéro gardens, more than two hundred acres of food, fun, and eye-popping mechanical inventions. The French were throwing a months-long party to mark the hundredth anniversary of the 1789 revolution but purposely played down the historic meaning—the overthrow and execution of royalty—to keep from offending the many kings and queens still sitting atop their thrones throughout Europe. Entertainment overwhelmed the politics: The very symbol of royal tyranny, the Bastille, was re-created not as the feared political prison it once was but as an amusement park with rides and colored fountains and shops tended by merchants in eighteenth-century costumes.

Apparently still touchy about the march of history, no monarch in Europe except the King of Belgium sent a representative to the exposition's opening ceremonies on May 6, 1889, prompting the president of France, Sadi Carnot, to declare pointedly in his dedication speech: "Our dear France . . . has the right to be proud of herself and to celebrate the economic and political centenary of 1789 with her head held high."

While his speech chided absent royalty, it also was meant to buck up his own beleaguered nation, which only the previous evening had barely escaped calamity. Setting off from the Élysée palace for an exposition ceremony at Versailles, President Carnot had ridden in an open landau through streets packed with revelers. As he moved along the rue du Faubourg-Sainte-Honoré, a deranged shopkeeper from the French colony of Martinque, believing he had been mistreated by the government, fired a single shot at Carnot's carriage, missing the president but delivering the message of national insecurity.

The opening went on as scheduled, and the exposition supplied spectacle on a grand scale. Fairgoers were awed by the largest enclosed building in the world, the iron-framed Gallery of Machines, which was possibly the noisiest too, with sixteen thousand machines clacking and clattering at once. In modern American terms, it was more than four football fields long and one football field wide. Among the many marvels inside was Thomas Edison's phonograph. The device so fascinated the men of the French Academy that they recorded the voices of their most gloried members so that years in the future, as a reporter put it, one would be able to hear "the dead speak."

The exposition was a contest of extremes. E. Mercier Champagne, which claimed to have the largest cellars in the Champagne region, displayed what was billed as the single largest cask in the world, a gargantuan oak barrel dwarfing the average man and containing enough wine for two hundred thousand bottles. On July 14, the centennial of Bastille Day, two thousand musicians performed a *concert gigantesque.* Another day, twelve hundred musicians played for an audience of twenty thousand in the Tuileries Garden; before the performance, thirty thousand pigeons were released into the air.

The most glorious achievement was Gustave Eiffel's iron latticework tower, created specially for the exposition as an emblem of French science and industry. It shot a thousand feet into the sky, higher than any other man-made structure in the world—so high it afforded a new perspective. "At a height of 350 feet," said a visitor ascending to the top, "the earth is still a human spectacle—an ordinary scale of comparisons is still adequate. But at 1,000 feet, I felt completely beyond the normal condition of experience."

Eiffel's tower was a marvelous but unsettling lurch into the modern world, a symbol of progress but also an inescapable reminder that humankind was hurtling toward the unknown. A fairgoer standing high atop the tower couldn't help but sense the loss of the Old World and shiver at what lay ahead.

Gouffé declined his companions' invitation to the exposition. He kept silent about his planned rendezvous for the evening, a lark that had come his way only that afternoon in a flurry of fortuitous coincidence. After lunching at home on rue Rougemont, as was his custom, Gouffé was strolling along boulevard Poissonnière on his way to his office when he ran into Michel Eyraud, a recent boulevard acquaintance. Eyraud burst into a display of theatrical surprise over their chance meeting, then informed his friend of some news: He was finished with his young mistress Gabrielle Bompard. Gouffé had had his eye on Gabrielle and listened with interest as Eyraud explained that she was now a free woman. And by the way, Eyraud snickered suggestively, Gouffé must have realized, hadn't he, that Gabrielle found him attractive? Then with a flourish of male bonhomie, Eyraud offered his mistress to Gouffé, giving him her address: 3, rue Tronson du Coudray.

Just the previous day, Gouffé had dined with the lovers at a boulevard brasserie, and Gabrielle had whispered in Eyraud's absence that she was fed up with the brute, and she was leaving him. Now, to Gouffé's delight, the breakup had come to pass.

Bidding his friend farewell, Gouffé continued on his way along boulevard Poissonnière and as he turned onto rue Montmartre, he was surprised a second time when Gabrielle herself appeared before him. He wasted no time.

"So is it true, what you confided to me?" Gouffé asked her.

"Who told you?"

"I just saw him," Gouffé told her. "He even gave me your address."

"Ah!" Gabrielle exclaimed. So the plot was proceeding exactly as planned. "Then come see me tonight," she told her admirer, setting the date for eight o'clock. As Gouffé sauntered off she called after him: "Don't forget: 3, rue Tronson du Coudray."

On the pavement outside Café Véron, Gouffé and his dinner companions had said their adieus, and his friends had climbed into a cab to join the slow procession to the fairgrounds. "Everyone is heading for the Exposition or is coming back or returning again to it," the writer Guy de Maupassant grumbled. "In the streets, the carriages form an unbroken line like cars of a train without end."

While mobs converged on the Champ de Mars, Gouffé found a cab and went his own way. Along the streets France was dressed up for a celebration. The national tricolor flag decorated lampposts and building windows, and centennial bunting draped the façades of department stores and hotels.

Gouffé's destination was a one-block-long side street not far from the *grands boulevards,* named after a minor figure of the French Revolution. Tronson du Coudray was one of two lawyers given the impossible task in 1793 of defending the deposed French queen, Marie Antoinette. But no legal magic could avert the queen's fate and she—along with her husband, King Louis XVI—lost her head to the guillotine. For his efforts Tronson du Coudray was hustled off to prison.

The apartment building at number 3 was an unremarkable three-story structure, its narrow windows overlooking the hushed street.

Gouffé rolled up at eight fifteen. No one saw him climb out of the carriage, no one saw him go toward the ground-floor apartment, no one saw the young woman in a dressing gown greet him at the door, so tiny was she that her head reached only as high as his chest. No one ever saw Toussaint-Augustin Gouffé alive again.

Chapter 2

At the Gouffé home on rue Rougemont, the cook Matilde Pagnon was the first to notice something was amiss. Matilde had worked for Gouffé for seven years and was acquainted with his idiosyncrasies. On Friday evenings, she knew, he didn't dine at home, preferring to take his meal with friends on the *grands boulevards* before setting off for one of his amorous liaisons.

That was all well and good by Matilde's reckoning, for Gouffé kept up appearances and nearly always was back in his bed by morning so he could have breakfast with his two daughters, aged nineteen and twenty. A third daughter, age sixteen, was at school in a convent. Gouffé's wife had died eight years earlier and Gouffé, with assistance from Matilde and a housekeeper-governess, Marie-Léontine Bullot, had brought the girls up on his own. If he needed a woman's embrace now and then, Matilde wouldn't begrudge him it, for he was punctual and proper and a doting father. Whenever he was delayed, he sent a telegram informing his girls and the household. But on this particular day, Saturday, July 27, 1889, no communication came.

When he failed to appear for breakfast, Matilde ventured into his bedroom only to find the bed undisturbed. Wishing to protect his daughters and preserve appearances, she devised a ruse: She threw the bed into disarray, opened the drapes, filled the basin with soapy water, and generally disrupted his belongings; then she informed the girls that their father had gone out early that morning on business. By lunchtime, however, her façade was crumbling and, unable to keep her worries to herself, she visited Gouffé's brother-in-law around the corner on rue de Trévise. Louis-Marie Landry speculated that after his night out Gouffé had gone directly to his office and was perhaps snoozing there before starting work as usual on Saturday morning.

Hurrying to the office at 148, rue Montmartre, Landry found Gouffé's clerks at their desks, awaiting the boss's arrival. Nothing was amiss. Indeed, sitting in plain view in a box on a countertop was fourteen thousand francs that Gouffé apparently had neglected to lock away in the safe the previous night.

But the husband of the building's concierge had some curious news for Landry. Claude Joly was standing in for his wife the previous night when at about nine o'clock a man in an overcoat and hat rang the bell and came up the stairs quickly two at a time, with a key chain jiggling in his hands. The man unlocked the office door and disappeared inside. Although Joly did not get a good look at him, he assumed the man was Gouffé, who sometimes worked at night. When the visitor came down a few minutes later, Joly offered him a bundle of mail and was surprised to see that the man was not Gouffé. Who are you? Joly asked, to which the visitor replied gruffly that he worked in the office. Then he vanished down the stairs and disappeared into the street.

Joly rarely assumed his wife's duties—he was a bread deliveryman—and hardly ever saw the building's tenants. So Landry assumed that the husband, who was a bit dim-witted, simply got it wrong: He just hadn't recognized Gouffé. For his part, Gouffé may have been surprised to see Joly and simply didn't want to engage with him.

Gouffé was a legal professional who performed a range of services. Often he collected outstanding debts on behalf of his clients as well as informing the clients' overstretched customers that their bills were past due and they faced potential legal action. In some ways, he was a more respectable species of debt collector. He had amassed a small fortune from these activities and was a member of the lucrative professional class, but he often found himself dealing with unsavory characters. To handle the worst cases, he had a longtime associate who himself had a shady past and a well-practiced talent for intimidation. Rémy-François Launé was a habitué of the meaner boulevards whom Gouffé called upon from time to time to shake loose payments from his toughest delinquents.

When Gouffé's brother-in-law tracked down Launé and informed him of Gouffé's unexplained absence, Launé went into a stagey display of shock that was certainly curious—and more than a little suspicious. He threw a hand over his heart, turned pale in disbelief, and cried out: "You did not have to announce it in such a brutal manner! Heart patient that I am I could have just dropped dead."

By eight o'clock that night, the missing man still had not materialized, so his brother-in-law, accompanied by Launé, brought his concerns to the police station serving the Bonne-Nouvelle neighborhood. Local police commissioner Michel-Émile Brissaud took statements from the two men and asked the usual questions: Was there anyone in the unsavory world of bill collection who posed a threat to Gouffé? A few names were put forward. Was there any reason Gouffé might have considered suicide? None, Landry insisted, saying his brother-in-law was well-off, his health was good, and he was happy with his life, and besides he would never cause such anguish to his daughters.

Brissaud learned from Landry that Gouffé had relationships with at least two demimondaines and that he was sometimes invited into the bedrooms of female clients desperate for leniency on their bills. Of all the collectors who might land on the doorstep, Gouffé was the one a woman most wanted to see. His gentle manner and willingness to hear them out endeared him to these women, and their gratitude for a small act of clemency knew no limits.

The shifty Launé volunteered that he was well-acquainted with Gouffé's private life and often accompanied him on his jaunts of pleasure, prompting the police commissioner to declare that to find the missing man it was necessary to find the mistress. Yes! Launé agreed. Find the woman! His friend, he feared, had fallen victim to a treacherous tart. Everyone knew Gouffé was rich, Launé said, and that he was not averse to accepting a dangerous rendezvous. "He was easy prey," Launé warned, "and may have been taken hostage."

Commissioner Brissaud worked the case through the weekend—he interviewed the concierge's husband and inspected Gouffé's office—then handed it off to the head of the Paris detectives, Sûreté chief Marie-François Goron.

Chapter 3

On that same Saturday morning of July 27, 1889, the morning Gouffé had failed to appear for breakfast, Michel Eyraud rolled up to the apartment at 3, rue Tronson du Coudray in a horse-drawn cab and hurried inside with the driver. Minutes later the two men carried out a large trunk and loaded it onto the carriage.

While they fussed over the trunk, Gabrielle Bompard appeared at the top of the steps, dressed for travel but looking tired and angry. She came down into the street, climbed into the carriage, and took her seat beside Eyraud. The driver flicked the reins and they rolled off amid a clattering of hooves.

Gabrielle was exhausted, having spent a sleepless night alone with a corpse, and she was furious at Eyraud for having deserted her. She nearly went mad in the darkness, knowing the dead man was there inside the trunk, tied up with rope and stuffed into the burlap sack she'd sewn. Though the cadaver was out of sight, the man was still alive in her mind. During the long night, she'd fallen prey to a ghoulish fantasy. She imagined herself getting dressed and going down to the boulevard and picking up a rube from the provinces. She'd bring him back to the apartment and just as she was about to sleep with him, she'd say, "Would you like to see a dead man?" And she'd throw open the trunk. While the poor guy screamed, or fainted, she'd run out of the apartment and lock him inside. Her fantasy took her out into the street again where she would find a policeman. "Monsieur," she would say, "please go see what has happened at 3, Tronson du Coudray. A crime has been committed." Her mind weak, she had laughed to herself imagining the look on the rube's face when the police arrived.

Inside the cab Eyraud, suddenly agitated, exclaimed that he had the wrong hat. Having rushed out of the apartment, he'd left his own hat behind and the one he now stared at in his hands belonged to Gouffé—it was a rich man's hat of shiny silk, and well-brushed. As fashionable as it was, Eyraud wanted his own hat. Feeling lost without it, he ordered the cabdriver to turn the carriage around. Gabrielle snarled that if they went back to the apartment they were sure to miss their train, and then what? Didn't they have to get out of Paris—now? Unhappily Eyraud gave in to reason, and the couple carried on toward Gare de Lyon.

It was one year, almost to the day, since Gabrielle had first encountered Eyraud. In late July 1888 she was a twenty-year-old runaway from Lille, a bourgeois girl, already broke after just three days in Paris, when she went to his office at the trading company Fribourg & Cie hoping for a job. In a fine black dress and veil, she poked her head around his door, which bore a brass plaque reading DIRECTEUR; and when he invited her to sit down next to him at his big wood desk, she'd had a bad premonition.

Something told her to turn back, not to go in there, but she was desperate.

Eyraud was more than twice her age, powerfully built, and meaty, with the neck of a bull and large, menacing hands. He had the manner of an overconfident businessman. As she sat down, he ordered her to lift her veil and then stared into her face with his dark, wolflike eyes. "This man," she would later recall for the police, "the way he looked at me—he stole my free will."

Eyraud informed her that if she wanted a job, she had to hand over five thousand francs as a security against employee theft. She had no way of knowing that the security deposit was a ruse—the money was to go directly into Eyraud's pocket. She told him she didn't have the funds, she had just left her family and had never been employed, at which point Eyraud barked that he had no job for her.

But that was not the end of it.

"You're nice," he told her. "I'll take you to dinner, would you like that?"

At the brasserie, he was charming, worldly, generous. He'd had an exotic life, serving in the French army in Mexico, working in Argentina, running his family's vineyard in Sèvres. He spoke French, Spanish, Portuguese, English. And my, how he could talk! Gabrielle felt her powers of resistance slipping away. "He could do what he wanted with me," she explained later. "He could make me do anything in an instant."

He asserted his control over her through a variety of tricks: hypnosis, guile, and terror. The degree to which Eyraud deployed the powers of hypnosis on Gabrielle would become a centerpiece of the later courtroom battle. Eyraud would insist that he was never able to hypnotize Gabrielle, that she fought him and did not once go into a trance under his command. Yet Gabrielle repeatedly argued that she was helpless under his influence, that she followed him like a dog; and her history of extreme hypnotic susceptibility would buttress her contention.

For a while, life as a mistress had its benefits. Though Eyraud had a wife and daughter at home, he lavished attention upon her. She got hats and high fashion, a new coiffure, manicures, fine liqueurs; he paid her rent and took her to cafés and restaurants. She enthralled him, gave him the flesh he craved, and he proudly showed her off on the boulevards.

But gradually the good life unraveled. At Fribourg & Cie, Eyraud was suspected of stealing funds, and then abruptly he was out, and of course, he claimed that the accusations were all lies. That lying Jew Fribourg! Gabrielle soon found herself trapped in her lover's twisted, claustrophobic world. Eyraud was vicious, a man like many others who subscribed to a popular maxim of the day: "Women are like cutlets. The more you beat them, the tenderer they are."

She ran away once but he found her, dragged her home, and nearly strangled her; she bore the red marks on her neck for days. Fear paralyzed her. She could not bring herself to leave him—and besides, where would she go?

One night, she lay at his feet after a pummeling, half naked, her shoulders bruised. She hugged his legs, tearfully apologizing, begging him not to leave her. Then, as usual, she gave herself to him, and sex sealed their reconciliation. "Don't be afraid," he told her. "Soon we'll be rich. It's my duty to you—so much I would kill someone for it."

Now, bound by that dead man, their lives were inextricably linked. Together they had killed and together they were to be fugitives. At Gare de Lyon, they got a baggage receipt for the trunk, and the agent attached a label: "From: Paris 1231. Paris 27/7/1889. Express Train 3.

To: Lyon-Perrache, 1." They were headed to Lyon, and Gabrielle had no choice but to be the traveling companion of this brute, the murder still fresh in her mind.

After the killing, he had drunk a bottle of cognac in the ground-floor apartment and forced himself on her right beside the trunk containing the corpse. Then he deserted her for the night.

At home, lying in his own bed next to his wife of nineteen years, Eyraud had snored so violently that she grew worried. She touched him lightly and he awoke with a start.

"What do you want?" he growled. "You're keeping me from sleeping!"

His wife, Louise-Laure, told police later: "He turned over and two minutes later his breathing was calm and measured."

The Paris Sûreté had its offices opposite the Palais de Justice and Prefecture of Police, a few steps from Notre Dame and Sainte-Chapelle on the Île de la Cité. Its chief, Marie-François Goron, was a stout bundle of energy, a showy sleuth with a thick mustache that he waxed at the tips. His hair was "tawny-colored," as his schoolmate, the novelist Émile Gautier, put it, and "cropped like a rat."

Goron devoted himself to his work, rarely slept a full night, grabbed quick meals at odd hours (suffering chronic stomach problems as a result), and did not take a day off unless dropped by illness. He was asthmatic but kept his cigarette case close at hand. He carried a magnifying glass in case he needed it to turn up an obscure clue but never carried a gun, trusting instead in his wits and despising violence. He was a devotee of the latest in criminal forensics and an unapologetic publicity hound—but only, of course, in the interests of stirring up witnesses and flushing out suspects.

When the Gouffé case landed on his desk, Goron had his mind on other pressing matters. Bands of pickpockets, a perennial Parisian annoyance, had multiplied like gnats at the exposition. In addition to putting in overtime at the fairgrounds, the men of the Sûreté routinely fanned out across the city to protect public morals, showing up incognito at café concerts and dance halls and watching for obscenity in song lyrics and indecency in the back rooms.

But those were minor tasks compared with the latest crisis: Gangs of teenage thugs were on the loose, slashing throats and terrifying city revelers. With the newspapers hounding him, Goron had little time to focus on trivial complaints like the weekend disappearance of a well-to-do bachelor. Besides, he'd seen enough in his years on the force to know what that meant. "Many people momentarily disappear," he explained in his memoir, "only to be found later eating frog legs on a lovely beach or at the edge of an azure lake savoring a guilty love affair, or just as likely in a prison cell."

Growing up in Rennes, the capital of Brittany in northwestern France, Goron had been an explosive young man who realized early that he'd never fulfill his mother's dream for him: He didn't have the inner peace for the priesthood. This became shockingly clear one day at school when a priest chastised him for a small infraction and the hot-tempered student erupted in a most ungodly fashion and punched the cleric in the face, smashing his glasses.

Later Goron joined the military and was sent to Mexico where, as a fresh recruit, he made the mistake of cursing at a belligerent sergeant. The outburst left him facing court-martial and a grim future. But he was saved when he happened to come before a benevolent officer who chose to instruct rather than punish him. Captain Deleuze sternly reminded the young Goron that a soldier's duty was to adhere to strict discipline and accept his inferior role within the ranks; patriotism and chivalry demanded it. Then, to Goron's astonishment, the captain turned on the sergeant, reprimanding him for neglecting a cardinal precept of the military code: respect for your inferiors.

Lady luck had kissed Goron, as she often would in his life, and he learned a lesson in justice he never forgot. He became a disciplined soldier, rarely reprimanded during his five years of service.

After the army, he came home to Rennes, got married, had two children, and worked briefly as a hospital pharmacist. But he had to leave the job when his superiors discovered he was too generous in dispensing opiates to ease patients' suffering. He tried his hand in the wine business, then wound up working in Argentina where tragedy struck. When his seven-year-old son became desperately ill, Goron sought every means of treatment but to no avail—the boy died in his father's arms. Devastated, Goron took responsibility on himself, wailing in his memoir, "I didn't have the power to save my son!"

Gathering his family, he fled Argentina and took a job as an officer of the peace in Paris. He was attracted to the work because he liked the uniform, which reminded him of his military days, and because he appreciated the military's dedication to discipline and mission.

In police work Goron found his calling and moved swiftly up the ranks. In the back alleys of Montmartre among swindlers and prostitutes he absorbed the ways of the Parisian lowlife, learned the slang, and saw suffering that haunted him. "Little by little," he wrote later, "I was initiated into the hideous and sad side of the great city." He was present when young girls gave up their infants because they couldn't properly care for them, admitting: "I had to turn my head to hide my emotion." He arrived at the sites of suicides, cutting down hanged bodies that were still warm. He raided child-prostitution rings, bursting in upon old men still wearing their Legion of Honor decorations.

Goron saw a side of Paris that left ministers and cultural watchdogs desperate over the health of the nation. "I penetrated behind the scenes of the magical city," he wrote, "where the outsider primarily perceived the splendor of the lights but did not recognize that the luxury and noisy good cheer hid despair, grief, and anguish."

Although he witnessed extremes of depravity, he never lost sight of the humanity he saw in many criminals; he understood that they were beings scarred by their grievous personal lives and by the lashes of society. If a suspect was hauled in and looked hungry, Goron fed him. In the antics of the criminal he may have seen vestiges of his own troubled youth. "I must confess," he explained, "that I have often felt pangs of genuine pity—such as have often surprised me—for men who have stolen or murdered and yet, at the same time, have retained in the depths of their souls some spark of good feeling which is often most touching."

That was not to say he went easy on evildoers. When he had a suspect in his grasp, Goron was a ruthless interrogator. Gautier said that Goron's eyes had "a look as sharp as a needle, penetrating, inquisitorial, a kind of Röentgen ray under which . . . criminals were to find themselves impotent to hide their secrets."

However much that description owed to friendship, or a novelist's imagination, Goron achieved spectacular success while tirelessly working the streets of Montmartre, and soon became the head cop in the Paris suburbs, first in Neuilly, then in Pantin. In October 1886, at age thirty-nine, he was named the deputy chief of the Sûreté.

Barely a year after his appointment, the head of the Sûreté, Hippolyte Ernest Auguste Taylor, an upright but choleric leader, was booted out of his job in the aftermath of a government scandal. In the shake-up, the position of Sûreté chief went to the once hotheaded youth from Rennes. As Goron settled into the job, he was noted for his honesty and for the amusing objects on display in his office. This "veritable museum" had a superb collection of weapons, according to one observer, and a "large frame filled with the photographs of a crowd of celebrated criminals."

If Goron hesitated at first over the Gouffé case, he had ample reason. No sooner had he solved one gruesome throat slashing in March than a second killing on July 15, shortly before Gouffé disappeared, sent another shock wave through the capital. In the latest murder, an elderly concierge was discovered in her apartment on rue Bonaparte slumped in an armchair with a handkerchief stuffed in her mouth and her throat sliced from ear to ear. Her rooms had been ransacked. A servant returning from an errand had stumbled upon the ghastly sight and was nearly knocked over by three young toughs fleeing the scene.

Goron was under intense pressure to capture the killers. Recognizing the need for a quick result, he sent two of his most wily detectives on a high-risk mission to infiltrate the criminal gangs. If the undercover agents were found out, the gang members would butcher them on the spot. As the days passed and no word came, Goron anxiously smoked many cigarettes. Then one day Sûreté agents hauled in five suspects. Three of them were young thugs aged seventeen to nineteen; the two others were older, filthy hooligans speaking the slang of the streets. But where were Goron's men? If these were the possible killers, what had happened to his detectives?

As Goron eyed the suspects, it dawned on him: What brilliant acting! What authentic disguises! The older gang members were his own men, so realistic in their thuggery they had fooled the arresting agents and the chief himself. Careful not to blow their cover, Goron questioned all five suspects hard, in his own demonstration of play-acting, until he wrested confessions from the teenagers and they were led away.

His own men, Goron learned, had been accepted as comrades by the younger men, and soon the teenagers were bragging of the concierge's murder, revealing vivid, incriminating details. The detectives then subtly provoked their own arrest along with the teenagers, bringing the case right into Goron's hands. The chief couldn't have been more delighted and, after sending his men off to get cleaned up, lavished them with handsome rewards for a job well done.

The Gouffé case, meanwhile, had moved into the hands of a *juge d'instruction,* or investigating magistrate. It had been three days since Gouffé vanished and, while Goron had hesitated, the investigating magistrate, a tireless Alsatian named Paul Dopffer, had already set to work. "Patriotic and conscientious, he is honesty itself," Paris court reporters said of him. He was noted for his quiet determination; he had "the steadiness of a pack horse, which moves slowly, but never stops to take rest on the way." His job was to root out the facts of a crime, working with police, detectives, doctors, forensic specialists, witnesses, and eventually the suspects themselves, to prepare the case for prosecution. He was free to carry out searches and seizures, call witnesses, order expert testimony, issue orders and warrants. Working out of an office on the upper floors of the Palais de Justice, Dopffer had unlimited powers. "The judge of instruction," the Paris court reporters said, "should leave no stone unturned that may lead to a discovery of the truth."

One of Goron's most trusted agents, the Sûreté's chief inspector Pierre-Fortune Jaume, suspected that the case of the missing wealthy man was going to be a tricky one. In temperament and tactics, Jaume was more like Goron than any other agent of the Sûreté. Potbellied, with a thin mustache, he was known for his wicked sense of humor and the easy laugh of a stage actor. He was an undercover genius who relished disguises and had mastered a vast repertoire of facial expressions. With his sharp eyes and ruddy face, he was, like Goron, a blistering interrogator and, also like Goron, he never carried a weapon.

Jaume was concerned now because the chief had assigned the footwork in the investigation to an agent named Léon Soudais. As a brigadier, Soudais was one of the highest-ranking officers in the department but, in Jaume's estimation, lacked the intuition needed to crack the case. While conscientious and obedient, Soudais was, in the inspector's view, "lacking in all psychological sense and initiative." Jaume noted in his diary that Brigadier Soudais "seems to me as capable of disentangling this business as I am of singing in the Sistine Chapel."

Chapter 5

By the time French justice turned its attention to the Gouffé case, Michel Eyraud and Gabrielle Bompard were on their way to Lyon, seated in a railway carriage like father and daughter in an uneasy truce, their backbreaking trunk stowed in the luggage car. Whatever their complaints with each other, the pair appeared utterly commonplace; they gave no reason for fellow travelers to raise an eyebrow at them.

That was far different from the impression Gabrielle had given a year earlier when, running away from home, she rode the train from Lille to Paris. Decent young women simply didn't travel alone; a girl on her own raised an immediate flurry of questions: Where was her family, or her husband, or her brother, or at least her governess? Why did no one care enough to escort her? A solitary girl, even in the finest of fashion, suggested a dark background: Gabrielle, alone in that railway car, attracted less a gaze of sympathy than of scorn.

She carried with her the scars of her youth, the boarding away from home, the convents, the bitter battles with her father and her governess. Her father, Pierre, was a small, robust man with a heavy black mustache and the affectation of a soldier, though he'd never served. His attention was lavished not on his daughter but on his flourishing metals business. Gabrielle's sickly mother, Louise-Sidonie, had given birth to five children, only two of whom survived: Gabrielle, who was born on August 14, 1868, and her younger brother. At age five, Gabrielle was living with nuns away from the family home in Lille when she was summoned to her mother's sickroom to watch her die. Very soon afterward, she was shipped off to her mother's brother in Ypres, Belgium, about thirty miles north of Lille, where she remained for eight years. Her uncle, Émile Vanaerd, was a dental surgeon who cared for his niece as though she were his own daughter and provided her with an excellent education; her letters demonstrated a keen command of French composition and a lively intellect.

Gabrielle came home in 1881, at age thirteen, and soon discovered the truth of her father's sordid living arrangement with the family's governess, Nathalie Bourgeois. Nathalie, taking advantage of Gabrielle's absence, had installed herself in Pierre's life and bed as his de facto wife. The family's physician, Dr. Sacreste, later criticized the scandalous arrangement, lamenting its impact on the impressionable teenager: "Her father gave her the example of the most immoral conduct and forced her to live in intimacy . . . with a concubine." For his part, Pierre bowed to his lover's wishes and, after Gabrielle's shocking discovery, Nathalie insisted the girl be banished from the house. Within days the teenager was on her way to a convent in Fournes, ten miles southwest of Lille.

By age fourteen, Gabrielle was enormously fat and had a reputation as a *méchante,* a bad child. She acted out, cursed freely, and was regarded as a dangerous influence on the other girls. One day in the middle of religious class she declared that the vicar had fondled her, a charge that swiftly ended the incorrigible girl's residence at Fournes after less than a year. Shipping her home, the convent warned Pierre that his daughter was in danger of a calamitous slide into degeneracy.

Pierre, who had no intention of keeping Gabrielle at home, sent her to board with a teacher in Lille, an arrangement that ended abruptly after one semester. Next she was deposited at a religious institution in Marq, and that, too, lasted just one semester.

As soon as she returned home from one failed boarding, her father began the search for her next destination in exile. But with each dismissal, it became harder to find an institution that would accept her; her prospects were frustrated by a stack of poor recommendations. Finally Pierre managed to get her into the Bon Pasteur convent in Arras, twenty-five miles from Lille, where she took up residence in late 1883. This was no average convent; it was a home for wayward girls and women—child-mothers and adulterers—a merciless environment, harsh and prisonlike, and Gabrielle languished there for three years. She mingled with other castoffs and learned the ways of fallen women and girl criminals. The head of the convent, Sister Marie Joseph Emphrasie, gave Gabrielle high marks for intelligence and obedience, even if she was sometimes mean-spirited. Another administrator, Sister Marie de Saint-Gabriel, said Gabrielle, who was plump and round and stood just four feet eight inches tall—was a submissive, docile girl, although she had mood swings that whipped her from genial to vicious in a flash. Sister Marie noted, with extraordinary prescience, that the troubled young girl had "a grand tendency to peculiar friendships."

In 1886, at age eighteen, Gabrielle was sent home with a note from Sister Marie Joseph advising her father to keep a close eye on her. Pierre now owned two adjacent buildings in Lille behind an iron gate at 216–218, rue Nationale. The gate opened onto a courtyard littered with the commodities of his trade: scraps of iron, cylinders, wheels, pipes—not a soft, cradling environment for a fragile girl. The buildings bore signs indicating the residence and the business: one read P. BOMPARD, the other METALS.

Gabrielle had spent so much of her life elsewhere that she was a stranger in her own home. None of the institutions she had inhabited was terribly far away but her father never once came to visit. During her eight years with her uncle, her father contributed not so much as a sou to her education, even though during that time he had become a prosperous metals merchant and had established himself as a respectable member of the community; while ignoring his daughter's needs, he donated to charity and bought memberships in prestigious institutions, such as the geographical society and the association for educational development.

At home, his concubine Nathalie made sure Gabrielle felt unwelcome. But the teenager fought back and asserted her independence. She lost weight, dressed provocatively, and took up with a Lille businessman named Jules who, embracing the current fad, had trained himself as an amateur hypnotist; in Gabrielle he had found an eager subject. Her father objected to her sassiness at home and her saucy displays in the street, complaining that she brought public shame upon him. Later he disingenuously told the press that it was trying for him to have a daughter like her—he had made so many sacrifices for her and paid so much for her education. He finished the interview by saying: "If one knew when they came into the world that children would turn out this way, one would break their neck."

The climax came when Nathalie warned Gabrielle that her father wanted to incarcerate her again in a home for wayward women. Instead of accepting another round of misery, Gabrielle chose to escape. In August 1888, she was on her way to the train station, with Nathalie escorting her to ensure she didn't change her mind at the last minute. Nathalie rode on the train with her as far as Arras, where she stuffed a handful of francs into Gabrielle's hand and bid her farewell. While Nathalie got on the next train back to Lille, Gabrielle, at age twenty, was on her way to Paris alone.

All that was a distant, year-old memory now. Since then Gabrielle had been sucked into the brutal world of Michel Eyraud: his rages, his scams, his chameleon way of life. Now, having murdered a man, they had little to show for it: The cash windfall that Eyraud had counted on hadn't materialized; he had nabbed only a hundred and fifty francs from Gouffé's pocket—a gold piece worth a hundred francs and a fifty-franc banknote—and he'd snatched the sapphire-and-diamond ring from the dead man's pinkie. The killing had left him more desperate than ever. He took on a new name, Émile Breuil, and posed as a businessman traveling by railway with his daughter. They arrived at the Lyon-Perrache train station late in the day on Saturday, July 27, 1889, around the time Louis-Marie Landry was informing police that his brother-in-law had disappeared.

At the Hôtel de Toulouse father and daughter were put in room number 6 on the upper floor, requiring considerable sweat from Eyraud and the hotel staff to get the trunk up the stairs. The next morning Eyraud rounded up a coachman, a busboy, and a housekeeper to bring the trunk back downstairs and hoist it onto the platform of a carriage he'd rented. The housekeeper, Jean Reyne, felt the contents shift inside; the sticky, wine-colored substance oozing from the bottom and staining his hands and smock, he assumed, was just paint. As father and daughter prepared for their journey, their tense relationship—he domineering, she aloof—was evident to everyone.

Eyraud climbed aboard, sat himself beside Gabrielle on a raised bench at the front, flicked the reins, and the horse set off at a leisurely pace. As soon as they were out of earshot, Gabrielle became frantic about the blood on the housekeeper's apron. He saw! He knows! He'll call the police. Eyraud shrugged it off. "Bah!" he growled at her, ready with a lie if anyone asked. "It's just an animal we caught in the woods."

The carriage with the bickering couple rolled out of Lyon and traveled along a desolate road above the Rhône River. From time to time, the horse balked, refusing to move until Eyraud climbed down and beat it into submission. The dusty route ran from nearby Millery to Givors and on to Saint-Étienne and saw little traffic except for Gypsies ambling with their dogs. Along the river, the embankment was thick with brambles and the air was rich with the scents of woodland and wildflowers. Gabrielle, emerging from a sulky silence, chattered gaily, taking in the sounds of the chirping birds and the beauty of the woods.

The carriage climbed a knoll and the river dropped from sight. At the summit, Eyraud stopped the horse and went for a look down the steep embankment: a fine spot to dispose of a body. With nature humming all around him, he worked the trunk off the platform and shoved it toward the edge. Tilting it up at an angle, he opened the lid and shook out the bulky burlap sack. Gabrielle held on to his arm as he booted the sack over the edge. Together they watched it tumble down the bank and come to rest at the foot of an acacia bush.

Eyraud then stomped on the trunk and broke it apart with a hammer, tossing the pieces onto the carriage platform. He climbed back up and rode on several miles before jumping down again and flinging the scraps of wood over the side. Then, with the dead man's fine silk hat still on his head, he got back onto the carriage, sat down next to his mistress, and guided the now-submissive horse—eager for the return journey—toward the Hôtel de Toulouse.

Chapter 6

Of the myriad pleasures of the belle époque, sex was among the sweetest—and sometimes the deadliest. The detectives on the Gouffé case were soon obsessed by a primary question: What role might a woman have played in his disappearance? With admirable depth of feeling, the widower had mourned the loss of his wife; but eight years on he was back into the fullness of life, most avid in his amorous adventures. Gouffé was a man of his era, one who appreciated the sentiment of another voluptuary who said, "Whoever has not undressed a woman [of the late 1800s] has missed one of the better refinements of love-making, from the first tiny pearl button of her rose-point cuffs, to the lacings of that inflexible bastion of honor, the corset."

Even bourgeois married women, pious in public, were crafty lovers, capable of navigating a logistical nightmare for a dalliance known as a Four to Five, named for the time of day when it customarily took place. As a social historian eloquently explained, "There was first the problem of giving the slip to her ever vigilant coachman, ordering him to wait outside some shop or tearoom while she escaped through a back door and scurried down a side street to her lover's flat. Once arrived in this bower of bliss, there arose the further and serious problem of her clothes . . . taking them off and getting them back on again without the assistance of her personal maid." And that was just the beginning. "After returning to her own house," this observer said, "there was the risk of facing the same maid whose all-seeing eye might note a button unfastened or a hook caught in the wrong eyelet. There would follow the lady's stammered explanation that she'd been for a fitting at the dressmaker's and had had to take off her frock . . . which did not explain, as sometimes happened, why she had brought back her corset concealed in her muff."

No one exemplified both the ecstasy and the agony of lovemaking more movingly than the famous writer Alphonse Daudet. At age twelve he lost his virginity during a weeklong sojourn in a brothel with a prostitute from Lorraine "whose skin," he told his friend the diarist Edmond de Goncourt, "was covered with freckles but was so soft to the touch that it had driven him mad." Daudet exulted over the "glorious frenzy" of sex "with a woman who is naked, a woman one rolls on top of and covers with kisses: copulation as practiced by artists, men of passion, men who really love women."

A mysterious disappearance naturally gave rise to the question of sex, and the offices of the Sûreté soon became the crossroads of Gouffé's paramours, who were all questioned intensively. Had a love affair turned sour and deadly? Was the bailiff lured to a rendezvous and attacked? Had Gouffé denied clemency to a seductress in debt and had she taken lethal revenge?

How easy it was to overspend in profligate Paris. The temptations were strewn along the boulevards. Giant display windows beckoned the curious into dreamy department stores "where one finds practically everything one can desire," as one awed provincial girl put it. Seductive advertising—women in the latest fashions, heads cocked, smiling beneath their parasols—raised the hopes of the less glamorous, but the dreams came at a cost: You had to empty your pocketbook.

The offices of the Sûreté overflowed with women, some in deep financial straits. But no matter how wretched their penury, they brought a sparkle to the eye of Inspector Jaume, who wrote: "I myself don't have any complaints about this extraordinary inquiry: the stairs and corridors have never been more perfumed. In Goron's office, one thinks oneself in a boudoir. A rustling of silk here, a whisper of gossip there."

In the first week Goron questioned more than twenty women—all of whom had slept with Gouffé just in the month of July. Nearly two dozen women in a single month, this harem of lovers, each one flouncing in and protesting she was innocent of any wrongdoing. Gouffé was a handsome man, with chestnut-brown hair, fine clothing, and a gentle, attentive manner. In Jaume's lively imagination, the missing man exuded a magnetic, even heroic, allure. Assessing the bailiff's sexual prowess, Jaume quipped: "Don't speak to me of the labors of Hercules. That was just a worn-out horse next to Gouffé."

By the end of the week, all the comings and goings, all the perfumes and protests in the detectives' offices had led nowhere. But while he had no suspects Goron had his suspicions. Gouffé's shady associate Rémy-François Launé was often in and out of his office, drawing up paperwork, stamping it with the bailiff's personal seal, and he sometimes had in his possession large quantities of money he'd collected from debtors. Goron questioned him hard, suspecting that Launé knew far more about Gouffé's disappearance than he was divulging, but the Sûreté chief came away with nothing he could pin on him.

Another suspicious figure was Louis-Marie Landry. In the days following the disappearance he had behaved curiously; he'd gone to his brother-in-law's office and carted off a stack of private letters and destroyed them. Landry, who was about fifty years old, had long graying hair and a mustache and goatee that, according to one description, gave him the "air of an ancient cavalry officer." Questioned about the letters, he asserted that they were written to Gouffé by assorted women and contained salacious information; if the details became public, he explained, they would have blackened his brother-in-law's reputation, harming the family and embarrassing his daughters.

Gouffé had been as industrious in his career as he was in his love life, amassing a tidy fortune that made him an ideal target for robbery or extortion. His lockbox at the Banque Parisienne, detectives discovered, contained a hundred and thirty thousand francs, and at Crédit Lyonnais, he had another two hundred thousand francs. (Three hundred and thirty thousand francs equals about $4.2 million in 2013 dollars.)

After a week of inquiry, Goron still had little to go on: no leads, no suspects, nothing. Just dead ends and wild speculation. Could the missing man have been the one who hanged himself from a tree in the Chevreuse woods? What of that corpse found floating in the Seine? Neither, it turned out, was Gouffé. He had vanished without a trace, and the longer he was gone, the more complicated the hunt became.

Sniffing a sensation, the newspapers flocked to the mystery, and Goron was soon facing tough questions. "The investigation so far is in vain," *L'Écho de Paris* sniped. "The agents of the Sûreté are not any further than they were on the first day."

The Sûreté was the most venerable and successful detective agency in the world. It was older and more sophisticated than its British counterpart, dating back to 1811 when Napoleon's prefect of police ordered the convict-turned-superlative sleuth Eugène François Vidocq to form a band of four ex-cons like himself to sniff out and pursue criminals; until then, police efforts had been largely directed toward rooting out dangers to the monarchy, not investigating criminal offenses. Vidocq's detectives knew the underworld and took whatever measures were necessary to haul in evildoers, but their unsavory personal histories and tactics left a taint on the Sûreté for years. By the time of Goron's arrival, the detective force had moved away from employing ex-cons and was now populated with men who were considered above reproach.

The public—recognizing the Sûreté's achievements but mistaking the literary world of crime for reality—regularly expected a swift, happy triumph over evil. Paris detectives were shaped in the popular imagination by the widely read novels of Émile Gaboriau, whose sleuths carefully analyzed clues and used reason and modern science to solve their mysteries. In the second half of the nineteenth century, the directors of the Sûreté were themselves devoted to the latest scientific methods, smarter forensics, and a new system created by Alphonse Bertillon for identifying and cataloguing criminals that was the envy of the world. The Bertillon anthropomorphic method of measuring criminals' body parts even attracted a high-ranking committee of admirers from London to study it and encourage its adoption back home. French newspaper readers had high hopes that the Sûreté would shine its light of reason into the dark corners of Paris and protect them from the malevolent class.

But Chief Goron had been a sleuth long enough to understand the mundane reality of solving crimes. He prized the hard work of shoe leather on the streets and the sleepless pursuit of every shred of information. What led to a villain's capture was the magic of the most ordinary skills and a smile from lady luck.

Goron was an avid reader of detective stories—Gaboriau, Edgar Allan Poe, and Arthur Conan Doyle, who in 1887 had published his first Sherlock Holmes mystery, *A Study in Scarlet*—and he enjoyed puzzling out those popular tales. But did they bear any similarity to real detective work?

"Like everyone else, I love to follow the twists and turns" of a good fictional mystery, he told the press. "It is a good intellectual sport—like playing chess. But do not imagine for a moment that it has anything at all to do with practical police work. Nothing at all. It is not by such subtle, opium-bred guesswork and fine-drawn deduction that criminals are detected."

Chapter 7

The last person Jean-Baptiste Eyraud wanted to see on his doorstep was his elder brother, Michel. A bitter memory still haunted him from their last encounter some five years earlier, and ever since Jean-Baptiste had kept his distance. All his life, he'd been tyrannized by Michel, and on this summer day in late July the cruelty was to begin again. So Jean-Baptiste was taken aback to find Michel darkening his door with a young female companion.

Michel and Gabrielle had traveled almost two hundred miles dead south from Lyon to Marseille, where Jean-Baptiste ran a café. Eyraud was comfortable in the south. His roots were here: His father was of Catalonian descent, a savvy businessman who, as one description had it, "could wheel and deal the stones on the street." He'd built a successful silk business in Saint-Étienne, about forty miles southwest of Lyon, where Michel was born in 1843, and owned a nearby inn. He eventually moved the family to Barcelona, where he established a fabrics business and later bought a vineyard near Narbonne.

Michel had the benefits of a fine education and had inherited his father's gift of wheeling and dealing—absent the old man's integrity. His errant ways presented themselves early in life to the dismay of his father, who prevailed upon authorities to lock his son up at age sixteen in a penitentiary in Oullins, just outside of Lyon, for two years. The cause remains a mystery, though the punishment was severe.

Eyraud's mother recognized that her eldest son, whatever his faults, was craftier and more intelligent than the younger, more loyal Jean-Baptiste. "Oh, this one here," she said of Michel, "has a well-organized head. He makes a lot of money. He is much more skilled than his brother."

Marseille was an old port town full of mystery and surprise, populated by tough and tanned natives, sailors, Gypsies, and crooks. The wind howled and seagulls squawked overhead. Church bells rang from morning until night. For generations ships from around the world carrying strange souls and exotic things landed here. The dispossessed and the fugitive knew the hidden alleyways; and the dark corners of Marseille kept their secrets safe.

The writer M. F. K. Fisher, who was drawn to the town again and again in the twentieth century, used the French word *insolite* to describe the people and the place. But, she said, it is a word as "indefinable as Marseille itself." She referred to the French *Larousse* dictionary for the meaning of *insolite*: "contrary to what is usual and normal." Then she turned to the *Shorter Oxford Dictionary* and to *Webster's Third International* and came up with three words to illustrate the term and the locale: apart, unique, unusual. "Marseille lives, with a unique strength that plainly scares less virile breeds," she wrote. "Its people are proud of being 'apart.'"

It was the kind of place that protected fugitives like Michel and Gabrielle, a hideout where they could contemplate their next move in comfort and security. They made themselves at home with Jean-Baptiste and lived off his sullen hospitality. Tensions lingered between the brothers from an ugly incident in the early 1880s when Jean-Baptiste was awarded the family vineyard in southern France. As the boys' mother told a newspaper later, Michel was consumed by a "ferocious jealousy" toward his brother. Although she recognized the intellectual skills of Michel, she had long favored the gentler and slower Jean-Baptiste and believed the brothers' relationship would survive "provided they didn't come to kill each other."

Jean-Baptiste accepted that his brother had the quicker mind and reluctantly turned to him for help when the vineyard was struck by an infestation of phylloxera, pale yellow insects that ate the roots of the vines. Phylloxera was attacking not just the Eyraud vineyards but was spreading to many properties in France, threatening the country's wine production. Jean-Baptiste's situation was particularly dire—creditors were hounding him and bankruptcy was imminent if he couldn't come up with fifteen thousand francs.

Michel's solution—which had a hidden motive—was for the brothers to visit their wealthy, aging mother in Paris and beg for the needed funds. She was fully aware of the crisis and had already doled out a considerable sum to battle the infestation, even staying on the property for six months to oversee the effort. But now her health was failing and she was still in mourning for her husband, the family patriarch, who had died three years earlier.

Her sons found her in bed in her apartment at 45, boulevard Saint-Germain. Seeing his mother so frail, Jean-Baptiste could not bring himself to ask for the money. But Michel had no such qualms. His entreaties did not sway the old lady, however, and she denied him repeatedly until his voice rose so loud and his language turned so vile that his mother ordered him to leave the apartment. He refused and drew a revolver from his pocket and pointed it at his mother as she lay in bed.

Staring him down, the tough matron called his bluff. He may have been a bully and a schemer but he wasn't fool enough to murder his own mother in her bed. Furious, Michel grabbed a photograph of his father from a bedside table and threatened to tear up the cherished memento and toss the pieces out the window. The old woman caved. Her devil of a son had exploited her weak spot: Losing the cherished photo of her husband would have been too much to bear.

She agreed to hand over the funds but only to Jean-Baptiste. Dismissing Michel, she informed Jean-Baptiste of where she kept her valuables and gave him permission to take the necessary titles to family resources that would cover the amount he needed.

Later, in private, Michel wore Jean-Baptiste down, convincing him that converting the titles into cash required considerable paperwork and that it was best if he handled the task himself. After all, he knew the bailiffs and notaries needed to complete the transactions. Promising to take care of everything, Michel left the apartment with the bundle of titles in his arms—and Jean-Baptiste didn't see his brother again until he appeared on his doorstep demanding hospitality. Nor did he ever see a franc of his mother's money. The family vineyard declined, went into bankruptcy, and was sold for a pittance.

Eventually Madame Eyraud moved from her Paris apartment into a hospice in the suburbs and from there to a convent in the south near Marseille, where she died in 1888. Jean-Baptiste brought her body back to Paris and buried it next to her husband's in a crypt in the tony

Père-Lachaise Cemetery. There the elder Eyrauds shared eternity with the remains of luminaries such as Balzac, Molière, and Chopin.

Meanwhile, Michel was growing anxious in Marseille. After imposing himself on his brother for a couple of weeks, he relieved Jean-Baptiste of three hundred francs and left with Gabrielle for Paris. Michel was still obsessed with his hat, so the first stop was to be the scene of their crime. It was a dangerous, even foolhardy venture. What if the police had traced Gouffé to the apartment and had an agent posted inside or others watching it from the street? But it was a gamble the killer was willing to take.

"A point is clarified for me," Inspector Jaume later confided to his diary. "I understand now why Eyraud went to find his hat at rue Tronson du Coudray. That hat he'd left at the scene of the crime, it could have served as a terrible piece of evidence against him."

Chapter 8

On October 6, 1886, the day Marie-François Goron became the deputy chief of the Sûreté, his boss, Hippolyte Ernest Auguste Taylor, warned him, "My dear Goron, you will experience some emotions on your debut."

That night, two murderers, Frey and Rivière, were to be marched from La Roquette Prison to the guillotine just before dawn with the two Sûreté officials in attendance.

"A little shudder ran through my veins," Goron recalled.

Taylor felt a pang of terror as well but not from the horror of an imminent beheading; rather he was afraid that he or the Sûreté might be dragged through the mud by the press for some unavoidable gaffe during the ceremony. Taylor lived in fear of the press and warned Goron to maintain the strictest discretion in public. He had good reason to do so.

The Paris press of the 1880s was an unruly mob, kicking a magistrate one day, hoisting a celebrity the next. The newspapers, having burst from the chains of government controls in 1881, were constantly testing the boundaries of their new powers. The "freedom of the press law," as it came to be known, threw out stamp duties, government deposits, arbitrary trials, and censorship. One observer described the new step as "a freedom law the likes of which the press has never seen in any time."

From inside their offices along the *grands boulevards,* editors sought to create a splash with every new edition, heralding the birth of the modern sensational media; the antics of the French press in the late nineteenth century pointed toward the yellow journalism of the early twentieth century and the tabloid frenzy of our own time.

In Paris, cheap newspapers blanketed the city, giving rise to what historians have called the city's "golden age of the press." In 1881, twenty-three newspapers could be had for a sou, equivalent to about an American penny; by 1899, there were sixty. *Le Petit Journal,* with a circulation of one million in 1886, and other mass publications defined Parisian culture and the reality of everyday life for their readers. The newspapers were in frantic competition to outdo one another in scandal, murder, and pathos.

There was no richer feast for journalists than an execution. It had it all: vicious murderers, bloody beheadings, swarming crowds, and lots of secrecy leading up to the event. Reporters circled, and Taylor, standoffish in the best of circumstances, was more aloof than ever. His stiffness had won him few friends. On principle he kept information from the press, believing that no good came from newspaper coverage. "This was well reciprocated," Goron observed. "Journalists were not slow to drag out their vengeance, which was inclined to be absolute." And Taylor was often aghast to find himself belittled in the papers, his successes ignored, his failures magnified.

When he finally left his post and was installed in another government department, the official ceremony was open to the public but not a single reporter showed up, indicating no love lost between him and the newspapers. *Le Temps* opined that the absence of reporters "must have rejoiced the heart of M. Taylor who, one knows, has an antipathy toward the press."

He was a nervous bureaucrat, out of place in the role of chief investigator of the Paris underworld. His approach was an object lesson for Goron, who, when he ran the Sûreté, sought to avoid his predecessor's mistakes and therefore broke all of his rules.

Taylor and Goron's appointment with the condemned wasn't until 3:00 a.m., so to pass the long hours, the Sûreté chiefs joined several other execution regulars for a night of theater and dinner. Their entertainment was a three-act comedy by Alexandre Bisson called *La Famille Pont-Biquet,* a light diversion about the family travails of an investigating judge. "I laughed with the professional insouciance that one slips into at certain moments," Goron wrote in his memoir. But the night's shadow weighed on him. The play, he noted, was "a preface to that bloody tragedy at which we were ordered to be representatives."

Over dinner Goron listened as the men shared stories of previous beheadings they'd attended. "I still have that memorable impression of us at the restaurant on the boulevard with our elbows on the table, smoking cigars, each man telling his own little macabre tale," Goron wrote.

At nearly 3:00 a.m., the chiefs returned to the Sûreté and climbed into an elegant landau for the trip to the prison. The luxury under the grim circumstances disturbed Goron: "The landau for a wedding party or a duel conducts the chief of the Sûreté to executions," he explained. "The rest of the time he takes a hackney or a hansom carriage—so why does he need a landau for this ghastly ceremony?"

Along rue de la Roquette the crowd was pressed against the police barricades. The landau maneuvered its way through the crush and rolled into place de la Roquette where workmen in overalls were erecting the guillotine in dim lantern light. A cluster of journalists hovered nearby, watching.

Climbing down from the landau, Goron caught some of the chatter of the workmen and journalists—talking of their sleepiness, of tomorrow, of a million little things. Some were laughing. The scene darkened Goron's mood. "I had a pang in my heart for the banality of death," he recalled in his memoirs.

A small, thickset man who had been meticulously checking the bolts on the guillotine stepped over to introduce himself. He was at least twenty years older than Goron and had soft eyes and a retiring manner. Louis Deibler had been the executioner in Brittany and had lived for many years in Goron's hometown of Rennes before taking up his duties as the executioner in Paris. He looked nothing like the fire-breathing monster of darkness one imagines of an executioner but rather like the kindly tailor he was during the daylight hours.

Growing up in Rennes, Goron—as well as every other child—knew that the executioner lived in a small house on rue du Pré Perché, set off from the others in what seemed morbid isolation. Young Goron and his friends had to pass by the house every day on their way to school and if, by chance, they had to come home after dark, they took a detour. "After nightfall," Goron remembered, "the sinister house seemed to our childish imaginations full of ghosts holding their heads in their hands."

Taylor and Goron and the other magistrates—a judge, a mayor, the police commissioner, the head of the prison—all in overcoats and top hats, trooped to the cells of Rivière and Frey, two pimps who had strangled and robbed a woman in her home. The murderers were led in a procession through the giant iron door of La Roquette and into the courtyard where early birds chirped in the trees and the guillotine loomed, its tall red uprights bright in the pale dawn.

"I had not known an impression more terrible," Goron recalled.

Now it was all business. Rivière went first: Deibler locked his neck in the lunette and, wasting no time, released the efficient blade. Next came Frey. As he was laid on the bascule he barked the slang of the streets, sneering at those responsible for his execution: *"Au revoir, tous les hommes!"* (Good-bye, all you tough guys!)

After it was over, Goron stopped at a snack stand in the Gare d'Orléans for a light breakfast, inaugurating what would become his post-execution ritual throughout his tenure at the Sûreté.

But he never got used to these bleak mornings. No matter how vile the condemned man was, he never accepted what he called "this butchery without grandeur." He rejected arguments that the guillotine was a deterrent to crime. "The truth is the guillotine does not scare those condemned to death," he said. "The criminal always believes he will escape punishment. He is not preoccupied with it, he is not terrified of it, except when it feels very near."

The guillotine did not protect society—it demonstrated a "contempt for human life," Goron believed. A beheading didn't exact justice but merely satisfied the public's bloodlust. "I confess," he wrote, "that personally the death penalty disgusts me."

On this night, two men died and Taylor was spared any public humiliation; the press found nothing in his actions to ridicule. Goron, meanwhile, was introduced to the darkest side of his job and to a boss who could not be more unlike him. When Goron took over from Taylor in late 1887, he immediately showed the press he was different from his predecessor. From his first day as the chief, Goron flattered and manipulated reporters. "I understood quickly that, damaging or useful, it would be necessary to live in concert with the press," he recalled. "The chief of the Sûreté had all to lose by not giving information to reporters. It was the nature of these times."

Acutely aware that the newspapers could be friend or foe, he played to reporters with a savvy unknown among his contemporaries. He used all of his considerable showmanship to win them to his side.

What reporters wanted most was exclusive information—descriptions of blood-soaked murder weapons, wild behavior of suspects in custody, ghoulish details from autopsies—anything to titillate their readers. Goron, the keeper of criminal secrets, handed out scraps and reaped the rewards.

At the same time, he appreciated that journalists could help his investigations. They were amateur sleuths digging up clues Goron's own agents might have overlooked. "How many times have I arrived at a murder scene," Goron recalled, "only to find reporters next to the cadaver with notebook in hand."

He accepted that he was a partner with the newspapers in sensationalizing coverage. "The press has a tremendous skill in whipping up the public spirit and enthralling the whole world in current events," he explained. Public enthusiasm over a case was beneficial to any investigation. In Goron's imagined perfect world, an engaged populace was always ready to deliver the case-breaking clue—something he sorely needed now in the Gouffé case.

In the first days of the investigation, Goron spoon-fed tidbits to the press in hopes of spurring the public's help and keeping press criticism at bay as the probe ran into one dead end after another. But after ten days, when the chief still knew next to nothing about the whereabouts of Gouffé or his possible attackers, the press turned on him. His fraternizing with reporters, his generosity in supplying details, even his charm proved inadequate for hungry editors and a restive public.

On August 7, the Sûreté chief was forced to defend himself publicly, telling *Le Gil Blas* that he was confident of success in what was now a very strange case. Cutting the chief a little slack, the paper allowed: "However arduous this case may be, M. Goron does not despair of bringing it to a good end."

Then came rumors of an imminent arrest. But the only arrest was of a con man who preyed upon Gouffé's grieving daughters; he claimed to have been a friend of their father and said he had important information, convincing the girls to part with a thousand francs for it.

The slow progress turned the chief into an object of ridicule: "M. Goron . . . marches through deception upon deception," *Le Gil*

Blas said. Goron was at such a loss that he began to reinterview everyone in the case, desperate for an overlooked clue, a careless word—
anything to put the investigation on track. But as he whirled vainly in
all directions, *L'Écho de Paris* summed up the situation: *"Rien, rien."*
(Nothing, nothing.)

Chapter 9

Barely two weeks into the investigation, an extraordinary gathering took place at the Hôtel Dieu, the oldest hospital in Paris, in the shadow of Notre Dame on the Île de la Cité. The event brought together nearly two hundred scientists, doctors, and experts for the First International Congress of Experimental and Therapeutic Hypnotism. The four-day conference, which opened on Thursday, August 8, 1889, held sessions on a range of issues from hypnotic hallucinations to hypnosis treatments for mental conditions.

Scholarship on hypnosis was at its peak. Books, magazines, and professional journals poured off the presses. In France there was the *Revue de l'hypnotisme*; in Germany, the *Zeitschrift für Hypnotismus*. Between 1885 and 1889, France led the world in publishing, turning out 37 percent of the 408 articles and books on hypnosis. Germany was home to less than half as many.

The most anticipated lecture of the congress would come on the final day when Jules Liégeois, a law professor at the University of Nancy, delivered his hotly contested theory of crime and hypnosis. That session would turn the amphitheater of highbrow academics into a schoolyard of squabbling children. Wisely, the organizers kept it for the close of the conference.

The site of the gathering, the Hôtel Dieu, had served as a refuge for the poor and the infirm ever since the church founded it in 651, five years before the first stone was laid on the Cathedral of Notre Dame next door. Despite the best intentions, for centuries the hospital was a chamber of horrors where patients in huge wards shared beds and breathed stagnant air, pungent with disease and death.

Although there were efforts to improve conditions—in the twelfth century King Philip Augustus donated straw from his stables to ease the bed shortage—the Hôtel Dieu remained notorious throughout the Renaissance. In the late seventeenth century if you showed up ill on its doorstep you had nearly a 30 percent chance of dying, double the rate at the more modern La Charité Hospital.

Disease and overcrowding weren't the only threats. A few days after Christmas in 1772 a fire broke out in one wing and raged for a week, killing scores. In the late eighteenth century, the philosopher Denis Diderot condemned the Hôtel Dieu, writing: "Imagine . . . every kind of patient, sometimes packed three, four, five or six into a bed, the living alongside the dead and dying, the air polluted by this mass of sick bodies, passing the pestilential germs of their afflictions from one to the other, and the spectacle of suffering and agony on every hand. That is the Hôtel Dieu."

By the time of the hypnotism conference a hundred years later no trace of the original Hôtel Dieu remained. Baron Georges-Eugène Haussmann, Napoleon III's prefect of the Seine, demolished the building in 1865, along with many other structures during his massive remodeling of Paris. The design of the new hospital stressed the importance of ventilation. Gone were the stuffy rooms and the stagnant air, and corridors were open to the outdoors. Planted courtyards, offering a breath of fresh air, served as gathering spots for both doctors and patients.

The two opposing schools on hypnotism assembled in the hospital amphitheater; on the one side were the Nancy theorists represented most prominently by Liégeois and the group's leader, Hippolyte Bernheim, and professing that the heart of hypnosis lay in suggestion, and on the other were the Paris academics, led in spirit by the neurologist Jean-Martin Charcot, who was represented at the congress by Georges Gilles de la Tourette, his fiercest acolyte.

A chief bone of contention was the matter of who among the general population was hypnotizable: The Paris school, associated with the Salpêtrière Hospital, believed hypnosis was a form of neurosis and hysterics were the most susceptible to hypnosis; evidence of the hysteric's hypnotic state was her neuromuscular reactions that occurred in a set pattern of contractions, anesthesia, and catalepsy.

The Nancy experts, based at the University of Nancy, had a broader interpretation; in their view, nearly anyone could be placed into a hypnotic state through the power of suggestion. Hypnosis had nothing to do with the narrowly defined sequence of physical reactions so crucial to the Salpêtrière school. The Nancy school's emphasis on suggestion implied that hypnosis was grounded in psychology rather than in neurology.

The two sides were already at war long before they gathered for the conference. Joseph Delbœuf, a Belgian philosopher and psychologist, questioned the scientific methods at the Salpêtrière, a grave charge given the towering authority of Charcot. The basis of the challenge was that the hypnotic behavior that supported the Paris school's conclusions—the pattern of muscular reactions—was nearly impossible to replicate outside the walls of the Salpêtrière Hospital. Delbœuf charged that what took place at the Salpêtrière was at best questionable, at worst outright fakery.

On a visit to the Salpêtrière, Delbœuf had watched two disciples of Charcot work with one of the star patients, a hysteric named Blanche Wittman, who obviously took pleasure in satisfying whatever the doctors wished to prove. Delbœuf concluded that her eagerness to provide the doctors with the behavior they sought tainted the credibility of the Salpêtrière research.

Challenging the Paris scientific community was a tricky matter. The majesty of French science resided in Paris, and any opposition to the capital's leadership was dismissed out of hand and often met with ridicule and disdain. But the hypnosis theories of the Nancy school were making inroads by the force of their own truths. Indeed, at several sessions of the congress, suggestion held sway as a key in understanding hypnosis. Some scholars believed the gathering was a turning point in the battle between the Salpêtrière and Nancy schools. "It is a remarkable fact that this Congress was dominated by Bernheim and the Nancy School," Henri F. Ellenberger wrote some years later in *The Discovery of the Unconscious.*

It was as if a fuse had been lit and was burning toward the explosive moment when Liégeois took the stage to present the Nancy views on crime and hypnosis in front of a restive army of Salpêtrière disciples poised to defend their positions.

Gilles de la Tourette was the commander of the Salpêtrière troops. In anticipation of Liégeois's appearance, he had stationed in the audience, young doctors and interns who were awaiting his order to attack.

The enmity between Liégeois and Gilles de la Tourette was both scholarly and personal. Gilles de la Tourette had reviled Liégeois for at least five years, ever since the law professor delivered his first major report on crime and hypnosis to the Academy of Moral and Political Sciences in 1884 and followed it up with an important book on the subject. Gilles de la Tourette had fired back with a book of his own, and now both men considered themselves preeminent scholars on crime and hypnosis and, like politicians on opposite sides of an issue, agreed on almost nothing. Although their books explored similar avenues of hypnosis and crime—cases of rape and experiments in simulated attacks and poisonings—they stood at odds on two key issues. Since Liégeois believed in the power of suggestion, he argued that almost anyone could be hypnotized and therefore could commit a crime under hypnosis, a view that implied a person's morality was malleable—under hypnosis, even the most upright citizen could be coerced into committing a crime. To Gilles de la Tourette, these were absurd propositions. In line with Charcot, he asserted that only people with severe hysterical neuroses could succumb to hypnosis and therefore the population of possible hypnotic criminals was limited; moreover, he and Charcot insisted that morality was fixed and could not be manipulated by a hypnotist.

The combatants were striking in their physical differences. Gilles de la Tourette was a neurologist at the Salpêtrière who had found a place in medical history for his work on a disorder characterized by motor and vocal tics, which has come to be known as Tourette's syndrome. He was an unattractive, argumentative man with skeletal cheekbones and heavy-lidded eyes. Lacking in social graces, he was loud and impulsive, foul to anyone who dared contradict him. He had no illusions about how he came across, describing himself as "ugly as a louse, but very intelligent."

Liégeois had the demeanor of an absentminded professor; he wore tiny, wire-rimmed spectacles, and his pants pockets were stuffed with notes. He was famous for boring his audiences, partly because his research was so voluminous and his recitation so detailed, but also because he was arrogant in supposing that his listeners hung on his every word.

Stepping to the podium on the final day of the congress, he opened by admitting to the delegates that he was undertaking a "perilous task" in speaking before them, but the risk was a worthy one. "Of all the questions submitted to the Congress," he told the amphitheater, "there are few as important as the reports" on crime and hypnotism.

And with that, he gave himself license to drone on as long as he wished. Launching into his presentation, he said, "In this case, the only thing that can be done, gentlemen, is a complete history of the subject." Then he strolled leisurely through the dusty archives of his own work until he finally came to his point: that his research proved an individual was capable of committing a serious crime in a hypnotized state. He'd seen it again and again in his laboratory. He had repeatedly produced what he described as "experimental crimes."

Crucial to his argument was that the hypnotized individual committed the crime without consciousness and therefore without responsibility. The hypnotized person was an automaton acting without free will under the command of the hypnotist. Liégeois told the audience that the spiritual father of the Nancy movement, the country doctor Ambroise-Auguste Liébeault, had confirmed his conclusions. "I am convinced as much as you, my dear friend," Liébeault wrote to Liégeois, "that certain somnambules will commit criminal acts by hypnotic suggestion and will do so irresistibly while asleep or while awake afterward—and therefore without any responsibility. They go to their goal the way a rock falls to earth."

Liégeois had argued for years that the guilty party was not the person who committed the crime but rather the hypnotist who instigated it. If the act was undertaken without consciousness, if the actor was indeed an automaton, then the hypnotist—the author of the suggestion—should be punished.

But how does one root out the author of the crime? It would be very difficult to do in some cases, Liégeois warned. If the hypnotist were crafty, he would ensure that his automaton had no recollection. The hypnotist would suggest to his subject that after the fact he would have total amnesia about the planning of the crime. It would simply never occur to the innocent perpetrator that the hypnotist had planted the crime in his mind. This, Liégeois concluded, made it nearly impossible to locate and punish the author of the criminal suggestion.

From his spot in the audience, Gilles de la Tourette listened, his fuse burning. Finally, unable to control himself, he shot to his feet and in a voice laced with contempt denounced Liégeois for speaking on medical matters that were beyond his qualifications as a mere law-yer. Gilles de la Tourette's cronies—the interns and medical students he'd planted in the audience—broke into wild applause. Then he ridiculed Liégeois's history of hypnotism and crime, and the gang erupted again.

Delbœuf was astonished by the rudeness of the Salpêtrière contin-gent, although he was awed by the eloquence of Gilles de la Tourette's harangue. "I had never heard someone use sarcasm with such mas-tery, such volubility, such aplomb," he recalled.

Delbœuf had seen the conspiracy forming around him. "It com-prised a crowd of young men, students of M. de la Tourette, without doubt," he wrote. "A young man who was in front of me had to have been one of the leaders because at each instant during the lecture of M. Liégeois he turned toward his master and made signs of collusion."

Now Gilles de la Tourette attacked Liégeois for unnecessarily stir-ring up the public's darkest fears. If, as Liégeois contended, hypnotists can turn anyone into an automaton, then a cunning devil could put the entire society under his spell. A political adventurer could stir up mass unrest. "You cannot look at someone too rigidly across the table or on a train for fear of letting yourself be hypnotized," Gilles de la Tourette scoffed. And then what? First one person, then another, and before you know it, the entire population is marching like an army of zombies in support of its hypnotic new leader. The country falls into the grip of a despot! At that, the Salpêtrière soldiers hooted and stamped their feet. They cried: "*Vive* Boulanger!"

It was only months earlier that a nightmarish coup had nearly befallen the nation. Georges Boulanger, a rugged general on horse-back, had won the hearts of the masses prancing about the streets atop his black stallion. He was the strong hand the country needed at a time of government weakness, rampant crime, and immorality. His admirers wanted him to seek a vacant Paris seat in the nation's legislative assembly known as the Chamber of Deputies. The news-papers sang his praises. His image was plastered everywhere. A nation hungry for renewal took pride in the powerful general. When he was elected in a landslide in January 1889, his supporters wanted more: A mob took to the streets urging Boulanger to march on the Élysée presidential palace and claim it as his own. The masses were as if mes-merized, and the nation stood on the edge of an uprising. The general, watching events from his headquarters at the restaurant Durand on the place de la Madeleine, went to the balcony to greet his supporters and heard the crowd chanting for him to seize power: *"À l'Élysée! À l'Élysée!"* Someone cried: "Say the word, *mon général,* and we march. Give the order!"

At the Élysée, President Sadi Carnot sat with his cabinet ministers in a state of gloom, worried that they were presiding over the death of the Republic. If Boulanger chose to seize power, there was little they could do to stop him. Most of the police force—including the few guards at the palace—were Boulangists. So were the Republican Guard and the army. There was nothing the ministers could do but await Boulanger's next move.

But the general didn't act. He was of two minds: He lusted for absolute power but also adored the companionship of his mistress, the Vicomtesse de Bonnemains, a striking beauty with long blond hair and sensuous lips who was about twenty years his junior. The vicomtesse, who was waiting in a private room at the restaurant, had a grip on the general that was more powerful than the cries of "*Vive* Boulanger!" Leaving his supporters, Boulanger went to join her. Later she would claim she gave him no advice. But after some time alone together Boulanger emerged with her, and the couple went downstairs and into the street. They climbed into a carriage, and the horses moved slowly through the crowd. The couple didn't answer the public outcry; the carriage didn't roll on to the Élysée. Boulanger and his mistress went to the apartment they shared as illicit lovers on the rue du Faubourg-Saint-Honoré and went to bed.

That night, Boulanger chose his mistress over the Republic. But his supporters didn't give up hope. Days passed with Parisians awaiting Boulanger's decision. Soon a month had elapsed. March arrived and still no action from the general. The government, sensing his hesitation, saw an opening and considered putting Boulanger on trial for plotting to overthrow the Republic. But turning on the general raised a host of delicate issues. His arrest could send his supporters back into the streets, and the result could be exactly the opposite of the intent—instead of quashing the threat, the action could precipitate a revolution that would sweep Boulanger into power.

In its impotence, the government instead chose to spread rumors that it was on the verge of arresting the general. For his part, Boulanger seemed paralyzed. Tipped off to his possible indictment, he lost his will. On April Fool's day 1889, he fled to Belgium with the lovely Vicomtesse de Bonnemains. The threat to the nation was over. Two years later so was his romance. The vicomtesse became ill—the diagnosis was tuberculosis and cancer of the stomach—and on July 16, 1891, she died at age thirty-five. Two and a half months after her death, the general visited her grave, sat with his back against her tombstone, put a revolver to his temple, and shot a bullet into his brain.

The cries of "*Vive* Boulanger!" at the congress were meant to highlight the lingering fears of a mass uprising at the hands of a hypnotic leader. But there was something else inherent in the outburst: It was meant to scorn Liégeois and put his theories in the darkest light. If everyone was hypnotizable, as Liégeois insisted, then the nation had good reason to fear a Boulanger or any similar opportunist who might follow him. The young doctors and interns pounding their feet and roaring seemed intent on literally stamping out the fear.

Delbœuf, white-bearded and balding, had never seen such a spectacle among intellectuals. "It was the noisiest occasion that I have ever been to," he recalled. "I could not imagine that these scholars belonged to France which had a reputation for politeness—no, never in my life."

Gilles de la Tourette wasn't finished, and he moved in for the final attack. He demanded proof of the absurd proposition that a person would kill at the command of a hypnotist. "Back in 1887 I asked M. Liégeois to cite me a single case of crime by suggestion," he reminded the audience. And what was Liégeois's reply? He admitted that the only way he could quiet his critics was for him to deliver not only a poor soul who was ordered to murder under hypnosis but the cadaver as well—and that was something he knew he simply could not do.

To Gilles de la Tourette, the absence of a body was conclusive: No cadaver, no truth to a preposterous hypothesis. Crime under hypnosis was a mere theory that would never burst out of the laboratory into the real world.

"And so," Gilles de la Tourette boasted to the audience, "we hasten to declare our triumph."

But Liégeois was not willing to go quietly. If Gilles de la Tourette wanted to breathe fire, Liégeois was ready to match him. "Would you want me to bring a somnambule on stage right now," Liégeois challenged, "and have him submit to a strangling?"

The taunt brought the young doctors and students back onto their feet, heckling and pounding their chests, shouting: "Me! Me! Take me!" It was a "deafening uproar," Delbœuf recalled a year later. "My ears still ring at the memory."

And so the theory of crime under hypnosis—unproved, unaccepted, little more than a hypothesis—left the scholars at a stalemate. With no real-life murder—no actual shooting, stabbing, or strangling, no blood, no body, no plea of hypnotic control—it was impossible to prove or disprove anything.

And yet, in an astonishing coincidence, the very next day, August 13, a ghoulish discovery nearly three hundred miles away set the stage for a final showdown, though none of the combatants at the time had any inkling. It would be months before an unidentified cadaver found on a riverbank outside Lyon inspired a real-world test for the theory of murder under hypnosis.

Chapter 10

The odor arose in late July and thickened day by day until soon the village of Millery, some ten miles south of Lyon, was suffocating. The townsfolk wondered if Gypsies migrating along this desolate stretch of the Rhône River had dumped a dog carcass in the brambles. Or perhaps a massive fish kill spewed a stink up the embankment. By mid-August the air had turned so foul that a local dignitary, the Comtesse de Bec-de-Lièvre, fainted while riding in her carriage to church. Something had to be done. So the comtesse ordered her valet to get to the bottom of it, and he in turn hurried off to the local road mender Denis Coffy, who agreed to take on the task, promising: "I'll find what stupidity could smell this way."

After delaying for two days, Coffy found the spot along the river where the stench was at its worst. Here the road climbed a knoll and the river dropped out of sight down a steep embankment. A guardrail protected carriages from tumbling over the precipice. The air, normally full of the scent of wildflowers, reeked of death.

Coffy made his way down the embankment, slashing through the brush with his billhook, until suddenly he was upon it: a lumpy sack lying at the base of an acacia bush in a frenzy of flies. Here was the source of Millery's torment. Coffy took a tentative step forward, then froze—he needed help. He made an about-face, scrambled back up the embankment, and raced into town.

Later in the day, Coffy was again on his way down the embankment, this time accompanied by local policeman Jacques Mange. The surroundings were deathly quiet except for the brush crunching beneath their feet and the buzzing of the flies. With a swing of his billhook Coffy sliced opened the burlap sack, revealing what appeared to be a human head hidden under an oilskin hood. Poking gingerly inside the sack, the men discovered a naked body tied up in a fetal position.

They dragged the sack up the embankment to the edge of the road. Then Coffy cautiously lifted the hood off the head, revealing a swollen, blackened face that was so decayed the eyes and nose were missing. Bloated lips bulged from a soiled beard and mustache. Having seen enough, the two men tossed handfuls of grass onto the corpse and hurried off to deliver the news.

At midnight Coffy was back at the scene again with the investigating magistrate Bastide and a young medical examiner from Lyon named Paul Bernard. Working under weak lantern light until 2:00 a.m., Bastide finally ordered Coffy to load the corpse onto a cart and take it to the morgue.

After a brief rest, Bernard began his autopsy at 8:00 a.m. A corpse in such an advanced state of decomposition presented a formidable challenge, particularly for an examiner of limited experience and skills. Alexandre Lacassagne, a professor of pathology at the University of Lyon and a giant in forensic medicine, would have applied his knowledgeable hand to the task, had he not been on vacation, and from the start the course of the investigation would have taken a radically different path. His former student Bernard did his best under the circumstances but his work was clumsy and imprecise. Making matters worse, the corpse by this time was barely intact. So fragile were the remains that hair and beard fell away at a touch. The internal organs—the spleen, kidneys, and bladder—had all been consumed by nature's maw. Bernard jotted in his notes that the brain resembled semiliquid boiled meat.

After laboring for several hours, he guessed that the victim had been dead for three to five weeks, which placed the murder between July 9 and July 23. That put the death just beyond Gouffé's disappearance on July 26.

Bernard estimated the dead man's age at between thirty-five and forty-five; his weight, at about a hundred and sixty-five pounds. His height, according to Bernard's best measurements, was five feet seven inches. The color of the victim's hair was black, the medical examiner concluded, ruling out a possible match with the missing Gouffé, whose hair was chestnut brown.

Despite the body's state of decay, Bernard surmised that the victim was most likely a man of means, for the nails on both the hands and feet had evidence of a manicure. In the dead man's stomach he found remnants of a final meal: partially digested pasta, carrots, and green beans. In a crucial dental clue, he determined that the first right molar in the upper jaw was missing. For the cause of death, Bernard concluded from two breaks in the larynx: "I think that the victim was strangled by hand." While the autopsy brought to light several important facts, the medical examiner was unable to attach a name to the body. The Millery corpse remained a mystery.

The next day, August 15, investigators received some new evidence. Alphonse Richard, a farmer, was hunting for escargot along the banks of the Rhône with his nine-year-old son when he stumbled upon a pile of wood scraps in a watery ravine. As he collected the pieces—about twenty in all—he realized they were the shattered remnants of a large trunk. At first he considered keeping them for firewood but was put off by their ghastly odor. He was aware of the corpse's discovery, news of which had traveled quickly through town, and now wondered if this trunk could have played a role in the death. Soon the scraps of sycamore and fir were in the hands of the police.

Two days later, on the morning of August 17, Coffy was back at the site, resting against the guardrail, when he spotted a metal object on the ground. Stooping down, he picked up a key and took it to investigators who tried it in the trunk's lock: a perfect fit. The key, the reasoning went, had been tossed away carelessly after the trunk was unlocked to dump the body; then the trunk had been hauled farther down the road where it was shattered, and the pieces were tossed over the embankment into the ravine where Richard found them.

But could that trunk, large as it was, carry a full-grown man? To find out, investigators ordered two craftsmen to rebuild it—no easy task given the scraps' poor condition and the stench of death that still clung to them. The craftsmen, François Duveau and Jean Cormod, went to work under such suffocating conditions that at one point Duveau became ill. Yet the men soldiered on and had soon pieced together their puzzle: The scraps formed a trunk that was about three feet long, a little less than two feet wide, and just over two feet high. Large—but large enough for a man? To test it, Cormod climbed inside and pulled his legs up into a fetal position like the victim. Duveau then lowered the lid, closing Cormod inside and proving that the corpse of a man not quite six feet tall with his legs drawn up could have been crammed into this undersized coffin.

One point was clear: The Millery corpse had once lain in the sycamore and fir trunk. But the Lyon investigators knew little else. The dead man had no name and his killer was on the loose.

Chapter 11

Police departments in nineteenth-century France were notorious for their failure to communicate with each other. Often it was provincial pride: Local cops wanted nothing to do with Paris; they were reluctant to assist the capital and abhorred interference in their own cases for fear of being ridiculed for their bumbling ways.

Chief Goron, for his part, tried to plug the gaps. He was assiduous in informing the provinces of criminals on the run from Paris and of other police matters in which he had an interest. But that didn't mean the provinces rushed to reciprocate. So Goron resorted to other means of information, and newspapers were his best source. To keep abreast of crimes in the hinterlands that could have a bearing on his own cases, Goron read every paper he could get his hands on from every corner of the country and around the world. He also kept a close eye on what came in from correspondents working for the Paris newspapers in other cities.

By mid-August, the Gouffé case had ground to a halt, and Paul Dopffer, the investigating judge, even admitted to *L'Écho de Paris* that he was discouraged. Goron was in desperate need of a break when two newspapers landed on his desk, each with a brief story about an unidentified body that had turned up in Lyon. The remains had been discovered on a bank of the Rhône River and delivered to the Lyon morgue. There was nothing in the reports to suggest that this corpse so many miles from Paris had anything to do with the Gouffé case. But Goron had a hunch.

He pressured Dopffer to telegraph his counterpart in Lyon for details but the judge demurred; he didn't want to chase after another dead end—the investigation had already suffered enough embarrassment. But Goron persisted—his relentlessness was breathtaking—

and finally Dopffer caved. But the Lyon investigating judge Bastide gave Paris the quick brush-off: The Millery corpse, he said, could not have been more different from Gouffé and, furthermore, Lyon had its investigation well in hand and required no assistance from Paris.

Not one to be denied, Goron telegraphed a reporter who had written about the cadaver and soon had a full account of the case. He learned about the stench that overtook Millery in July, the body's discovery in August, the inconclusive autopsy, and the recovery of the trunk. The victim, Goron read, was five feet seven inches tall, between thirty-five and forty-five years old, and had black hair; his larynx was broken in two places, suggesting death by strangulation.

One other piece of evidence intrigued Goron. A railway baggage label had been found on a scrap of the shattered trunk. It indicated that the trunk rode aboard an express train from Paris to the Lyon-Perrache railroad station. But the label was frustratingly incomplete. It was missing the last numeral on the date of the journey: 7/27/188—

Goron, however, had no trouble completing the label: To him, the conclusion was indisputable. Gouffé had disappeared on July 27; a few weeks later a rotting corpse and a smashed trunk showed up on a Lyon riverbank. In what year could that have occurred except 1889?

But Bastide and his cohorts in Lyon, including a special police commissioner named Ramonencq, were of another mind: They had decided, for reasons that baffled Goron, that the missing numeral was an eight, not a nine, and therefore, that the trunk had come to Lyon a full year earlier, in 1888, and had only now been used in the commission of a local crime.

Goron was stuck. The reasoning of the Lyon investigators was absurd but he had little chance of persuading them to see things his way. Besides, Bastide and the Lyon contingent had one piece of evidence that was impossible to contest. Everyone who saw the rotting corpse had the same opinion of the hair: it was black. Protest all he might, Goron could not change Gouffé's hair color from its now well-publicized chestnut brown.

Of all the people who had seen the corpse—villagers, investigators, police, the medical examiner—no one had known Gouffé. What, Goron wondered, might have been missed by this parade of strangers? If Goron could send a relative of Gouffé's to Lyon for a private viewing, perhaps something would leap out, some jarring feature of the corpse, maybe a trait that only an intimate would recognize. Despite its terrible decomposition, the cadaver had to have its chance to talk.

Goron now had the difficult task of convincing both investigating judges, Dopffer in Paris and Bastide in Lyon, that a family viewing was essential. At the very least, a proper investigation demanded such thoroughness. Not only that, officials owed this courtesy to the anguished Gouffé family. Goron kept pestering until he wore down his opposition and, grudgingly, both judges granted his request. Dopffer gave in only to placate Goron, while Bastide believed he had nothing to lose and saw an opportunity to humiliate Goron and the Paris Sûreté.

Goron assigned Brigadier Léon Soudais to accompany Gouffé's brother-in-law Louis-Marie Landry to Lyon. Both men, expecting a chilly reception, a gruesome corpse, and probable failure, were less than enthusiastic. Before departing, Brigadier Soudais, a man who usually kept his complaints to himself, told Goron he was ready to carry out the mission as ordered but doubted its chance of success. His gloom irritated Goron, who demanded blind obedience from his troops. To him, any pessimism from an agent impaired the fortunes of the Sûreté. "Faith is indispensable in police work, as much as it is in art or in literature," he wrote in his memoir. "Sadly, it frequently is lacking in agents, especially when it's the boss who asks it of them . . . So Soudais left in a bad humor and his skepticism was only made worse in Lyon."

Goron's prognosis was quickly borne out. Arriving at the Lyon police headquarters, the two Parisians were subjected to hours of bureaucratic formalities. Worse, Soudais had to fend off mocking questions from local officers: Had he come to Lyon to learn how to solve crimes? Did Paris police know so little they needed lessons from the provinces? The sting of ridicule only sharpened Soudais's criticism of Goron. "Naturally," the chief wrote, "this attitude of Lyon encouraged my brigadier to think that I was completely misled."

Landry and Soudais arrived at the morgue after nightfall. What would have been a ghastly viewing in daylight was a horror in the dark. The morgue sat on a barge in the Rhône and was reached by a wooden gangplank. The visitors were met by a filthy attendant with an untamed beard and hair hanging down almost to his waist. Père

Delaignue guided them over the gangplank by the light of his swaying lantern, his pipe smoke slightly mellowing the thick odor of rotting flesh.

Inside, Delaignue pointed out which of three nude bodies lying on the stone floor was the Millery corpse. Landry, with a handkerchief pressed to his nose, glanced at the wretched remains, which flickered in the reddish beam of the lantern. He gazed just long enough to convince himself that the putrid flesh on the floor was not that of his brother-in-law. It looked barely human. And the hair, as expected, was as black as the dismal night. If Landry's verdict was hasty, it was, he believed, the best he could have done under the circumstances. As he explained later to Goron, "If you are in a sinister place like this your single preoccupation is to get out of there as quickly as possible."

By the next morning, Goron had Soudais's telegram in his hand and frustration in his breast. The Millery corpse was slipping out of reach. On August 24, *Le Petit Journal* resolved the matter, announcing that the body had been identified as that of a Monsieur Peillon, an architect in Lyon. Three days later, however, the question apparently was still open as the same newspaper reported that the corpse was not that of Monsieur Peillon but rather that of a Monsieur Martin, the long-missing husband of a Madame Martin.

Whoever the unfortunate soul was, it wasn't the missing Parisian. "It is at present established that the cadaver in Millery is not that of the bailiff Gouffé who, it is believed, has been spotted in good health in London," reported *L'Éclair*. "M. Goron has vainly invoked the gods, including the god of luck who is often so amiable to the police but who does not know anymore what murder to devote himself to."

Chapter 12

Michel Eyraud was on his way back to the murder scene—and no appeal to reason could dissuade him. His obsession with his hat was just the latest example of the crazy ideas that filled his head. His wrecked life was a testament to his blind pursuit of ill-advised schemes. In the early 1860s, when he was with the French army in Mexico, he became enamored of a local young woman. Fluent in Spanish and glib of tongue, he considered himself quite a ladies' man—as the French put it, a *coureur de jupons,* a skirt chaser. One day he used his charm and language skills to set up a date with the girl. But his commanding officer nixed the rendezvous and ordered him to stay in camp. So Eyraud plotted his escape. On the appointed evening, he slipped away on a stolen army horse.

His fool idea got him charged with desertion and suddenly he was in legal limbo. If he returned to France, he risked arrest. So he roamed South America, careful to evade French troops, who along with the British and Spanish armies had invaded Mexico in response to the country's delinquent debt payments. In 1869, Eyraud got lucky when the French government offered a general amnesty for military deserters. He returned to Paris long enough to marry a woman from a respected family in 1870, and soon he and his wife, Louise-Laure, had a daughter. But ever restless, Eyraud helped himself to his wife's dowry of forty thousand francs and deserted mother and baby to resume a life of adventure.

By 1872 he was in Córdoba, Argentina, where he passed himself off as the personal business emissary of Napoleon III. By then, Napoleon III was in exile in the British village of Chislehurst after France's defeat in the Franco-Prussian War of 1870. Nonetheless, the fraudulent use of his name allowed Eyraud to attract thousands of francs for nonexistent business opportunities until the Argentine deputies and senators he duped realized his deception. Eyraud vanished and next appeared in the Paris suburb of Aubervilliers where he represented a London glassworks company in 1875 and 1876. The following five years found him back in South America in the employ of the English fabric manufacturer Thomas Adams & Cie, until he was dismissed in the early 1880s for what the company characterized as dishonesty.

Now he was running again, this time from his most serious crime yet. He and Gabrielle Bompard arrived in Paris from Marseille as the newspapers were reporting the discovery of the corpse near Lyon. They enjoyed a moment of relief when the press declared that the remains were not those of Gouffé, the slow progress in the case giving the fugitives some breathing room. Neither Eyraud nor Gabrielle had surfaced in the press. Nearly a month after the crime still no one had any idea they had played a role. It seemed a remote possibility that the apartment at 3, rue Tronson du Coudray had figured at all in the police investigation. Indeed, when Eyraud arrived at the building he found no detectives staking out the place—no sign of any activity at all. The block was as quiet as when he had left it. Inside the apartment nothing had been disturbed. His hat awaited him.

Cocky as ever, with his own hat now back on his head, Eyraud set off to visit his wife's brother, Léon-Guisbert Choteau, a shirtmaker, and walked away with two thousand francs in loans. Now he had enough money to flee Paris with his mistress and start a new life far beyond the clutches of French justice.

Before setting off, however, he took some precautions: With a pair of scissors and a new wardrobe, the middle-aged man and his mistress transformed themselves into father and teenage son. Gabrielle chopped her hair as short as a boy's, put on a pair of pants and a shirt, and the murderers headed for England under the name Labordère, the same name they had used to rent the apartment at 3, rue Tronson du Coudray.

At just four feet eight inches, Gabrielle could pass convincingly as a teenage boy. As doctors examining her later noted, she had a child-like physique, with narrow hips and rudimentary breasts. "One can understand," the doctors wrote in their report, "how easily she was able to be taken for a young boy of about fifteen."

Eyraud and his son took a steamer across the Channel to Dover and went from there to London and then on to Liverpool. On the train, Eyraud bunched into his hand a gold watch and chain he had stripped from the corpse and tossed them out the window. After a wait of several days in Liverpool, the travelers set sail for Quebec, Canada, aboard a transatlantic steamer, plowing across the sea at about seventeen knots. It was time now for the duo to cast off one fake identity—the name Labordère—for a new one—Vanaerd. Gabrielle discarded her role of the Labordère teenage son and transformed herself into a blond-haired girl, Berthe, the daughter of Monsieur E. B. Vanaerd. To cover their villainy as international fugitives, Eyraud had appropriated the name of Gabrielle's uncle, Émile Vanaerd, the kindhearted dental surgeon who had looked after her for eight years in Belgium.

Eyraud had several options for his new sham life in North America. He could present himself as a Paris businessman involved in international trade; his facility with Spanish and Portuguese and his experiences in South America provided him with good cover. Or he could pretend to be a sophisticated French vintner. Although the management of his family's vineyards ended in failure, he had gained a textbook education in wine and winemaking. He was at his best on the move, relying on his wiles and quick wits. He was a garrulous storyteller, a showman, a man of easy impersonations and no scruples. His repartee suggested a successful businessman, an honest Frenchman with an admirable command of English. With Gabrielle at his side, he was the picture of the doting father.

After nearly three weeks at sea, the steamer landed at the Port of Quebec on September 7. Eyraud and Gabrielle checked into the Hotel Richelieu in Montreal where, according to one report, "they lived riotously" for a couple of weeks. Eyraud surprised Gabrielle with a pair of earrings he'd had made in Paris using diamonds from Gouffé's pinkie ring.

Posing as E. B. Vanaerd, international trader, Eyraud inserted himself into Montreal society. "Vanaerd was a hail fellow well met," one newspaper said, "and made several friends, to whom he introduced the woman who was traveling with him simply as 'my daughter.'" He was on his way, he said, from Paris to Vancouver where he planned to establish a branch of his company.

The couple boarded the Canadian Pacific Railroad and rode across the continent, reaching Vancouver in the latter part of Septem-

ber. There, they met a French adventurer and businessman, Georges
Garanger, who was just back from the Far East and who was destined to play a decisive role in their lives. He was tall and blond, with
"blue eyes of incomparable softness," as one report put it. Forty-nine
years old, he was still youthful and handsome, "one of those men who
didn't seem to age." His family had made a fortune in jewelry, particularly diamonds, then lost a substantial portion of it during hard
times in the mid-1880s. Garanger then spent time in the Far East and
Africa, becoming a wealthy man again thanks to lucrative new businesses he established in Algeria and Burma.

Eyraud boasted to his new acquaintance of his own success in the
cognac business and of his plans to establish a distillery in California.
He and his daughter, in fact, were on their way to San Francisco.
Was Garanger aware of the fortune that could be made by export-
ing cognac from the Napa Valley to France? Why not join them in
San Francisco? Sensing he'd found a potential dupe, Eyraud invited
Garanger to invest in his new distillery project. The wealthy adven-
turer was intrigued but noncommittal, saying he regretted he couldn't
go on to San Francisco just then; he had business to attend to in
Vancouver.

This brief encounter ignited an explosion of passions in all parties and set in motion a chain of events that would shape the outcome of the Gouffé case. For his part, Eyraud, reckless and greedy,
had designs on Garanger's fortune, whatever violence was required
to get it. By now, Gabrielle had begun to despise Eyraud and longed
to escape; in Garanger she saw her savior. And Garanger, unattached
and trusting, had an eye for Monsieur Vanaerd's lovely daughter. He
promised to meet up with the family in San Francisco in a few days.

Chapter 13

Étienne Laforge was a twenty-one-year-old coachman who had been jailed for attempted fraud in 1885 and now, to stay in the good graces of the Lyon police, served as an informant. He was a large, dim-witted peasant but also just smart enough to recognize a golden opportunity when it presented itself. Like everyone in town he'd heard the stories of the mysterious body and trunk that turned up on a riverbank in Millery. He also knew that the case baffled police.

Thinking he could help, he went to police headquarters and started talking. He revealed that on the night of July 6 he had picked up three men with a trunk and took them in the direction of Millery. On a deserted road along the river he agreed to wait in his cab while the men carried the trunk off into the distance. He shut down his lanterns, as they demanded, and lazed in the dark for an hour and a half until the men finally reappeared, still carrying the trunk. After they loaded it onto the coach Laforge took them back to Lyon, arriving at about 10:00 p.m. And he hadn't seen the trio since.

The large peasant obviously hadn't read the newspapers carefully enough, if he could read them at all. Had he paid attention, he'd have known that the trunk did not come back to Lyon with the murderers but was left in a shattered state on the banks of the Rhône. But he got the story almost right, and Commissioner Ramonencq, whose chief concern was simply to wrap things up as quickly as possible, helpfully nudged Laforge in the right direction. The commissioner suggested a few convincing details to fill out the tale—such as the exact condition of the trunk—and in his corrupt mind justice crept closer to being served.

Soon Laforge had refashioned his story. In its latest telling, he transported the men and their trunk nearly to the spot where the body was found; the men still lugged the trunk down the road, and Laforge still waited in the dark, but when the men came back, this time they were empty-handed. Now Laforge's memory conformed to the published realities. The peasant also embellished for the sake of drama. Before climbing out of the coach back in Lyon, he recalled, one of the men warned him: "You tell anyone where we got rid of the trunk and I'll break your neck. I have a habit of doing that, you know." And the thug flashed a set of brass knuckles. The young toughs were between twenty and twenty-five, Laforge told police; the leader had a small, bronze-colored mustache and a scar above the right eye.

But what were the names of these suspects? Ramonencq wanted to know. Laforge hesitated, claiming the men never called each other by name. Ramonencq was not pleased and instructed Laforge to search his mind: One did not gain anything for oneself without divulging crucial information. No sooner was the warning issued than three names flew off the peasant's lips: François Revol, Paul Michel Chatin, and Adrien Apollinaire Boubanin. All were underworld figures who were in jail for stabbing a restaurant manager to death just three days after Laforge said he drove them to Millery. If Laforge were to be believed, these young men were very busy murderers.

Laforge's testimony set the police into action. They visited the killers' landlady, who affirmed that her three tenants were out all night on July 6, the day Laforge claimed to have transported them in his cab.

Laforge's interrogation made its way to Chief Goron in Paris. A witness? It was the last thing he wanted to hear. And this witness fingered three suspects? Impossible. One report portrayed Goron as receiving the report from Lyon "with bad grace," adding that "with his peculiar type of obstinacy, he refused to let it alter his opinion." A look at the calendar, Goron insisted, destroyed Laforge's time frame. He could not possibly have met the three mysterious men on the date he claimed. If the men dumped the body on July 6, then the stench of its decomposition should have swamped Millery around the middle of the month. But the odor didn't surface until late in the month or even into early August. So Laforge's timing was off, making his testimony, in Goron's view, a despicable lie.

The Sûreté chief could do nothing but watch while provincial rogues turned their backs on justice. Having begun as a trifling weekend disappearance of a rich man, the Gouffé case had swelled into one of the greatest frustrations of Goron's career.

The chief had only one suspect, Gouffé's business associate Rémy-François Launé, but Launé had repeatedly dodged his clutches like a pickpocket on a crowded boulevard. The robust Launé had become a familiar face at the Sûreté offices and always had a smooth answer for every question and never said more than was necessary.

Launé was forty-two, the son of a distiller who had disappeared after driving the business into bankruptcy. As a young man he'd emulated his father, falling afoul of the law at age fifteen and spending three years in jail. A cunning businessman, he briefly changed the spelling of his name to Launay, a move possibly intended to disguise his illicit activities. A short time before Gouffé disappeared he had been hauled into court for charging illegal high interest rates on loans he provided and, again thanks to his silver tongue, had managed to escape jail. Gouffé had recognized Launé's craftiness and put him to work on one of the more unpleasant tasks of his business: shaking loose delinquent debt payments. Their business relationship dated back to 1871 and was understandably rife with tensions. Launé collected thousands of francs on behalf of Gouffé but often was slow to part with the money. On July 25, 1889, the night before Gouffé vanished, the two men were overheard on the terrace of Café Véron arguing over eighty thousand francs in Launé's possession, which belonged to Gouffé. The men were drinking absinthe when Gouffé insisted loudly—and he rarely raised his voice: "I do not like money to lie idle. I wait for you to reimburse me."

Other circumstantial evidence pointed to Launé. Goron's detectives had questioned a woman who claimed she walked into Gouffé's office just as Launé threatened to kill the bailiff. And he had good reason for wanting Gouffé out of the way. He owed his first interest payments on loans he'd taken from Gouffé for construction of a building in Sèvres, about eight miles from the center of Paris. The payments were due at the end of July but Launé was short of cash—so much so that a few days before Gouffé disappeared he had to halt construction on the project. But the stoppage didn't last long. Soon after Gouffé disappeared, Launé somehow had come up with the funds to resume construction.

Inspector Jaume wondered if Launé had a large sum of money

he'd collected for Gouffé but hadn't yet handed over. Suspiciously, a ledger containing notes on the amounts in Launé's possession was stolen on the night of July 26—the night of Gouffé's disappearance, the same night a mysterious man entered his office. More curious still, Launé showed up at Gouffé's office the following day and engaged in a bizarre conversation with the concierge. He apparently was aware of the mysterious visitor and the disappearance of the ledger; indeed, it was tempting to surmise that Launé was acquainted with the thief and that he wanted to ensure that his identity remained unknown.

"You are incapable of recognizing him?" Launé asked the concierge several times, anxiously pressing the point, and only relented when the concierge insisted he'd barely had a look at the man and had no idea who he was. "With this," one report said, Launé "left like a man reassured."

As this cloud of suspicion settled over Launé, detectives reinterpreted his dramatic reaction on first learning of Gouffé's disappearance. The exclamation of surprise and the clapping of his hand over his heart were now seen as a flagrant display of poor acting intended to disguise his own role in the crime. But what was that role? Did Launé have a hand in the deed, or was he just a conspirator? Inspector Jaume suspected Launé had an ulterior motive for wanting Gouffé killed. To get to the bottom of the matter, Jaume invited the shifty suspect to lunch and chatted idly until the dessert arrived. Then he brought up the Gouffé case.

"It is well-proven," the inspector said, sipping his coffee, "that you didn't take part in this crime. But," he added with a laugh, "you could have profited from it." Jaume suggested that Launé had cash belonging to the bailiff still in his possession. "That would have put some butter in your spinach!"

At that, Launé smiled slyly but didn't say a word.

If he played a role, Launé had made sure to cover his tracks. From morning to night on the day of July 26 he had made a point of being seen all around Sèvres, as one account put it, "going from one person to the next as if to say hello to the whole town." He even joined in a meeting of the local gymnastics society from eight to ten that evening, during which everyone could have vouched for his attendance. His appearance at the meeting ruled out any possibility that he was on the boulevards in Paris to meet Gouffé after his dinner at Café Véron.

Still, Goron kept the pressure on him, summoning him repeatedly for interrogations at Sûreté headquarters. As one session was nearing its end, Launé suddenly tossed out a tantalizing lead.

"There is a man who disappeared at the same time as Gouffé," he began. But after dropping this bombshell, Launé immediately backpedaled. He was not pointing toward a suspect; no, he was only indicating a certain coincidence. "This has nothing to do with the disappearance of Gouffé," he explained. "But since the case is so complicated I just give you the idea."

So why mention it at all? What was his motive? Was he hoping it would get detectives off his own back? Goron came down hard, demanding to know who this person was. And then for the first time the chief heard a name that would trouble his days for months to come: Michel Eyraud.

Chapter 14

Inspector Jaume was leery of this new lead. Considering the source, he gave it little credence. The last thing the Sûreté needed was another dead end. "Could it be one of the useless rumors that we've heard enough of?" he jotted in his diary.

But the following day brought a change of heart. "Hold on! Hold on!" Jaume cautioned himself. "The story of the person named Eyraud . . . starts to seriously intrigue me." Eyraud, Jaume had learned, was a cash-strapped businessman who had met Gouffé for drinks at Café Gutenberg the night before both men disappeared. Launé, who was present, told the detectives that as Gouffé sat down he warned Eyraud, "I don't know if I should drink with you since you've gone bankrupt." Eyraud had a ready answer. He glibly accepted no responsibility for his financial straits and, if his conditions were a bit tight, that was because his company had fallen on hard times. "It's not me who went bankrupt! It was my boss." A convenient lie, for the truth was, his former employer Fribourg & Cie had chased off the embezzler Eyraud, and the firm's finances were sound.

Gradually Eyraud began to occupy the detectives' minds. For one thing, he fit the description of the man in the overcoat who slipped in and out of Gouffé's office on the night of July 26. On that same night, investigators learned, he stumbled home at 1:00 a.m. and then hurried away again at 7:00 a.m. His wife, Louise-Laure, admitted that her husband had numerous affairs, and he often disappeared for long periods after which he returned in a fugue state unclear about where he had been and what he had done.

Eyraud's latest mistress, according to his friend Launé, was a twenty-one-year-old named Gabrielle Bompard. The forty-five-year-old Eyraud and his girlfriend were habitués of the boulevard cafés and brasseries, and were well-known to the maître d's; but when questioned, none had seen them for weeks. Launé divulged other curious facts. The night before Eyraud disappeared, he used English currency to pay his restaurant bill, raising questions about whether he had been to England recently and why, and suggesting where he might be found now. Launé described a business partnership he and Eyraud had formed in Sèvres in the mid-1880s. In his telling, the two men were wine merchants, although police later discovered that they in fact had created an elaborate scheme to defraud wine distributors.

At the outset of each scam, Launé presented himself to a distributor as an independent businessman who had relationships with many reputable wine buyers. Then Eyraud visited the same distributor under a fake name and posed as one of Launé's buyers. The distributor would then contact Launé, who would sing Eyraud's praises, assuring the distributor of Eyraud's golden reputation and rock-solid credit, and advise the distributor to sell his wine to him. He then recommended an excellent winery where the distributor could purchase his wine to sell to Eyraud; this winery, called Joltrois and Eyraud, happened to be a front set up by the two con artists.

After the distributor bought the wine from Joltrois and Eyraud, he would ship it to the Bercy train station to be picked up by Eyraud under his assumed name. But Eyraud would never show up, and the wine would sit at the station until the distraught distributor called Launé for help. Feigning surprise, Launé would generously offer to buy the lot at a steeply reduced price. The difference between what he offered to pay for the wine and the much higher amount the distributor originally paid left Eyraud and Launé with a handsome profit. What's more, they got the wine back, which they could now sell again to another dupe. Clever and wicked, the scam was unsustainable and by 1887 had run its course.

And now, two years later, Launé was at the Sûreté headquarters dragging his former partner into the Gouffé case. But while casting suspicion on Eyraud in one breath, Launé tried to protect him in the next. "You can't accuse him of anything," he told Goron. "He's an honest man. I know him."

The police pieced together a portrait of Eyraud as a middle-aged man clinging to pretenses. He wore a toupee to hide his baldness, favored cameo cuff links and high silk hats, and thought of himself as a Don Juan. But just as police became intrigued by him, the leads dried up: The newest suspect was nowhere to be found in Paris. "One sees that it's not necessary to put great hope in this new trail," one newspaper commented. "The double and simultaneous disappearance of the bailiff and his friend the trader could be nothing more than a simple coincidence."

Eyraud's wife stepped forward in his defense. Although she'd had no word from him, Louise-Laure insisted on his innocence. His disappearance, she told the newspapers, was easily explained: He had gone to Rio de Janeiro on business.

The newspapers beat up on Chief Goron—his handling of the case was in a shambles. His obsession with the Millery corpse was indefensible, and the papers demanded he give up on the hunch. Agreeing to an interview with *L'Éclair,* Goron said what the public wanted to hear. "I tell you frankly," he insisted, "that I never thought that the cadaver was that of Gouffé." But, he added, if there was the slightest chance the corpse might have played a role in the bailiff's case, he had to pursue it; he sent Soudais and Landry to Lyon to demonstrate that he was neglecting nothing in his investigation. Privately, however, he still clung to his hunch, and his trusted sidekick, Inspector Jaume, stood staunchly by his side. From the outset, just like Goron, Jaume never doubted the importance of the corpse in the Lyon morgue. "In learning of the discovery of the cadaver of Millery, I did not hesitate one second," Jaume wrote in his memoir. "I said to myself: 'That's Gouffé's cadaver there! I bet the universe against a bunch of carrots.'"

The reporter from *L'Éclair* challenged Goron on the search for Eyraud. If he had been a potential suspect, why hadn't the Sûreté chief known about him sooner? Goron grew testy. "What do you want?" he said, then added in an obvious slur on Launé: "In this case, one must confess that Gouffé's acquaintances have not been very valuable in our assistance." Careful not to alienate the press, Goron claimed he wasn't displeased by any of the criticism in the newspapers. In fact, he insisted, the press attention only drove him and his men to work harder. "The more the newspapers occupy themselves with this case, the more information will come to us," he said. Indeed, he had received two hundred letters from the public thanks to press coverage. "There are some idiots among them," he pointed out, "but some of the letters are full of very useful observations."

With little reason for optimism, other than his unwillingness to accept defeat, Goron finished on a note of bravado: "I have the strong hope that I will straighten out this mysterious business."

The case already was shaping up as a sensation. As *Le Figaro* declared: "Opinion continues to follow with passion the twists and turns, which are more moving than the best-framed novels."

Goron was wracked by his failure. He stayed up into the night obsessing over botched leads and new angles. Inspector Jaume detected the signs of stress in his boss. "I see," he noted with lighthearted concern, "that Goron's mustache has lost its symmetry."

Chapter 15

Chief Goron had no corpse, no suspects, no solid leads. Weeks after Gouffé's disappearance, the investigation was at a standstill. In late September *Le Figaro* asked: "Where does the Gouffé case stand?" Ten paragraphs later the reader understood there had been no progress.

The Gouffé family took matters into its own hands. In a plea for help, they offered ten thousand francs to anyone who provided details that led to Gouffé's whereabouts. Goron soldiered on. He sent photographs of Michel Eyraud and Gabrielle Bompard to police throughout France and around the world and awaited a response. But nothing came.

Then startling news arrived from Lyon: The case had taken a sudden turn—it was now in the hands of a no-nonsense investigating judge named Vial who, unlike certain other Lyon magistrates, prized justice and was determined to get to the bottom of the mystery. Vial relentlessly questioned the coachman Étienne Laforge until he broke down in tears. "All right," Laforge blubbered, "I did not tell you the whole truth." But the new version of his story deviated from the original only in small details: He still claimed to have picked up the three men with the trunk and taken them to the riverside on July 6.

Unconvinced, Vial tossed the coachman into prison so he could stew over his half-baked testimony. He then turned his attention to the incomplete baggage label found with the shattered trunk. Here was a vital—but disregarded—clue. Did the trunk depart from Paris in 1888, as Bastide and Ramonencq believed? Or did it come to Lyon in the current year, 1889? Vial knew there was only one way to get the answer: Someone had to pore over the baggage registry at Gare de Lyon in Paris. So he sent a note to Goron requesting help. For a provincial magistrate, Judge Vial showed uncommon courage in reaching out to Paris. In his note, he requested that Goron dispatch a detective to the train station to examine the registry. To the chief's astonishment, the Lyon judge also sent along the baggage label.

With the label between his fingers, Goron was confident he was closing in on the discovery of Gouffé's body. The scrap from the trunk read "From: Paris 1231. Paris 27/7/188. Express Train 3. To: Lyon-Perrache, 1," indicating that trunk number 1231 had left Paris on July 27, the day Gouffé vanished. The only question remaining was to prove the year was 1889. Goron was so intent on the answer that he took the label to the station himself and waited while the railway agent searched the 1888 registry for bag number 1231. When nothing turned up, he asked the agent to try again for the year 1889.

The second search took quite some time because tens of thousands of baggage-toting visitors had poured into Paris for the International Exposition. Normally an impatient man, Goron was content to wait while the agent flipped through the registry; he smoked cigarettes and toyed with the ends of his mustache, convinced he was on the verge of the most important breakthrough in the case.

At last the railway agent delivered the news: There was indeed a trunk numbered 1231 that departed Paris on the day Gouffé went missing. The notation in the baggage registry read: "27 July 1889, Train No. 3, 11:45 a.m., No. 1231. Destination: Lyon-Perrache. One trunk, weight 105 kilograms [230 pounds]."

For Goron, the conclusion was inescapable: the body of Toussaint-Augustin Gouffé had ridden from Paris to Lyon inside that trunk. But Goron still had to prove it. In order to do that he needed the Lyon corpse to be exhumed. Only a second autopsy could reveal the truth. Only the body, indisputably identified as Gouffé's, could save the case.

Moving swiftly, Goron begged Dopffer to arrange a visit to Lyon for Inspector Jaume and himself. Was this not a fool's errand? Dopffer worried. By now, he supposed, the corpse was so badly decomposed its identity could never be known. Nonetheless he agreed to inquire, and on November 9, 1889, Goron and Jaume were on their way to Lyon. As the train cut through the countryside heading south, the two Sûreté men laid out their battle plan. Their ambitions were huge: They wanted to dig into the dossier; they wanted to interrogate the coachman Laforge; most of all, they wanted a new autopsy to prove they were right all along about the corpse. Echoing their hopes, *Le Gil Blas* wondered whether Gouffé's brother-in-law hadn't missed something when he viewed the rotting remains on the morgue floor. "Was he mistaken?" the paper asked. "Was his examination too superficial? Anything is possible."

The detectives arrived in Lyon braced for rude treatment similar to that which Brigadier Léon Soudais and Louis-Marie Landry had received. There was no assurance that Vial, while cultivated and welcoming, could control the animosity that inflamed the rest of the Lyon investigative force. But the alarm was unfounded. Vial was as accommodating as he could be. He brought the peasant Laforge from his prison cell to an interrogation room where Goron and Jaume were waiting. Informing the coachman of the latest developments, Vial advised him: "Now search inside yourself and tell us the truth." How could he have picked up the three men with the trunk on July 6 when that trunk had not even arrived in Lyon until July 27?

But the peasant didn't budge. He twisted his hat in his hands, seeming guileless and asserting that what he had said was the truth. The monkeying around infuriated Jaume, who lost his temper and grabbed Laforge by the arm. "Listen, my friend, you are not going to do this to us," he hissed. "We are not from Lyon."

The outburst not only startled Laforge but also insulted the entire legal system of Lyon. Jaume knew exactly what he was doing; his hotheadedness was a calculated act, and Goron, who was secretly delighted, had to bite on his mustache to keep from laughing. He later explained that the inspector was "a good man but an incorrigible rascal." To salvage appearances, however, the chief drew a stern face and disciplined his underling with some sharp words and a rough shove. But the display fooled no one in Lyon. "From this moment on," Goron recorded in his memoir, "I think I was no longer in their hearts."

Judge Vial was the only man in the room not offended, and as a show of camaraderie handed the interrogation over to Goron, who was famous for his brutal grilling of suspects. So intense were his sessions that his interrogation rooms were dubbed "Monsieur Goron's cookshops." Now, with the Gouffé case hanging in the balance, the chief went to work on the peasant coachman, who burned in the Paris hot seat. He quickly admitted that everything he had said was a lie and threw himself on Judge Vial's mercy. He fell to his knees before the judge and burst into tears. "What do you want?" he whimpered. "*I* am just a coachman."

His confession was abject and thorough—he recanted everything. He never picked up the three suspects, never took them to Millery, never even saw them on the night of July 6. And he never laid eyes on the trunk. If he was to suffer for his lies, he wasn't going alone. He now dragged the unscrupulous Lyon magistrates into the mud with him. "If I was able to give a fairly exact description of the trunk," Laforge said, "that was because Monsieur Commissioner Ramonencq helped me." At the time he gave his testimony, he explained, he didn't even have a permit to operate his hackney. It had been revoked more than two weeks earlier after a run-in with the law. And the officials encouraging his false story didn't even realize it. Laforge had shown up at headquarters knowing police were hungry for a lead. "So I thought I would please these gentlemen and give them one," he continued. "To tell you frankly, I saw quickly that what I said had the effect of pleasing them a lot. And the nicer they were to me, the more I talked."

Why had he lied? That was simple: to get into the good graces of the police. "I hoped that as a reward for my service," he said, "the police would rehabilitate me and return my permit."

And how did he come up with his three suspects? He chose the three young thugs because they were already in jail charged with a separate murder. "It seemed to me," he reasoned, "that another crime more or less would not much aggravate their situation."

The magistrates' actions were reprehensible—and farcical. One local paper likened the case to the zaniness of Eugène Labiche's play *The Italian Straw Hat,* a famous farce that became a model for the Keystone Kops. "The entire inquiry tumbles like a house of cards," the newspaper wrote.

Amid the ruins, Chief Goron saw an opportunity to grab control of the investigation, prompting a local newspaper to ridicule him for "an attitude that his position doesn't justify." The chief "arrives in Lyon," the paper chided, "not relying on anyone but himself to do the inquest." Goron wanted to start the case over from the beginning, with a new autopsy. But no sooner had he broached the idea than he ran into another wall of provincial ineptitude. Judge Vial informed him that another autopsy was impossible because no one could locate the body.

The coffin containing the unidentified corpse had been tossed into a communal graveyard at La Guillotière cemetery with nothing—no marking, no cross—to distinguish it from any other. There were no records of where unidentified bodies lay. The remains became part of a jumbled heap in this confused mass burial site. These were indeed lost souls. Finding and exhuming a specific body from this loners' resting ground would require nothing short of a miracle. No one even knew where to begin.

Goron was appalled, but still he plowed ahead hoping other evidence would build his case. He and Inspector Jaume rode out to the desolate riverbank where the corpse was recovered and peered over the parapet at the shrubbery below. In nearby Millery they chatted with locals, uncovering more evidence of malfeasance by Lyon authorities. When the Lyon police came out to speak to residents, the locals said, they were interested not in digging up the truth but in simply confirming Laforge's story. The police posed leading questions: "It's since the beginning of July, isn't it, that you smelled the stench of the corpse?" and obliging locals gave the answers the police wanted.

Goron took the opposite tack: He encouraged the people of Millery to draw on their memories, as best they could, to tell him when the odor overtook the town. Undirected and unintimidated, they produced a timeline starkly different from the one insisted upon by Laforge and the Lyon investigators.

At Restaurant de la Tour, a popular gathering spot in Millery, Goron bumped into a Paris journalist from *Le Petit Journal* who had come to conduct his own investigation. "M. Cornély came, like me, instinctively, to find out," Goron wrote in his memoir. "The procedures of a good reporter do not differ much from that of a policeman. For one, like the other, there are no small details in a case: all should be searched to the core. This was not unfortunately the doctrine of some magistrates."

It was a cold November Sunday and the restaurant was packed. Goron sat at a table with the owner, Antoine Thiebaudier, and asked him to recall when the putrid odor had invaded the town. "No doubt is possible," Thiebaudier said, "it's only after the fourth or fifth of

August that one started to smell bad odors in the countryside." Others confirmed Thiebaudier's account. These new recollections made sense. If the trunk arrived in Lyon on July 27 containing the body of a man killed the previous day and the corpse was dumped soon afterward on the riverbank, probably on July 28, an odor of decomposition would likely have swept over the town in another week or so. That would have lent accuracy to Thiebaudier's estimate of August 4 or August 5. It also destroyed Laforge's story that three men dumped a body on July 6.

Next Goron visited Paul Bernard, the medical examiner who had performed the original autopsy. Although the earnest young doctor had largely botched the inquiry, he had shown a flash of foresight by setting aside some hair from the corpse. "I had the excellent idea to save a few tufts," he told Goron, putting them into the chief's hand. The clump of coal-black strands were coated with blood and a greasy substance from the decomposing scalp. Nothing about them suggested they'd been clipped from Gouffé's chestnut-brown mane. Goron rolled the hairs between his fingers, his mind working. These hairs, he reasoned, came from a corpse exposed to the environment and the action of decomposition for possibly two weeks. Did those conditions have any impact on the coloring? No one, Goron realized, had questioned whether these slimy strands were in fact originally black. Goron, who was a leading proponent of the scientific investigation of crime, proposed a simple experiment.

"I asked for a bit of distilled water," he recalled later in his memoir.

When Bernard produced a basin, Goron plunged the hairs into the water, and the men waited several minutes; then Goron lifted the hairs out and combed them through his fingers, removing grease and dirt. He dropped the hairs back into the water and retrieved them again several minutes later, combing away still more grime. He repeated the process one more time. He then presented the hairs to the young doctor. "He recognized immediately that he had been oddly mistaken," Goron remembered. "The hairs were, in fact, brown."

Of course any number of victims could have had brown hair. What was it about these particular hairs that said they belonged to Gouffé? Without a body, there was no room for doubt. Goron needed an exact match. He telegrammed his agents in Paris to contact the Gouffé family: Had anyone saved a hairbrush belonging to the missing man? The next day, hairs from Gouffé's brush were on their way to Lyon.

When Goron placed the hairs side by side—the cleansed strands and the ones from the hairbrush—he and Bernard were astonished by the similarity in color and texture. An encouraging breakthrough, but was it enough to build a case?

Inspector Jaume understood now why Gouffé's brother-in-law did not recognize the missing man on his visit to the morgue. The corpse's matted hair darkened by blood and dirt left Landry "naturally mistaken about its true color," the inspector surmised in his diary. He applauded Goron for his determination and cleverness, then took the opportunity to ridicule Lyon authorities for their idleness: "Why had no one had the idea for this new and so simple, controlled experiment?"

That Dr. Bernard had saved a few tufts of hair from the corpse was fortuitous. But it was nothing compared to the twist of fate that next came Goron's way. As he wrote in his diary: "Decidedly, luck returned to me, and, as always, good luck and bad luck come in a streak." It was at this time that he made the acquaintance of a medical apprentice who had assisted Dr. Bernard in the original postmortem. The young trainee had followed the Gouffé case in the newspapers and wondered if Goron's hunch about the Millery corpse might not be right. The autopsy had disappointed him: The failure to identify the remains, he believed, would haunt the case. He suspected that before this drama played out the corpse would need to see the light of day again. He also knew that remains buried in La Guillotière cemetery were lost forever. And as he was accompanying the body to its unmarked resting place, he got an idea. "At the moment of the burial," the apprentice told Goron, "I made marks on the coffin." Then he added: "I did better than that." He took one more step to ensure that this body could be singled out from all the others. "I left an old hat of mine with the corpse," he explained to the speechless Sûreté chief. "In that way, I was sure that one wouldn't be mistaken on the day one wanted to exhume the Unknown of Millery."

The Gouffé case suddenly roared to life. As a local newspaper put it: "Without this hat . . . the case was definitely buried like the cadaver." Ecstatic, Goron stuffed five hundred francs from the Gouffé daughters' reward fund into this ingenious assistant's hands, which he accepted with humility. "This modest one," Goron gushed in his memoir, "had the trait of a genius."

On the evening of November 11, the state prosecutor ordered the body of the Millery unknown to be exhumed from the communal grave in La Guillotière cemetery and an autopsy to commence the following day.

Chapter 16

In San Francisco, Michel Eyraud was safe. Here on the far side of the world he was free to remake himself, establish his false identity, and renew his prospects. He had come to the right place. Here, he could pose as a sophisticated French vintner. To the north lay the Napa Valley, where nearly a hundred and fifty wineries dotted the fields. If there was an American wine, it was Californian, and the vintage flowed abundantly. Right now, wine production was so strong it was causing an oversupply, pushing down prices, and forcing some vineyards to close.

But Eyraud had no reason to fret over that; realities were meaningless to him. He moved in a fantasy world of shadows and lies. To anyone who listened, he was scouting California for just the right site to build a distillery. He was eager to produce volumes of cognac for export to France. He planned a big investment, a sizable operation with at least a dozen stills. Putting fine California cognac in the hands of the French guaranteed an open spigot of profits. Of course, there was no truth to any of it; he meant to build nothing. This smooth-talking French winemaker was just a scam artist whose only aim was to bilk investors and make off with their cash.

San Francisco gave Eyraud cover. It was a freewheeling place, an outlaw kingdom on the bay, with a forest of masts in the harbor and steep hills and sand and dust. He mixed easily with the swagger and wealth, the poverty and drunkenness and degradation. Here was Paris, reimagined San Francisco–style. Rudyard Kipling captured the mood when he visited in 1889 as an unknown twenty-three-year-old newspaperman working for the Indian publication *The Allahabad Pioneer*, several years before the fame of *The Jungle Book, Kim,* and *Just So Stories*. An odd creature to the Americans—short, arrogant, and British with a mustache and spectacles—Kipling strolled the cobblestone streets marveling at the liberal use of electric lighting and the wondrous operation of the cable cars. "If it pleases Providence to make a car run up and down a slit in the ground for many miles, and for a twopence-halfpenny I can ride in that car, why should I seek the reason of that miracle?" he wrote. He disparaged "the 'dives,' the beer halls, the bucket shops and the poker hells where humanity terrible and unrestrained was going to the Devil with shouting and laughter and song and the rattle of the dice boxes." In sum, he wrote, "San Francisco is a mad city—a city inhabited for the most part by perfectly insane people."

While San Francisco gave Eyraud license to imagine vast criminal horizons, it inspired Gabrielle Bompard to yearn for freedom. She'd had enough of Eyraud, his empty talk and brutal eruptions. When she first arrived in Paris, Eyraud had protected her. "I am certainly grateful to him," she'd written to her lover in Lille. "But to love him, never. Poor man, he lives on illusions." Now she wanted out. But she was unable to desert him. If she ran and he tracked her down—what then? She feared he would kill her. It was safer to placate him than to provoke him. Here in San Francisco she had hope of escape. Even if she fell into the hands of the police, she was safer than with Eyraud. She could convince them of her innocence—for she *was* innocent. She was not even complicit, for she had been manipulated into committing that awful crime.

She relied on her wiles for survival, drawing on an animal instinct of self-preservation, a mixture of viciousness and deceit, honed by her years alone in the convents. But she realized she needed help, and she placed all her hopes in one man: Georges Garanger. If only he would come to San Francisco, as he had promised—she dreamed of putting her life in his hands. She dreamed of running away with him. In her mind, he had taken the shape of her handsome liberator.

But would he come? She worried that Garanger was not nearly as interested in her as she was in him. Perhaps he sensed what kind of man Eyraud was—and he had good reason to be wary. Eyraud had his own designs on Garanger. To him, the gentleman was the perfect mark: rich, adventurous, and naïve. Eyraud wanted a good portion of his fortune and was desperate enough to do whatever it took to get it.

As the days flicked past, with no sign of their visitor, Eyraud and

Gabrielle each veiled their private disappointment behind a tense silence. What could be keeping him away? Had he seen their story in the newspapers? Had he gone to the authorities? Even thousands of miles from the scene of the crime, out here in the Wild West, the French fugitives knew they weren't safe.

And then just as hope was fading, their quarry arrived, courtly, calm, and open-minded. Now the two schemers were in dangerous competition with each other, and the unsuspecting Garanger was trapped in the middle.

Eyraud went to work on him, charming his new friend with tales of his winemaking talents, sermons on the advantages of the California fields, and promises of the waiting market in France. Bit by bit he reeled the rich man in. He tantalized Garanger with his ambitious and wholly bogus distillery project.

Gabrielle, meanwhile, played the enchantress, provocative yet subtle, and the gentleman's eyes gradually came to rest on her with a rising intensity. Garanger showed his affection for the young Berthe in only the most dignified manner, careful not to offend her father, Monsieur Vanaerd. When the trio was out shopping in the chilly San Francisco air, Gabrielle cooed over a sealskin coat. No sooner had she expressed her wish than Garanger stepped forward with $100 to put it on her back.

For ten days, the new friends toured the Napa Valley, drinking the wines and studying options for Eyraud's distillery. The con man displayed a sophistication that surprised the local experts. "He is a regular brandy sharp," raved V. Courtois, a winemaker in Larkmead. "If we had more like him the grade of our wines and brandies would be raised 100 percent."

The owner of the Inglenook Vineyard in Rutherford, Captain Neibaum, at first took Eyraud as a charlatan but was soon won over and escorted him into the cellar where in the dark Eyraud correctly graded the brandies. Neibaum was so impressed he invited the sophisticate to return. "He was way ahead of me on the subject," the owner admitted months later. "It was a liberal education to hear him."

One day Eyraud showed Garanger an order he'd placed for twelve stills that would establish his new operation. Then he sheepishly confessed that he had miscalculated the initial costs. He thought the first payment would be only for one-quarter of the total cost but realized that the bill required a payment of one-third, and to his great embarrassment, he didn't have that amount available.

Garanger generously advanced Eyraud $200.

What an easy mark he was! Eyraud wasted no time in laying his trap. He told him that his brother-in-law in France had fifty thousand francs belonging to Eyraud's wife that he was preparing to send to San Francisco. Eyraud's brother-in-law also was planning to raise an additional five hundred thousand francs for the new business. What's more, Berthe stood to inherit nine thousand francs when she came of age, and she was eager to invest the funds in the business.

Eyraud then outlined how much money could be made by producing cognacs in California and shipping them to France. Now that Garanger understood the soundness of the business, Eyraud had an offer for him: Why not get in at the beginning? It was a rare, and lucrative, opportunity. Here was how the partnership would work: Eyraud would put up two-thirds of the three hundred thousand francs (roughly $3.9 million in 2013 money) needed as capital and take an equal amount of the profits. Garanger would kick in the rest, roughly a hundred thousand francs in loans, and collect the remaining third of the profits. And in time, Eyraud promised, he would pay back all the money he borrowed.

Eyraud played his dupe flawlessly. Garanger was eager to dig into his accounts and lay down significant backing for a can't-miss undertaking with an experienced and savvy businessman. Eyraud drew up a contract and Garanger signed it, making him a partner in an imaginary distillery with a man he believed was named E. B. Vanaerd.

Chapter 17

After four months of decay, the corpse of the Millery unknown was a nauseating sight. Its humanity had been lost to the ravages of nature. Flesh and organs had been eaten away, leaving behind tufts of hair and a puzzle of bones. The task of extracting an identity, a verifiable link to a once-upright mortal, fell to France's premier forensic scientist, Dr. Alexandre Lacassagne.

Lacassagne was chief of forensic medicine at the University of Lyon, a chair created for him in 1880. Originally from Cahors, southwest of Lyon, he was educated at the École Militaire in Strasbourg and developed a passion for forensic medicine while serving as a young army doctor in North Africa. In the slums of Tunis and Algiers he discovered the popularity of tattoos—and their value in identifying corpses. His treatise on the subject marked the beginning of his extensive writings on criminology and forensic medicine. He founded and edited a highly regarded journal on the subject called *Archives d'anthropologie criminelle* (Archives of Criminal Anthropology), where for nearly thirty years experts from around the world debated the latest research in the field.

Lacassagne was charismatic, intellectually nimble, and widely versed in medicine, biology, and philosophy. He was well read in subjects far beyond his specialty, amusing friends with passages he memorized from literature and drama. Students flocked to his lectures and colleagues sought out his opinions. He had a heavy mustache and looked older than his forty-six years. One contemporary said the professor had a "strong, rhythmic step and ever-cheerful eye."

While his work was grim, Lacassagne kept his friends laughing. He was known for his macabre sense of humor—his summer cottage outside of Lyon had a door knocker that was a bronze casting of a female criminal's hand. At his apartment in Lyon, he had a set of plates that bore reproductions of the criminal tattoos that so intrigued him. As charming as he was, there was no escaping the fact that his work was repulsive. He spent so much time up to his elbows in corpses in an era before refrigeration and rubber gloves that he sometimes carried about him a faint odor of rotting flesh.

His contribution to forensic medicine was vast. He researched how blood settled in bodies of the deceased, paying close attention to the formation of the purple splotches known as lividity, and helped pave the way toward a method for estimating the time of death. He had the scientist's inquiring mind and was often heard to say: "One must know how to doubt."

On November 12, 1889, at 4:00 p.m., Lacassagne stepped up to the slate table in his medical amphitheater at the University of Lyon and, with bare hands, began work on the Millery corpse. Clustered around the table were Chief Goron of the Sûreté; Paul Bernard, the medical examiner; Lacassagne's colleague Dr. Étienne Rollet; Lacassagne's assistant, Dr. Saint-Cyr; and a state prosecutor named Bérard, who at first sought to prevent the exhumation but finally acquiesced.

It was here in the amphitheater that the professor performed dissections as he lectured to students seated on ascending benches. Now the benches were empty, except for Inspector Jaume seated alone at the very top. The sight on the table was awful enough, but it was the stench that drove Jaume far away to the upper reaches of the room. A corpse's impact on the nostrils was "a mixture of every repulsive odor in the world," as one author has put it, "excrement, rotted meat, swamp water, urine."

Goron steeled himself: He also was weak in the presence of rotting flesh, a debility that dated back to his days as the police chief in Pantin. Called to an apartment by distraught neighbors, he had discovered two young lovers decomposing on a bed after having carried out a suicide pact two weeks earlier. He managed to stay on his feet only by racing to a broken window and sucking in air.

Now he was so intent on proving his hunch about the Millery corpse that his revulsion was nothing to him. "I had such eagerness to know if science would confirm my prediction that I forgot the insurmountable repulsion of cadavers that I'd had all my life," Goron noted in his memoir. "I was only a bit sickened by the odor of the

decomposing flesh but I did not hesitate to stay engaged to better follow Dr. Lacassagne's learned demonstration."

Lacassagne's task was a formidable one. The advanced decomposition was trouble enough, but more annoying was the way Bernard, Lacassagne's former student, had hacked up the body in the first
autopsy. Obviously Bernard had failed to heed a warning the professor had repeatedly delivered in the classroom: "A bungled autopsy
cannot be revised!" The professor was angered at the way Bernard
had manhandled the body: The throat had been needlessly butch-
ered; the chest had been ripped apart; the skull was smashed and
sections were missing; and the breastbone had been torn away. Had
Bernard learned nothing from his professor's lectures? In the face of
this mangling Lacassagne redoubled his efforts and devoted himself
to the task with such clear focus that in years to come his work on the
Millery corpse would rank as a landmark in forensic medicine.

To determine the victim's height, he relied on the latest work of
his colleague Rollet, who over many years had made significant con-
tributions to the understanding of badly decomposed bodies. Rollet
came up with a method for determining a corpse's height based solely
on the size of the bones, findings that he had just published. He studied fifty males and fifty females and discovered that he could correlate
with remarkable precision the height of a body from a limited number
of remaining bones.

For instance, a humerus—the bone of the upper arm—that measured 13.8 inches usually suggested that the body was five feet nine
inches tall. Based on that one bone—if no others were present—Rollet
could make a reliable guess. If more bones were available, the guesses
became a detailed calculation that was notably accurate. In the first
autopsy, Bernard concluded that the corpse was five feet seven inches
tall, a guess based on less-detailed measurements.

Lacassagne used a special high-precision instrument to measure
the corpse's arms and legs. Based on the arm bones, he thought the
body was five feet seven inches tall; based on the legs, he put it at five
feet nine. Rollet had determined that an accurate body size could be
calculated from the mean of the bone measurements. By that standard, Lacassagne came up with a body height of five feet eight inches.

When Gouffé went missing, his family had told investigators that
he was five feet seven inches tall, a discrepancy that sent Goron racing

to the telephone. Using a recently installed national telephone line, the Sûreté chief soon had his agents in Paris chasing after Gouffé's military records. Within two hours, the answer came back—Gouffé, the soldier, had been measured at precisely the height Lacassagne had calculated: five feet eight inches.

Lacassagne's observation of the corpse's right leg turned up another curious clue. The bone suggested that that leg had suffered from some kind of disease, causing stunted development in the lower part. Lacassagne looked closer: The knee had signs of some inflammation, as did the right heel bone. He surmised that the victim was afflicted in the heel during his youth, a condition that weakened the right leg. Indeed, the right, according to Lacassagne's measurements, was much lighter than the left.

Did anyone know whether Gouffé had a leg problem?

Goron raced back to the telephone to launch his agents into action. He also sent out a flurry of telegrams in search of Gouffé's medical history. He wanted to probe the recollections of Gouffé's daughters, his shoemaker, and anyone who knew the bailiff when he was young. Soon he was fielding the replies. He learned that Gouffé had had a childhood accident: He fell over a pile of apples that for years left him with an ankle inflammation in the right leg. One of Gouffé's doctors revealed that he had treated his patient for water on the right knee. Another confirmed that the patient's right leg had weakened over the years—it was so weak that Gouffé limped slightly, though he disguised it well.

Lacassagne was so rigorous that the autopsy consumed three days. At last he turned his attention to the ghoulish head—minus its eyes and nose. He dug into the mouth and discovered the victim was missing a molar in the upper right side of the jaw, which sent Goron off to the phone again. The chief ordered Brigadier Soudais to track down Gouffé's dentist, who corroborated the finding: Some years ago Gouffé's upper right molar had been extracted.

Lacassagne lingered over the teeth, analyzing the buildup of tartar at the roots and the amount of wear in order to estimate the victim's age. Bernard's guess on the age ranged from thirty-five to forty-five. To Lacassagne, the teeth reflected those of a man of about fifty, which was a year older than Gouffé's forty-nine.

Next Lacassagne went to work on the corpse's black, greasy hair, washing it several times, revealing what Goron had discovered: The hair was in fact not black but chestnut brown—just like Gouffé's. But was this the corpse's true hair color? If the victim had dyed his hair chestnut brown, then the match with Gouffé's would be merely coincidence, not conclusive.

Lacassagne left nothing unexamined. He subjected the hair to chemical analysis, looking for copper, mercury, lead, bismuth, and silver—all elements found in dyes. None turned up, suggesting the true hair color was indeed chestnut brown. Next, under the microscope, he studied strands of the corpse's hair next to strands taken from Gouffé's brush: The thickness of the two samples was identical.

The professor had exhausted all avenues of exploration. He was now satisfied. Bit by bit he had teased out the human life that once animated the putrid remains. Lacassagne set down his instruments and proclaimed to the assembled spectators: "Gentlemen, I herewith present you with Monsieur Gouffé."

Chapter 18

"Light is shed," cried *Le Petit Journal,* "and this time it's definitive." At long last the body had surrendered its secret. Goron was triumphant, returning to Paris on November 15 aboard the express train from Lyon, in a shower of press accolades. "We were given to see yesterday the face of a happy man," *L'Écho de Paris* reported. "We speak of M. Goron, who arrived, face glowing in the company of principal inspector Jaume, no less radiant than his chief." His reputation salvaged, Goron was now, in the words of *Le Figaro,* "the very skilled chief of the Sûreté."

Newspapers displayed photos of Gouffé's gruesome remains next to images of the man himself in full life, and reporters held back nothing in their revolting descriptions of the autopsy. The reading public was appalled and delighted, swarming newsboys on the streets. The editions rapidly sold out.

Finally Goron had a body—and proof that Gouffé had been murdered. The bailiff's brother-in-law, Louis-Marie Landry, acknowledged his mistake at the Lyon morgue, telling *L'Écho de Paris* he was resigned to Gouffé's death: "Yes, there cannot be any more doubt, it's him."

Now, four months after the man had disappeared, the murder case was only beginning. With no suspects in hand and no leads, Goron turned his single-minded obsession to the trunk. It was the only tangible evidence he had. It had moved through public places, it was at Gare de Lyon, on a train, in the streets of Lyon—it was notably large and had some distinguishing features, such as reinforcing metal bands. Someone somewhere had to have seen it, someone had to have noticed it—and the travelers who accompanied it.

Goron needed the public's help. He needed to get the trunk in front of a large number of people. But how? Soon he would introduce a sensational solution.

But first, the trunk had to be restored, as closely as it could be, to its original appearance. It needed to look as it did when it was brand new, before it was smashed to pieces and lay in the dirt on the riverbank, exposed to the elements for weeks. When Goron returned to Paris he brought the reconstructed trunk with him. He disapproved of the craftsmanship of the workmen in Lyon; their work was so slapdash no one would ever recognize the trunk. So he hired fine Paris craftsmen to take the trunk apart and reassemble it, this time with artistry. "I assigned some workers—I even called upon some true artists—to do a reconstruction that would give the complete illusion that this could have been the parcel by all appearances that left the Lyon station on July 27," Goron wrote in his memoir.

While the craftsmen worked, Goron turned his attention back to two curious figures in the case: Michel Eyraud and Gabrielle Bompard. There was little to connect them to the crime but that didn't stop Goron from speculating. Newspaper stories with their photographs began appearing around the world. *L'Écho de Paris* reported: "The police search with feverish activity for Eyraud and his mistress against whom charges seem to accumulate."

Now back in favor, Goron had little trouble playing the press. He reminded reporters that Eyraud was born in Saint-Étienne, just forty miles from Lyon, and therefore was familiar with the area. And as *L'Écho de Paris* dutifully explained: "Whoever dumped the cadaver knew the countryside and carefully chose the site." The newspapers portrayed the fugitives like heroes in a mystery novel. Gabrielle was "a petite, attractive brunette, with large eyes of velvet in a rosy face," said one paper. Another called her "a ravishing brunette with large black eyes and a childlike face." Eyraud, readers learned, had a full brown mustache and was between forty-five and forty-eight years old. Insights into their Paris relationship emerged. As one report revealed, "Eyraud presented himself as very proud of his mistress and he never neglected an occasion to show her off to his friends." Reporters traced Gabrielle to a hotel on rue Beauregard where she had lived under the name "Mme. Eyraud." She also apparently spent time at the Hôtel de Mulhouse on rue la Ville-Neuve, where she was known as Lucie Doria. In May, Eyraud was paying for an apartment for her in Levallois-Perret.

The couple was known to frequent a house on rue de Rome where small groups gathered for hypnosis sessions and Gabrielle was the star performer. "She was adored there, the one who wanted to be put to sleep," *Le Petit Journal* reported, adding she was "extra-responsive" to the commands of a hypnotist. But the society lady who held the salons discovered something about Gabrielle she did not like—and her participation ended. The paper didn't specify what it was, referring only to "the spiciness of this young person."

Speculation turned to the murder. "How could Eyraud have attracted Gouffé into an ambush?" Inspector Jaume wondered in his diary. "One can well guess: he was helped by his mistress, Gabrielle Bompard, young, pretty, vicious—completely ideal for a philanderer like the bailiff of rue Montmartre." The hypothesis making the rounds was that Eyraud strangled Gouffé—the autopsy had revealed that the bailiff's larynx was broken—and the most tantalizing theory was that Gouffé was attacked while in the throes of his lovemaking with Gabrielle. But afterward, how did the killers carry the trunk, stuffed with the victim, weighing more than two hundred pounds? "Gabrielle Bompard could not have been much help to her lover in that regard," Jaume reasoned. "Was there a third accomplice?"

While suspicion fell on Eyraud—partly for the lack of any other suspects—his faithful wife, Louise-Laure, still defended him vigorously, telling police she could not imagine he was involved in an act as vicious as this. She described him as a man who would do anything to ease another's misery. "He was so good, so charitable that it is impossible . . . [he] has become a criminal," she said. "Of course he has made mistakes in his life. He might have compromised his honor, he has not always acted properly, but from there to become a murderer—I don't want to, I can't believe it."

All the speculation, however, proved nothing. And as the trunk's reconstruction dragged on, the public became restless. *L'Écho de Paris* complained that the success of the autopsy inspired hope that the Gouffé case would gain momentum but the opposite had occurred:

"The investigation advances slowly, very slowly, threatening to be eternal."

When at last the craftsmen finished their work, they had reconstructed the trunk with reasonable fidelity, even covering the interior with the original white paper dotted with blue stars. But they could not overcome the ravages of nature. No one could have made the trunk look exactly as it did when it was new; the shattering of the wood and the long exposure to the elements were simply too much. So Goron had a second trunk built to the exact specifications of the original. Parisians would see the battered original in all its ghoulish glory and compare it to a brand-new replica.

Now Goron began preparing to exhibit the two trunks in dramatic fashion at one of the city's most popular attractions: the Paris morgue. He needed frenzied participation of the masses to elicit clues, and he understood better than most that Parisians hungered for gruesome entertainment. Who hadn't seen drunken spectators surge toward the guillotine at public executions? Sigmund Freud, who came to Paris in 1885 as a medical student, wrote home: "Suffice it to say that the city and its inhabitants strike me as uncanny; the people seem to me of a different species from ourselves; I feel they are all possessed of a thousand demons." Freud battled his own demons—massive anxiety and apprehension—applying "a little cocaine," he wrote in early 1886, "to untie my tongue" in the face of his mentor, the imposing Jean-Martin Charcot. He toured the city, catching glimpses of Parisians indulging their dark impulses. A daily stream of visitors strolled through the morgue's exhibit room where unidentified children pulled from the Seine or unknown women murdered in back alleys were laid out for viewing—sometimes with touching scenic effects. One four-year-old girl discovered in a stairwell in 1886, with no apparent injuries except a bruise to her hand, sat in a dress on a red cloth-covered chair that accentuated the paleness of her skin, and attracted fifty thousand viewers. Police relied on the visitors to identify the anonymous dead. Do you know this child? Do you recognize the clothing on this brutalized woman?

The morgue's spectators came from every social strata—workmen, grandes dames, tourists, all strolled by for a look. "All day long a multitude of the curious, of the most diverse ages, elbow and jostle one another from eight in the morning until nightfall in the public gallery," wrote a contemporary medical inspector. Neighborhood merchants relied on the steady stream of gawkers. Children broke off their games in the street to dash inside on the arrival of the latest corpse. Commentators described the morgue as theater for the masses. "It is nothing but a spectacle *à sensation,* permanent and free, where the playbill changes every day," explained a journalist.

Freud's perception of the French was informed by their love of such spectacle. "I don't think they know the meaning of shame or fear," he wrote. "The women no less than the men crowd around nudities as much as they do round corpses in the Morgue or the ghastly posters in the streets announcing a new novel." All of it fed into the Parisian lust for outrageous sensation. Just the previous month, the city had thrown the doors open on the raunchiest, loudest, most unpredictable dance hall anyone had ever seen. There were already plenty of decadent nightspots in Montmartre, such as Moulin de la Galette, where the working class whooped it up, and Élysée Montmartre, where a man calling himself Father Modesty tried to dissuade innocent youth from indulging in the temptations of the night, though his work was in vain. Or Reine Blanche, where an acrobatic cancan dancer one night suddenly walked on her hands, revealing no underclothing and prompting the policeman on duty to exclaim: "Cré Dieu! Les belles cuisses! God! What beautiful thighs!" And so was born Nini-la-Belle-en-Cuisse—Nini of the Beautiful Thighs.

But of all these places none rivaled the Moulin Rouge, which opened on October 6, 1889. If one establishment reflected the Paris of the belle epoque it was this riotous dance hall, known for its slowly revolving red windmill in front and its daring freedom inside, a mood captured by Henri de Toulouse-Lautrec, a radical young artist whose name would become forever synonymous with the outrageous nightclub. Toulouse-Lautrec depicted the pathos of the music-hall life: gay, high-kicking dancers and joyous patrons alongside dark, mournful souls. Inside the raucous hall he found the hopeful reveler and the sad-eyed drunk, the promise and the doom of Parisian society.

The new attraction was the brainchild of Joseph Oller, an enterprising Spanish businessman who created extravagant circuses, the first heated indoor swimming pool in Paris, an aquarium, and an

amusement park. The brilliance behind many of Oller's projects
was the handiwork of the man he now installed as the director of
the Moulin Rouge, Charles Zidler, a tannery worker at age ten who
eventually showed an inventive genius as an impresario; he discovered many stars, such as the mad dancer Jane Avril, the distinct
warbler Yvette Guilbert, and Joseph Pujol, better known as Le Pétomane, who sang from his behind and told Zidler at his audition, "I
have an elastic anus that I can open and close at will . . . If you
would be so kind, I will perform a remarkable musical program for
you."

Inside the Moulin Rouge was a cavernous hall softly illuminated
by gas jets shaded pink and white and by electric lightbulbs colored
cream and rose and shaped like tulips. On all sides of the immense
dance floor stood refreshment tables where patrons sipped cherry
brandy, champagne, and absinthe. National flags from around the
world ringed the room.

The evening began with variety shows on several stages: trained
seals and caterwauling female singers in pink tights. Outside was a
large garden, presided over by a two-story-tall stucco elephant saved
from the International Exposition, where patrons wandered past fountains and flowery nooks and watched bare-breasted women riding
donkeys in a ring. Singers, dancing girls, and vaudevillians performed
on a small stage. Climbing the spiral stairs inside the elephant's leg
brought you to the creature's roomy belly, where young girls in Arab
dress swayed and wriggled in what was described as "supersalacious
entertainment" for gentlemen only.

Then back inside the club at 10:30 p.m., with the throng num-
bering perhaps two thousand, "the overcrowded, overheated, over-
perfumed hall was ringing with laughter and conversation," as one
writer put it, when a drum roll announced the start of the chief
entertainment of the night. "The quadrillistes would run in and take
their places, and from then to twelve-thirty, to the loudest music ever
blared out in Paris, the big show was on." These were the famed cancan dancers who performed their high-kicking steps at eye level, titil-
lating customers with peeks at their bloomers beneath the ruffles of
their petticoats.

The Moulin Rouge satisfied an unhinged abandon among Parisians, the wild liberation of souls in need of release. Tapping into that public mood, Goron aimed to unleash a frenzy over the Gouffé case by displaying the two macabre trunks at the morgue. To build anticipation he courted the press. He gave interviews, described preparations, explained his hopes for the exhibit. He enlisted the press as his partner in whipping up enthusiasm. "It was necessary," he conceded, "to stir up a lot of noise."

Finally, on Friday, November 22, readers of *Le Figaro* learned that the trunks would go on display the following morning at nine. The two pieces were to be placed just inside the morgue's entrance near a large window to capture the best possible light.

By the expected opening time, some three hundred Parisians were in line, bundled in their overcoats against the chill. By noon, the doors still hadn't opened and the crowd had swollen to a thousand. As the hours dragged on, the grumbling intensified along quai de l'Archevêché, not far from Notre Dame. When rumors spread that the attraction had been canceled, the horde grew restless. Police were called in. At 3:00 p.m. word filtered out that, despite earlier promises, the trunks were only then being installed. At 4:00 p.m., guards were posted at the entrance and at last visitors were waved inside, ten at a time.

As spectators filed into the hall, exclamations were heard, some sincere, others jocular. "Many women were very pale and very happy at the same time from the emotion of seeing the sinister package," *Le Petit Journal* wrote.

Each trunk had a label. The one on the original read: "This trunk transported the body of M. Gouffé of Paris to Tour-de-Millery (Rhône). It was broken into about twenty pieces and was discovered in the bush about ten kilometers from the corpse. It has been rebuilt." The posting on the replica read: "This trunk was made with materials resembling those of the authentic trunk, displayed opposite. It is fairly certain that before departing Paris the trunk that transported the corpse was in the condition of the specimen found here."

Another placard instructed anyone with information relating to the corpses to visit the morgue office where a Sûreté inspector was stationed or to contact Goron himself at Sûreté headquarters, 36, quai des Orfèvres.

The crowd kept coming until the doors closed at 6:00 p.m. In *L'Écho de Paris,* the show garnered a rave review: "There was last night at the morgue a grand premiere—a sensational premiere. For the first time, the trunk that transported Gouffé's cadaver was exhibited in this lugubrious monument."

So stirring was the first day that the papers predicted a deluge of visitors for Sunday—"a veritable traffic jam," as one put it.

But what was to be gained from the crowds, and who among the public would break the case? *Le Petit Journal* laid out the quest: "Amid the innumerable curious who file in front of the trunk, will we find one who can reveal anything meaningful about its origin? A secondhand goods dealer—will he remember having sold it? And when? Can he give a physical description of the buyer? Does a coachman remember having loaded it onto his coach? A neighbor, would he have seen it being brought into a home that he can name? One must hope. One can only support the magistrates for trying everything to discover the authors of this mysterious crime."

By Monday, the papers estimated that twenty-five thousand people had swarmed through the morgue. On Tuesday, the figure climbed to fifty thousand. But so far, not a single useful lead came to light. To jog people's memories, the Gouffé family offered five hundred francs to anyone, particularly coachmen, who recognized the trunk. That brought a caravan of coachmen into Goron's office claiming they'd carted the crate to the train station. "It took an interrogation of just a few minutes to convince me that all these drivers were influenced by the suggestion of the promised gift and that none of them had any useful information to give," Goron recalled. "It's necessary to have spent time as a detective to appreciate the extraordinary number of true practical jokers, crazies, idiots, and blackmailers that fill a great city like Paris."

Still, coachmen were suddenly important personages—deemed the best bet to deliver a golden nugget. So they earned priority entrance at the morgue. If you showed up driving a coach, you were escorted to the front of the long line to make your way right in, while those who had waited for hours jeered.

Each evening, as the autumn darkness fell, gas jets were lighted inside the morgue, casting shadows over the gloomy scene. "Illuminated by a reddish light, the trunk . . . seemed to take on a tragic aspect," wrote a reporter for *Le Petit Journal.* He imagined Gouffé's body, its arms and legs crushed into the coffin, and, perhaps speaking for himself, reported: "More than one of the curious left with the shivers."

Chapter 19

And the crowds kept coming. The line formed at eight in the morning and by nine it stretched to the Pont Notre-Dame. Inside, spectators strolled through the hall gazing at the trunks as if window-shopping at the grand department stores; in place of price tags were the placards outlining the merchandise's morbid history. Visitors went home with mini-trunks as souvenirs, and in the cafés the French raised their glasses in a rousing toast to *la malle sanglante*—the bloody trunk. "They are people given to psychical epidemics, historical mass convulsions," the young Freud observed in a letter home, "and they haven't changed since Victor Hugo wrote *Notre Dame*."

Moving slowly through the exhibit hall, the voyeurs each had a wide-eyed look at the trunks; some were respectful, others crude. Tourists added the morgue to their itinerary. British elites rolled up in fancy carriages and, "as common mortals," *L'Écho de Paris* explained, "these curious exotics had to get in line and wait their turns."

And the days rolled on. The sensation never cooled, and yet no one came forward. The newspapers rang similar notes. *Le Gil Blas,* November 27: "No news from the morgue." *L'Écho de Paris,* December 3: "In the eight days the trunk has been on display . . . no new information has arrived."

And the bloody trunk kept its secrets.

In the meantime, the public devoured any tidbit on the suspects. A concierge remembered an encounter with Eyraud in the days before Gouffé disappeared. Eyraud was distraught, he said, his frock buttoned up to his neck—which was unusual for him because he liked to show off his fancy clothing and jewels.

On seeing him, the concierge had said, "You look unhappy, Monsieur Eyraud."

"I'm ruined," Eyraud replied. "I don't have a sou. I've barely had a scrap of bread in three days."

"Don't let misfortune beat you down," the concierge sympathized.

And suddenly Eyraud flew into a rage. "I'll take vengeance on those who ruined me! You'll see. I'm going to remake my fortune in America."

Stories like this one, true or not, added currency to the impression that Eyraud had fled across the Atlantic to America or points south.

More reliable was Eyraud's wife, the distraught Louise-Laure. She told reporters she had prepared a valise for her husband around the time of the murder, packing it with twelve shirts and other items for a trip he said he would be taking to South America. "That he has abandoned us," she told *Le Figaro*, "to go live in a strange country with the one whom he has made his mistress! I must admit it alas!" But she still refused to believe her husband could have been involved in a murder. He was a loving father, she insisted: "He adored his daughter and certainly he will write to her, if he isn't dead."

Then, in late November, the procession in front of the trunk finally shook loose an important lead: A cabinetmaker named Paul Cathrin who studied the piece carefully came forward to say that without doubt it was made in England. Cathrin, who had spent several years in London, said the trunk's dimensions were based on the English yard, not the French meter, and the original nails used in its construction were found only across the Channel.

Then came this: A man named Liénard, who knew Gabrielle in Lille, said she stayed with him in Paris for two days—and she had a large trunk that was identical to the one at the morgue. Brigadier Soudais was dispatched to Liénard's apartment. He measured the space where the trunk had rested on the floor—and the dimensions were a match.

Goron wasn't satisfied by the measurements alone. He ordered Inspector Jaume to take the trunk from the morgue to Liénard's apartment and place it in the exact spot where it had sat. A perfect fit: the trunk scratched the wall again right where it had done so earlier and left scratches on the floor identical to previous ones.

There was more to Liénard's story: When Gabrielle arrived at his apartment, she told him she'd bought the trunk in London before abandoning her lover there because he beat her. She returned to Paris on July 14 for the celebration of Bastille Day.

So Gabrielle could now be placed in Paris about two weeks before Gouffé disappeared, and she had a large trunk that she bought in London matching the one at the morgue.

Next with some news was a Frenchman living in London, Georges Chéron, who kept up with life in Paris through the French papers. Chéron was a regular reader of *Le Petit Journal,* whose recent flood of stories about Michel Eyraud and Gabrielle Bompard had reminded him of an experience he'd had several months earlier. Chéron described it in a letter to Monsieur Berthe, a business associate of the Gouffé family whose name had appeared in one of the newspapers. Reading the letter, Berthe realized its importance and passed it on to Chief Goron, who in turn informed Paul Dopffer, the investigating magistrate.

The letter's circuitous route into the right hands exposed the tensions that existed among investigators—not to mention the haughtiness and pettiness rife within the hierarchy of the French justice system. As the lead justice official, Dopffer expected to be the first contacted with fresh news pertinent to the investigation. He was miffed not only that the letter was not originally addressed to him but that its arrival on his desk seemed something of an afterthought by everyone in the chain. Jaume took Dopffer to task for his snit. Did he plan to arrest Chéron for addressing his letter to the wrong party? Was he planning to retaliate against poor Monsieur Berthe for the crime of receiving a letter? "The magistrates, like the agents of the Sûreté, are overworked, nervous, and irritable," the inspector noted in his diary.

The letter contained some explosive new evidence. Having read about Eyraud and Gabrielle in the newspaper, Chéron wrote: "I am nearly certain I had these two persons as lodgers."

Chéron rented out furnished rooms in his small house at 151 Gower Street. When Marie-Alexandrine Vespres, a thirty-year-old Frenchwoman also living in London, told him her uncle was looking for lodgings he was most happy to take him in. This man, a Monsieur Michel, arrived in late June with a small trunk and two handbags. Chéron was not particularly pleased by his lodger, whom he described as a braggart with a penchant for bawdiness. Michel presented himself as a businessman who was familiar with Parisian café and boulevard life. He spoke decent English, explaining that after French his best languages were Spanish and Portuguese, for he'd lived in South America and traveled extensively in Argentina. He had a heavy mustache and balding head which he sometimes hid under a wig that he parted in the middle. He told Chéron he was married with one daughter. When he laughed, Chéron noticed the gold rim of a false tooth.

Several days later, on July 7, a tiny young woman showed up at the Chéron home wearing a hooded overcoat and a black veil. She had no bags, no money, nothing except a piece of paper on which was scrawled the address 151 Gower Street. She informed Chéron that this was where she was told to meet Monsieur Michel. As she didn't have money for the coachman, Chéron's wife covered the fare for her. The young woman waited in the kitchen, and when Monsieur Michel returned the Chérons noticed how coolly he greeted her—no one could miss the tension between them. A few days later, however, Michel and the woman went to a department store on Oxford Street, where he bought her a new wardrobe.

Monsieur Michel rarely stayed with the young woman at the house on Gower Street; he told Madame Chéron that a friend of his wife's had offered him a room in her home and he was obliged to avail himself of it. He explained that the young woman lodging with them was waiting to reach legal age so she could claim a considerable fortune from her father in Lille, who was a wealthy merchant of used metals. They could sense that the young woman was afraid of Michel. On at least one occasion she pointed out to Madame Chéron patches of her blackened flesh where he had beaten her. When Madame Chéron cautioned her to stay away from him, the woman seemed helpless, pointing out: "He is capable of anything."

On July 11, Chéron wrote, Michel and his young companion returned to Gower Street with a large trunk they had bought at a shop called Zwanziger's at 251 Euston Road. "I can still see it," Chéron remembered, "all dark brown, and the interior decorated with blue stars on a white background." A few days later, on July 14, the young woman was off to Paris alone, taking the huge trunk, packed only

with a dress or two and a hat. Monsieur Michel accompanied her to
Victoria Station and put her on the train.

Less than two weeks later, that same trunk was again on a train,
this time to Lyon, with the murdered Gouffé inside.

The Paris newspapers went crazy over the letter. Now there were
two tantalizing suspects linked to the bloody trunk. The portraits of
the conspirators wasted no time on psychological subtleties: Eyraud
came across as a dangerous degenerate while Gabrielle was a cheeky
young coquette. But Eyraud was portrayed not only in shades of evil.
His brutality was given a romantic tint; though he was ill-mannered
and balding, Eyraud was depicted as something of a ladies' man who
had attracted a saucy young mistress. Aghast at the coverage, Jaume
exclaimed in his diary: "The reporting rises to the height of the most
epileptic novels!"

The Sûreté now bustled with activity. Goron wanted to know
more from the Chérons: Did they overhear the lodgers plotting a
crime? Did they see anything that might reveal where the suspects
fled? He sent an agent to track down the Frenchwoman living in
London, Marie-Alexandrine Vespres, who had directed Eyraud to the
Chérons. What did she know about him? Where did she think he
might be now?

Goron also needed someone to interview workers at Zwanziger's:
What did the trunk buyers reveal while in the shop? What did they
look like? Where were they heading? The man for the job was Brigadier Soudais, who was chasing leads on the Channel Island of Jer-
sey. He was ordered to London, where he was to meet another agent
named Emil Houlier.

By December 6, the agents stood inside Zwanziger's surrounded
by trunks, listening to salesman Hermann Lauterback describe his
encounter with the suspects. The male customer, who had a heavy
mustache, was not satisfied by any of several pieces Lauterback had
showed him: one wasn't wide enough, another wasn't long enough.
They were on the point of leaving when Lauterback brought out one
last trunk—a piece so large that it had sat around the shop for two
years. No one had had any use for this behemoth.

"That's the one!" the customer cried. "That's just the size I want."

When Lauterback pointed to exactly where the trunk had sat in the shop, Soudais took string measurements for the length, height, and depth of the space and pocketed the evidence to show Goron.

Next Soudais made his way to 151 Gower Street to visit the Chérons and found the couple greatly upset over their role in this heinous case. Gazing at a photo of the famous trunk, Madame Chéron said in tears, "Oui, monsieur. That's it."

Soudais then pounded the pavement in the Cherons' neighborhood, looking for leads on the lodgers, and discovered they had shown up several times at a nearby saloon. Several regulars recalled one shocking incident. Eyraud and Gabrielle were drinking in the saloon when he decided he wanted to show off his hypnotic prowess. He told patrons he was going to put Gabrielle to sleep and demonstrate how he could control her completely. But when he started to talk her into a trance Gabrielle resisted and clawed him in the face. Eyraud reflexively grabbed her and smacked her, causing an uproar among the surprised inebriates. Those who witnessed it remembered the tussle for its bizarre mix of hypnotism and brutality.

Eyraud's barbarity also was recorded by the London correspondent for *Le Petit Journal,* who was doing some of his own sleuthing. Witnesses told him that one night Eyraud climbed into a coach and tried to prevent Gabrielle from entering. When she jumped onto the running board he pushed her off, sending her stumbling into the street as the coach departed. Another time Eyraud tried to strangle Gabrielle but she managed to break free and yell for help; the next day she displayed the tracks of his fingers on her neck.

Back at the Sûreté offices in Paris, Soudais's string measurements didn't satisfy Goron. While the width and height were accurate, the length failed to match the trunk exactly. The chief refused to let this pass, insisting that the smallest discrepancy left an opening for his critics. Inspector Jaume took a different view. "This is not a big thing," he reckoned privately in his diary, "as all the other measurements agree exactly. That suffices for certain people who would say, '*Vive la petite différence!*' "

But Goron demanded absolute certainty and he reckoned there was only one way to ensure it: He shut down the morgue exhibition and prepared to take the original bloody trunk to London himself. The three-week run had served its purpose, shaking loose some leads and reinvigorating the investigation. On December 11, the trunks were moved out of the morgue and Goron and his sidekick, Inspector Jaume, were set to travel immediately to London.

But then an intruder from Lyon swept into Paris and the departure was put on hold.

Chapter 20

Georges Chenest, the Lyon prosecutor, forced his way into Paul Dopffer's office, claiming he had come on an important legal matter. The trunk, he reminded the Paris investigating judge, was officially under the jurisdiction of Lyon because it was found there; it was only on loan to Paris. Chenest demanded it be returned because it may have played a role in a separate case officials in Lyon were now investigating. Dopffer was dubious: How could the same trunk have figured in a second, unrelated case—especially now that its history had been confirmed? Dopffer recognized the demand for what it was—a ridiculous attempt to obstruct the Gouffé inquiry—and he rejected it out of hand.

But Chenest wasn't finished. Here was the real reason for his visit: He wished to lodge a complaint against Chief Goron and his sidekick Inspector Jaume who, the prosecutor charged, had publicly criticized the Lyon justice system and ridiculed the Lyon prosecutor's office. Apparently the provincial authorities were still smarting from Goron's coup in Lyon: The Sûreté had shown local investigators how to solve a mystery and embarrassed everyone associated with the corrupt interrogation of the coachman Étienne Laforge and inept handling of the Millery corpse. Chenest, in fact, had reason for his complaint: It was true that Goron and Jaume had spoken to the press and denigrated the work of the Lyon authorities. For Chenest, the humiliation ran so deep that he traveled to Paris to insist that Judge Dopffer issue a public reprimand of the Sûreté slanderers. And by the way, Chenest added for good measure, that macabre exhibition of the trunk at the morgue was, in his estimation, an abomination.

Dopffer yielded nothing; he did not take kindly to Chenest's high-handed buffoonery: In any showdown between Paris and the provinces, there was no doubt of Dopffer's loyalties. Informed of the complaint, Jaume jeered in his diary: "Chenest is going to return empty-handed to Lyon."

The disruption delayed Goron and Jaume's departure for London by more than a week. Finally they left Paris on December 20 aboard an 11:00 a.m. train for the coast. Goron had the flu, the victim of a virulent pandemic that had erupted in Russia and was sweeping across the world: Paris, Berlin, Vienna, London, and much of Europe along the Mediterranean, and as far away as the United States. Over the next two years, the disease would touch nearly half the human race, killing an estimated one million people. But nothing was to stand in the chief's way. "I was very sick at this time," he noted, "but I reckoned it was necessary to move quickly and I left without waiting for the authorization of my doctors." London's subfreezing temperatures didn't help. "Brr!" Jaume exclaimed. "It's cold. I can no longer find myself in the fog of London."

To keep the murder trunk from creating public alarm, Goron hid it inside a specially made sack tied closed with string and stamped with an official seal indicating it was evidence of a criminal investigation in Paris. He also doused it with disinfectant to mellow the stench of rotting corpse that still clung to it. But his scrupulous preparations weren't enough to prevent what Goron described as a "burlesque incident" at the hands of English customs agents at Victoria Station. Despite his protests, the British agents broke the French seal, untied the strings, and pulled the trunk out of its gray canvas sack. The officious agents, who, Goron noted, "were almost as annoying as our own," got a nasty surprise when they lifted the lid. If they expected to cast their eyes on a mountain of smuggled tea or layers of tobacco, they were disappointed to discover, as Goron had told them, that the trunk was entirely empty. They were taken aback, however, when the opened trunk exhaled the stench of death. "They found," Goron was pleased to report, "that it had an extraordinary odor. I'd think so! It smelled of the cadaver!"

After the comedy at customs, the detectives made their way to Scotland Yard, where the London witnesses—the Chérons, Marie-Alexandrine Vespres, and Hermann Lauterback of Zwanziger's—were assembled for a 2:30 p.m. inquest. Presiding was the eighty-five-year-old judge Sir James Taylor Ingham, and seated beside him was a representative of the minister of the interior, a man named Edward Leigh Pemberton. The trunk, still in its wrapping, was placed in full view.

Goron was to lead the questioning. He rose, kissed the Bible, and swore to tell the truth.

"May God be of aid to you," the elderly judge said.

Fighting back the ill effects of the flu, Goron invited Lauterback to examine the trunk closely: the lock, the nails, the leather covering, the interior lining. An interpreter was on hand to make sure the Frenchmen and the Britons could understand one another.

Lauterback said he had no doubt this was a trunk from Zwanziger's, for it bore two characteristics found nowhere else: the interior lining marked with blue stars and a unique manufacturer's notch on the lock. He recalled that he sold the trunk on July 11 to a man fitting the description of Michel Eyraud.

"Do you know where the trunk went after it left your store?" Goron asked.

"Gower Street, the home of Monsieur Chéron," he answered without hesitation.

When the Chérons were asked to inspect the trunk, they also recognized it beyond doubt. Georges Chéron remembered being struck by the large, uncommon nails used in its construction.

And what of the two lodgers? Goron wanted to know. In the eyes of Monsieur Chéron, they were as perfect a fit to Eyraud and Gabrielle as he could imagine.

So a man who looked like Eyraud had purchased the trunk. But Lauterback didn't know Eyraud personally; he'd never seen him until he stepped off the street into his shop. And Chéron had never seen Eyraud until he rented a room to him. Yet he claimed he was certain a couple matching the description of the fugitives spent time at his home. Could these witnesses have been mistaken? Goron needed someone who knew Eyraud and could place him definitively at the Gower Street residence, with the trunk.

Marie-Alexandrine Vespres, the woman who had recommended the lodger to the Chérons, stepped forward and placed her hand on the Bible. Goron peppered her with questions. How did she know the lodger? Why did she act as his intermediary? Was this man really her uncle, as she had told Chéron? Wilting under the interrogation, Vespres admitted that she was not the lodger's niece but rather had been his lover in Paris fourteen years earlier, at age sixteen. She had since moved to London, and they had stayed in touch. Goron asked how she came to send the lodger to the Chérons? In June, she said, the man wrote to her asking if she could find a room in London for his daughter. Vespres said she now knew the young woman with him was not his daughter but his mistress Gabrielle Bompard. Vespres was acquainted with the Chérons, who she knew had a vacancy, so she sent the man along to them.

She had yet to utter the lodger's name. So Goron pressed her. Name the man. Vespres wavered and then at last acknowledged that the lodger was in fact Michel Eyraud.

Goron was now satisfied on one point: There was no question that the trunk belonged to Eyraud and Gabrielle. But other questions still had to be resolved. Were they the authors of the crime? Did this man and his mistress kill Gouffé and stuff him into the trunk? In hindsight, the Chérons noticed some behavior that seemed suspicious. It always baffled Madame Chéron why Gabrielle needed such an enormous trunk; the young woman had so little clothing—why not just a travel bag? When she asked about it one day, Gabrielle chirped: "Oh, we'll have plenty to fill it with in Paris!"

Then on July 14, Eyraud received a telegram from Gabrielle, who was already in Paris. In light of what occurred less than two weeks later, the terse message now sounded sinister to anyone seeking evidence of a crime; though not conclusive, it raised the possibility of a premeditated killing. In the telegram, Gabrielle told Eyraud: "Come. All is ready."

Five days before the murder, on July 21, Eyraud left London.

While there was still no proof the couple killed Gouffé, some facts were clear. In early July, Eyraud and Gabrielle were in London, where they rented a room at 151 Gower Street and purchased a large trunk at Zwanziger's. Later in the month they returned to Paris with the nearly empty trunk. On July 26 Gouffé failed to return home from a night out. Eyraud and Gabrielle also vanished that same Friday evening. And on the following day, July 27, they traveled aboard a train to Lyon, with the oversized trunk from Zwanziger's, which weighed 230 pounds. As Gabrielle had promised, they found plenty to fill it.

Goron telegraphed the results of his mission to the Paris prefect of police, Henri-Auguste Loze, who immediately sent back a note of congratulations. Loze told Goron he would inform the prosecutor, who would issue arrest warrants for Michel Eyraud and Gabrielle Bompard. "From then on I had certitude about the case," Goron noted. "I had only to finish it. It was necessary to find the scene of the crime and to get our hands on Eyraud and his mistress."

London was in the throes of its own grisly murder mystery. A vicious killer was stalking prostitutes and slashing their throats, so violently their heads were nearly severed from their bodies. Women were dying in Whitechapel, Spitalfields, and Stepney, and though Scotland Yard was out in force, the killer remained at large. The count so far: nine women dead.

Before leaving London, Goron got a firsthand look at the crime scenes. Robert Anderson, a brilliant barrister who was head of the Criminal Investigation Department, escorted the Paris detective around Whitechapel as the two men traded theories about who might have been Jacques l'Éventreur, or as the British called him, Jack the Ripper.

London provided amusement both high and low. Inspector Jaume was especially enamored of his Charing Cross hotel, which reminded him of a feudal castle minus the knights and pages. Since he kept the trunk in his room, the hotel staff would enter, he said, with a "dreadful expression." Noting their discomfort in his diary, he recorded: "They appear flabbergasted by my audacity: I dare sleep in my room, alone, together with the bloody trunk." But Jaume wasn't spooked by it in the least: The trunk, after all, no longer contained a cadaver. It was simply extraordinary evidence in a criminal case unlike any he'd ever pursued. He confided: "I'm living the most fantastic macabre tale that is offered to the imagination of man."

Chapter 21

One day in December, Michel Eyraud came to his new business partner Georges Garanger with some bad news. His daughter's extremely rich aunt had died and now Berthe had to return to France immediately. The timing of the death couldn't have been worse, Monsieur Vanaerd explained, for he was needed in California to work out details of the distillery. Would Garanger, by chance, be willing to escort Berthe back to France in his place?

How it would sadden him to be alone without his daughter, Eyraud said, but he would find a way to bear it. And if there was one man he could entrust her to, it was the estimable Monsieur Garanger.

The wealthy Frenchman had taken a fancy to the young woman—a weakness Eyraud had noticed and intended to exploit—and to be offered the chance to spend weeks alone with her seemed a delightful prospect. Garanger happily consented. Eyraud then had one other request. Having learned that Garanger had considerable money available at a bank in Canada, Eyraud wondered whether his partner might not stop there to collect the loan he'd promised for the distillery and transmit the funds to Eyraud before setting off for France. Once the money was safely in San Francisco, Eyraud said, Garanger and Berthe could head out to New York to catch the transatlantic steamer.

If Garanger wished to collect on the loan, at least in part, Eyraud encouraged him to visit his brother-in-law in Paris, who would willingly provide some repayment. Eyraud put on such a good show, he was so sincere in his deception, that Garanger had no reason to doubt him.

When it came time to go, Monsieur Vanaerd escorted the travelers to the train station and as they boarded he burst into tears, like any good father would, wishing them well and declaring he'd miss his girl. At the last minute he asked Garanger for another $200 loan, which he pocketed with profuse thanks.

Eyraud's plot was unfolding just as he intended. It was a bold ruse—if all went as Eyraud wished, Garanger would never make it to Paris, would never have the opportunity to seek repayment, would in fact never leave New York. Gabrielle was to travel with him, first to Canada, then to New York, where Eyraud—having hopped aboard the transcontinental railway—would be waiting. In New York Gabrielle was to lead the unsuspecting Garanger into Eyraud's clutches. Then Garanger would disappear just like Gouffé.

Success, of course, depended on perfect obedience from Gabrielle. Eyraud took for granted that she was under his command, faithful to him without question, that she would again blindly play the role of sexual bait to trap a rich man. One thing he hadn't reckoned on was her turning on him. But not only did she despise Eyraud, she had fallen hard for Garanger, this tall, blond, blue-eyed aristocrat whom she'd grown to trust. With him, she was safe from Eyraud's bullying and beatings; she felt free. And aboard the train she was soon warning Garanger about his new business partner. Monsieur Vanaerd, she told him, was a brutal con man. The distillery operation: a sham. Vanaerd's investment in it: laughable. Beware, Georges. Monsieur Vanaerd is following us to New York—he'll trick you out of thousands of dollars and even kill you.

Garanger took swift action. There would be no stop in Canada; no withdrawal of funds—nothing sent to San Francisco. They would bypass New York and go instead to Halifax, Nova Scotia, where they would depart for Liverpool and from there go on to Paris.

Gabrielle confessed that E. B. Vanaerd was a phony name, and she was not Berthe. Her next admission was a delicate one: Would Garanger recognize their real names? Had he read any news? Did he know anything of the Gouffé case? When she revealed that she was not Vanaerd's daughter but Gabrielle Bompard and that Vanaerd was not her father but in fact Michel Eyraud, she was relieved to see that Garanger did not react to their notoriety. He'd been traveling in the Far East and Africa, shielded from news about the fugitives. His concern was the deceit that both she and Eyraud had played on him—what else did Gabrielle have to reveal? He suspected there was more, and she wanted to divulge everything—but later. Later she would confess all.

On the cross-country journey they became lovers. Gabrielle told investigators later that she cared for Garanger and wanted to protect him from Eyraud. And Garanger was charmed by her. He was an intrepid businessman who had roamed exotic lands; he was drawn to the darkness that haunted the young woman, to her tangle of anguish and lightheartedness. Inspector Jaume liked Garanger the moment he met him months later. Gabrielle's newest amour was "an intelligent, honest, ingenuous man," in Jaume's estimation, but he was "in love with an adroit and audacious woman."

While the new lovers snuggled, Eyraud was making his way to New York, unaware of his fatal miscalculation. Had he not been so vain he might have sensed Gabrielle's faithlessness. As she would tell investigators, "I am not aware of any sentiment that Eyraud inspired in me. It was fear—that's all. He disgusted me."

Arriving in New York on December 26, Eyraud became furious when he was unable to locate his mistress. Gradually it dawned on him that he was the dupe. Indeed, two days later, on December 28, Gabrielle and Garanger departed from Halifax for Liverpool. In a crazed fit, Eyraud scrawled out a letter to her on December 29 but had nowhere to send it. He began on a note of concern for her, then moved into self-pity, and at the close issued a subtle threat. "My dear Berthe," he wrote, still imagining their aliases were in play. "What could have happened? Leaving you at the station [in San Francisco] you held my hand and you said to me: 'Do not be sad, we will see each other again.' Alas! There is nothing . . . What misfortune could have come to you? . . . I no longer sleep, nor eat. Are you sick? Are you dead? Have you disappeared? . . . M. Garanger, has he mistreated you? I must know! Ah! Berthe, don't let me die of despair. I am crazy. You do much evil to your benefactor. If you return I will pardon you."

Two days later, in a second letter, he raged at Garanger. "You do not have the right to keep this woman," he warned his rival. "While I did not think of you as a coward you have acted as one. This woman, she is mine, I gave her my fortune and my honor . . . She does not have the right to be happy while I suffer . . . She is lost . . . I promise you . . . you will lose her and perhaps yourself. I am not making any threat. I pose conditions. Return Berthe and I will pardon her."

While Eyraud fumed in New York, Gabrielle and Garanger steamed across the Atlantic on a two-week passage to Britain. She pondered what more to tell her new lover but realized she couldn't speak of her darkest secrets just yet. For now she wanted to enjoy the gracious Garanger and the tranquillity at sea.

But there were hints of the turbulence ahead. Garanger, himself an amateur hypnotist, was eager to see if Gabrielle was as easy a subject as she claimed. He hoped to understand her better through hypnosis and possibly unlock some morbid truths he suspected lurked within her. She went quickly into a trance and the session was unspectacular, revealing little, until Gabrielle became agitated and cried out: "Murderer! Murderer!" Garanger was surprised by the outburst but chose not to attach great significance to it. By now, he knew Gabrielle's flair for the dramatic—and hypnosis was an invitation to the actress in her. So he tucked her shriek into the back of his mind. But after their arrival in Paris its meaning would become shockingly clear.

Chapter 22

Goron returned from London, still in the grip of the flu. It was a nasty strain that attacked the body, the mind, and, in Goron's case, also the eyes. He had been in so much discomfort in London that he consulted an English doctor who clumsily probed his left eye with a pointed instrument, causing a serious threat to his vision. From the train station in Paris, Goron headed directly to his own doctor. "Without doubt I would have lost my sight if it weren't for the good care of my eye specialist, the kind Dr. Dehenne," he wrote in his memoir. There were other dangers from the flu. Some patients succumbed to crippling psychosis. The following year, 1890, the number of suicides in Paris attributed to influenza shot up 25 percent.

Although he badly needed to convalesce, Goron refused to take to his bed and pursued Eyraud even though all traces of the man had vanished. Others around town were less concerned with justice than with financial gain. In early January 1890, Goron was visited by an ambitious trunk maker who wanted to manufacture small replicas of the murder trunk, stuff them with chocolate, and sell them as mementos. The craftsman wished to know if Goron thought that there was anything illegal in the enterprise. The chief brusquely dismissed the man, saying he had no authority in the matter. Not long afterward, sightseers along the boulevards were tempted by tiny Gouffé trunks stuffed not with a replica cadaver but with sweets.

Eyraud's wife, Louise-Laure, was deeply distressed by the incriminating details that had emerged at the London inquest. How much more could she take? Having stood by her absent husband for six months, she'd finally had enough. In early January she marched down to the Palais de Justice to file for divorce. Her reason, she said, was "family considerations," and although she was breaking her marital ties to her husband, she reiterated that she still had absolute faith in his innocence.

Goron had found no one in Paris who had any contact with the fugitives since they had disappeared months ago. They had vanished without a trace—until one day a bizarre letter appeared at Sûreté headquarters. It landed on Goron's desk on January 16, addressed to *M. Gorron,* the name misspelled; the chief's assistant had to pay forty centimes to take delivery because the envelope lacked sufficient postage. Inside Goron found a twenty-page ramble dated January 7. He thumbed through it quickly, stopping now and then until he came to the signature on the last page: *M. Eyraud,* underscored by a confident upward slash at the letter *d.*

Initially Goron was skeptical; so extraordinary was this thunderbolt—and so full of crank leads was this case—that his impulse was to dismiss the letter out of hand: "I thought I had before my eyes the flights of fancy of a farceur." After reading the letter page by page with care, he was intrigued. It had the markings of a desperate man on the run. Eyraud was outraged at what was reported in the Paris newspapers, how the press had misrepresented him. Monsieur Gouffé, he insisted, was his friend and his bailiff. "To think that I murdered him? But why?" Eyraud wrote. "I was neither accomplice nor murderer and know nothing of the affair except what I read in the papers, I swear to you." His family, he complained, had to be devastated by the lies printed in the newspapers. He acknowledged that he and Gabrielle traveled together to Canada and then to San Francisco before he wound up in New York. But he was as surprised as anyone to discover that he had left Paris the same day as his friend Gouffé. He assured Goron that it was nothing but a coincidence.

"Ah! Monsieur, how I suffer—and such sadness for my family," he wrote. When he read that he was a suspect in a murder, he said, "I cried like a baby, day and night. I thought of my daughter, my wife, my whole family."

He described his trip to London prior to Gouffé's disappearance as a way to escape his troubles at the trading company Fribourg & Cie. He had been unjustly accused of pilfering funds, he said, and could not stay in Paris to face punishment at the hands of the Jew Fribourg. The night before he left Paris, he slept soundly. In the morning he told his wife: "I am lost. I must go—I don't know where—but the

Jews have ruined me." His wife packed a small trunk for him and he left on the 9:00 a.m. train for London. Yes, he admitted, he'd made big mistakes in his life—but murder, never! "I have deserted my home, and yet my wife is an angel. Ah, how I suffer."

If Eyraud was, as he depicted himself, just a thoughtless but well-meaning rascal who was incapable of murder, who then was to blame for Gouffé's death? The fugitive had a ready answer. He explained that after he had been in London a few days Gabrielle showed up with no baggage, no travel clothes—nothing. He took her out to buy her a few things but soon he'd had enough of her and ordered her to leave. First she demanded that Eyraud buy her a trunk. Then at last she was off, back to Paris with her new luggage. "I never saw that trunk again," Eyraud wrote.

Soon Gabrielle wrote to Eyraud whimpering that she missed him and was on her way back to London. Somehow she had managed to rustle up two thousand francs. By Eyraud's reckoning, she arrived in London around August 20, without the large trunk. She claimed she had sold it for nearly as much as he had paid for it. The couple then set sail for Canada and from there went to San Francisco.

So who killed Gouffé? Was laughter a sign of guilt? In San Francisco they saw a French newspaper in which Eyraud was described as a suspect. "She burst into laughter," he scoffed. Then he bought another paper, *Le Petit Journal,* and there again was his name. "I was crazy with anguish," Eyraud wrote, "and she laughed. What does that say?"

In San Francisco, the couple met a man Eyraud identified as Monsieur Garanger. One day, Garanger asked about the case. "Did they find the bailiff?" he wondered. The innocent inquiry caused Eyraud's throat to tighten. But, the fugitive wrote, "Gabrielle broke into a peal of laughter, saying the bailiff was alive—he was right then probably amusing himself with a woman." From this, Eyraud asserted, it was clear that Gabrielle was the real murderer.

In the letter Eyraud revealed that he was alone, his mistress having set off from San Francisco in the company of Monsieur Garanger. That gentleman was escorting Gabrielle back to France to visit her sick aunt, and Eyraud was to have reunited with them in New York. But now he realized they had ditched him—and he was furious.

Goron understood his rage: Not only had he lost Gabrielle but he'd lost control of her. But were these histrionics the grief of a wronged lover or the jig of a con man? "We have not seen each other again," he informed Goron. "I wrote more than twenty letters to her. I was a fool. I pleaded with her to return. I cried. I wanted to kill myself. I inhaled chloroform. The manager at my hotel called the doctor."

One moment he was anguished at losing her, the next he was condemning her for murder. "Ah! Ah! I am dead," he wrote to Goron. "I write to refute all the rumors. It's necessary to find Gabrielle, the most sly woman in the world. What could she have said to Garanger? I don't know but they have gone. Does she have reason to fear the light? . . . You must find Garanger. Gabrielle will be with him. Her hair is now cut like a boy's and is dyed red. The sadness of this creature is that she lies too much and has a dozen lovers."

Continuing his mad ravings, Eyraud wondered: Could Gabrielle have killed Gouffé on her own? It wasn't likely, but any one of her many lovers could have assisted her. Eyraud vowed he would never return to France to be unjustly accused. "I am not guilty and will never bear shackles," he declared. But he promised to rush home as soon as that guilty young woman was arrested, and he would place himself at the disposal of the police to resolve any lingering mysteries.

Goron set the letter down. He was certain it came from the pen of Eyraud. But to make sure, he compared the handwriting with specimens taken from the fugitive's home, and the match was exact. While it had been impossible to find Eyraud, Eyraud had no trouble finding Goron. The fugitive expressed no remorse, indeed, lacked any conscience whatsoever. He even seemed indifferent to his own fate if he were caught. Goron regarded the letter as a clumsy self-defense—and a supremely stupid undertaking. By writing it the suspect put himself at great risk. While he believed he was turning the spotlight onto Gabrielle, he had instead provided a wealth of clues that heightened the chances of his own capture. "It was possible that Eyraud did not understand the danger of this letter," Goron explained, "but he sent it anyway. His jealousy was stronger than reason."

What disturbed Eyraud the most was that his mistress had run off with another man. He was enraged and would do anything—even send her to the guillotine—to wreak vengeance. "His Gabrielle was taken from him," Goron noted. "She was in the arms of another and he could not abide that. He had only one thought: to prevent his mistress from being the lover of another man. For him, the rest no longer mattered."

Goron soon received two more letters from Eyraud. One was dated January 9, 1890, postmarked Montreal. The other was written on January 11 and bore a Philadelphia postmark. Eyraud was roaming the East Coast, and his long-winded letters were evidence of a desperate, solitary fugitive. Goron considered the series tantamount to a confession of murder. But just as the trail was heating up, Goron's health took a turn for the worse. He was still weak from the flu and his eye was irritated. On doctor's orders, he was forced against his mighty will to retreat to a dark room for a period of recuperation. Inspector Jaume would keep the chief informed.

On the streets, the talk everywhere was of Gabrielle Bompard. Eyraud's letters had turned her into a figure of fascination. A day didn't pass without her name shouted in the headlines. At least one newspaper filled its entire front page with an engraving of the infamous new celebrity. Soon everyone was familiar with her saucy, childlike face. Parisians felt they knew her as they might a wayward cousin; they saw her pictured in different poses; they read about her youth, her brutal affair with Eyraud. Some gossipmongers expressed sympathy for the poor girl. But mostly it was her wickedness that mesmerized the city. A woman of her age ought to have been sweet and demure—traits that were attractive to a reputable husband. But Gabrielle ignored the norms. She was France's greatest fear: a woman on the loose, a dangerous murderess, a threat to the stability of the French family—and precisely for all that, Parisians found her tantalizing.

Chapter 23

After docking at Liverpool, Georges Garanger and Gabrielle Bompard made their way to London then crossed the Channel a few days later, arriving in Paris on Saturday night, January 18, 1890, to discover a city abuzz over the Gouffé killing. The elusive suspects—Gabrielle Bompard and Michel Eyraud—were splashed across the newspapers. Obviously Gabrielle could no longer evade the subject. Ensconced in their hotel room she finally acknowledged the truth—at least part of it. She told her lover that Eyraud had murdered Gouffé—and she was there, but she was entirely free of responsibility. If she were guilty of anything, it was the crime of silence—she had kept her terrible secret to herself. She begged Garanger to understand and, full of his affection for her, he accepted her story of innocence. She urged him to go out in the morning and get all the newspapers he could find. He needed to read everything; then, she promised, they would talk.

The next day, Gabrielle hid inside the hotel room while Garanger went about Paris in no great hurry. First he lunched with a friend; then he went to see Eyraud's brother-in-law, hoping to collect on some of his loans to Eyraud. But the mere mention of Eyraud's name enraged the brother-in-law: Why in the world would he cover the man's debts? He was waiting for Eyraud to repay him thousands of francs. Did Monsieur Garanger not realize the cold truth? He too had been swindled.

When Garanger returned to the hotel, his arms were filled with recent editions of *Le Petit Journal*. He read them patiently while Gabrielle watched and waited. Finally it was time to talk. But again Gabrielle only wanted to prove her innocence. She implored Garanger to believe she had no hand in the murder. If she were an accomplice, she was an involuntary one. As Goron later described her attitude:

"In her mind she had erected a system of defense that she thought was infallible."

Garanger was disappointed, and decided there was only one course of action: Gabrielle had to tell her story to the prefect of police. She agreed, believing in her innocence and trusting in Garanger to protect her. For his part, he placed his faith in French justice. Her innocence would save her.

On Tuesday afternoon, January 21, at about four o'clock, Gabrielle and her gentleman approached the office of the prefect. Her name was in every newspaper and her face stared out from the photos; she was the woman all of Paris wanted to see. But when she presented herself to the bailiff, he asked dryly, "Do you have a letter of introduction?"

"No," she replied. "But I am Gabrielle Bompard."

The name meant nothing to him, and the bailiff had his rules. "Get a letter of introduction," he told her. "You will not be received otherwise." And he sent her away. Goron was astounded. "The prefect's bailiff was the only person in Paris who was ignorant of the Gouffé case," he recalled. This daft guard let France's premier fugitive slip away. "With him," Goron scolded, "rules took precedence over other observations."

Gabrielle and Garanger tried again the following day, returning to the prefecture at 10:00 a.m. A cold wind had blown in overnight and rain had come. Gabrielle was in an elegant black dress and veil; she had pushed her dyed-red hair up into a soft fur hat. Garanger at her side was a bearded, distinguished-looking gentleman in a top hat. A different bailiff was on duty but was as much a dullard as the previous one. He, too, mindlessly demanded to see a letter of introduction, and Gabrielle again admitted that she didn't have one.

"But I need to see the prefect," she pleaded. "It's extremely urgent."

"Please state your name."

"I am Gabrielle Bompard."

The stunned look on the bailiff's face showed he had read the newspapers. He shot to his feet and raced out from behind his station. Staring hard at the young woman, he escorted her into the office of the prefect, Henri-Auguste Loze. Her companion followed closely behind.

That morning Inspector Jaume had visited the ailing Goron, whose recovery was slow and painful. The Sûreté staff was deeply concerned. "He is sick," the inspector wrote in his diary. "His eyes haven't worked since the trip to London, and we are very upset because the doctors do not offer us assurances."

A short time later, Jaume rushed to Prefect Loze's office on an urgent summons and found two visitors on the prefect's sofa: a respectable-looking middle-aged man and a young woman whose face was turned away.

"Tell me, Jaume, do you recognize Mademoiselle?" Loze said.

The woman swiveled toward the inspector.

"Perfectly, Monsieur le Préfet," Jaume replied calmly. "That's Mademoiselle Gabrielle Bompard."

She was a slight woman with pretty eyes and matchstick arms and legs. But the fur hat, Jaume thought, it did nothing for her—it was slightly out of fashion.

"How can you be sure?" the prefect wanted to know.

"Very simple, Monsieur le Préfet. I have close to three thousand photos of Mademoiselle Bompard on my desk. It is not surprising her features would be engraved in my memory."

Gazing at her companion, Jaume wondered privately "who the devil the bearded man was."

If Gabrielle was innocent, Jaume didn't see it. She had a sly, kittenish look and, when she smiled at him, Jaume was inspired to exclaim in his diary: *"O monstre!"*

For weeks, the inspector had carried a document inside his portfolio, hoping for this day. He smiled back at Gabrielle and dipped into his case, saying, "Mademoiselle, I have something for you."

It was a warrant for her arrest.

Chapter 24

Gabrielle Bompard's entrance was, in the words of *Le Petit Journal,* a *coup de théâtre,* a dramatic turn of events, a scene only a novelist could invent, but in this case "the reality . . . surpassed fiction."

Gabrielle was a real-life character who fed the public's fascination with the criminal mind. Encouraged by the lurid press, the French had a passion for the otherness of killers popularized by the Italian criminal anthropologist Cesare Lombroso, who claimed to have discovered a new human subspecies: the born criminal. After first focusing on men, Lombroso turned his attention to criminal women, and later he would draw on Gabrielle as proof of his theories (which are now largely discredited). Her confession to Garanger fit the Lombroso model. "We find that while [criminal women] often obstinately deny their guilt," the criminologist wrote, "they also often spontaneously reveal it. This complex psychological phenomenon is caused in part by that need to gossip and that inability to keep a secret which are characteristic of females." In recounting Gabrielle's case, Lombroso described her travels with Georges Garanger, their arrival in Paris, the newspapers' vigorous coverage of the crime, concluding that "she could not refrain from revealing her own and her accomplice's identity." Lombroso distinguished born killers by their physical defects, and Gabrielle, he said, had "all the characteristics," noting her tiny stature and small breasts and hips. Furthermore, Lombroso deduced, "she had an asymmetrical and flattened face as in Mongolians."

None of it, however, detracted from her allure to Parisians. Her charm and unpredictability only enhanced the mystery of her criminal nature. She took to her public role instinctively, stepping eagerly into the spotlight and playing to the masses; her life suddenly acquired meaning thanks to the glare of the press and the readers' obsessive curiosity. Shamelessly self-promoting, she laid the foundation for the modern criminal celebrity. "Her biggest concern," *Le Petit Journal* marveled, "is to know, Is she getting good press?" She repeatedly asked her keepers what journalists were saying about her and when she heard they were portraying her as a spoiled child, "she could not suppress a smile of satisfaction."

From the prefect's office she was taken in a hackney to the home of Judge Dopffer, with Inspector Jaume and Garanger at her side. She seemed lighthearted, even happy. Rolling along the Paris streets, she delighted at the sights while Jaume and Garanger sat in silence. "No one said a word," Jaume recorded in his diary. "Only Gabrielle Bompard from time to time let out a joyous exclamation at seeing some lovely ornament of Paris. Were we on a pleasure outing? The devil take me if I'd ever seen a similar arrest."

Her behavior was mystifying: Did she not realize the gravity of her situation? Was she a child overjoyed at being the center of attention? Was she relieved her long flight from justice was over? Was she mentally unstable? Or did she possess the indifference of a born criminal?

In front of Dopffer's residence, a flower girl thrust a bouquet of violets at Jaume, mistaking his relationship with Gabrielle: "Flowers for your madame, my good monsieur. It will bring you happiness." Quickly seizing on the peddler's confusion, Gabrielle turned puppy-dog eyes on Jaume, trapping him between embarrassment and disgust. "Voilà," he wrote later, "Gabrielle addressed a mute prayer to me, and I was compelled to read the desire in her eyes. I paid for the violets."

Gabrielle gaily pinned the flowers to her bodice and the trio went up the steps to the door. But Dopffer, who had not been informed of the big news, was out at lunch. So, with time to kill, Jaume walked his charges to the nearby Café de l'Observatoire on boulevard de Port-Royal. The place was in high spirits. Four young men played a noisy round of billiards, and a group of students and some "pretty ladies from the Latin quarter" were laughing and singing together, Jaume wrote. To his great relief, no one so much as glanced at the notorious murderess. Happily, he wrote, "they had no more care about us than might Queen Victoria or the Grand Mughal." Gabrielle slipped into the mood of the place and was as animated as a girl out for lunch with friends.

Back at Dopffer's home, Jaume felt the weight of the moment. Presenting Gabrielle would be no ordinary introduction. Here was the young fugitive detectives had chased for six months, the woman who had run from Paris to America and back and who stood at the center of an abominable crime that had shocked all of France and a good part of the world.

When Dopffer entered the room, Jaume was concise—no preamble, no narrative. He simply announced: "La belle Gabrielle."

As if already acquainted with her, Dopffer turned his eye on the accused and uttered: *"Voilà, voilà, petite menteuse!"* (There she is, the little liar!)

Jaume was taken aback. He knew Gabrielle was slippery; he knew she was likely to color the truth. "But she hadn't said a word yet," he observed. "No one had asked her a question. How the devil did Monsieur Dopffer already size her up as a liar?"

The judge ordered Gabrielle to his office at the Palais de Justice, and there over the next five hours she withstood his aggressive questioning. Throughout it all she remained calm. Sometimes she delivered the truth, and at other times she lived up to her nickname, *petite menteuse,* little liar. When she spoke accurately she merely confirmed what police already knew: that she had been Eyraud's mistress, that his money had run out, that they had bought a trunk in London. And then she revealed something new: that she and her lover had rented an apartment at 3, rue Tronson du Coudray. When the address hit the newspapers, hordes flocked to the quiet, one-block-long side street to gawk at the scene of the crime. Some fanatics were not satisfied just to look; they put their hands on the building, and they reached up to touch the apartment's shutters. Neighbors debated how a murder could have taken place on a warm summer evening when the windows were open and "the least cry, the lightest noise" would have been heard. "All the neighbors shake their heads with an air of incredulity," *Le Petit Journal* reported. The number of pilgrims grew daily, congesting traffic in the intersecting streets and forcing police to maintain order.

When Gabrielle first told Dopffer about the events on the night of July 26, she lied: She concocted a story featuring a new accomplice. She said she'd gone out to run some errands and when she returned Eyraud was inside the apartment with a tall man with a red mustache. Eyraud announced that their financial troubles were now over, though he didn't explain why, and Gabrielle had no idea what he meant. She noticed, however, that the trunk, which had been in the kitchen, was now against the wall in the sitting room. According to her story, Eyraud told her that he and the man had to go out for a while and off they went carrying a set of keys she'd never seen before. Sometime later he came back alone in a manic state. When she asked what was the matter, he just rambled. Nothing he said made any sense. Then he started drinking and at eleven he went home to spend the night with his wife.

The next morning at eight o'clock he arrived at the apartment in a cab with two horses. They had to flee, he told her, then Eyraud and the coachman loaded the trunk onto the cab for the trip to Gare de Lyon, where they boarded a train for the south. In Lyon, they stayed at a hotel next to the train station, and the trunk leaked what looked like blood, leaving a large red stain on the floor. As Eyraud mopped up the mess with his jacket, Gabrielle told Dopffer, she began to suspect the worst. In the morning they rented a horse-drawn cart and took the trunk into the countryside. All the while, Gabrielle tried to get Eyraud to tell her the truth but he just waved his revolver in her face until she stopped nagging him. At a deserted spot along the Rhône River, they came upon another carriage—and there, to her surprise, was the man with the red mustache. She was ordered to wait at the side of the road while the two men carried the trunk off in the second carriage. About half an hour later they returned without the trunk, and they told her nothing.

Gabrielle, Dopffer realized, was manufacturing her innocence: She wanted him to believe she couldn't have had a hand in a crime she didn't even know existed. Eyraud and the man with the red mustache were responsible for everything, and they kept her in the dark. In Gabrielle's imagining, she had a whiff of some terrible deed but she had no idea what exactly had taken place. Frustrated by her storytelling, Dopffer called an end to the first day's session.

Gabrielle was sent off to a dusty corner of the prefecture of police for a meeting with Alphonse Bertillon, the slow-moving but meticulous cataloguer of criminals. Bertillon was a repellent genius, given to nosebleeds and crippling headaches, who created a revolutionary system for identifying lawbreakers by measuring their body parts.

Using his tape measure he noted the size of the head, feet, fingers—everything—and carefully cataloged the length and circumference of each part. He kept his anthropometric calculations of each criminal on a filing card, with mug shots attached, and stored the records in a massive cabinet. He was convinced that no two people had identical measurements. If he had a card, he could determine a criminal's true identity; his cabinet could break the alias of anyone. His inventive system laid a cornerstone of modern criminal science.

Gabrielle endured the tedious process and, despite her long day, was cooperative throughout. She seemed unaware of the meaning of the experience. On command she raised her arms, and Bertillon noted the length of her extended reach. She tilted her head to allow her left ear to be measured. She put her middle finger on a ruler. She rolled up her sleeves and her forearms were measured. She removed her shoes so the tape measure could be extended along her foot.

She was a model prisoner, her composure exquisite, until it came time for her mug shot. She wanted to look her best and insisted on returning to her hotel for her favorite hat. Apparently she did not understand, or refused to accept, that she was under arrest and not free to come and go as she pleased. She had such a beautiful hat at the hotel, a grand thing festooned with feathers.

"I look spiffy in that," she told the guards, striking a Sarah Bernhardt pose.

Of course it was a ludicrous request—she was going nowhere. Well, perhaps someone could go to the hotel for her. No, no one would be sent to pick up her hat.

Finally she crumbled. The despair of the past year and a half weighed on her: the murder, the fleeing, the beatings, the arrest, and now the obstinacy of the police. She sobbed hysterically. And no one offered her any sympathy. At last she pulled herself together and posed for the mug shot hatless.

Next, she was taken to the Dépôt, the prison at the Palais de Justice usually for criminals just passing through the legal system. In rare cases suspects took up residence there. Gabrielle was to be housed at the Dépôt throughout her interrogation so the judge and detectives could keep a close watch on her. She was deposited in a tomblike cell about twelve feet long and six feet wide with an eight-foot ceiling. Two louvered windows high on the wall at the front opened inward;

in the daytime, the slats let in a pale slanting light that died on the floor near the door while the rest of the room sat in shadowy half-light. On her arrival the cell was in a murky gloom. There was an iron bed, an oak stool, and a small board that served as a table—all fixed to the walls. "One thus avoids a furious defendant who cannot use the furnishings as bludgeons," *Le Petit Journal* explained. There was a small stove that brought heat in from the basement. Some prisoners occupied their time by rubbing the stove to a shine, adding a splash of brightness to the room; others filled the long hours by sweeping the floor with a handleless broom.

With Gabrielle's capture, the press speculated that additional arrests were imminent: A major breakthrough was coming. At long last the pieces of this drawn-out saga were falling into place. "The emotion was great yesterday in Paris when the public learned . . . that the Gouffé case was finally on the eve of being clarified," *Le Petit Journal* reported. *Le Gil Blas* added its own optimism: "It is thus now permitted to hope that we will soon have the solution to the mystery that has impassioned public opinion for so long now."

But poor Goron, the man who drove the case through its darkest hours, watched the excitement unfold from his sickbed. He wanted badly to be in the center of the interrogation; he wanted to question the suspect himself and soak up some glory. But he remained, on doctor's orders, recumbent in a dark room, contenting himself with reports delivered by his trusted aide, Inspector Jaume. Goron was pleased that Gabrielle was under arrest but his own frustrations ran deep, as *Le Petit Journal* noted: "A man who should be quite unhappy right now is Monsieur Goron, who has an affliction of the eyes that stops him from all work."

Chapter 25

On the second day of questioning Judge Dopffer bore down on the *petite menteuse.* His patience grew thin, his manner severe, and Gabrielle teetered at the edge of a psychological abyss, laughing, then crying, and then laughing again. Gradually Dopffer coaxed out a new story, one that transformed her from a mere witness to an active participant.

What turned her, Goron later hypothesized, was the power of a night in jail. Behind bars, in the silence of the cell, she probably heard the judge's first day of interrogation pounding in her head, and she lost her confidence. By day two, she realized she needed to cooperate. The first thing she recanted was the tale of the man with the red mustache. There was never any man with a red mustache in the apartment on rue Tronson du Coudray, nor did he reappear on the road outside Lyon. Some newspapers had been skeptical of the suspect's storytelling from the start; now they patted themselves on the back: "We were right yesterday when we said that it's not necessary to accept all that Gabrielle Bompard says," *Le Gil Blas* wrote.

Dopffer methodically peeled away the young woman's lies and bit by bit brought to light a more credible scenario. At times, Gabrielle seemed distracted, uninterested, or simply lost, forcing her interrogator to swing between sternness and sympathy to maintain her attention and draw her out. Gabrielle took Dopffer back to the beginning of July when Michel Eyraud was running out of his plundered cash. With Fribourg & Cie on his back, Eyraud told Gabrielle they had to get out of Paris. But first he needed to strike a big blow, a robbery so lucrative it would set them up and send them on their way. He considered killing an elderly jeweler, and when that proved too risky he set his sights on Toussaint-Augustin Gouffé. Here was a man he knew was vulnerable to the lure of sex, and Eyraud had Gabrielle to dangle before him. She insisted she had no choice but to take part in the tawdry scam. Eyraud had seized control of her; she no longer had any free will.

At first she believed Eyraud planned just to rob Gouffé, who, he had discovered, often carried a large amount of cash and wore a very expensive gold ring. But soon she realized Eyraud had something far worse in mind. With cold-blooded calculation, he planned to leave no trace of his crime; he had to eliminate any possibility his victim could point a finger at him. So Eyraud set about his task. For a man lazy in the traditional ways of work, he was a remarkably diligent schemer. The trap, he knew, had to be carefully laid. He learned Gouffé's habits, discovering that the bailiff kept large sums of money in his office on Fridays after a week of collections. Gouffé also stayed out late on Friday night, usually in the arms of one of his many paramours. So no one would begin to miss him until the morning, giving the killers a cushion of time to make their escape.

On the afternoon of July 26, the day of the crime, Eyraud sprung the trap: He tricked Gouffé into believing that his own affair with Gabrielle was over, that she was free to entertain other men, and that she was looking for a new lover. And Gabrielle abetted the ruse by bumping into Gouffé on the street, at Eyraud's direction, and inviting him to visit her that evening at 3, rue Tronson du Coudray.

At eight fifteen there was a rapping at the door.

Gabrielle greeted the visitor naked except for her dressing gown, which she'd tied closed with a red silk sash. The room had been prepared for romance: candles burned, and some biscuits and bottles of champagne and cognac were on a table. The trunk was out of sight in the kitchen. With her eye for fashion, Gabrielle admired Gouffé's top hat, which he removed and placed on a side table. "A beautiful hat," she told Dopffer. "Shiny—not the hat of a bailiff!"

"So, little demon," Gouffé began. "We have left Michel?"

She sensed that he didn't believe it.

"Yes," Gabrielle lied. "That's over."

"Not very big-hearted," he said.

Gabrielle invited him to have a seat.

Looking around, Gouffé saw there was nowhere to sit. All the chairs had been removed, leaving only a chaise longue beside a curtained alcove. And out of sight behind that curtain was Eyraud, seated on a wooden chair, lying in wait.

The room had been prepared for a hanging: In the ceiling of the alcove—hidden by the curtain—was a pulley, and running through the pulley was a length of rope. If all went as planned, Eyraud would soon yank down on the rope and feel the weight of Gouffé on the other end, his neck in a makeshift noose fashioned from the red sash around Gabrielle's waist.

"Sit there," Gabrielle said, indicating the chaise longue.

"Oh I'm not tired," he said, adding suggestively: "On the contrary."

"Sit down," Gabrielle begged. "Please." She had to get him onto the chaise longue.

"I wish you would sit down," she repeated.

Gouffé remained on his feet.

Gabrielle offered him a glass of cognac. He declined.

Gouffé sensed her anxiety.

"Are you afraid of me?" he asked.

Gabrielle again begged him to sit on the chaise longue and at last he did. She climbed onto his lap, she told Dopffer, and chattered about her red silk sash. Eyraud had coached her in what to say. She told Gouffé that the sash was very expensive—didn't he think it was lovely? And then she removed it from her waist, allowing her dressing gown to fall open. Gouffé began to fondle her breasts and kiss her neck.

While he was distracted by his lovemaking, she quietly trans-formed the sash into a noose—Eyraud had doctored it and showed her what to do—and she discreetly reached through a break in the curtain, passed one end of the sash to Eyraud, and he connected it to a clasp on the rope. She was marching through her orders like an automaton, just as Eyraud had instructed her. Now she raised the sash—shaped like a noose—and playfully chirped: "What a nice necktie it makes." Gouffé, absorbed in Gabrielle's body, paid no attention to her chatter.

The moment had arrived: Gabrielle knew what she had to do. Recalling the scene for Dopffer, she sounded distant, as if reciting the actions of someone else. She told the judge that she started to drop the sash over Gouffé's neck but then froze. She panicked, her mind was exploding, she was paralyzed. Somehow Eyraud sensed her hesitation and burst out of the alcove, grabbing the noose out of her hands and throwing it over Gouffé's head. The bailiff was startled but had no time to react. Eyraud was already pulling on the rope and the red sash was tightening around Gouffé's throat. Eyraud yanked down ferociously and Gouffé slowly rose off the floor. The bailiff's hands went to his throat, his fingers clawing at the sash, trying to get underneath it. He cried out but he was choking. Eyraud threw all his weight onto the rope, jerking Gouffé upward and draining the color from the bailiff's face.

Then, Gabrielle said, she heard a loud snap—the pulley had popped out of the crossbeam. Suddenly the rope was cascading down and with it came Gouffé, who tumbled to the floor, still alive. Eyraud dove on top of Gouffé like a panther and grabbed his throat. Gouffé was too winded to resist. Maniacally Eyraud drove his large thumbs into the bailiff's windpipe, pressing with every ounce of his strength.

To Gabrielle, time stood still—Gouffé's strangulation took only seconds but the horror seemed to drag on forever.

When it was over, Eyraud fell backward on the floor red-faced and out of breath.

"*C'est fait,*" he said. (It's done.)

A dramatic tale, no doubt. But was it the truth? Eyraud committed the murder, and Gabrielle, she was just a terrified witness. But was she as disengaged as she suggested? What was Eyraud's story? He was not here to defend himself, he was unable to challenge Gabrielle's recollection. Dopffer realized it was going to be difficult, if not impossible, to arrive at an indisputable account of what occurred inside 3, rue Tronson du Coudray on July 26, 1889.

Newspapers reported details of the interrogation: Gabrielle's intense sobbing, her outbursts of mad hilarity. She was described as a spoiled child, a street urchin, a deranged woman. And there was her aloofness, her detachment, as if she were anywhere else but at the scene of the crime. To Inspector Jaume she displayed "a disconcerting aplomb." She was as slippery a wench as he had seen. "To embarrassing questions, she responds with a burst of laughter," he noted. But he warned that she should not be dismissed as a lightweight. "This woman is not a scatterbrain. She thinks. She calculates. She has extreme self-possession and audacity. A cunning devil, yes. A fool, no!"

She had seduced the masses and prompted a guessing game: Who was Gabrielle really? What drove her? Why did she return to Paris? Why come back if only to face certain prosecution? Paris intellectuals dug deep in search of profound answers. One essay compared her to the tormented souls who populate Russian literature, characters created by Dostoyevsky, Tolstoy, and Turgenev. "She shows the need for confession which is the pivot in so many celebrated dramas and novels," the essayist wrote. "It is necessary that she speak, the miserable girl, that she shakes off the load of her crime, that she tells it, perhaps to be able finally to sleep in peace."

The little demon threw the nation into a frenzy, as *Le Petit Journal* put it: "She is a suitable heroine in this sad drama that preoccupies all of France."

Her arrest redeemed Jaume and the ailing Goron. The newspapers had lacerated them for their handling of the case; Parisians had snickered, and some magistrates had publicly scolded them. But the two men stuck to their hunches, risked their reputations—and now who dared to doubt them? They were, in fact, the cleverest of all sleuths. Henri-Auguste Loze, the prefect of police, told Jaume he was pleased by the turn of events. "I am especially very happy for you because the public was saying that Goron and Jaume are phonies."

The men were lionized. Without Goron, *L'Écho de Paris* declared, the case had been destined to founder in the hands of incompetents in the provinces. What kind of a man had such courage to stick by his beliefs? It was Goron, the paper said, who "proved in the Gouffé case the remarkable qualities that others seemed to totally lack." *La Presse* praised Goron for his relentless pursuit of the truth. Every one of his steps now seemed a masterful stroke. He was "certainly right" when confronted by the unidentified cadaver in Millery to declare: "That's the bailiff Gouffé!"

Chapter 26

Each day Gabrielle was greeted in her cell by Brigadier Soudais and another Sûreté agent and escorted to Judge Dopffer's office for her interrogation. She faced the judge alone, without a lawyer. French law did not require that suspects have counsel present during questioning; the investigating magistrate was empowered to interrogate anybody and to do so in private. Gabrielle and the guards climbed several flights of stairs to the top three floors of the Palais de Justice. Along the enormous corridor leading to Dopffer's office she was able to pause and gaze through the windows at Sainte-Chapelle, home for more than six hundred years to relics from Christ's crucifixion: a nail, his blood, his crown of thorns.

The vast corridor was thick with people. Here Gabrielle was among the accused who had come to protest their innocence or confess their guilt and the witnesses who had come to provide testimony. On any average day the eye took in a kaleidoscope of impressions: "Here a cook in a white apron talks lovingly to a municipal guard," a court reporter wrote of the scene. "There, with their arms folded in the attitude of blind men waiting for alms, the witnesses of some accident bide their time, leaning against the wall . . . One of them sighs and keeps looking at his watch . . . another reads his newspaper . . . another, possessed by an irresistible desire for movement, walks up and down, counting his paces, and feverishly biting the points of his moustache."

They were each summoned to their session by a clerk in a dark blue uniform with copper buttons who sat officiously at a desk lighted by a gas lamp covered in a green shade. Every so often an electric bell sounded, rousing the clerk, who scrambled into the judges' quarters for his orders.

Gabrielle sat on a bench to await her turn. Lost in her own thoughts, she did not notice that standing nearby was Georges Garanger, whom she had not seen since her arrest a week earlier, and who was talking with his legal representative, the famed attorney Henri Robert. Since the couple had appeared at the prefect's office, Garanger had managed to evade the spotlight. For a few days he had been the unnamed mystery man who escorted the young woman on her way to justice. He had been subjected to a round of questioning by police, which revealed he had a business relationship with Michel Eyraud in America—and that revelation had kicked up a swirl of suspicion around Garanger himself. So he had hired the formidable Robert, who at twenty-seven was already considered one of France's brightest legal minds, and soon any doubt about Garanger's honesty and integrity vanished. *Le Gil Blas* highlighted the gentleman's wealth and exotic business ventures in China, Burma, and Cambodia and his membership in the Legion of Honor. It concluded that "his role in this affair had been in all respects honorable."

Garanger provided police with a statement that described his initial encounter with Eyraud and Gabrielle in Vancouver, then elaborated on seeing them again in San Francisco, and touring the wine country of Napa for ten days together. He recounted being drawn into a phony distillery project that Eyraud promised would produce staggering returns. He recalled buying a sealskin coat for Gabrielle for $100, advancing Eyraud $200 here, another $300 there, and hearing Eyraud prattle about the huge sums of money needed for the distillery. Garanger told police about setting off with Gabrielle from San Francisco and then avoiding Eyraud on the East Coast and sailing across the Atlantic. "Eyraud had the real intention of murdering me," he told police. Gabrielle had told Garanger about threats against him. "The swine had better watch out," Eyraud had said. "I'll have to kill him to get his money." Gabrielle said she warned Eyraud to keep his hands off of Garanger: If he murdered Garanger, she vowed to go to the police.

While Garanger had captured the respect of the nation, he seemed an odd match for a troubled, lost girl. What did he see in this volatile coquette? Could it be that Garanger, who had spent years in remote, mysterious lands, thrived on the exotic and was intrigued by her inconsistencies? Was he the sort of man who found impulsive behavior amusing? In his statement to police, he was unconcerned that his "voyage companion was a bit eccentric." She had charmed Garanger's wandering soul: She was young and pretty and always surprising.

The writer Émile Zola felt compelled to weigh in on their relationship, seeing in Gabrielle the deadly deceit of the femme fatale. Her conduct, in Zola's eyes, exemplified the distrustful nature of all women. So easily she turned from one lover to the next, forsaking Eyraud in a heartbeat for Garanger, and then denouncing her former lover to the police. "Ah, they are all like this, women," Zola declared. "All! Whatever their social condition, their education, their character, all break up like this—the next day forgetting the one they loved the day before." Zola believed that Gabrielle's decision to go to the police was not an act of remorse or courage—there was nothing admirable at all in it. In Zola's world, women did not behave honorably. "It's part of a need to create talk about themselves, to occupy the public attention," he said. "Gabrielle Bompard is delighted to know that her name is in the newspapers every day. It's the profound indifference they reserve for those who have ceased to please them."

Inspector Jaume also found Gabrielle about as trustworthy as a starving street cat. "The rascal knows men well," he confided to his diary. "She plays the ingénue with the good Garanger to ensure he accepts her innocence—the perverse little woman." Now that she had revealed her role in the murder, she needed the support of the virtuous Garanger all the more. "The interest he shows in her is a shield which she has to preserve," Jaume reasoned. "If he abandons her, her situation before the jury will be infinitely worse." Once, when Jaume had both of them in his office for questioning, Gabrielle had sweetly begged Garanger to forgive her for failing to tell him the whole truth right from the start. But by this time her honeyed words did not impress Garanger, and he remained stoically silent. Jaume suspected Garanger was seeing Gabrielle for what she was: "a vulgar prostitute and accomplice in murder." He recorded in his diary: "Garanger is beginning to understand that Gabrielle has fooled him."

While awaiting her session with Dopffer, Gabrielle caught sight of Garanger standing several paces away with his lawyer, and she sprang off the bench and raced toward him. With wild abandon she threw herself into his arms, hugging and kissing him. Her display was childish, dramatic, deranged. For his part, Garanger was visibly moved by her passion, but he maintained his dignity and gently disengaged himself. He held her in his outstretched arms, his voice quavering. "My child!" he said. "My child, have courage."

What gave rise to Garanger's emotions? Genuine affection for Gabrielle, empathy for her plight, sadness at the impossible barriers now between them? "Let me . . ." he began but then stopped, unable to find the words. Finally all he could manage to say was: "Please."

Gabrielle clung tightly to him until Brigadier Soudais intervened by tapping his walking stick on Garanger's leg. Soudais signaled with his head for the gentleman to move away, and Garanger followed orders, delicately extricating himself from her embrace and taking a few steps backward. Soudais then piloted Gabrielle back to the bench.

Was this outburst a contrived performance? Or was Gabrielle a weak child craving attention in the cold confines of the Palais de Justice? Was she fluttering at the edge of psychological disintegration? So many questions: Who was this baffling lost soul? Was Gabrielle the *petit démon* conning the world, or was she a damaged girl facing the wrath of French justice? Jaume had his own answer: "The play-acting of this young woman," he groused to his diary, "irritates me more than I can say."

Chapter 27

A world away in San Francisco, Gabrielle Bompard was a local story: The young woman who'd once roamed the city was now implicated in a shocking murder. The *San Francisco Chronicle* carried a page-one story: "A Criminal Heroine: Gabrielle Enjoys Her Notoriety." Michel Eyraud also became a figure of fascination. Reporters trekked out to the Napa Valley to retrace his steps, sending back dispatches head-lined: "He Can Tell Good Brandy—One of the Accomplishments of Eyraud, the Paris Strangler."

In Paris, Gabrielle had the limelight all to herself, and her out-bursts and droll observations flooded the papers as if she were a stage star. One day, while eating lunch, she glanced at the scrap of news-paper wrapped around her cheese. Studying the fragment, she saw a few words about the Gouffé case. "Ah, there's something here about me," she commented to Jaume. "What are they saying about me in the newspapers?"

"Woman! The newspapers speak only of you. You are *l'héroïne du jour*," Jaume told her.

"Ah, that's very nice." And she burst out laughing.

Although some worried that Gabrielle's mental state was deterio-rating, Jaume was convinced she was in full control of her faculties and was manipulating a willing Paris audience. "I do not hide what I believe: that her laugh rings false, that her unconscious gaiety is cal-culated, and that she does not at all merit in any way to monopolize the attention of the public."

The public wanted to know everything about her. Newspaper readers learned that her fine fashions, in which she appeared each day on the staircase of the Palais de Justice, had been supplied by her gentleman friend Georges Garanger. "We have seen her in black, blue, tobacco-brown and beige," reported *L'Écho de Paris.* "Yesterday, she wore a simple and elegant dress in a shade of brown. But always the same hat, a small, velvet toque."

The reporting was obsessive. Journalists revealed not only what came out of her mouth but also what went into it. After she was interrogated in the morning at the Sûreté, the newspapers published what she had for lunch: *"côtelette de mouton avec de la purée de pommes, un morceau de fromage de Brie et une pomme. Comme boisson, une vulgaire chopine de vin"* (lamb chop with mashed potatoes and a piece of Brie cheese and an apple, along with an ordinary glass of wine). "She ate with a very good appetite," *Le Figaro* said, "although complaining that her lamb chop, brought in from a neighboring restaurant, was cold and hardly appetizing."

Isolated in her barren cell at the Dépôt, she managed to cling to some of the finer things in life. She had with her a flask of Eau Circassienne, a special water created by a Dr. Wiloff, which was said to preserve a woman's skin tone.

In his daily interrogations, Judge Dopffer wrestled with Gabrielle to tease out the truth. On some days he was the harsh inquisitor; on others, a paternal adviser. Gabrielle, he realized, could only be led to the truth through a maze of lies. "La belle Gabrielle . . . recounted a new fact to the judge every day, which was often a lie but also sometimes a confession," Goron wrote in his account of the case.

Piece by contradictory piece, her sordid tale took shape. The concierge at the apartment on rue Tronson du Coudray confirmed that Eyraud and Gabrielle had been seen coming and going. But he found nothing suspicious about the couple. "I would have never thought that this monsieur and this mademoiselle were murderers," he told *Le Figaro.* The businessman Fribourg confirmed Gabrielle's descriptions of Eyraud's scams to rob the trading company. Her account of how she and Eyraud dumped the body in Millery provided the map for a later trip to the south to retrace the killers' steps.

There was, however, an unanswerable question that loomed over all the proceedings. Dopffer could amass details; he could create a giant dossier; he could describe every train ride, every shopping trip, every ruse. But no matter how many facts he assembled, the answer to one mystery still was just out of reach: How was it that this young woman from a bourgeois family could have taken part in a series of dreadful acts that ultimately ended in murder? The plotting. The trips to London. The theatrical killing. To everyone, her conduct was inexplicable. How could she have stayed with the brutal Eyraud for so long and then gone with him on the run across the sea to America? She was either an immoral degenerate or a bullied young woman dragged along like a chained dog by a manipulative older man. Her motives, her adventures, her essence were a mystery.

Whatever frailties lay within Gabrielle's soul, Inspector Jaume had no sympathy for her. He wanted a conviction and the most severe sentence. His cop's obsession left little room for mercy and scant understanding of female oppression. Abuse and its crippling impact meant nothing to him. "Gabrielle tells stories that Eyraud terrorized her," he wrote in his diary. "He could. But when one lets oneself be terrorized into becoming the conscious instrument of a crime, one does not merit much pity."

Her volatile emotions suggested something else was at work. Day by day, outburst by outburst, a theory emerged to explain Gabrielle's submission to Eyraud. In the interrogation room, she laughed one moment, cried the next. She chattered then fell silent. At times she was carefree, oblivious to the gravity of her circumstances, to the fact that she was under arrest for murder. Her utter indifference to the crime was evident in her bizarre language. She said that after killing Gouffé, Eyraud cut the clothes off of the body and trussed it with a rope to make it fit into the trunk. She chirped that they had "tied up Gouffé like a chicken!" Remarks like that revealed a profound detachment. Gabrielle, it was feared, was separating from reality. "This woman is a nervous person, sick, with an unstable mind, a broken woman," reported *Le Gil Blas*. Still, she deserved no leniency, the paper said. "She is far from meriting a light judgment."

Reporters, doctors, judges, police, and the public dissected the character of this unhinged spirit and soon a new word entered the discussion. *La Presse* explained the diagnosis: Gabrielle, it said, "offers attentive observers some very curious symptoms of well-developed neurosis." She was very intelligent and at times was capable of providing thoughtful, precise answers to Dopffer's probing inquiries. But some other responses revealed a deeply troubled psyche. "It's the attitude taken by this woman, speaking first in a tone very disengaged, offering a first version, then another, finally a third, a bit closer to the truth," the paper wrote. "At times, she was wracked by intense agitation. Then she interrupts herself to laugh without reason and these outbursts of mad hilarity last several minutes." *La Presse* then offered a diagnosis that began to gain currency: Gabrielle, it stated, was "affected by a sort of hysteria."

"Hysteria" conjured images of madwomen inside the hysterics ward of the neurologist Jean-Martin Charcot. But hysteria was far more complicated than that, more elusive, not just a flipbook of contortions, convulsions, and frozen states of catalepsy. It could be subtle. "Like a globule of mercury, it escapes the grasp," one writer has said. From the earliest days, the irrational behaviors designated as hysterical—ranging from a flare of anger to ravings—were misinterpreted as peculiar to women. The men who first defined hysteria located the problem in women's reproductive organs. The word itself was derived from the Greek *hystera,* meaning uterus. But in fact it was impossible to locate the seat of the problem: Was it the soul, the passions, the brain, or a mere "acridity in [women's] sexual organs," as one male observer put it?

The hysteric label stuck to Gabrielle and soon defined her. She had what were believed to be the classic traits: She was deceptive, weak-willed, changeable, and she had an insatiable craving for attention.

The psychologist Edgar Bérillon saw in Gabrielle undeniable traits of hysteria—the laughter and tears, the contradictions—all quite typical in a hysteric who otherwise presents a healthy-looking appearance. Bérillon studied her portraits and photographs, read all the newspaper reports, and was fascinated by her moods during her interrogation. Gabrielle, he said, mixed up truth and imagination. She told lies with "the most unnerving impudence." In sum, Bérillon said, "I do not doubt we are in the presence of a hysteric."

Jaume came to accept the popular conclusion. "Each time I see Gabrielle Bompard," he wrote in his diary, "I ask myself: How did she help Eyraud to murder Gouffé? How much responsibility falls on her shoulders?" Of one thing, he too was certain: "I allow that Gabrielle Bompard is a hysteric."

What came next transformed this grisly murder into a landmark criminal case—a first in legal history. Hysterics, Charcot argued, had a particular susceptibility to hypnosis, and in a hypnotic trance, the law professor Jules Liégeois contended, a person could commit terrible crimes, even murder. These theories took shape in the person of Gabrielle: Her submission to Eyraud and her participation in the killing now were blamed on the powerful influence of hypnotism.

It was Garanger who first proposed that Gabrielle had fallen prey to a force she could not resist. Whether he had the idea himself or Gabrielle had cunningly placed it in his head is impossible to know. But he suggested a murder defense that had never been introduced in a court of law. The question he put forward for a jury to decided was this: Did Gabrielle engage in murder while under the hypnotic control of her middle-aged lover, Michel Eyraud?

Garanger was an amateur hypnotist himself—he had hypnotized Gabrielle on the transatlantic journey—and he knew what happened to a subject placed into a trance: She surrendered her will, she had no consciousness of her actions, and afterward she had no recall of her behavior. In her telling of the Gouffé murder, Gabrielle consistently asserted that she had acted against her will—in essence, she was sleepwalking through the horrors. She said repeatedly that Eyraud had a bizarre control over her. Garanger knew firsthand how deeply she fell into a hypnotic state. With a woman as susceptible as she, were there any limits to what she might do in a trance?

Once Garanger's speculation arose, a critical question entered the case: If Gabrielle had committed murder under hypnosis, was she responsible for her actions? "Monsieur Garanger does not believe in the culpability of his mistress," *Le Petit Journal* revealed, noting that he contended she was forced into the role of a hypnotic intermediary and therefore not culpable. "She is, he says, a hypnotic subject of exceptional sensitivity, and if she played a role in the murder of Gouffé, she was pushed by a suggestive force against which the poor girl was incapable of resisting."

La Presse chimed in: "Gabrielle submitted her free will to a spirit much stronger than her own."

The hypnotism theory rapidly gained credence—and in no small measure because of Garanger's impeccable standing. What's more, he had a special intimacy with the suspect—he was her lover and he had hypnotized her. He knew about her hypnosis obsession while a teenager in Lille and about her performances at the hypnotism salon in Paris. No one knew Gabrielle quite as well as Garanger: He was endowed with unique insight into her character. All this lent weight to his pronouncements. And so it came to be accepted that Gabrielle had killed a man while under hypnosis. All at once Garanger had introduced the notion and legitimized it. Soon it stood at the center of the case. Exerting its bizarre power, hypnosis in the Gouffé murder investigation took on a life of its own.

Gabrielle herself didn't have to press the hypnotism issue—the men around her leapt to her cause. Once the possibility of a hypnotism defense was raised, lawyers and academics converged on the question, seeking to enhance their own positions or win their medical and scientific battles. With her history, Gabrielle was the perfect candidate to bring the criminal aspect of hypnosis to the courts and to the public; but she spoke rarely, if at all, of her role as a hypnotic in the commission of the crime—the men were ready to speak on her behalf, positively or negatively, shoving her into the expected role of a passive woman. Her own life was on the line but doctors, lawyers, and professors were to determine her fate.

Garanger's attorney, the wunderkind Henri Robert, sensed the potential of a spectacular courtroom drama. What better way to enhance one's fame than to test the boundaries of justice with an unprecedented hypnotism defense? If Robert should prevail in such an endeavor, it would not only influence court proceedings for years but also assure him a place in legal history. Even if he failed, his celebrity would be guaranteed. His decision to take on the case raised the stakes by putting the state on notice that Gabrielle would come to court with a brilliant legal mind at her side.

Though still young, Robert was a formidable opponent. Few attorneys were as intellectually nimble and as eloquent on their feet. If he escorted you into the courtroom, you had an excellent chance of walking out free. He had once considered entering the priesthood if only for the chance to address a congregation inside Notre Dame cathedral, but he chose the law instead. He brought clarity into the courtroom; he had no patience for the esoteric language of the law. He was eloquent and had a quickness of repartee. "For this reason he is the favorite advocate of the criminal classes," one observer said. He had saved many men from the guillotine, "to say nothing of having secured the acquittal of a large number of the most thorough rascals in the capital."

Eyraud was still on the run and the state's case against Gabrielle was yet to be completed. But Paris was already eagerly anticipating an extraordinary trial in criminal court, the Cour d'Assises, focused with great fanfare on the question of hypnotism. "It's a new theory, very much in favor at this time, which opens a large door for the defense attorneys," *Le Figaro wrote. Le Petit Journal* considered the historic nature of the case: "For the first time, the mysterious question of suggestion will find itself clearly posed in the course of a criminal investigation."

Jaume was disgusted by all the hoopla. Gabrielle was, in his view, a degenerate liar who stuck by Eyraud's side by her own choice and took part in the vile murder with her eyes wide open. "These stories of hypnotism get on my nerves," he complained. "They take on a greater importance day by day."

He found it impossible to accept that Eyraud had hypnotized Gabrielle to act out his every command to the point of killing Gouffé. How then did she suddenly awake from her stupor to run off with the tall blond adventurer Garanger? One moment Gabrielle was Eyraud's hypnotic pawn, the next she is fighting him to protect her new lover—such contradictions revealed her ugly duplicity. "Gabrielle, inert thing when it's about the life of Gouffé, suddenly recovers her lucidity when it's about Garanger," Jaume said. "She resists, she refuses, she threatens. She yells at Eyraud: if you touch Garanger, I'll tell."

The investigation, Jaume protested, was spinning out of control. "There is truly hypnotism in the air," the inspector bristled. "Only it's Gabrielle who magnetizes public opinion."

Chapter 28

If hysteria and hypnotism were the topics of the day, then the man of the hour had to be the formidable Jean-Martin Charcot. What would the world's leading neurologist make of Gabrielle Bompard's condition—and, more important, her chances of a successful hypnotism defense?

Charcot's climb to the pinnacle of the medical world had been gradual and far from certain. He was a man of contradictions, a bookish, restrained figure of subtle movements and precise language. He had an artist's soul, a sympathy for the suffering, and an eye for detail. His father created beauty with his hands as a working-class artisan, a highly regarded designer and decorator of coaches. Charcot, too, was an artist: His sketchbook showed considerable talent. In his youth, he had to choose between two passions, two paths: one led to a life in art, the other to medicine. He was a bright young man from a modest background, aching with ambition. In the Paris of the 1840s, the medical profession made room for men of his circumstances. So he chose the healing arts for their promise of wealth and prestige.

His gift of observation followed him into medicine. It went with him into the classroom, the clinic, the wards. He was an innovator and sought to see beyond what men of medicine had become accustomed to seeing. His former student Sigmund Freud wrote that Charcot "described how wonderful it was suddenly to see new things—new diseases—although they were probably as old as the human race."

Shyness, however, nearly crushed him, particularly in his youth. It was the weight in his shoes, the clamp on his tongue. At the University of Paris Medical School in the 1840s, he had to compete for honors by written and oral exam and, on his first application for a coveted internship, was passed over, although his work was rated as above average. He threw himself into arduous studies and grotesque lab work—anything, as long as he could prove himself without speaking. In the dissection room he got his first exposure to the study of anatomy—at which he would later excel. An American student in Paris described a typical dissection: "Here, the assiduous student may be seen, with his soiled blouse, and his head bedecked with a fantastic cap. In one hand he holds a scalpel, in the other a treatise on anatomy. He carries in his mouth a cigar, whose intoxicating fumes, so hurtful on most occasions, render him insensible to the smell of twenty bodies, decomposing, putrefying around him."

As a student Charcot showed a fondness for bizarre images and strange behavior, the kind of phantasmagoria that would come to life for him later in the Salpêtrière's hysteria ward. He smoked hashish experimentally and while high took to his sketch pad. As a fellow student described it, "The entire page was covered with drawings: prodigious dragons, grimacing monsters, incoherent personages who were superimposed on each other and who were intertwined in a fabulous whirlpool bringing to mind the apocalyptic conceptions of Van Bos[c]h and Jacques Callot."

In his early years, Charcot was more at ease in the stench of the dissection room than before an audience delivering his findings. His shaky verbal skills still plagued him, and he failed in his first try to win an associate professorship in 1857. But with an indomitable will he overcame this weakness, winning the post three years later. He was no rising star in the Paris medical world, however. He published fairly widely and was considered erudite. But destined for greatness? His career until the age of thirty-seven did not suggest it. Then things changed. In 1862 he was appointed head of medical services of the Salpêtrière Hospital, near quai d'Austerlitz in the thirteenth arrondissement.

The Salpêtrière, once a small arsenal, had been transformed into a vast hospital, home to nearly five thousand live-in patients, mostly women—a third of them insane and the rest so ill they couldn't function in society. Behind its walls were dozens of structures, narrow lanes, stone walkways, gardens and squares, and an enormous domed church. It was a world of its own, known as the city of incurable women. Charcot's was largely an administrative job that others before him accepted in hopes of moving on to a more modern and prestigious institution with a better address. But Charcot had other ideas. It was this "grand asylum of human misery," as he called it, that set him on his journey probing the mysteries of the nervous system.

When Charcot took over, conditions were grim for the institution's destitute and disturbed women. A report in 1863 detailing the previous year at the hospital recorded two hundred and fifty-four deaths from "causes presumed to be due to insanity." Among the reasons cited were masturbation, debauchery, erotomania, rape, blows and wounds, alcoholism, joy, love, and nostalgia. But there were glimmers of hope, too. The report contained the news that during the year a garden was planted in a courtyard and a piano was purchased. Of the women who were able, many were put to work to burn off the boredom and aid the economy of the institution. Their chief task was sewing in small workshops: making bonnets and blouses, mending sheets, and stitching lace.

Jules Claretie, who later portrayed the Salpêtrière atmosphere in his novel *Les Amours d'un Interne,* explained in a journal article: "Behind those walls, a particular population lives, swarms, and drags itself around: old people, poor women, cripples and convalescents awaiting death on a bench, lunatics howling their fury or weeping their sorrow in the insanity ward or the solitude of the cells. The thick gray walls of this *città dolorosa* seem to retain, in their solemn dilapidation, the majestic qualities of Paris under the reign of Louis the Fourteenth, forgotten by the age of electric tramways. It is the Versailles of pain."

Charcot designated himself the curator of what he called this "museum of living pathology." Until then he had demonstrated little interest in the pathology of the nervous system. Now in the face of it he found his calling. In eight years he produced a flurry of groundbreaking studies, paving the way for the creation of a new, separate discipline called neurology. His achievements in such a short span were extraordinary for a man who took on the study of the nervous system only after his appointment in 1862. "While unquestionably he was considered by his contemporaries as a very well-trained worker in his field, no one would at that time have predicted that, a few years later, he would become one of the founders of neurology," wrote Georges Guillain, a neurologist at the Salpêtrière who would succeed Charcot as the professor of clinical diseases of the nervous system.

Some of his achievements still stand. Before Charcot no one had observed order in the chaos of the degenerating nerve cells that control muscles. He identified lesions on the spinal cord that correlated to various symptoms, including muscle contractures, atrophy, and flaccidity. Perhaps the disease was as old as the human race but on the basis of his observations Charcot named it "amyotrophic lateral sclerosis"—known in France as *maladie de Charcot.* For Americans nearly seventy years later, Lou Gehrig became the poster boy of courage in the face of the ailment, which then became known as Lou Gehrig's disease.

Charcot also turned his eye on a scourge that raged unabated until the discovery of penicillin in the early twentieth century. Syphilis caused a torturous slow degeneration in the nerves that send sensory information to the brain. Charcot discovered the role played by damage to the spinal cord.

In another seminal insight, he detected that tremors thought to be associated with Parkinson's disease were actually something else. His eye was sharper than anybody else's and his minute clinical observations revealed a distinction: Certain tremors indicated a separate ailment entirely, something no one had ever identified before, which he called multiple sclerosis.

His curiosity drove him. He wrote on a range of neurological topics, among them aphasia, epilepsy, hysteria, intracranial hemorrhage and stroke, meningitis, migraine, neuropathy, sleep disorders, tics. Somber and meditative, and obsessed with personal glory, he set the standard for modern practices in neurological science. Brain, spinal cord, nerve, and muscle diseases—he built the foundation on which they were defined. He became the uncompromising, sometimes dictatorial, father of modern neurology.

By 1870 Charcot had turned in a new direction, again partly by happenstance. This shift came as a result of a long-needed remodeling at the Salpêtrière. The building housing epileptics, hysterics, and psychotics had become so dilapidated that the patients had to move to new quarters. The epileptics and hysterics went together into a new ward, and the psychotics were placed elsewhere. The hysterics became Charcot's responsibility. He'd had only a passing interest in hysteria, but now he was drawn to the enigmatic behavior of his new patients. With hysteria Charcot moved away from the study of disease with purely organic roots into a realm where anatomical origins were impossible to observe. When studying spinal cord disturbances in his earlier work, he could rely on visible lesions found during autopsies to aid his analysis. With his hysterical patients he was on less firm ground because no physical evidence was discernible in their postmortems. He had only symptoms and behavior to guide his research.

Charcot approached hysteria in the same manner with which he'd tackled previous medical questions: He concentrated on the observable. By its nature, however, this question was among the trickiest he had encountered. Hysterics were known to dissimulate even in the throes of an attack; they also were great imitators.

Working with an intern named Paul Richer, a gifted medical artist, Charcot established the patterns of a hysterical attack. He laid out the recurring phases of what he called an attack of *grande hystérie.* It began with palpitations, pain in the ovaries, uncontrollable coughing or yawning, loss of consciousness, then erupted into muscular contractions similar to what an epileptic experiences. The attack progressed into spectacular contortions on an acrobatic scale that Charcot dubbed "clownism." A patient lying in bed would shoot up into a sitting position then fall back again and repeat the action over and over in what was called "salutations." In another variety, the patient would arch her back so dramatically that her body would rise up and form a semicircle, an *arc-en-cercle,* with only the head and feet touching the bed. The attack then passed into a theatrical phase where the woman expressed a range of emotions. During these *attitudes passionnelles,* Charcot heard love, hate, fear, and anger and saw acts of bold sensuality. Sometimes the young women launched into diatribes or imaginary conversations. The attacks climaxed in a delirium that could last hours or days.

Charcot relied on a handful of women hysterics to develop his concepts. Among them was a young woman named Augustine who was admitted to the Salpêtrière on October 21, 1875, when she was fifteen years old. She was prone to spasms, convulsions, and loss of consciousness. Hospital records showed she had a stunning 2,239 attacks in a single year. Some were sexually charged. During one episode, Charcot noted that her breathing was noisy and rapid. Suddenly she screamed and wriggled her body as if struggling to escape someone's grasp. She then threw her arms out in the shape of the crucifix, saying, "What do you want? Nothing. Nothing." Then she smiled and declared, "Well done!" She looked to the side and lifted herself up and kissed the air. "No no, I don't want him!" Then she kissed the air again. She smiled and opened her legs. "You're starting over again. This isn't it. This isn't it." Her face then took on an expression of regret, and she began to cry. Charcot ended the notation in his records with the words "Abundant vaginal secretion."

In the mid-1870s, Charcot became intrigued by the work of a French doctor named Victor Burq who had worked with hysterics for twenty-five years. Burq had discovered a way to relieve numbness in the limbs of such patients. He found that if he placed certain metals on the skin he was able in some cases to revive sensation. He had his patients wear bracelets of gold, copper, or iron. The key to the treatment, known as metallotherapy, was discovering the right metal for each patient. If the metal was chosen correctly, Burq reported that sensation returned in stages. First came a tingling, then a feeling of heat and weight, and finally of pins and needles. Sometimes, in this way, Burq said he was able to relieve cases of complete paralysis.

In 1876 the Society of Biology agreed at Burq's request to look into metallotherapy for possible scientific validation. It chose Charcot as president of a commission of inquiry. Burq's treatments were replicated at the Salpêtrière. One phenomenon in particular grabbed investigators. They observed that when sensation was returned to one limb by use of metals it simultaneously was lost in another. Magnets, in particular, were found to stimulate a transfer of anesthesia from one leg to the other. Overall, investigators found that repeated use of magnets had an ameliorative effect on the body. Charcot and the commission gave metallotherapy a stamp of approval.

Over the next few years Charcot introduced metallotherapy into his own work with hysterics at the Salpêtrière. Around this time he was drawn to the work of the British surgeon James Braid, who some years earlier had experimented with a phenomenon he called "neuro-hypnotism." He put subjects into a trancelike sleep by having them lock their gaze on an object, such as the top of a wine bottle or a sugar bowl. He recorded the changes in pulse, respiration, and muscular activity in these somnambulists. Over time the term that described the phenomenon of induced sleep would lose its prefix, and it became simply "hypnotism."

Braid's work fascinated Charcot. With metallotherapy and now hypnotism he saw an opportunity to move from merely observing and describing symptoms to experimenting on patients. In 1878 Charcot described his own use of hypnosis for the first time, though he didn't mention the word. His report focused on two young hysterical women at the Salpêtrière. Like Braid's subjects, Charcot's women fixed their gaze on an object, in this case a bright light.

It was at this time that Charcot began to believe in a link between hysteria and hypnotism, and he set about formulating what he thought were the stages of a hysterical attack under hypnosis. Hysterics put into a hypnotic state experienced a sequence of symptoms that Charcot identified as lethargy, catalepsy, and somnambulism. A woman who passed through these three stages in strict obedience to Charcot's classification was said to have suffered an attack of *grand hypnotisme,* or major hypnotism. Charcot asserted that a woman experiencing such an attack had physical reactions that were impossible to simulate. He was able to assert then that his work with hypnotism was grounded in the science of physiology. He had also discerned a smaller-scale reaction that he dubbed *petit hypnotisme,* or minor hypnotism. This attack had a psychological component and lacked the clear physiological markers Charcot required. It was therefore harder to pin down and of less interest to him.

Charcot's classification of the stages of *grand hypnotisme* would dominate the field and eventually ignite intense controversy. According to his rules, a patient experiencing the lethargic first stage of an induced hypnotic attack seemed to fall into a deep slumber and become unresponsive and even unable to hear; in this state, however, the muscles were alive and could be stimulated to contract by a light blow or massage. Next came catalepsy, in which a kind of paralysis set in, allowing the investigator to manipulate the limbs into any frozen position. The final stage was somnambulism, in which the patient could hear and speak and respond to commands.

The reactions of these women, in Charcot's view, were involuntary—the result of physiological eruptions that the women could not control; therefore, there was no reason to doubt their behavior. "For Charcot, a neurologist accustomed to the examination of patients suffering from locomotor ataxia or lateral sclerosis, the definite symptoms—which could not be counterfeited—were changes in the condition of the muscles, variations in the reflexes, and modifications of sensation," wrote the psychologist Pierre Janet. "Thus it was that Charcot, in his endeavor to work out a strictly scientific method [for hypnotism], devoted himself to a study of the movements and reflexes of the subjects."

Hypnotism became Charcot's life, his career, his obsession in the clinic. It was fundamental to his investigations into the mysteries of the nervous system. But hypnotism maintained a tenuous status in the world of science, a fragile legitimacy. The French Academy of Sciences had repeatedly rejected any claim of scientific validity. Relying on his own prestige, Charcot brought the matter before the academy on February 13, 1882. Inside the wood-paneled chamber, adorned with the marble figure of Molière, curly locks falling to his shoulders, and a portrait of Antoine-Laurent Lavoisier, the father of modern chemistry, Charcot addressed the sixty members of the academy, including Louis Pasteur, who several months earlier had demonstrated his vaccine for treating the fatal sheep and cattle disease anthrax. He had the enormous task of reversing the longstanding damage Mesmer had inflicted on the discipline. Speaking in the most sober tone, Charcot emphasized his "prudent and conservative" approach in the study of hypnotism. "Every attempt was made," he told the assembly, "to avoid being attracted by the esoteric or the extraordinary, a peril which in this scientifically unexplored field was encountered, so to speak, at every step of the way."

He assured the members that he was unwilling to be led by "the unexpected and the mystic" and instead pursued "intense physiologic and neuropathologic studies" of hypnosis. He stressed that he didn't bother with the most obscure aspects of hypnotism or with anything he did not correlate to a known physiological mechanism. He argued that scientific progress would benefit from a change in perceptions about hypnotism. Proper studies of hypnotism, he concluded, "are certainly destined to bring eventual light to a whole host of questions, not only from a pathologic standpoint but also from the standpoint of physiology and psychology."

When the members of the academy came back with their answer

in November 1883, Charcot was rewarded: Hypnotism had won approval as a legitimate subject for scientific research from France's highest academic body after a hundred years of rejection. To bring his investigations to a wider audience, Charcot conducted public lectures on Tuesdays, with hypnosis demonstrations using women from the hysterics ward. Medical students and doctors packed the wooden benches of the amphitheater, eager for a peek into the brain of the eminent neurologist. On any given Tuesday journalists, writers, politicians, and philosophers joined the medical men to witness Charcot's performance. Charcot, sober as ever, would appear in a dark suit and bow tie, the unflappable medical luminary. He was clean-shaven in a culture of bearded men. His hair was combed straight back over his head and tucked behind his ears. His eyes were deep-set and brooding, bordered underneath by heavy bags. A strong Roman nose gave a hint of his intellectual despotism. "The arch of the mouth, ironic and taut, bent up slightly higher on the right than the left, as one sees in someone bitterly disappointed," wrote his student Léon Daudet, the son of Charcot's close friend the novelist Alphonse Daudet. Another pupil recorded Charcot's "frowning eyebrows" and "lips that bespoke silence." Charcot guarded his emotions behind what Daudet called an "imperious masked face." He was so aloof one did not approach without trepidation. But he was also fiercely loved and admired, and his disciples were staunchly loyal.

But the real stars of his lectures were the women hysterics—delusional, vicious, obsessed, haunted. In action, they were unforgettable. There were stars among them: Blanche Wittman, *la reine des hystériques*—the queen of the hysterics. After Charcot blandly walked the audience through his method of diagnosis, prognosis, and treatment, the patient—the living, suffering prop—performed on command. Blanche took to her role with gusto, delivering astonishing trance-induced convulsions, hallucinations, paralyses, numbness. It was always compelling theater: patient and doctor, in an extraordinary dialogue and performance. "Just like plays," as one scholar said, "with lines, soliloquies, stage directions, asides by the hero."

Now the newspapers sought out the hero to hear him expound on the question of murder under hypnosis. *L'Écho de Paris* sent a correspondent to his home at 217, boulevard Saint-Germain in the elegant neighborhood of Faubourg Saint-Germain. The journalist was appropriately awed by Charcot's mansion known as Hôtel de Varengeville, which was "furnished in perfect taste," with "tapestries, stained glass, Japanese crafts." Here was the man whose private consultations were sought after by the wealthy and illustrious from Eurasia to South America. He counted among his patients the novelist Ivan Turgenev, the emperor of Brazil, the queen of Spain, and Grand Duke Nicholas of Russia.

"I know what brings you here," Charcot affably greeted the reporter, "and I have my lesson all ready."

Charcot warned that he could not say anything definitive about Gabrielle's condition because he had not personally examined her. But as a matter of principle he was reluctant to go along with the press and the public's rush "to see everywhere the irresponsible and the mad." He explained that there are degrees of madness, or levels of hysteria, just as there are degrees of responsibility in crimes. It had still to be determined, he pointed out, how ill Gabrielle was. It would then be up to the jurors to decide what sentence to mete out relative to her illness and responsibility in the murder. But, the correspondent asked, could her incessant lying and her mood swings from joy to tears denote an extreme form of hysteria? And if she were a profound hysteric, could hypnotism have influenced her participation in the crime?

Charcot explained that the most susceptible hypnotic subjects were those who exhibited *grand hypnotisme*. For some newspaper readers, this would be their first encounter with the phrase. While popular aspects of hypnotism were well-known, as were some medical applications, the Gouffé case brought highly detailed academic research on hypnotism before the public. The professor was at pains to explain in clear and simple language how a hysteric responded to the commands of a hypnotist. "The mind of the hypnotized plunged into sleep could be considered as absolutely empty and incapable of any personal will," Charcot said. "The operator/manipulator could then imprint on the subject sensations and images of his liking and could direct the will to take a designated action."

If Charcot were to indicate an object—any object—on the floor and tell a hypnotized subject it was a snake, he would get a reac-

tion of terror. Tell the subject it was actually a hummingbird and the
response would be fascination and a desire to caress it. A hypnotized
person could also commit small crimes: steal the money purse of a lab
assistant, for example, after first resisting, even if the subject were an
honest person; or commit the crime several days later at a designated
time if this was suggested during hypnosis.

Behavior could be manipulated, Charcot assured his visitor, but,
he added, one must interpret this phenomenon in the most limited
sense. A major crime committed outside of a controlled experiment
in the hospital was another matter altogether. Charcot could induce
a hypnotized hysteric in his ward to act out killing the professor himself, but he was adamant the subject would not commit an actual
murder. A subject, even under hypnosis, did not lose sight of right and
wrong. "That means," Charcot explained, "that if I ordered one of my
subjects to kill the director of the Salpêtrière because he serves bad
kidney beans at the lunch table, he would hit him with an ordinary
blow on the back with whatever was at hand but it would be done
without real conviction and in spite of himself."

Charcot summoned the words of his colleague Georges Gilles de
la Tourette to assert that so far there had only been crimes committed in the laboratory under experimental conditions. The courtroom
had never witnessed a case claiming a role for hypnosis in a real murder. "Until now," Charcot said, "there has not been a single hypnotic
crime." That's not to say, he continued, that a clever defense attorney
would miss this chance to argue for Gabrielle's lack of responsibility
due to her obedience to commands from an unscrupulous hypnotist.
But it would be a difficult thing to prove. The defense would have to
establish scientifically, Charcot said, that Gabrielle became a submissive accomplice in the premeditation and execution of the crime. It
would have to be shown that Gabrielle was a hypnotic automaton
responding unconsciously to the will of Eyraud. Should the defense
be able to prove such a theory, Charcot acknowledged, the crime
would represent a major step in the science of hypnotism.

He didn't hold out much hope of that, however. He rejected the
influence of hypnosis in the murder of Gouffé. Gabrielle was not
Eyraud's marionette dancing blindly to his whims. Like any other
common criminal, she knew she was on a dangerous path and that

her actions would have dreadful consequences. "This girl seems to me simply a perverse being," Charcot concluded. "She could very much have participated consciously in the crime."

After visiting Charcot, the *Écho de Paris* reporter sought out the thirty-one-year-old psychologist Edgar Bérillon, who was expected to oppose Charcot's conclusion. Bérillon was a founder of the *Revue de l'hypnotisme* and had been an organizer of the International Congress on Hypnotism at the Hôtel Dieu the previous August; he also had been a student of Charcot's but had since fallen in with his opponents, including Hippolyte Bernheim and Jules Liégeois. The two camps, which had clashed so bitterly at the congress, were headed for another confrontation, this time on a public stage—and egged on by the press.

"Wouldn't it be your opinion," the reporter asked Bérillon, "that Gabrielle's role in this lugubrious affair could have been imposed by a will stronger than her own?"

Bérillon smiled, and behind his spectacles his face was lean. "You will greatly embarrass me," he said, "if you put me on notice to make a legal decision in this case."

He acknowledged that murder under hypnosis was a seductive theory, but now that it had taken on such profound application he was hesitant to leap to a conclusion. Hysterics, he pointed out, often bend to a strong will even without the use of hypnosis. Bernheim, for instance, used the force of his will and a stern voice to suggest actions to his patients. There was a fine line in some cases, Bérillon implied, between the effects of pure suggestion and hypnotic control.

Bérillon had studied the accounts of Gabrielle's relationship with Eyraud and raised a fascinating question: Was it possible that his brutality could have affected Gabrielle's behavior as much as the power of hypnotism? The men who interrogated Gabrielle, who examined her medically and psychologically, gave little importance to her lover's tyrannical dominance. Violence against women was commonplace. There was always a vague supposition that any woman who got pummeled might have deserved it. In Gabrielle's case, the thinking went, she was a saucy imp who ought to have been at home under her father's roof in Lille instead of carousing on her own in Paris.

Bérillon's perspective was extraordinary—and a disheartening one for the hypnotism defense and for the state of French society—for he was virtually alone in suggesting that Eyraud's cruelty played a role in Gabrielle's behavior. "As to her participation in the crime, I do not think she was acting under the influence of a hypnotic suggestion," Bérillon told the reporter. "She could have been to a certain degree terrorized by her lover and obeyed him without knowing much about what she was doing."

The Musée Grévin opened in 1882 behind a stone arch façade on bou-levard Montmartre in a direct challenge to Madame Tussaud's, the famous wax museum in London. It took its name from its art direc-tor, Alfred Grévin, a well-known caricaturist and theater costume and set designer. To distinguish itself from its London rival, the Musée Grévin strove for a gay Parisian flair, as Grévin himself described in a letter: "Grévin must be to Tussaud what Paris is to London, what our boulevards are to Regent Street, what the Parisian woman is to the London woman, that-is-to-say, charm, taste, spirit (and if I dare say so) to vastness and bad taste." The museum catered to the popular tastes of the boulevards, its displays re-creating the sensations of the day as if the newspapers had sprung to three-dimensional life. When some fresh atrocity captured the public's attention, an old display was rushed out the back and a new one moved in. International revolts and Paris murders ranked high on the Musée Grévin entertainment scale.

The writer Jules Claretie satirized how the museum pandered to a fickle mass audience. "O glorious transitory wax figures!" he wrote. "Celebrities of the day! Pantheon of the moment!" But what drew crowds was the exhibits' fidelity to real life. If a scene depicted the arrest of Russian nihilists, the samovar and tea glasses in the stag-ing were imported from Russia. And the wax figures were so lifelike, some visitors believed that pinching them would make them jump.

If ever a crime was destined for the Musée Grévin, it was the Gouffé murder. Not only did it have shock value and glamour but there was the eerie coincidence that the victim, Toussaint-Augustin Gouffé, had last been seen alive directly across the street at the Café Véron. In early February, just weeks after Gabrielle returned to Paris, the museum created a rendering of the murder scene at 3, rue Tronson du Coudray, an identical replica of the apartment with the alcove, the chaise longue, the red silk sash, the cognac bottle, and the rope dangling from the pulley in the ceiling—a haunting tableau in dim lighting. Standing in the room where Gouffé was strangled the spectator could imagine his every groan. Crowds who swarmed the display gazed upon the "famous trunk . . . reproduced with complete fidelity," *Le Gil Blas* reported, noting that the scene was skillfully reconstructed from the latest revelations. It was an impressive depiction, the paper said, that gave "the greatest honor to the artist who so rapidly executed it."

Around this same time Judge Dopffer turned his attention to the crime scenes far from Paris: the hotel in Lyon, the riverbanks where the body had landed and where the shattered trunk was found. He wanted to comb the Millery area in person, and he wanted Gabrielle as his tour guide. He needed her to show him exactly where the deeds took place and to describe in detail what she and Eyraud did. She was to be put to the test: Would her tales hold up, or would she prove to be the little liar, the *petite menteuse*?

When Jaume told her she was to travel south, Gabrielle was elated. "I was beginning to go moldy here," she said, and immediately turned her mind to her wardrobe. What to wear? Silk? No, it would be too cold for silk. She was to be on tour like a French celebrity and had to impress the public with her fashionable attire. Jaume bristled at her sense of self-importance but he'd resigned himself to it. She was now part of French culture. "Her fame is immense," he wrote in his diary. "From what has happened so far, Gabrielle will never be forgotten. People compose songs and write columns and put on scientific conferences about her. Artists, photographers, and caricaturists seize on her petulant little face."

On February 7, after several postponements, the trip to the south was set. Two Sûreté agents, Wahlen and Robert, collected Gabrielle in her cell at 5:30 a.m. and found her as excited as a child. She was fussing at the last minute over whether to wear the same beige dress she had lately displayed at the Palais de Justice or another outfit of a darker shade. She chose the latter but was so high-strung the men expected her to change her mind again. "There will be a lot of people at the station to see me leave," she chattered at her guards. She was anxious to win plaudits for her public appearance. "And when we arrive in Lyon I'm quite sure the crowd will be large."

Wahlen and Robert escorted her out of her cell into a frigid, overcast morning and to a waiting carriage. The delays had confused the public about which day she was to depart and, arriving at Gare de Lyon, the trio found the station largely deserted. No one had turned out at that early hour to gawk at her in her black dress and velvet hat and long brown overcoat. No one paid her any attention except a journalist from *Le Petit Journal* who was assigned to stalk her incognito throughout the trip.

While Agent Wahlen went off to get the tickets, Gabrielle stood with Robert and prattled loudly, hoping to turn the heads of the few sleepy-eyed stragglers on the platform. Her liveliness, so out of place in the early morning, attracted the attention of a group of young military officers who encouraged her by ogling, wholly unaware that the object of their clowning was the celebrated little demon.

"Had they only known!" Jaume exclaimed in his diary.

The travelers settled into a first-class compartment aboard the 6:25 a.m. train. Although she was disappointed by the poor turnout, Gabrielle reasoned it was probably best that no journalists were begging for her time. With the rush to board she could not have properly entertained them. "They would have wanted to question me and I would not have been able—to my grand regret—to respond to them," she commented to her guards.

"I pity Wahlen and Robert," mused Jaume, who stayed behind in Paris. "They will not have a minute of rest between Paris and Lyon. If they do not compliment her thirty times on her outfit, she will be in a bad humor and say she won't talk anymore and then suffer ridiculous mental crises."

Goron, to his unending frustration, was still in bed, confined to his house, unable to participate in any way in the expedition. Dopffer traveled on the same train as Gabrielle but in a different compartment.

As the train lumbered out of the station, Gabrielle was in high spirits. The *Petit Journal* reporter, who hid himself in an adjacent compartment, could hear her bantering gaily with her escorts. "She burst out laughing," he wrote, "and seemed absolutely unconscious of the gravity of the situation."

When the train pulled into Gare de Perrache in Lyon at 5:44 p.m.,

Gabrielle was greeted like an arriving conqueror. Her tour had been well-publicized, and a mob packed the station. An army of journalists was on hand, some having waited an hour. A committee of local dignitaries was ready to welcome her: the head of the Lyon Sûreté, the Lyon prosecutor, and other officials, including several police commissioners. Jaume sardonically observed: "Only Napoleon's entrance into Berlin, perhaps, was on par with that of Gabrielle into the Gare de Perrache."

Despite the long journey Gabrielle looked fresh and well-coifed when she stepped onto the platform with a small travel bag in her hand. Seeing the swarm of reporters and spectators, she cried, "So many people! There would not be as many for the Queen of England." She scanned the faces and swelled with delight: "Ah, I've had a success!" As she moved through the station the crowd tagged along. In the jostling and pushing, a few unfortunates were knocked over and trampled. Gabrielle picked up her pace and suddenly her leg buckled beneath her and she nearly fell over as a heel broke off one of her boots.

Before climbing into her hackney she stopped to greet local officials, then she was off for the short ride to Saint Joseph Prison, located just behind the train station. And suddenly reality hit. Sitting in her cell on the prison's second floor she had no one gawking at her, no one chasing after her for a look. She was alone. She didn't feel famous at all. There was an iron bed with a wool blanket, a water jug, an earthenware basin, and a wooden chair. In this stark setting she had time to think about the crime scenes she was to see tomorrow and the interrogation she faced. Her eyes moved along the bare walls and she lost her composure and sobbed. Worst of all, she wept, "There's not even a mirror for me to do my coif."

Chapter 30

Paul Dopffer was close to wrapping up the case. As the investigating judge, he was entrusted to gather the facts about the crime and prepare the dossier, which contained all the testimony not only from the accused but from a battery of witnesses. So in addition to interrogating Gabrielle, he interviewed dozens of people with any information that could shed light on her character and the commission of the crime. Wielding his enormous power, the investigating judge shaped the primary evidence in the case in a way that set the tenor of the trial and guided the performances in the courtroom. Since he worked for the state, his dossier aimed to prove the guilt of the accused, and because of the great respect accorded him, his conclusions were not contested in court. The trial was not a pursuit of the truth but a public exposition of the dossier proving the criminal activities of the defendant.

But Dopffer still needed to fill in some crucial pieces on Gabrielle and Eyraud's movements after the murder. He'd carefully courted the Lyon magistrates to gain their cooperation and impressed upon them the need to treat Gabrielle with special care to ensure her compliance. A happy Gabrielle was, in Dopffer's view, a truthful Gabrielle. His courtesy quieted the bulldogs in Lyon, and in a rare show of amity, Parisian and provincial authorities questioned Gabrielle together on her first morning in Lyon. Dopffer was joined inside the interrogation room at Lyon's Palais de Justice by Judge Vial, who had shaken the truth out of the coachman Étienne Laforge; the special police commissioner Ramonencq, who had encouraged Laforge in his lies; and the prosecutor Georges Chenest, who had lodged the complaint against Goron claiming he'd ridiculed the Lyon justice system.

After the questioning, Gabrielle was escorted by a parade of officials to the Hôtel de Toulouse, where she and Eyraud had stayed with the trunk. There she encountered the hotel carriage driver, a man named Novel, who recognized her. Gabrielle explained that Novel and three hotel boys were needed to haul the trunk to room number 6. Inside the room she pointed to the spot where the trunk had sat against the window. Then the procession was off to the Hôtel d'Orient, where the murderers stayed after disposing of the body and the trunk. The manager, Madame Descombes, recognized Gabrielle right away. "Only," she said, eyeing her red hair, "you were brunette at the time." Gabrielle burst out laughing: "You are not the first person, madame, who has made that observation today."

A caravan of eight carriages then made its way to the location along the riverbank where Gouffé's body had lain. Gabrielle faithfully pointed to the exact spot near a small wall where she stood lookout as Eyraud opened the trunk and turned it upside down, shaking out the sack. She described the way Eyraud heaved the body over the edge: "He threw it like one would throw a heavy package, helping it with his knee." And she pointed to the spot where it landed. Dopffer was pleased that the location she indicated was precisely where the cadaver was discovered. The little liar was telling the truth.

On her way back to her cell that evening Gabrielle joked with the Sûreté agents. Her mood had markedly improved from her first night when she had refused to eat and a nun had to talk her into having two eggs. There was no problem with her appetite on this night: As the newspapers dutifully reported, she polished off a meal of escargots, *saucisson de Saint-Symphorien-sur-Coise, pieds de mouton, veau chasseur, bifteck cresson, macaroni gratiné, dessert varié, café,* and champagne. She also insisted on éclairs and, over the course of her brief stay, was reported to have eaten more than a dozen. To her great delight she was offered after-meal cigarettes, remarking: "Well, you are more gallant here than they are in Paris!"

She spent the night smoking cigarettes and reading a book called *Artists' Wives* by Alphonse Daudet. Each of the twelve stories illustrated how wives harmed the lives of their husband poets, painters, musicians, and sculptors and pointed up the tensions between men and women generally. The artists, Daudet revealed, were distracted from their important work by troublesome domestic concerns. Some of the pieces were light, others serious—but all made the case that artists should never marry.

The next day, climbing into the carriage at the prison for the ride to the Palais de Justice for more questioning, Gabrielle playfully commanded: "Coachman, to the palace!" People filled the streets hoping for a glimpse of her and, as a carriage pulled up to the curb, the crowd closed in. A cry went up: "It's Gabrielle!" But jubilation quickly turned to disappointment when someone other than the celebrated murderess stepped out. Yet some of the spectators skipped away calling out: "It was her! Gabrielle! For real!"

Among her many interrogations, Gabrielle sat for an hour-long session with Alexandre Lacassagne, the esteemed criminologist whose autopsy had saved the case. He wanted to hear her describe the pulley breaking free of the ceiling and the rope falling to the floor; he wanted to hear her say that Gouffé was not hanged but strangled, as the autopsy showed. She reiterated what she'd told Dopffer: that after the pulley gave way, Eyraud threw himself on Gouffé and strangled him bare-handed. Her recounting of events intrigued Lacassagne not so much for its content but for its style. Her manner was offhand; she was untroubled by the depravity of the actions she described. Lacassagne said she sounded like a ten-year-old child describing a play she'd seen in the theater. She showed no sign of shock or deep emotion. What she described did not seem real to her. "I didn't do anything," she told Lacassagne. "I did not touch Gouffé. I did what Eyraud told me to do. If I thought about it too much he would beat me."

Lacassagne believed Gabrielle was conscious of her actions during the murder. But was she a full accomplice? He allowed that her mind was so fragile she could only be held partially responsible for what she did.

For Dopffer, the Lyon trip was a success. He'd gotten Gabrielle to lay out in detail what happened after the killing; he'd studied the locations, heard the witnesses, and was able to stitch all of the evidence together to prove step by step the accuracy of her account. The man who once sneered that she was the *petite menteuse,* the little liar, now was gratified that she had so willingly helped build the case for him. He revised his opinion of her, telling the local press that "he had rarely seen a witness enlighten justice in a fashion so clear and so precise."

A crowd swarmed the train station for Gabrielle's departure. Some admirers tossed her bouquets of flowers, prompting one cranky spectator to say: "We have come to assist in the glorification of a crime." Mostly, however, the throng was fascinated by the petite show-off. As she mounted the steps of the carriage, the mob surged forward and Gabrielle stood in the doorway shaking hands like a *grande artiste*. At last she boarded, and once she was settled inside her compartment, she pulled back the drapes and waved to her fans, who blew her kisses. The antics disgusted Jaume. "Should one laugh?" he asked. "Should one soil oneself? Or should one philosophize on the inexplicable excitements of the provinces? The departure of Gabrielle Bompard surpasses all that the most sour misanthrope could imagine in order to scoff at humanity." The behavior of both the criminal and her admirers was beyond anything Jaume could countenance. "If the train had not gotten under way, the devotees would have undoubtedly asked Gabrielle to give them her blessing," he wrote. "This infatuation with a criminal is the most droll phenomenon I have ever heard of in my whole life."

Inside the train, Gabrielle charmed the battery of officials seeing her off. She handed a bouquet to the head of the gendarmes and announced: "I am enchanted by the Lyonnais people. They have covered me with flowers. I have pockets filled with bouquets!" She asked to shake hands with the police chiefs and agents, and no one refused her. She left a strong impression on the special police commissioner Ramonencq, who in his long career, punctuated by many strange cases, had never encountered a woman as extraordinary as Gabrielle, a woman he described as both perverse and naïve. "There is an unconsciousness so profound, an unawareness of remorse so absolute," he said, "that one is left stupefied."

Before departing, Gabrielle held a mini press conference aboard the train. She spoke candidly, providing a rare glimpse into her motivations in public. "I did everything to be gracious and to present myself well," she told *Le Lyon Républicain*. "But in my cell at night I cried very often. I thought I would falter during the confrontations in the judge's office. If a tear had gushed from my eye, that would have been the end, my courage would have abandoned me."

The papers printed her claims that she was little more than an unconscious instrument of Eyraud: "I never loved him. But he dominated me completely." And: "I am unconscious." And: "I didn't do anything. I was forced to do ill. I am more a victim than I am guilty."

Jaume exploded at such statements—she was plainly duplicitous. "Very skillful," Jaume said. She cried that Eyraud robbed her of her free will, that she had no will left, that she was the irresponsible instrument of crime. But since her arrest, Jaume pointed out, she had miraculously "rediscovered her free will, her personality, her joie de vivre."

The crowds, the flowers, the blown kisses—the case had become a vulgar spectacle. The Lyon press blamed Dopffer and the Sûreté for indulging Gabrielle just to obtain her confessions. Their lenience, complained *Le Lyon Républicain,* unleashed the public's infatuation with "this sad heroine. Enough is enough. It is time this stopped."

Far more pressing, the newspapers agreed, was the question: Where was Eyraud?

Chapter 31

Sûreté chief Marie-François Goron lay in a darkened room at home, frustrated and restless, recovering too slowly from his nasty bout with the flu and subsequent eye affliction. However powerful his resolve to direct the hunt for Michel Eyraud, his debility proved stronger. "I was gravely ill," he recalled in his memoir.

The search for Eyraud centered on New York. He had posted his letters from there, and reports had come from guests at hotels and boardinghouses who had encounters with a man fitting Eyraud's description, and from New York City police who were doing their part to reel him in on behalf of the Paris Sûreté.

But where Eyraud was hiding now was anyone's guess. American detectives had found traces of him in both New York and Montreal. But those trails led nowhere. Was he still in New York? Was he hiding in Canada? The anonymity of big cities could help protect him. Had he gone south to Mexico or farther, into Colombia or Argentina? His potential playground was vast. He spoke the languages of Europe and the Americas, and changed identities with the ease of a stage actor. There was another possibility: In his letter to Goron in January he had vowed to rush back to Paris to defend himself if Gabrielle ever showed up and accused him of the crime. Had he read Gabrielle's testimony in the newspapers? Was he headed back to Paris? Taking no chances, French police put the nation's ports on alert.

The press aided the dragnet: Eyraud's photo was everywhere; police and the public across the world knew his face; his celebrity would make it impossible to hide. "The truth is, Eyraud is very actively sought: be it in London or in America," *Le Gil Blas* wrote. "It's possible that in the coming days Gouffé's assassin will be behind bars."

The prefect of police, Henri-Auguste Loze, acting in Goron's stead, dispatched two Sûreté agents to New York. Léon Soudais and Emil Houlier—the former balding, the latter with a walrus mustache—set sail on February 2 aboard *City of Paris,* the roomiest, most luxurious steamer on the seas. The vessel stretched 560 feet and accommodated 1,371 passengers on its four decks. The main saloon had a vaulting ceiling and stained glass, and was illuminated by incandescent lights. In the smoking room 200 passengers lounged in red leather chairs.

On February 12, as the agents docked at New York, news came from London that Eyraud's arrest was imminent in a local pub. Parisians braced for a big break. But the following day, *Le Figaro* cooled expectations: "Yesterday, rumors circulated of the arrest of Michel Eyraud in London. This information is wrong. One is still without news of Gouffé's murderer."

Meanwhile, Soudais and Houlier had checked into the Hotel Martin on University Place, signing the registry under the pseudonyms Léon Jolivet and John Johnson to avoid tipping off the press and alerting Eyraud. At the French consulate they introduced themselves to the consul general, Viscount Paul d'Abzac, who put his resources at their disposal. Next they climbed into a cab and went to police headquarters, where Chief Thomas Byrnes briefed them for an hour on his detectives' work on the case. Among his efforts, the chief had stationed detectives incognito at the main post office and several branches where Eyraud was known to check for mail, and the clerks were told to give a signal if the suspect appeared. Byrnes handed Soudais and Houlier a large dossier and promised any assistance they needed during their stay.

The next day, the Sûreté detectives were alarmed when they opened *The New York Times* to discover that their cover had been blown. A reporter who had tailed them from place to place snidely commented that anyone could have picked out the French sleuths: "They advertised their errand by their garb, appearance, language and luggage." Although the reporter misidentified them as Inspector Jaume and an assistant, he still had the substance right: These were French detectives on the hunt for Eyraud. The writer apparently had sneaked a look at the Hotel Martin registry and then scoffed at the agents' phony names. How could a Frenchman try to disguise himself as Johnson? It was as absurd for a French detective to hide behind an Anglicized name, the reporter wrote, as it was for an ostrich to hide its body by poking its head into the sand. Now a game of cat and mouse ensued, with journalists chasing Soudais and Houlier as the men attempted to shake off their pursuit. By February 17, they assured Loze in a dispatch to Paris that they had tricked the newspapermen into believing they had left town, when in fact they were still lodged at the Hotel Martin: "The journalists here no longer occupy themselves with us."

The French detectives checked hotel rooms and whorehouses that Eyraud was believed to have frequented. Their search was complicated by the many names the fugitive used: Bertheir, Labordère, Vanaerd, Deporte, Avrarad, Moulié. A man fitting Eyraud's description was remembered at various locations under these names. "We do not yet have any indication of the hiding place of the individual we seek," the French detectives wrote to Loze. But they said the search of his lodgings raised the hope that the rooms "could be precious help in providing us with a trail to follow."

The agents were now fairly confident Eyraud had arrived in New York from San Francisco in the last week of December, expecting to meet up with Gabrielle and do in Garanger. But the couple had evaded him, leaving Halifax, Nova Scotia, on December 28 for Liverpool. By January 2, 1890, Eyraud had taken up residence at a boardinghouse at 28 Waverly Place posing as Miguel Garico, a wealthy planter from Mexico. The lodging was owned by a married woman named Susan Martin who soon became the lover of this exotic traveler.

Living upstairs was Florence Stout, a twenty-one-year-old actress, and her playwright husband, George Stout. One morning, the couple was going out when Garico called them into his room. Ever since he'd arrived, the Mexican, as he was known around the boardinghouse, seemed a troubled man: unshaven, restless, and overcome by some deep grief. He was often groaning and crying. He didn't eat with the other boarders and didn't seem to sleep. "At night he was heard pacing to and fro until the people in the surrounding rooms were nearly driven to distraction," George said. Sometime later, when Florence had discovered who he was, she said, "Except for his eyes, he was not an evil-looking man." That morning, he sat the couple down in his room and told them his story. He said he was traveling from Mexico to Paris with his wife and a neighbor's son. In Philadelphia, his wife and the young man deserted him, making off with a satchel containing $12,500. He was certain they had eloped together to Paris. "My god!" the Mexican sobbed. "After twenty years!" Stout panicked when Garico pulled a revolver out of his pocket, shrieking: "I will kill myself, but first I will kill that false woman!" Stout persuaded the Mexican to put the gun away but the man was still raving that he had to go back to Mexico—an impossible journey because he was now penniless. "I have plenty of money in Mexico," he told the couple.

"Why don't you telegraph for money?" Stout asked.

The Mexican said his home was a four-day ride from the nearest telegraph station.

It was quicker just to go to Mexico and bring the money back himself. Right now he was so broke he had only twenty dollars in his pocket.

Stout offered to take him to Chief Byrnes, who could telegraph to Paris and have his wife and neighbor arrested. In this way, perhaps he could recover his money. Visiting Byrnes was the last thing Eyraud wanted. He told Stout the money didn't trouble him as much as the disgrace. The Mexican's tale moved Stout so much that he, too, began to cry. He asked how much Garico needed to get home. The distraught man gestured to the clothing scattered on his bed and all around the room, petite dresses of Gabrielle's that he had hauled with him from San Francisco; Eyraud had been trying to sell them to anyone in the boardinghouse. "Here are dresses that cost hundreds of dollars," he told Stout. He offered to let Stout take the clothing as collateral for a seventy-dollar loan. The Mexican signed a receipt with a bold flourish, promising to return in a month and pay the lender back twofold.

As a playwright Stout appreciated a good performance, and when he learned later who the Mexican was, he declared: "I never saw such a well worked-up scene in all my theatrical career. The detail was perfect and the stage business was worthy of a Booth." He applauded Eyraud's skill in eliciting emotion. "I look back upon the fellow's acting with a feeling that closely approaches awe."

Having acquired the murderess's clothing, including a dainty hat and a small handbag, and the couple's trunk, Stout had an inspiration. When a reporter visited him a few months later, his little daughter skipped around the room with the hat atop her curly hair and the small handbag swinging at her side. "I shall make the story of Eyraud's crime into a drama," the playwright said, proposing a theatrical tribute that never made it to the stage. "I shall play the strangler, and my wife will act Gabrielle Bompard in Gabrielle's own dresses."

Chapter 32

Eyraud had disappeared from the boardinghouse on Waverly Place on January 12 after a ten-day stay, making off with a hat from one of the tenants. His next stop was a lodging at 54 Washington Place, a few blocks away in Greenwich Village, where the landlady took him in even though he refused to give his name. Just as he did on Waverly Place, Eyraud paced in his room throughout the night, sometimes erupting into sobs. Gesturing wildly, he raged over a man who had stolen his mistress and taken her to France. Day after day Eyraud made excuses for his failure to pay his rent, until finally the landlady lost her patience and threatened to call the police, causing the strange tenant to vanish.

At his next lodging, the Hotel America on Irving Place, Eyraud cast himself as a jovial Mexican merchant on a business trip. He delighted guests with his bonhomie, acting out wonderful tales, smoking the finest cigars, drinking an entire bottle of wine at dinner, and borrowing money freely from his new fans. Around this time he responded to a newspaper ad placed by a French piano teacher, telling her he wanted to arrange lessons for his daughter. Two days later he returned to say that his daughter had gone to Chicago but in the meantime he was interested himself in learning to play. Soon the teacher had become his lover. For Eyraud, women not only satisfied his lust but also gave him cover. "This man finds himself in areas where there are women and he loses himself there," wrote *L'Écho de Paris*. He was charming and skillful at seduction. After his capture, it was said, he "had in his life an incalculable number of mistresses. He gloried in seducing many married women and even some virgins."

He charmed the lodgers at the Hoffman House Hotel at Broadway and Twenty-Second Street, known for its glamorous bar and posh clientele. Although he resided at the Hotel America, Eyraud was often found in the common rooms of the Hoffman, acting as though he was a resident. While hobnobbing there he learned that the Hoffman was Georges Garanger's place of residence whenever he visited New York. Soon he had smooth-talked his way into Garanger's room, number 46, where he discovered two black trunks, one with a nameplate that read G. GARANGER. Eyraud talked the staff into allowing him to move the trunks out of the Hoffman to his room at the Hotel America, where Soudais and Houlier found them; inside the trunks were a note signed by Gabrielle, three pairs of shoes, two shirts monogrammed with the letters G.G., and a baggage claim receipt for a San Francisco train journey under the name Vanaerd. Somehow, possibly by impersonating Garanger, Eyraud conned the Hoffman staff into handing over his mail, which contained checks that Eyraud cashed.

Pretending to live at the Hoffman House gave Eyraud entrée to the elite. He met two wealthy Frenchmen, Monsieur Potier and Monsieur Laffeit, who owned businesses in Honduras. "With a top-flight address," a newspaper explained, "he pussyfooted in the society of these gentlemen." One evening, when Eyraud joined his new friends for dinner, he was introduced to a Turkish gentleman named Dr. Pardo who had just arrived from Constantinople. Eyraud posed as a wealthy businessman, rather free with his money, who was considering a business proposition in New Orleans. He told his dinner companions he was recently in San Francisco and was on his way to Europe. When Dr. Pardo described a beautiful Oriental robe he'd just acquired, Eyraud expressed interest in it after learning it was worth about five hundred francs.

"I will buy it from you," Eyraud told his new friend.

When Dr. Pardo agreed to the sale, Eyraud told him the robe was so gorgeous he wished he could photograph it. Would Dr. Pardo be so kind as to allow Eyraud to borrow it briefly to take a few photographs? Dr. Pardo, fully flimflammed, had no hesitation. And off Eyraud went with the robe, promising to return shortly with the cash. Dr. Pardo never saw the wealthy businessman, or his robe, again.

Around February 8, four days before Soudais and Houlier landed in New York, Eyraud vanished from the Hotel America. He had been seen reading a foreign newspaper; then he suddenly dropped it on the table and rushed to his room. He scooted out of the hotel, leaving behind his own trunk and Garanger's, along with an unpaid bill of $45. The last sighting of Eyraud in New York was at a whorehouse at 120 West Thirty-First Street where he had a liaison with a petite woman named Marcelle. She told detectives that the man talked movingly about his tiny mistress who was stolen from him.

"We have determined," Soudais and Houlier informed Prefect Loze on February 20, "that we are not going to see him anymore in this area and that very probably he fled from New York."

The agents followed a few leads pointing in several directions but the hope of finding Eyraud in the vast territory of North America was fast dwindling. In Montreal, they learned, Eyraud passed himself off as a silk merchant, met the editor of the newspaper *Le Monde de Montréal,* and presented him with a business card that read: "E. B. Vanaerd, Paris, Brussels." Eyraud was eager to learn about business opportunities in the city and, more important, what the editor was hearing in the news from France. Soudais and Houlier shivered through the bitter Montreal weather, telling Prefect Loze in a March 4 dispatch: "There is no less than two feet of ice on the streets. We have been obliged to do our research in sleds." And then they happily set off for the warmer climate of California.

In San Francisco, they retraced the journey that Eyraud, Garanger, and Gabrielle had made into the wine country. But the trail in America had gone cold, so the detectives began making plans to return to Paris. While their sweep of North America had deepened the portrait of Eyraud, the French press painted the agents as bumbling fools. Eyraud, by contrast, came across as a savvy renegade always one step ahead of the law. The papers romanticized him, portraying the murderer as a folk hero. Here was a ruthless fugitive who easily outwitted the Sûreté. He was a seducer, a ladies' man, a raconteur with too many paramours to count. One newspaper declared: "Decidedly, Eyraud has turned into a legend."

Smarting from the ridicule, Soudais and Houlier slunk back across America and sailed for France on March 22 aboard the five-hundred-foot steamer *La Champagne.* Inspector Jaume was sympathetic to the travails of the agents, knowing that the odds in the hunt favored Eyraud: The criminal watched the newspapers for the detectives' movements and benefited from knowing the New York terrain far better than his French pursuers. Jaume was confident that the agents' work would help pave the way for Eyraud's eventual capture. "They learned many things about Eyraud but they did not see him," he wrote in his diary. "There is nothing surprising about that: the game has the advantage over the hunters."

Goron was less charitable. When Jaume briefed him on the failed mission, the Sûreté chief was annoyed that "Houlier and Soudais had toured a bit more than half of the world and yet returned empty-handed." But he saw one positive result: The hunt for Eyraud was now a cause for many people across the globe—and for some, an obsession. Goron was confident that all the publicity, particularly the photos of Eyraud in foreign newspapers, would prompt someone to step forward: "People were as passionate about the Gouffé case in New York, Canada, and Mexico as they were on rue Montmartre or boulevard des Italiens." But the Sûreté couldn't shake off the fiasco. When a French-language newspaper in the United States reported that Eyraud was probably still in New York in early March, a month later than the detectives had determined, *Le Gil Blas* asked: "If these facts are true, why did inspectors Houlier and Soudais return in fail-ure? These fine bloodhounds must have given American detectives a feeble opinion of the French police."

If Eyraud were to turn up, many surmised it was to be on his own terms—killed by his own hand. Suicide seemed the only way the chase would end. Reports of his self-inflicted death poured in. In early April, a body with a bullet hole in the head was discovered on the banks of the Meuse in Maastricht, Holland. A wallet found in a pocket was stuffed with French newspaper clippings about the Gouffé case. In a coat pocket was a handkerchief embroidered with Eyraud's initials: M.E. The dead man's hat bore the same initials. Here apparently was the end of the case. News reports said the body had a striking resemblance to Eyraud. And the French press took the opportunity to slap the Sûreté yet again: "Once more has luck put police on the trail that their finest bloodhounds were unable to dis-cover." Yet the excitement was unwarranted—the case did not end in Maastricht. The corpse, it turned out, belonged to someone other than Eyraud.

Later in the month a crowd formed outside the New York City morgue when rumors spread that a suicide fitting Eyraud's descrip-tion had been carted inside. But it too proved to be unrelated.

Suicide mania had taken hold. In the western Paris suburb of Suresnes a sailor came upon a bottle on the banks of the Seine that contained a purported final note from Eyraud. But again, hopes were dashed. Finally, on April 28, *Le Figaro* tried to halt the craze. It declared that it would now doubt any report until it was proved true: "Several times already Eyraud's suicide has been announced and yet suicide is so little in the nature of Gouffé's murderer."

The publicity had some grisly consequences. In Copenhagen, a soap maker named Philipsen was arrested for the murder of a bank clerk by the name of Meyer who, like Gouffé, disappeared without a trace. Philipsen confessed to police that he had robbed and strangled Meyer and then stuffed the body in a crate that he shipped to America. The box sat in the New York port for two months. Who else but the Paris strangler could have inspired such a crime? Eyraud, commented one paper, was the school principal to students of murder seeking a method for disposing of a body: "The simple expedient is to ship it quickly to a faraway address."

For Gabrielle, Eyraud suddenly loomed large again. His picture in the papers revived the reality of the man—and terrified her. If he were found dead, then she could rest. But his possible capture was a source of intense anxiety. Even if he were brought back to Paris in chains, she still would not feel safe. She lived in terror of his finding a way to kill her. Even from a distance Eyraud haunted her. "This man exerts such an influence on her," *Le Figaro* explained, "that she seems to think she is in his presence even when she is protected by police."

Chapter 33

No one wanted Gabrielle to stand trial alone. But there was no choice: Eyraud had vanished, and the public was impatient for a resolution. Although Eyraud undoubtedly had a hand in the crime, if not the dominant role, the authorities began making plans to bring Gabrielle into court as the sole defendant in the murder of Toussaint-Augustin Gouffé.

Judge Dopffer appointed a trio of doctors to assess her mental health. Leading the examination was Paul Brouardel, who was the top figure in the legal-medical world in France. If there was a celebrated crime, Brouardel was the expert called in; he was a preeminent voice in forensic science and the head of medical investigations at the Paris morgue, where he oversaw the newly created toxicology lab. He also occupied the chair of legal medicine at the University of Paris. For the examination of Gabrielle, he was joined by two leading French psychiatrists, Auguste Motet and Gilbert Ballet.

Mentally unstable criminals did not have a friend in Paul Brouardel. In an earlier case of a man who raped and dismembered a four-year-old boy, Brouardel, Motet, and another expert overlooked his obvious mental illness. As a historian wrote of the case, "for these men he was nothing more than a degenerate. They were unwilling to see him consigned to an asylum and seemed little troubled by the probability of his execution."

Steeped in such bias, the three doctors began their assessment of Gabrielle. They met with her several times a week, questioned her, hypnotized her, physically examined her, studied her testimony and her letters to Eyraud and to her lover in Lille, interviewed her family and acquaintances and the nuns at the convents where she had boarded in her youth.

Was Gabrielle mentally impaired and therefore not responsible for her actions at the time of the murder? To answer this question, the doctors searched for insanity in her family, discovering a paternal uncle given to bizarre behavior and a maternal uncle who, it was said, died crazy. As a baby Gabrielle had had convulsions. By age eight, she was in puberty; early menstruation, according to Italian criminologist Cesare Lombroso, suggested degeneration and a tendency toward prostitution. And until age eighteen, Gabrielle was very fat. The doctors looked into her troubles at home, the tensions with her unsympathetic governess, Nathalie, who was her father's mistress, and made note of Gabrielle's unruly behavior, her loose tongue, her interest in men and fashionable clothing. The family physician, Dr. Sacreste, informed them that he had been asked by Gabrielle's father, who claimed his daughter was deranged, to alter her behavior by hypnotism, an effort that failed.

Brouardel's committee weighed Eyraud's influence on Gabrielle's behavior. She asserted that she followed him blindly, not because of affection but from sheer terror. She recounted one time when she tried to leave him but he found her on the boulevard after two days. "He hit me," she said, "and I had to return with him." Another time, she said, he found her and beat her so badly she was sick for fifteen days. "I followed him like a dog follows his master," she explained. "I would have let him kill me. When I think about it now I tremble."

But the doctors did not believe she was quite as browbeaten as she suggested. She was, they said, given to exaggeration. They questioned her sincerity, particularly in how she depicted her own role in the planning and execution of the crime. Gabrielle told them she had no idea of the intended use of the sack she stitched. The trunk? She thought they bought it for clothing. The sash for her dressing gown? She said Eyraud demonstrated the slipknot he'd made in it and told her she had to put the sash over Gouffé's head; Eyraud had said he only wanted to convince Gouffé to sign some bank notes—that was all. Not kill him. But with Eyraud hiding right behind the curtain, she was so terrified she could scarcely speak to Gouffé as he sat on the chaise longue.

The doctors made much of the fact that during their interviews Gabrielle demonstrated an utter indifference to the murder itself. When relating details she did so without the slightest sign that she was personally engaged in what had occurred. She showed no remorse. She was merely a witness imparting information about a crime. She gave no indication that she was a direct participant or even an accomplice. The doctors had a ready explanation for Gabrielle's apathy, and it had nothing to do with mental impairment. Quite the contrary: The young woman had a robust intelligence, but also a flawed character. In the eyes of the doctors, she was a born criminal of the lowest type: she had failed to develop a moral sense. She was egotistical and vain and demanded to take center stage. She was capable of doing ill with complete indifference. She personified an Italian proverb: "Woman is rarely wicked, but when she is, she is worse than a man."

Her physical exam revealed another feature of the born criminal: a large lower jaw. But she also had neutral characteristics, such as a symmetrical face; large, almond-shaped eyes; irises of gray-blue; white, well-spaced teeth; and small ears. The doctors described her hip and breast development as rudimentary and said, in a reference to her disguise when she and Eyraud fled France: "One can easily understand how Gabrielle Bompard could have been taken as a young man of fifteen." Her facial expression was intelligent, the doctors observed, adding, "the bright look takes at times a hard fixity."

To assess her susceptibility to hypnosis, the doctors tested her under Charcot's guidelines for symptoms of hysteria. Hysterics, according to Charcot, suffered from a form of hyperesthesia, abnormal skin sensitivity on the neck, under the breasts, on the abdomen above the ovaries, inside the thighs, and on the arms. Using these tests, the doctors were able to affirm that Gabrielle was a hysteric. They further discovered that, like a typical hysteric, she was easily hypnotized. Even though she had not been in a trance for several months, she went quickly into a hypnotized state and like one of Charcot's star performers experienced a profound hysterical attack in the investigators' presence. Her arms and legs went stiff. She succumbed to hallucinations and tried to bat away tormenting visions that rushed in on her. Even these thick-skinned doctors, who had seen so much, acknowledged that her horrors were terrifying. After she calmed down—and was still in a trance—the doctors ordered her to perform specific actions when she awakened, testing her ability to carry out posthypnotic suggestions. They didn't reveal what those actions were but, they noted, "these acts were exactly realized at the moment desired."

Gabrielle indeed proved herself an extraordinary hypnotic subject. She was pliable and responsive, and she acted without any conscious thought. In a trance she lost her free will. In the hands of other investigators, these conclusions might have entered the dossier as support for the argument Gabrielle intended to put forward in court: that Eyraud was the author of the crime and she was his unconscious automaton. But, as adherents to the Charcot school, the doctors were quick to head off any claim that hypnotism played a role in the crime. Brouardel had written a preface to a book on hypnosis and the law by the Charcot disciple Georges Gilles de la Tourette, in which he said that hypnotic suggestion could induce action—but only within limits. "If a hypnotized person is given agreeable or indifferent suggestions, he submits himself to them," Brouardel wrote. "But if the suggestions challenge his personal beliefs or natural instincts he opposes them with an almost invincible resistance." Such was the power of one's moral convictions: Hypnosis could not turn a moral person into an immoral killer.

Even in the case of an amoral person such as Gabrielle, hypnotism could not induce criminal activity, Brouardel asserted. Gabrielle's behavior resulted from her own personal failings and was separate from any hypnotic suggestion. "It did not enter, it could not enter, an instant in our minds that hypnotism and hypnotic suggestion could have intervened as a determining factor in the reproachable acts of Gabrielle Bompard," the doctors asserted. Although Gabrielle presented symptoms of hysteria and was easily hypnotized, the doctors sided firmly with the Charcot camp and delivered a warning to those who would defend her at trial. Offering a preview of the testimony Charcot's experts would give in support of the prosecution, the doctors said: "We repeat it, neither hypnotism, nor suggestion, is linked to the accomplishment of criminal acts."

How, then, was the court to view Gabrielle? The doctors conceded she was a complex, incomplete woman, lacking a moral compass. She was a hysteric but she was not crazy and should not—on account of her mental condition—be excused from appearing in court. There was nothing in the doctors' view that should prevent her being brought to trial and held fully accountable for her actions. "Gabri-elle Bompard is not a sick person," the doctors concluded. While she was impaired morally, she was intelligent enough to know right from wrong. "She should not then be considered as irresponsible of the acts that are attributed to her."

Chapter 34

At long last, chief Goron marched back into the Sûreté offices at 36, quai des Orfèvres in mid-March. He'd gotten back on his feet in late February, then took a couple of weeks in the south of France to regain his strength. Now he was welcomed with a round of press accolades. *Le Figaro* reminded its readers just how much his leadership had been missed. He'd shown foresight, daring, and consummate skill in his direction of the case: "He knew by a series of inductions and deductions that were sharply contested how to reconstruct the entire crime in such a way that is proven correct today by the confessions." Now this audacious bulldog was needed more than ever in the search for the phantomlike Michel Eyraud.

Tips poured in to the Sûreté but Eyraud's scent had vanished. On a hunch Goron dispatched a couple of detectives to Mexico, where they wandered aimlessly. On April 26, *Le Gil Blas* declared that the fugitive was "unfindable."

But Goron's hunch was not so far off base. While Soudais and Houlier had been ambling around New York, Eyraud had been tracking their movements as much as they were tracking his. He was avidly reading the newspapers, keeping tabs on the agents, and cagily staying ahead of them. Finally he realized New York was too hot for a hunted man. In February he fled to Mexico and, unable to stay put, he made his way first to Havana.

He arrived at the height of carnival, and the streets were filled with music and dance. Bonfires roared, street performers entertained the crowds. Everyone gorged on empanadas and omelet fritters and roast pork and boiled plantains, and the rum and aguardiente flowed. Mysterious-looking men and women roamed the city in masks and costumes.

How easy it was to vanish here! Eyraud donned a disguise of his own. He was now a Polish silk merchant named Michel Gosski, and he had some fine pieces to sell—silks, fabrics, lace—articles he'd stolen in New York. He visited a dressmaking team, Michel Pucheu and his wife, Marie, and impressed them with his knowledge of the craft. He discoursed on the value of lace, both antique and modern. Madame Pucheu and her assistant, Albertine Biemler, were charmed by the newcomer. The Pucheus bought several items and begged the salesman to show them another piece he had praised at length. This one was an exquisite Oriental robe, unlike anything they would have ever seen, a masterpiece of fine Turkish handicraft. Unfortunately, Gosski told them, he didn't have the robe with him, having left it with his other samples in Mexico. He'd forgotten it was carnival, and this extraordinary gown was perfect for the festival; any woman draped in it would attract many eyes.

Shortly after Gosski left, news reached Cuba that the Sûreté was searching for Eyraud in New York. The Pucheus read that the killer was believed to have fled to Mexico with some beautiful fabrics and silks he'd stolen. Their eyebrows rose when they saw that the fugitive had made off with a gorgeous Turkish robe exactly like the one their visitor had mentioned. They compared the newspaper's description of Eyraud to the garrulous merchant they had entertained and realized that both men had large, powerful hands.

The Pucheus closely read the newspapers for developments in the Gouffé case, and soon they knew all the details of the Paris killing. Now they were curious about Gosski and slightly alarmed, but they didn't see him for three months. Then, in the middle of May, he showed up and tried to talk Michel Pucheu into joining a partnership in a tobacco business in Mexico, an invitation Pucheu politely declined. Gosski then tried to write some fabric orders and take payment, saying he now represented a British company. But when the Pucheus asked to see his samples, he said he didn't carry any; it wasn't necessary because the British company was so well known around the world. Sprinkled in with his sales pitch were fascinating tales of his journeys in Mexico over the past several months.

When Gosski was asked about the beautiful Turkish robe—did he still have it?—he apologized, saying that he had sold it. But he promised to return the following day, this time with more details about the tobacco partnership so the Pucheus could better understand its value.

Still uncertain whether Gosski was Eyraud, the Pucheus decided on a subtle strategy to find out. When he came back, Albertine asked him if on his adventures through Mexico he had encountered the elusive Eyraud. Michel and Marie Pucheu watched his reaction closely. At first, Gosski betrayed nothing. Oh, he knew about the case, he said, and went on at length about the Sûreté agents' travels across America, even praising how skillfully Eyraud seemed to evade them. Then his face lost its color and he seemed dazed for several moments, before he recovered and resumed the conversation. But now he was preoccupied, as though something was racing through his mind. Marie and Albertine told Gosski they wanted to see a picture of this man Eyraud. "All the newspapers have published it!" Gosski exclaimed. But the women insisted they hadn't seen it.

Gosski stayed away for the next few days. In the meantime a horrific tragedy struck Havana. At 11:00 p.m. on Saturday, May 17, 1890, a fire erupted in a hardware store called Ysasi's, sending volunteer firefighters racing to the scene. A crowd gathered to watch the brave souls—all from leading families of Havana—fight the inferno that lit up the night sky. Four fire chiefs directed the battle: the Venezuelan consul, Francesco Silva, looked on from the street. Inside the shop, the flames gradually crept toward a barrel of gunpowder and, without warning, a gigantic explosion rocked the neighborhood and incinerated the building. Flames leaped to nearby houses and the fire burned out of control. The four fire chiefs and the Venezuelan consul were killed, along with twenty-nine others. More than a hundred people were injured. Some locals were never accounted for. The governor-general and other top officials raced to the scene and their fancy carriages were used to cart away the injured. The next day charred limbs were still being carried out of the ruins. Shocked Cubans feared that hell had swept across the earth. Every year afterward, the catastrophe was marked with a solemn remembrance full of music and flowers. Houses were draped in mourning, flags were displayed, and the largest parade of the year would move through the city to the cemetery.

Two days after the disaster, Michel and Marie Pucheu and Albertine Biemler joined nearly the entire Havana population for a funeral service honoring the thirty-three known dead. The dressmakers were in a miles-long procession when suddenly Gosski approached with a newspaper in his hands. Ignoring the tragedy—and obsessed by only one point—Gosski held out the paper, saying, "Look, the portrait of Eyraud." He explained that he had found the paper lying on a table at a Havana spot called Café du Louvre. It was a poor likeness that bore no resemblance to the man who stood in front of them. "Doesn't he have the look of a scoundrel!" Gosski said. The paper was dated February, and even though it was three months old, it was in near-perfect condition, raising the Pucheus' suspicions. How could the newspaper have been in such fine shape if it had been lying on a café table since February and passing through the hands of hundreds of patrons? Could Gosski have hoarded it himself, saving it in his private belongings? Did he have a special interest in the Gouffé case that drove him to collect newspaper clippings about it?

Gosski's behavior was certainly peculiar, but the Pucheus still weren't convinced that he was the fugitive murderer. This Polish silk merchant was alarming enough, however, that they brought their concerns to François de Ripert-Monclar, the French consul general.

Chapter 35

Immediately the consul general flew into action, first by alerting the Havana police. Then he started searching consular records for a Frenchman living in Havana who might be able to identify Michel Eyraud if he were hauled in, and by a miraculous coincidence just such a man existed: Ernest Gautier had worked for six months at the Joltrois and Eyraud winery in Sèvres, unwittingly assisting Eyraud and his friend Rémy-François Launé in their scam. Gautier would certainly recognize his former boss.

But how to find Gautier? The consul general remembered that a former consulate employee named Hagerman was friendly with Gautier and likely knew his habits. So Hagerman was put on the prowl and caught up with Gautier as he was going into the Café du Louvre. Hagerman informed the former winery worker that the consul wanted to see him immediately. Rushing off to the consulate, Gautier was alarmed to learn that Eyraud was possibly in Havana. He had read about the Gouffé murder and, having already lived through the disaster of the distillery, preferred never to see Eyraud again. But he promised the consul that he would keep his eyes open.

It turned out that Gautier didn't have to look far. At around ten that very same evening, he got the surprise of his life when he suddenly found himself face-to-face with the murderer in a Havana park. Eyraud identified himself not as Gosski or Garico or Vanaerd or Moulié but by his real name. Wary, Gautier pretended not to know him. But Eyraud persisted, rattling off details about the Joltrois and Eyraud winery and Gautier's work there. When Gautier finally acknowledged his former boss, Eyraud leaned on their past relationship to beg him for help. Eyraud needed money—and he needed to flee. Frantic, he hurled questions at Gautier: How could he get loans in Cuba? Would he have to establish a fake name to do so? And would he need to visit the consulate to prove his identity? And would he need a witness to go with him? Gautier didn't like the direction of the conversation. And Eyraud refused to let him go.

"Gautier, I saw you earlier at the Café du Louvre," Eyraud said. "I heard a man with a black beard tell you the consul wanted to see you right away." Gautier realized that Eyraud had seen Hagerman, the consul's messenger. "I've been following you," Eyraud said. He had trailed Gautier to the consulate and waited outside, then followed him to the park.

Feeling trapped, Gautier tried to reason with Eyraud, but the murderer was desperate. Gautier agreed to go somewhere to talk— someplace public, Gautier thought, a crowded place, the Café du Louvre.

"I don't have any illusions," the fugitive told Gautier at the café. "I am a marked man." He needed to get out of the country, but he had only thirteen francs. He begged Gautier to give him some money. Gautier, protected by the crowd in the café, felt safe putting him off, saying he had very little cash with him. Tomorrow, he promised, he would bring Eyraud enough money to send him on his way. Wild-eyed, Eyraud asked what Gautier would do if he found himself in a similar position. And then he cried: Help me!

As they left Café du Louvre, around midnight, Eyraud took Gautier's arm and tried to steer him toward the quiet side streets. Gautier stood his ground. Alarmed yet trying to keep his composure, he explained that Havana wasn't a safe place and they had better keep close to the crowds. But the powerful Eyraud was dragging him, and Gautier realized the man was beyond reason. Gautier had only one thought: to get away. But he had to be crafty—who knew what Eyraud might do? As a free hackney rolled by, Gautier seized the moment. He bolted from Eyraud in one sudden move and climbed into the carriage, leaving the murderer abandoned on the street. But Gautier was so terrified he didn't go to the police and didn't seek out the consul. Eyraud had so unnerved him that Gautier could not think straight: He just went home and trembled. The next day he was still too frightened to go to the consulate, fearing that Eyraud would be lying in wait for him. Finally he went instead to see the president of the French Chamber of Commerce, a man named Dussaq, who alerted the Cuban civil governor, Rodríguez Batista, who also served as the prefect of police.

Dussaq informed the French consul of Gautier's encounter with Eyraud. So now it was a fact: The murderer was in Havana. But the consul could not arrest a French citizen on Cuban territory without a warrant from France, or a telegram indicating that a warrant existed. It would take at least a day to secure the necessary paperwork and by then Eyraud might have fled. Understanding the urgency, Batista dispensed with formalities and ordered Eyraud's arrest on his own authority. Havana's second chief of police, Antonio Pérez-López, was put in charge of hunting down the fugitive and bringing him in. Pérez-López and his men swarmed the Hotel Roma where, Gautier had gleaned, Eyraud was staying. The hotel register showed no one by the name of Eyraud, but Pérez-López discovered that a Michel Gosski who fit the description of Eyraud had left the hotel at ten that morning with two trunks after paying his bill of eighty francs. It was curious that a man so used to skipping out on his bills stopped to pay this one—and it raised a troubling question: Did Eyraud have enough money to flee Havana? Clearly he had lied to Gautier about his dire financial condition.

Police fanned out into the neighborhoods, kept an eye on the ports and the rail station, and checked out boardinghouses and brothels. Guards were assigned to the Pucheus' home.

Gautier was hauled in to the consulate and forced to remain there in case Eyraud was nabbed and denied his identity. But when Eyraud was still on the loose at midnight Gautier insisted on going home, and he was set free. He declined a police escort and set off alone. He'd gotten only as far as a nearby brothel before he was suddenly accosted by a frantic Eyraud; the fugitive had gone to the whorehouse in hopes of spending the night with a favorite of his, a dark-haired young woman from Toulouse named Margot. But she was otherwise engaged and Eyraud was wandering the streets in a distracted state. Later, when it was all over, Goron commented: "Again, it was this satyr's exaggerated passion for women that did him in." Wearing a coarse, beat-up jacket and a straw hat, Eyraud tried to engage Gautier, who dodged him and sprinted away, and kept running until he found two city policemen, Hernández and Crusado. In his poor Spanish he tried to explain the situation but he was so distraught the police thought they had a crazy man on their hands. Finally they realized he was a foreigner and obviously very worked up over something.

Only the police under Cuba's civil governor had been notified of the hunt for Eyraud; these municipal officers had no idea the international fugitive was in their midst, but they recognized the seriousness of Gautier's rantings and went with him to the French consulate. Hearing Gautier's tale, the consul urged Hernández and Crusado to rush back to the area where Eyraud was seen. Back in their district the officers were joined by another policeman named Lecal and the threesome combed the streets. At 1:15 a.m., on Calle Villegas Amargura, they came upon a man loitering in the neighborhood of the brothel. When they approached him, the idler said, *"Buenas noches."* The police noticed he fit the description of Eyraud and his Spanish was spoken with a French accent. Lecal said, "Who are you? Where are you going?" When the man replied "Gosski, Hotel Roma," the officers grabbed him. Eyraud struggled and it took all three officers to subdue him and bind his wrists with rope. Since Gautier had gone home, the police brought the suspect before the Pucheus who, roused from sleep, looked upon the dirty, disheveled Eyraud and nodded: Yes, that was the silk merchant Gosski.

The suspect, who still needed to be positively identified as Eyraud, was taken away and locked up while the police hurried off in search of the trunks Gosski had carted away from the Hotel Roma. The hunt went on through the night until the trunks turned up at a cabaret near the train station. Inside were documents bearing the name Michel Eyraud and a wallet embossed in gold lettering that read M. EYRAUD.

At 5:30 a.m., the French consul general was informed of the arrest and set off immediately for the prison, where he was joined by Pérez-López and Dussaq. Opening the cell, the men were shocked to see the suspect lying on the floor in a puddle of blood mixed with shards of glass from his pince-nez. With his hands bound Eyraud had managed to smash his eyeglasses and slice himself with the pieces.

Roused from bed, the consulate's doctor, Louis Montane, bandaged the suspect's legs and left arm and pronounced him weakened from the loss of blood but in no mortal danger. While examining the prisoner, Montane discovered a healing gunshot wound on his right side, which the fugitive claimed he'd suffered in Mexico when he was attacked by five Indians. Still strong enough to boast, Eyraud said he survived the ambush by killing three of the Indians. His identity seemed certain enough from the many photographs in circulation and from documents found in his trunk, but the consul wanted to hear it from the murderer's own lips.

When asked, the bedraggled and bandaged prisoner admitted: "Yes, monsieur, I am Eyraud, Michel."

Chapter 36

In Paris, banner headlines announced the news: "Arrestation d'Eyraud." But Parisians were leery: There had been too many false reports. Was this one for real? *L'Écho de Paris* addressed the skepticism. "This time it's not a lie," the paper declared. "The murderer of the bailiff Gouffé is in fact arrested." *Le Petit Journal* assured its readers: "The news is very official this time." The paper explained that the French consul general in Havana had sent a telegram to Paris on Wednesday, May 21, alerting officials that Eyraud was sighted in the country. That dispatch was followed by a second the next day announcing the capture. The newspapers printed whatever tidbits they collected: that Eyraud had tried to kill himself rather than face justice; that his trunk contained a pistol, a knife, and French newspapers about the Gouffé murder.

By the afternoon of May 24, Léon Soudais and another Sûreté detective, the Spanish-speaking Inspector Gaillarde, were aboard the steamer *La Bourgogne* headed for Havana to bring the fugitive home.

At first Gabrielle rejoiced. "Ah good news," she told Judge Dopffer. "Good news." Now that he had the real killer in custody, she insisted that he no longer needed her; he could let her go. Did she truly believe her legal travails were over? Or was her plea merely theatrical? Or was it perhaps further proof of her detachment from reality? Following fast on her joy came a fit of panic, for Gabrielle now feared for her life. Deranged scenarios whipped through her head. "Don't leave me alone with him! Not for a minute!" she pleaded, obsessing on the nightmarish chance that guards would put the two of them together unattended. "He'll kill me!"

Jaume believed Gabrielle had other reasons to fear Eyraud. For weeks she had been the star of this sordid drama, the sole defendant shaping perceptions of the crime in her own way. Now that Eyraud had stepped onstage, the real danger to her was his portrayal of the murder. Wouldn't he argue in person, as he had in his letters, that she was the chief architect of the killing? And even worse, perhaps, was that his entrance would steal attention from her. "Another sentiment, obscure, unspoken, difficult to express, agitates her," Jaume noted in his diary. "She thinks that Eyraud will take away her popularity, because it is very evident that he will, in his turn, benefit from the great spotlight."

A reporter visited Eyraud's wife and nineteen-year-old daughter at their apartment and found them very sad, their faces drawn, though he noted the younger woman was extremely pretty and genteel. Both women sobbed and admitted that they wished Eyraud had succeeded in killing himself. To his daughter he was a coward; he was lost to her forever.

In Havana, Eyraud was under a twenty-four-hour suicide watch in his empty cell: no cot, chair, stool—nothing but four walls. He lay on the stone floor in his filthy white pants and straw hat with one guard posted at his head, another at his feet, and a third watching from outside. His eyes were closed. Was he sleeping? The guards were on alert, the slumber may have been a ruse: No one wanted to be caught flat-footed if he tried to escape or kill himself again.

Soudais and Gaillarde docked at New York on June 3, putting up at the Hotel America, Eyraud's last known residence in the United States, in hopes of taking possession of any belongings he'd left behind. But the hotel owner refused to surrender them without a New York court order. Unable to wait, the detectives set sail the next day aboard the steamer *Le Seneca,* arrived in Havana on June 9, and checked in to the murderer's former lodgings, the Hotel Roma. They rested barely an hour, then headed to the French consulate where they handed over Eyraud's arrest and extradition papers, setting in motion the legal formalities for his release.

But no sooner had the gears started turning than they ground to a halt: Under a French-Cuban treaty, France was prohibited from taking possession of its own prisoner on Cuban soil. So Eyraud had to be escorted onto a French steamer by Cuban police and officially transferred to the Sûreté agents waiting on board. But there was no French steamer in port. So Eyraud's departure would have to wait until June 16 when a French vessel, the *Lafayette,* already en route from Veracruz, Mexico, was expected to reach Havana.

Eyraud was kept in the dark about his extradition. His greatest fear was to return to France for a show trial, a pronouncement of guilt, and execution. When a newspaper reporter, visiting him in his cell, asked if he liked Havana, he replied: "Yes. Two thousand miles away." But he was annoyed by the prisoner in the next cell, a Jesus look-alike soon to be hanged for murder, who kept a rooster that crowed at all hours.

On June 16, at four in the morning, a Cuban entourage tramped along the prison corridor: Second Chief of Police Pérez-López, the prison superintendent, a battery of police officers, and soldiers armed with swords. Eyraud's neighbor, the Jesus-like murderer, awoke with a start. Had the hangman come for him? But the procession passed his cell and he heard the next door clang open: They wanted the French-man. Eyraud was roused and told it was time for a court meeting, just a formality, something about arranging his extradition. But he was suspicious: It was too early for the courts. He refused to speak as they locked his wrists and ankles in iron chains, hustled him into a carriage, and rode in a caravan toward the wharf. His suspicions were right—he was sailing for France. Defeated, he accepted his departure with equanimity, breaking his silence. "Farewell, Cuba," he muttered, "I am content." He was escorted across a plank onto the *Lafayette* and taken to a lower deck where the consul general along with Sou-dais and Gaillarde awaited the handoff, and in an instant it was over: Eyraud, still in irons, was in French custody. Exhausted and filthy, he buried his face in his hands and wept. Real tears? Or the first scene in a con man's drama? "The world thinks I am an assassin," he cried. "I know I am not—and when I think of my little daughter, my heart breaks." He asked the consul for news of his family and when the consul assured him his wife and daughter were well, he groaned: "My greatest punishment is to be deprived of knowing about their lives." The shame he had caused them—it was too painful for him.

Then his mood took an ugly turn and he snorted that the Cubans had deceived him into thinking he was going to see a judge today.

And taking a slap at Soudais, he boasted: "The first time you were in America you would have caught me, but I read about your arrival in the *Herald* and fled to San Francisco."

Eyraud's lodging for the long journey home was a cage eight feet long and eight feet wide, a cell for mutineers, with Soudais and Gaillarde on a strict schedule of guard duty, each on a four-hour shift twice a day. Eight sailors on one-hour shifts were enlisted to cover for the agents the rest of the time. The regime allowed the detectives time to sleep and to dine with the other passengers as the steamer set a course for Santander, Spain, then Saint-Nazaire along the west coast of France.

Soudais and Gaillarde's single-minded obsession was to get Eyraud back to Paris alive and healthy so he could stand trial. They were among the Sûreté's finest, and they knew the nation was watching. Gaillarde was a small man in his fifties with a dark complexion, who in Paris headed a squad of forty detectives. He was older than the powerfully built Soudais. On the job he was deadly serious but off duty he was a vivacious bon vivant, full of merriment and jokes.

On the agents' orders, no one was permitted to see Eyraud except a doctor and an enterprising *New York Herald* reporter who had arranged exclusive access for himself. "This very wise and proper decision on the part of the detectives," the reporter wrote, "was a great disappointment to all on board who had hoped to see Eyraud on exhibition like a wild beast without any Barnum to charge for admission."

Down below, Eyraud was under constant suicide watch. "He has nothing to live for," the journalist explained, "and if he does not kill himself it will be due to the vigilance of the French detectives." In the stifling heat the reporter offered Eyraud his hand fan, which passed Soudais's safety inspection. But the prisoner could barely wave it in front of his face because of the chains on his wrists. Even still, after a couple of hours, Soudais had second thoughts and confiscated it.

On two occasions, early in the voyage, the electric lights in the lower deck suddenly blinked out and, each time, Soudais and Gaillarde leaped forward in the darkness to seize Eyraud. At mealtime, the prisoner had to eat without a knife or fork and when he asked for some wine it arrived in a tin cup, causing him to growl about the absence of a wineglass.

Although the famous prisoner was invisible to the passengers, his presence on board buzzed throughout the ship. Here right below deck was the brutal killer whose thick hands had been at Gouffé's throat. The *Herald* reporter dubbed Eyraud "the *Lafayette*'s bugaboo," adding "the children on board have been told that if they were naughty Eyraud would strangle them."

Chapter 37

As the days wore on at sea, the *petit oiseau* (little bird), as Soudais and Gaillarde called their caged prisoner, swung through a range of moods. He lay for hours on the stone floor silent, with his eyes closed, then suddenly came alive and talked nonstop, usually to defend himself against the charge of murder. In one story he claimed Gouffé was already hanging in the makeshift noose when he arrived at the apartment on rue Tronson du Coudray. No, he proclaimed, he would never go to the guillotine! At other times, he was morose, resigned to his fate. When a barber came to shave him, he shooed him away, announcing that only the Monsieur de Paris—the executioner— would shave his neck hair. Three miseries awaited him: "My trial, my sentence, then the guillotine."

His daughter and wife were often on his lips. His girl—she was an exceptional artist and pianist, Eyraud boasted, then wept and rubbed his eyes with his manacled hands. "Thank God, she can't see her father now." He cried out: How happy he and his wife were ten years ago. She had a carriage and servants, and they traveled in style to London. And in the next breath he was bragging about his many female conquests. How many mistresses he'd had in France, England, the United States, and Mexico. He revealed all the salacious details, then suddenly swerved in the other direction and dredged up a sweet memory of his wife, which launched him into another crying jag. His lurid tales revolted the *Herald* newsman. Eyraud, the reporter wrote, "is utterly incapable of understanding a moral obligation and in this respect appears to be at once a brute and a fool, although intelligent enough in other matters."

One day Eyraud fell ill and lay on the floor of his cage groaning. An examination by the ship's doctor, Paul d'Hoste, revealed a bladder affliction, which only got worse. The patient didn't eat or drink for twenty-four hours; he just lay there moaning in pain. Dr. d'Hoste tried everything—special baths and the application of leeches—but all to no avail. Eyraud grew so weak that Soudais and Gaillarde deemed him no longer a danger to anyone and at no risk of attempting suicide, so they removed the shackles from his wrists and ankles. Freed of his irons, Eyraud lay motionless as though dead, except for the occasional muffled groan.

Gossip floated up from the hold: Something was wrong with Eyraud, although on the upper deck no one knew exactly what. Then one evening, when neither detective showed up in the dining room, a rumor swept through the ship: The prisoner was dead. But that was soon discounted as a new fear took root: Eyraud was faking an illness in order to be free of his shackles—and what if he got loose among the passengers? The imagination ran wild.

But his ailment was real, and it was only by the assiduous care of Dr. d'Hoste that Eyraud gradually recovered. When he finally began eating again, the guards cut his meat and bread into tiny pieces as if for a child. He was a limp specimen of a man, but some women on board imagined him as the romantic outlaw; they were beguiled by the tales of his adventures across America and Mexico. One bold young woman got an apron by bribing a ship worker and, posing as an attendant, carried a jug of hot water to the prisoner. But the sight she came upon shocked and disappointed her. "He presents a very pitiful spectacle," the *Herald* explained, "not at all like the dashing, gay Lothario they seem to think him."

On Saturday, June 22, the northern coast of Spain came into view, and as the *Lafayette* steamed toward Santander, the passengers were alerted that a cholera outbreak had overwhelmed the port. No one was to be allowed off the ship except those staying in Spain. The steamer eased into the wide bay, dropped its passengers, and didn't linger. Soon it was heading up the coast of France toward Saint-Nazaire.

Now fully recovered, Eyraud was full of brash talk again, asserting he had proof of his innocence, and he would present it in court. He would show that he was not to blame for Gouffé's murder. On the contrary, the responsibility lay entirely on the tiny shoulders of Gabrielle Bompard.

On the night of June 29, the *Lafayette* approached Saint-Nazaire and the passengers, braving a chilly wind, collected on deck. When rain cut through the darkness, they bowed their heads but no one ran for cover. At 4:00 a.m. on Monday, June 30, the ship moved into the harbor and announced its arrival with two blasts from a cannon. The *Lafayette* dropped anchor, and a tug called the *Belle-Île* came up alongside ferrying doctors, government officials, and representatives of the steamer company. About a half hour later, the *Lafayette* had passed its cholera inspection.

Soudais and Gaillarde escorted Eyraud onto the tug and sat on either side of him for the brief excursion to shore. The prisoner wore a light jacket, dark blue pants, and his straw hat with a black silk ribbon around it. His beard was trimmed short, and his hands were manacled. On shore he rode with his guards in an open carriage to the train station, where he waited in the police office for the 6:37 a.m. departure for Paris.

Soudais and Gaillarde took comfort in the knowledge that they had reached the last leg of their long mission, and ten hours later, at 4:21 p.m., the train pulled into Gare Saint-Lazare in Paris to a waiting mob. When Eyraud appeared at the door, there was scuffling and shoving on the platform; police were unable to hold back the crowd, and a few aggressive gawkers pushed their way on board. A cry went up: *"Le voilà! Le voilà!"* (There he is!) Arms shot into the air, fingers pointed. A chant broke out: *"À mort! À mort! À mort!"* They wanted him dispatched to his death. Eyraud, pale and weak, was shaken by the commotion; his eyes shot left then right as if fearing what might come next; his legs were ready to collapse under him.

A carriage, protected by a cordon of guards, waited nearby. Standing beside it in triumph was the man who had chased the murderer for nearly a year at serious risk to his career and health: the head of the Sûreté, Marie-François Goron. This case had tested him like no other; it drew on all his sleuthing skills; it forced him to stick by his controversial hunches; and it laid him low for months. But now the killer was within his grasp. Goron and his quarry climbed into the carriage and set off toward the prefecture of police.

First stop was the chief's office, where Eyraud was put through a series of formalities—papers had to be filled out. Dazed and fatigued, the prisoner took off his straw hat and held it submissively in his hands. Sweat beaded on his bald head.

By 5:10 p.m., he was in a cell at the Dépôt where, like Gabrielle, he would stay while the judge and detectives did their investigation. Soudais and Gaillarde basked briefly in the glow of a job well done and then were dismissed to the comfort of their homes. Eyraud lost his chattiness. He was sullen and silent and refused food. He had the night to ponder his fate before his first interrogation in the morning.

Chapter 38

Michel Eyraud had a rough night. For a man who loved his freedom, who was happiest gallivanting across the open spaces of Mexico, here he was back in Paris locked up in a stone cell, his future looking bleak. Adding to his woes, his bladder attacked him again, the pain striking at five in the morning and rousing him from a fitful sleep. The Dépôt physician, Dr. Jules Voisin, came to his aid; he learned of the bout the patient had suffered during the voyage; he listened to Eyraud's heart and, noticing the bullet wound in his side, heard the tale of his gun battle with Mexican bandits. The doctor prescribed a cup of bouillon and, over Eyraud's loud protests, prohibited him from drinking wine.

Dr. Voisin also looked after Gabrielle while she was at the Dépôt and had hypnotized her repeatedly to explore her memory of the crime. But none of his findings filtered out to the public: Voisin was adamant about the confidentiality of the sessions; they would inform the state's investigators and no one else.

Later in the morning, Goron took Eyraud to Alphonse Bertillon's police anthropological service, where the murderer was photographed and measured. The details of his work-up—the size of his head; the length of his fingers, forearms, and feet; the width and depth of his ears and nose; the thickness of his nostrils; the gradations of his eyes through every zone of the iris—were jotted down carefully on a registration card and filed with his photo in the catalogue of the criminal class.

By three thirty in the afternoon, Eyraud found himself in an interrogation room surrounded by Judge Dopffer, Chief Goron, and Sûreté agents Wahlen and Houlier. Weakened by his illness and months on the run, Eyraud had little fight left. After forty minutes of grilling, he was a broken man: *"Je suis cuit."* (I am cooked.) He confessed that he had murdered Gouffé but made sure to implicate Gabrielle: He had not acted alone; the girl played her part.

Describe the murder, Dopffer demanded.

Gouffé was hanged, Eyraud said, suggesting Gabrielle's active role.

Not entirely true, Dopffer countered. There was evidence that the victim was strangled.

Eyraud dismissed the accusation, as though it were an insult to him personally, and his mood darkened. For a man who bantered easily, his words suddenly stalled. He claimed he was too exhausted to speak, he needed time to think things over. He shut down so completely that the investigators ended the interrogation. Judge Dopffer gave him a couple of days to regain his health and gather his thoughts. Whatever his defense, Eyraud realized his past was closing in on him. He had put it just right: He was cooked.

Back in his cell, he brightened, slipping into his comfortable role as raconteur, and he regaled his guards with his globe-trotting adventures. He was an expansive storyteller, taking his time, rolling out the drama scene by scene, and lingering over his sexual escapades. So many mistresses, the guards lost count! If it weren't for the cell's stone walls, they might have imagined they were enjoying an aperitif in a boulevard café.

Eyraud maintained his bonhomie even as blood appeared in his urine and his appetite vanished. One morning he sang a Portuguese song for his guards, then translated the verses for them. "Whatever one says, there is nothing sinister in his manner or in his language," *Le Matin* wrote. "His joviality and his large laugh brought joy to his guards and his continuous pleasantries allowed the agents to pass many hours without boredom."

By his next interrogation Eyraud had spruced up his appearance. Gone were the shabby overcoat and straw hat. Although his wife and daughter were in no mood to visit him, they sent along a new wardrobe and, when he came before the investigators, he appeared in a magnificent black overcoat with a velour collar and on his head was a chestnut-brown bowler. When Gaillarde complimented him on his new look, Eyraud implored him to send his thanks to his wife and daughter. But, the prisoner added, please tell them not to visit: He couldn't bear the shame.

With the trial looming, though still months away, the public prosecutor, Jules Quesnay de Beaurepaire, ordered that journalists be kept at a distance from the accused. Strict measures were taken. When Eyraud was transferred from his cell to a carriage, the courtyards were evacuated and doorways shut off. An enraged press fought back. "Permit us to remark," *Le Matin* reminded the keepers of justice, "that it's thanks to the immense publicity that journalists gave this case that the Havana police captured the murderer of Gouffé."

At his interrogation Eyraud tried to save his own neck and shift responsibility onto Gabrielle. Although he claimed he neither hated her nor sought to destroy her, his testimony showed otherwise. He asserted that he would not sacrifice himself for Gabrielle. She caused him too much anguish, for she abandoned him and denounced him to the police. "If we had been captured together, I would have taken all the responsibility and I would have saved her," he told investigators. But because she deceived him, he added, "I will not clear her. I will tell the truth about the role she played before, during and after the crime, and if she must take the fall, too bad, she will take the fall."

It was Gabrielle, he said, who proposed the crime, Gabrielle who insisted on robbing Gouffé, Gabrielle who was in control of the planning and execution of the murder. She had a strange hold over him. In her presence, if investigators were to believe him, this brutal, dominating tyrant was as weak as a lamb. He was so in love with her, he could deny her nothing. "It is said that I terrorized her, that I hypnotized her," Eyraud declared. "On the contrary, it was she who drove me like a lapdog."

She willingly undertook her part in the murder, Eyraud charged. She had no qualms about placing the red silk sash over Gouffé's head: She instigated his hanging. She was as callous as an animal, he said, a vicious woman who was untroubled by spending a night alone with the cadaver. When Eyraud returned the morning after the killing, having slept in his own bed at home beside his wife, he asked Gabrielle if she was afraid during the night.

"Moi?" the young woman replied. "Why would you think I'd be afraid? He's slammed shut in there." Then laughing hysterically, she kicked the trunk. "Look inside," she ordered Eyraud, kicking it again. "See if he turned over!"

Eyraud denied he was ever able to control Gabrielle through hypnosis. He'd read the newspapers: He was surprised by the charges that she acted as his hypnotized automaton. Yes, he'd tried to hypnotize her, but no, he'd never succeeded. Once, when he tried to put her to sleep in a London pub, she slapped his face. "The newspapers say that I hypnotized this girl, that I had suggested the crime to her and that she acted unconsciously!" he cried. "What lunacy!"

Chapter 39

Michel Eyraud and Gabrielle Bompard were now at war, and neither backed down on the critical question of who put the silk sash over Gouffé's neck. That action demonstrated murderous intent. To place a noose over a man's head left no doubt you wanted the man dead. Gabrielle maintained that she never completed the action, that she had the *cordelière* in her hands, and had raised it over Gouffé's head, but then froze—she could not carry out the final step. In her telling, Eyraud sensed her hesitation, came out of hiding, grabbed the noose, and dropped it over Gouffé's head. Then he'd yanked down hard on the rope that was connected to the *cordelière,* and the act of murder had begun.

But as savagely as she disputed him, Gabrielle was deeply shaken by Eyraud's return. His presence shoved her to the edge of hysterics. His assertions sent her mind reeling. She proposed the crime? It was her idea to rob Gouffé, to murder him? She raged against Eyraud. How could he say such things?

The suspects' contradictory testimony muddied the investigation. Building a reliable scenario of the murder became all but impossible. Who was lying? Who was telling the truth? Investigators needed to break through the defendants' stubbornness and get at the facts. Goron believed the stalemate called for dramatic action. Only the two suspects knew what took place in that apartment on rue Tronson du Coudray. Why not bring them together, let them confront each other in that very same room? What better place to shake loose the answers than the crime scene itself!

"She detested him, he hated her," Goron observed. "It was necessary to put the two lovers face-to-face. That was the only way to discover the truth amid their lies."

The rooms had been vacant for months. One tenant, a well-known acrobat named Leona Dare, had moved in unaware of the apartment's history and, as soon as she made the shocking discovery, she vanished. The last occupant, reputed to be a woman of questionable morals, hoped the notoriety of the site would enhance her business. Whether men came to her out of morbid curiosity or for all the usual urges was impossible to know, but she didn't stay long either.

In preparation for the suspects' rendezvous, the scene of the murder was re-created down to the smallest detail: A chaise longue was placed next to the alcove, a rope was dangled out of sight behind the curtain, brandy appeared on a table, and the trunk was positioned against the wall in the kitchen. The accused were to reenact the murder before Judge Dopffer, the forensics specialist Dr. Brouardel, Chief Goron, and other magistrates and detectives. There was to be a stand-in for Gouffé, played by a Sûreté agent. Planning for the event was splashed across the newspapers, prompting one enterprising spectator to rent the apartment across the hall in hopes of a front-row seat. When it was announced that the murderers' reunion would take place on Tuesday, July 8, the curious began assembling in front of the apartment the day before to stake out their places.

At 7:30 a.m. on the appointed day Eyraud and Gabrielle were taken from their cells at the Dépôt and escorted separately along bare, monotonous walls and down dismal staircases. Eyraud, looking proud and combative in his fine overcoat and bowler, was conducted to the offices of the Sûreté where a barber gave him a quick haircut and shave. The illusion was complete: He now looked just as he had almost a year ago on the night of the murder. Gazing at himself in a wall mirror, he was satisfied. "I am reborn," he said. "I'm sure to attract a lady at Tronson du Coudray." Jaume was aghast, and wondered if Eyraud really believed his wild fantasy. "The heart of a man is an unfathomable abyss," he confided to his diary, "and a man might very well yearn to the point of humiliation!"

Gabrielle also got a sprucing up. She wore a black silk dress pinched at the waist, accentuating her petite figure. She had her coif remade to match the sweet, childish style she wore when she'd guided Gouffé toward the chaise longue.

The former lovers climbed into separate carriages outside the Dépôt several minutes apart, Eyraud departing first, accompanied by

Judge Dopffer. As Gabrielle stepped up into her coach she daintily lifted her skirt, keeping the hem out of the mud, then rode off with Goron at her side.

The carriages made their way from the Île de la Cité to the *grands boulevards* in about twenty minutes. As they neared boulevard Haussmann the scene was like a carnival. People watched the coaches pass from their apartment windows, and shopkeepers waited expectantly outside their doors. The crowd thickened along rue Pasquier, and on rue Tronson du Coudray the mob had crashed through police barricades at both ends of the one-block-long street and thronged in front of number 3.

At about 9:00 a.m. police parted the crowd and Eyraud's hackney rolled to a stop in front of the apartment. When he climbed out, there was some commotion before he quickly disappeared through a double door at the street level. A crowd awaited inside the small apartment. Jaume counted nineteen people: besides Dopffer and his clerk and Goron and a few Sûreté agents, there were representatives of the prosecutor, two medical examiners, a few Paris magistrates, a couple of select journalists, the building concierge, and the doctors Brouardel, Motet, and Ballet, who were there to assess Gabrielle's mental condition. "Eyraud seemed emotional," Jaume observed. "Was it the memory of the crime? Was it the certainty that he would soon see his beloved again? It could have been the two sentiments striking him at once."

Two minutes later, Gabrielle's carriage eased through the throng in front of the building. As she stepped lightly onto the street, the mob surged forward. Pleased by the turnout, Gabrielle calmly gazed at the faces. She was in no hurry to go inside and instead went leisurely to the sweating horses and stroked their backs. "Poor animals," she purred. "They're hot." She lingered in the spotlight, absently running her fingers through the horses' manes until Goron piloted her toward the double doors. But when she gave a push, the doors didn't budge—the star of the show was locked out. "Why . . ." she cried dramatically. "How is it that it doesn't open?" Goron rang the bell impatiently, and after several moments the doors parted and he and Gabrielle slipped inside. Two journalists sneaked in behind them but retreated on the threat of arrest.

Inside, Gabrielle immediately recoiled when she caught sight of her former lover. Whipping her head away, she hissed in a stage whisper that everyone heard: "I can't see this man. He disgusts me."

Dopffer stepped into the center of the room amid flickering candlelight, and everyone fell silent for a moment as if suddenly remembering the tragedy that had befallen a man in this room. Gouffé's murder was something more than macabre entertainment, it was real and brutal. And now it was time for the truth to emerge.

Dopffer addressed Eyraud. "Some enormous contradictions exist between your statements and your accomplice's," he said. "We want to know if it was she or you who passed the *cordelière* over Gouffé's neck. I beg you to tell the truth."

Eyraud spoke in a loud voice, his eyes dark and fierce: "I did not strangle Gouffé. I hanged him, or better, we hanged him, Gabrielle and I. She took off the *cordelière* that closed her dressing gown and she passed it over his neck, with it arranged in a slipknot. Then she put the *cordelière* in the snap hook I prepared. I pulled the rope. It rode through the pulley, and Gouffé found himself hanged."

"But," the judge remarked, "we found the signs of fingers on the larynx." Dopffer clearly had reached his own conclusion. The ragged marks in the crossbeam overhead were proof enough that the pulley had snapped out of the wood, and that the hanging was interrupted. But Dopffer needed to hear it from Eyraud himself.

"I assure you," Eyraud replied, "I hanged him and did not strangle him. The pressure of the *cordelière* was sufficient for that."

Across the room Gabrielle stamped her foot angrily. "You lie, monsieur!"

"I tell the truth, mademoiselle, and I advise you to do the same."

It was clear why Eyraud insisted on a hanging rather than a strangling. He was guilty in either case, but a hanging, as he portrayed it, also implicated Gabrielle. If he wanted to take her to the guillotine with him, he had to prove she placed the noose over Gouffé's head. He had to dispel any possibility of a strangulation, a deed he could have accomplished alone.

Dopffer directed the players to their places to begin the reenactment. Eyraud went behind the curtains into the alcove. Gabrielle moved toward the door to admit a Sûreté agent playing the role of Gouffé. And so the seduction began. Gabrielle recounted her conversation with the bailiff, her story of her breakup with Eyraud, her attempts to get Gouffé to sit on the chaise longue, his initial resistance at first, and his fondling of her breasts. She had told this story before but never in the presence of Eyraud. Might he react in a way that proved the truth of her words? That was the gamble of this exercise: that someone in the heat of the moment would lose their composure and shed some new light. Continuing her tale, Gabrielle said Gouffé was preoccupied with his lust when Eyraud burst through the curtain, grabbed the noose from her hands, and threw it onto his neck. Then Eyraud pulled down on the rope and began to hang the bailiff until suddenly the pulley leaped out of the crossbeam and the two men both tumbled to the floor. "Eyraud strangled him with his hands," Gabrielle said.

"Mademoiselle lies," Eyraud growled, emerging from behind the curtain. "It's she who put the *cordelière* around Gouffé's neck saying to him, 'This would make you a beautiful necktie.'"

Gabrielle lunged toward Eyraud and was restrained by two agents.

Eyraud confidently repeated his story. Gabrielle placed the noose around Gouffé's neck while Eyraud, behind the curtain, pulled down on the rope. "I came out of hiding crying: 'He's taken,'" Eyraud declared, looking back and forth between Dopffer and Goron, reading their reactions. "Then I saw the bailiff was inanimate," he went on. "Gabrielle hanged him."

Eyraud turned a ferocious gaze on Gabrielle; his lips trembled and malevolence filled his eyes. In this frothing state, he was a terrifying devil. "You could see that a last hope made the wretch's heart beat," Goron recalled. "At this moment I was sure that Eyraud would have joyously placed his head on the rim of the guillotine, if only he could see Gabrielle guillotined next to him."

"Liar! Liar!" Gabrielle shrieked. "Coward! Coward!" Furious, she tried to shake herself free of the agents restraining her. Her face was a mask of demonic possession. If released, she seemed entirely capable of strangling Eyraud with her tiny hands. "She merited well, at this moment, the nickname of *petit démon* that had been given to her," Goron observed.

The staggering sadness of their lives was on full display. There had been such promise in these two lost souls. Both intelligent, born to opportunity, yet they slid with a carefree glint in their eye into degradation, deceit, and murder. Consumed by greed and lust, Eyraud was finally done in by his hunger for a crafty femme fatale. Gabrielle, cast out by her family, drifted to the edge of madness and resorted to cunning to survive.

She shrieked—she insisted she was telling the truth: Eyraud strangled Gouffé. "That's true, absolutely true!" she cried. "That's just how it happened. Monsieur is a liar."

"It's mademoiselle who lies," Eyraud persisted. "She's a liar, a dirty liar. *I* tell the truth."

"What nerve he has! He's a liar! He's the one who did it all!"

Gabrielle was close to a hysterical breakdown, and this reunion was in danger of a quick end. To pilot her back from the brink, Dopffer addressed her in the calming, paternalistic tone he'd used at similar moments during her interrogations.

"What did you do then," he asked in a tender voice, "when one of your lovers was strangling the other?"

"I hid in a corner," she answered meekly. "I turned away so I didn't have to see."

Eyraud interrupted, declaring again what he had already told interrogators in private: It was Gabrielle who conceived the murderous plan. It was she who put the notion in his head. He was a man in love and could deny her nothing. Yes, he would kill for her!

"Oh! What cheek!" Gabrielle snorted. "This is not true! Was I the one who knew that Gouffé always had lots of money on him?" She stamped her foot: "Liar! Liar!"

Sadly, Dopffer realized the rendezvous had accomplished nothing other than inciting the accomplices, and he called a halt to the farce. The truth of the night at rue Tronson du Coudray was still hidden, perhaps forever, by the mutual loathing of the former lovers.

The press seemed to side with Eyraud. Though he proved nothing, he somehow implicated the petite demon. "Gabrielle seems to have taken an equal part to that of Eyraud in the murder of Gouffé," wrote *Le Matin,* "and the general opinion is that the two merit the same punishment."

As Gabrielle left the apartment, she grabbed Soudais's hand and placed it on her chest, declaring: "How my heart beats!"

Riding back to the Dépôt with Goron, she raged at Eyraud: "He's a liar! He lies all the time. Nothing can be done with his dirty type!"

Back in her cell by 10:30 a.m., Gabrielle descended into a full-

Completed in March 1889, the Eiffel Tower soared 1,000 feet into the air on the Champ de Mars, higher than any man-made structure in the world, and served as the centerpiece of that summer's Paris International Exposition.

Wealthy ladies' man Toussaint-Augustin Gouffé slept with twenty women in July 1889 and disappeared late that month after a liaison.

Marie-François Goron *(below left)*, the head of the Paris Sûreté, and his chief inspector, Pierre-Fortune Jaume, defied skeptics and clung to the belief that Gouffé's body had turned up on a riverbank near Lyon, about 250 miles south of Paris.

LE BRIGADIER JAUME

Gouffé was positively identified from his badly decomposed remains by means of groundbreaking forensic techniques.

Twenty-one-year-old Gabrielle Bompard, the fabled "Little Demon," and her middle-aged con man lover, Michel Eyraud, the murderers of Gouffé.

After killing Gouffé at the apartment at 3, rue Tronson du Coudray, Bompard and Eyraud stuffed his body into a trunk, carried it downstairs to a waiting carriage, and eventually dumped both trunk and body on the banks of the Rhône river.

The *malle sanglante*, or bloody trunk, was painstakingly reassembled after being smashed to bits by Eyraud and was displayed before thousands of curious Parisians and tourists.

The killers fled to New York, Vancouver, and then to San Francisco, making the acquaintance along the way of a wealthy Frenchman, Georges Garanger *(left)*, who was smitten by Gabrielle. She returned to Paris with Garanger and turned herself in to the police.

(Below) After his capture in Havana, Eyraud attempted suicide. Back in Paris, he posed for his mug shot and had his anthropomorphic measurements taken.

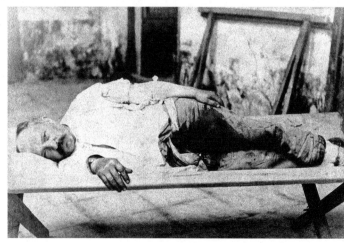

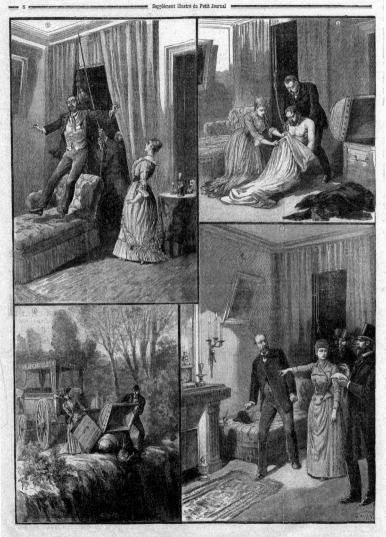

AFFAIRE GOUFFÉ
1. Le crime. — 2. Le sac et la malle. — 3. A Millery, près de Lyon
4. La confrontation rue Tronson-Ducoudray

With both Eyraud and Gabrielle once again in Paris to face justice, the press sensationalized the case to an eager public. Illustrations in *Le Petit Journal* depicted the murder, the dumping of the body, and Eyraud's and Gabrielle's return to the murder scene to reenact their crime for investigators.

Le Petit Journal

TOUS LES VENDREDIS
Le Supplément illustré
5 Centimes

SUPPLÉMENT ILLUSTRÉ
Huit pages : CINQ centimes

TOUS LES JOURS
Le Petit Journal
5 Centimes

Première Année   SAMEDI 20 DÉCEMBRE 1890   Numéro 4

AFFAIRE GOUFFÉ
LA COUR D'ASSISES

Gabrielle was tried in a courtroom packed with diplomats, dignitaries, famous artists, writers, and scientists, and she became so overwrought she had an hysterical attack that halted the proceedings while she was carried out for treatment.

Gabrielle's defense attorney was the young Henri Robert (pictured here in later years), a renowned, intellectually nimble advocate who had already kept many accused criminals from the guillotine.

Félix Decori, noted for his Mephistophelian mustache, had the difficult task of defending Michel Eyraud.

The courtroom drama turned on the question of whether Gabrielle had committed the murder under Eyraud's hypnotic influence. The world's leading expert on hypnosis and crime, Jules Liégeois *(left)*, appeared as an expert witness on behalf of Gabrielle, arguing she could have become the plaything of her hypnotist lover. The prosecution put forward the theories of the prominent neurologist Jean-Martin Charcot *(below left)* and his disciple Georges Gilles de la Tourette *(below)*, who contended that murder under hypnosis was impossible.

blown hysterical attack. She became incoherent, raved like a mad-woman, and writhed in convulsions. The nuns who looked after her tried their best to calm her, undressing her, cradling her, and finally putting her to bed. At last she was resting, sobbing quietly to an old nun who had an affection for her: "Do you think, my sister, this is not abominable? That man said I did everything—and they believe his lies. Now he's the one everyone listens to."

Then, during the night, she went wild again, becoming deliri-ous. In the morning, Dr. Voisin visited, pronounced her in a state of "grand weakness," and had her transferred to the infirmary.

The old nun was worried about her young charge. So charmed was she that she disregarded her prisoner's dark side and saw only a clever, industrious girl who had been wronged. She had put Gabrielle to work on worthwhile projects, making good use of the sewing skills she'd acquired in the convents. Gabrielle embroidered shirt collars for charity and had stitched a beautiful piece that was delivered to a needy orphan. But once it was learned whose hands had created it, the accursed collar was immediately sent back.

Chapter 40

The confrontation on rue Tronson du Coudray proved good business for the Musée Grévin. In the aftermath, visitors crushed into the wax museum's basement exhibit to see the remarkable likenesses of Michel Eyraud and Gabrielle Bompard. "It is true to say that these personages are of a gripping resemblance," observed *Le Petit Journal.*

The couple's barbed bickering found a home in French folklore. At the famous Montmartre cabaret Chat Noir, patrons sang a ditty called "The Reconstruction of the Crime," by the poet-performer Jules Jouy. In twenty two-line stanzas, Jouy lampooned the crucial questions of the case: Was Gabrielle conscious of her actions during the crime, and who placed the *cordelière* over Gouffé's head?

> *Gabrielle, elle est innocente;*
> *En esprit, elle était absente?*
> *C'est pas vrai!*
> (Gabrielle, she's innocent;
> In spirit, she was absent?
> It's not true!)

> *Elle ment, la sale vipère;*
> *C'est elle qu'a mis la cordelière.*
> *C'est pas vrai!*
> (She lies, the dirty viper;
> It is she who placed the *cordelière.*
> It's not true!)

Goron was criticized for demanding the reenactment, which the newspapers called a "useless experience" that "did not advance the investigation one step." The only result, some critics observed, was that the newspapers were again filled with lurid details of the crime. Goron wrote in his memoir: "Some political men were concerned about what they called the indiscretions of the police—or more, the indiscretions of M. Goron—because I was the one always targeted in this case."

Days after the confrontation Gabrielle was still morose and constantly a hairsbreath away from an emotional breakdown. When she was summoned to Dopffer's office for further questioning, she needed assistance going up the stairs at the Palais de Justice and was supported on a guard's arm while walking the wide corridors overlooking Sainte-Chapelle. On July 14, Bastille Day, she begged her keepers to raise her spirits by taking her out to see the celebrations. She wanted to ride through the streets in a carriage and take in the dancing and drinking, the laughter, and the French flags draped over the window ledges along the avenues. If she were lucky she might catch the parade of schoolboy rifle battalions. "Since I am suffering you could afford me this favor," she pleaded with her guardians. When her request was denied, she sobbed and was comforted by the old nun. To kill time, she read and sewed, and on Sundays she went to hear the prison chaplain deliver mass.

Gabrielle was allowed to order food from outside the prison at her own expense, and for several months she had money thanks to the kindness of Georges Garanger. By now, he had turned away from her and discreetly left the scene. His absence meant that Gabrielle now had to get meals from the prison canteen like everyone else. Her wardrobe suffered, too. She passed her days in an old black wool dress and with the help of the nun kept her hair properly coifed.

In his cell, Eyraud entertained his guards with his tales of adventure. He was as lewd as a drunken sailor, holding back nothing, joking and swearing in four languages: French, Spanish, Portuguese, and English.

Throughout July and August both suspects had sessions with Dopffer as he worked to wind up his investigation; they were summoned separately and were kept out of each other's sight. By the end of August, Dopffer had everything he needed and at last declared he had completed his dossier. The two suspects were to face justice together in a trial set to begin October 27. Félix Decori, a Mephistopheles look-alike who had a pointed beard and a mustache with twirled tips, was named to represent Eyraud. The formidable Henri Robert was to defend Gabrielle. Dopffer, exhausted and deserving of a rest, set off on an extended holiday.

As the trial approached, Eyraud appealed his arrest, his lawyer offering a flimsy, indeed absurd, argument, but one that nevertheless was taken seriously. The appeal contended that the minister of the interior, Ernest Constans, who headed the national police, had Eyraud arrested to settle a political score. Constans had been instrumental in staving off a potential coup by Georges Boulanger the previous year, forcing the popular general to flee the country under the fear of arrest. Eyraud, who had been a strong supporter of Boulanger, asserted in his appeal that Constans had him arrested because of his political sentiments. Given the evidence of Eyraud's role in the murder, the appeal of his arrest on political grounds amounted to little more than the ravings of a man with nothing left to lose. Yet the Court of Appeals took up his request and, on October 28, rejected it. The gambit had one effect: It pushed back the start date of the trial to November 25.

Jury selection began in early November. Juries in the French legal system had evolved to offset the power and indiscriminate sentencing of the judge, and therefore played a vital role in the courtroom. The punishment for individual crimes was determined by the French legal code—for instance, the guillotine for murder—but the jury ruled on the existence of extenuating circumstances. For Gabrielle, the jury was entrusted to determine whether some extenuating circumstance—hypnotic control or mental illness—should lessen her punishment or even acquit her. But while the jury had considerable influence, it was hampered by the incomplete picture it got of defendants during a trial. Juries did not read the full dossier prepared by the judge of instruction; and French trials did not reveal all facts related to the case. Often the evidence was not presented in an orderly fashion but was jumbled and confusing. The presiding judge controlled the dissemination of information and tilted it to his own bias, resulting in a lopsided picture for the jury to consider. But juries, to their credit, were often of a fairly high intelligence. The pool for Eyraud and Gabrielle's trial swiftly narrowed to thirty-six, including a pharmacist, a retired sea captain, an architect, a fruit seller, and an engineer. From that group twelve were to be chosen to sit in judgment.

The steady march toward the trial halted suddenly two weeks before the opening. The freewheeling press, which had pulled almost every trick to sensationalize the case, now overstepped its legal bounds. On November 13, *Le Matin* published an article titled "Nos bons jurés" (Our Good Jurors), in which it revealed many of the potential jurors—twenty-one in all—and had polled them on their opinions. Were you inalterably for conviction? Did you want to see Eyraud die? Did you want to send Gabrielle to hard labor for life? Did you believe in leniency? Were you convinced hypnotism played a role in the crime? Did you think Gabrielle should go to an asylum rather than to prison? The article destroyed the juror pool, forcing dismissal of everyone under consideration and requiring a fresh start. Another delay ensued. Now the courtroom doors weren't scheduled to open until December 16, once a new jury was seated.

In the meantime, *Le Matin* had its own trial to cover. The court went after its editor, Monsieur Moro, for interfering in the judicial process. His case became its own mini cause célèbre. Editors of other newspapers came to his defense. How could the court so blatantly infringe on their press freedoms? Didn't these freedoms separate the Republic from the monarchy? Moro presented his own arguments on the freedom of the press at his trial on November 26, and the court swiftly rejected them, contending that divulging jurors' impressions prior to a trial was an assault on the judicial system. The editor got a month in jail, and the court was pilloried in the newspapers. Magistrates, the writers declared, were happy to grant the press its rights only when the papers published material flattering to the magistrates.

All the hyperbole, however, was a mere sideshow to the main event that lay ahead. The French were turning nearly as one toward the coming performance at the Cour d'Assises, with the expectation of grand theatrics. Everyone knew the characters, the grisly details, the major questions to be resolved. *L'affaire Gouffé* had been so mythologized it needed no introduction. The case had dragged on so long some people were eager for the denouement. "Everyone has had enough," groused *Le Petit Journal.* "It is necessary to have it finished." One Frenchman clearly had had enough. On December 12, a man burst into a newspaper office in Bordeaux, claiming he was Eyraud and the editors were Gabrielle. Armed with a baton, he swung out crazily, knocking some of the journalists to the ground before police carted him away. Others sought to capitalize on the trial. A tailor on the *grands boulevards* approached Eyraud's lawyer, Félix Decori, with a proposition. He would make the accused a fine suit for his appearance in court. He would deliver the ensemble at a very reasonable price for the cachet of having his handiwork displayed on the famous murderer during the proceedings.

As the trial neared, the lawyers met with their clients to review strategy and coach them on their public appearances. Decori impressed upon Eyraud that he must behave in the courtroom, or he would make things worse for himself. The biggest risk, in Decori's view, was that his client would lose control when he caught sight of his nemesis Georges Garanger. Eyraud despised the man who stole his mistress and became livid whenever his name was mentioned. He wanted nothing more than to exact revenge.

Henri Robert advised Gabrielle to strive for proper decorum whenever in public view. She was widely regarded as a degenerate and, far worse, a murderer, so she had to project an image of virtue and innocence. Gabrielle promised she would be well-behaved. For his historic defense, Robert would strive to convince the jury that Gabrielle was not conscious of her actions during the murder because she was under the hypnotic control of her lover. Experts from the Nancy school would explain to the jury how a person in a trance submitted their will to another being and how it was the hypnotizer—in this case Eyraud—who was the guilty party. The contention would be that Gabrielle was a victim, used by Eyraud in the same way a gun was used to commit a crime. And if Gabrielle failed to remember her hypnotization, the explanation was simple: Eyraud had ordered her to forget everything once she was out of her trance.

Inspector Jaume was dismayed that the defense strategy was gaining credibility among Parisians. How could learned, respectable people believe that Gabrielle acted against her will? Her defenders, Jaume wrote in his diary, "make Gabrielle not responsible." He ridiculed their attempt to present her as hypnotized by Eyraud, her will crippled. "For them, one should not punish Gabrielle any more than one should punish the dagger of a murderer. Do these philanthropists, who deplore the horrors of war, lock up cannons, bayonets and bullets in prison?"

Chapter 41

The trial was scheduled to take four days, beginning on Tuesday, December 16, with the reading of the charges and interrogation of the accused. The following day was for testimony of the witnesses. On the third day came the experts: doctors Brouardel, Motet, Ballet, and Lacassagne for the prosecution; Dr. Hippolyte Bernheim, the leader of the Nancy school, on behalf of Gabrielle and the role of hypnotism in the murder. Friday was set for the verdict.

A trial in the Cour d'Assises was presided over by three judges, ostensibly to prevent any one of them from imposing his own whimsical justice. But in practice only one judge guided the proceedings—the president of the court—and the other two sat mute and ineffectual. In the trial of Eyraud and Gabrielle, the president of the court was Judge Robert, a querulous, red-robed figure with a high-pitched voice and sagging, fatigued posture. Yet he asserted a fearsome authority. "The president of the Court of Assize was not a simple man," explained Albert Bataille, an influential journalist who reported on the courts for *Le Figaro*. "He was a demigod." Once he assumed his throne in the courtroom, Bataille said, "an aureole appeared around his brow. He no longer walked, he advanced; he no longer spoke, he pronounced."

Gabrielle's lawyer, Henri Robert, suffered a setback just a few days before the trial's start when his hypnotism expert, Hippolyte Bernheim, fractured his leg and was unable to travel to Paris. It was a huge loss for the defense. Bernheim's name carried prestige in legal and medical circles; that, along with his eloquence and incisiveness, had been expected to carry considerable weight with the jury. In his stead, the Nancy school put forward the legal scholar Jules Liégeois, a shift that meant a vastly different presentation for the defense. Liégeois was a rambler, obsessive about details, an easily distracted professor of law. But there was a benefit to his substitution. He was recognized as the world's leading authority on hypnotism and crime. No one had conducted more experiments. No one had written more voluminously on the subject. No one—not even Bernheim—could put together a more thorough demonstration of the subject. *Le Petit Journal* praised his "veritable passion for hypnotism." It was Liégeois who had legitimized the study of crime and hypnotism with a groundbreaking lecture before the Academy of Sciences in 1884. "We wait with great curiosity to hear the explanations given by Liégeois," the newspaper added. "He is a specialist whose competence one cannot contest and with whom one must reckon."

Some commentators weren't waiting for Liégeois's seminar to reach their conclusions. The *Figaro* reporter Bataille had had enough of the Gouffé case and the suppositions about the role of hypnotism. "The public waits for the denouement . . . like it waits for the last episode of a serial that has been dragged out for eighteen months," he wrote the day the trial opened. In Bataille's eyes, Gabrielle was a perverse child whose corrupt nature explained her actions. It was no surprise to him that the doctors who prepared her medical report rejected the influence of hypnotism. Gabrielle had succumbed to evil, Bataille contended, an evil that existed long before Liégeois or Bernheim or Mesmer ever experimented with hypnosis.

As the day neared, a severe cold snap gripped Paris. Giant blocks of ice choking the Seine were a threat to river traffic. Clocks on storefronts stood idle, their internal mechanics frozen. In the wooded Bois de Boulogne skaters glided across an ice-solid pond, the women ditching their usual cumbersome attire and ridiculous large hats in favor of sensible wool skirts and small caps. Counts, viscounts, and barons braved the cold to snack at a rink-side restaurant nestled in the trees.

On the morning of the trial, the sky was gray and misty, the temperature at twenty-eight degrees Fahrenheit. The curious, ignoring the chill, streamed toward the courthouse, where police and soldiers were in place. "What a spectacle!" declared Jaume. "All of Paris came—a mélange of bizarre personalities." *Le Matin* denounced the frivolity, declaring that it detracted from the gravity of the occasion and stained France's reputation: "They must laugh abroad at the mental state of a society where such spectacles are possible!"

There was intense competition for seats. Judge Robert had received two thousand requests in a single week. The lucky spectators were ambassadors—Lord Lytton, the British ambassador, and his wife, Lady Lytton; the Italian ambassador and the Turkish ambassador—and members of the French Chamber of Deputies, actors and actresses, luminaries from the worlds of literature and science, representatives of the French elite: dapper men and their much-perfumed women in extravagant hats toting opera glasses. Some ticket holders were less interested in sitting through the trial than in turning their seats into gold; they circulated among the crowd offering entry at a scalper's price, which had shot up as much as 500 percent in the final days, according to some accounts. The British sneered at the rush for tickets. "Few people of real refinement would care to intrigue, wheedle, or pay, a heavy sum for admission to the Old Bailey during a murder trial," *The Royal Gazette* wrote. "Here it is different. The *procès* is looked upon as a kind of comedy, which fashionable people attend, just as they would the first night of a new play, with the exception that their behaviour in the theatre is much more decorous than their conduct in the Assize Court."

The ticketed spectators arrived at around ten, munching on their breakfast, and jostled their way inside when the doors opened. Lawyers eager to witness the proceedings were required to come dressed in their legal robes and ready to prove they weren't ordinary citizens masquerading to steal a seat. Journalists settled on their benches next to the dock, along with the sketch artists, pads in hand. There was standing room at the back for the riffraff, packed in shoulder to shoulder, unwashed, stinking of sweat and onions.

In front of the judge's dais stood the evidence table, a sight certain to sober jovial spirits. There lay the revolver seized from Eyraud in Havana, his suitcases, Gouffé's silk hat that Eyraud mistook for his own, the Turkish robe, the red silk *cordelière*. The notorious trunk also was present, covered in a yellow cloth. The wooden table's long history was evident in its scratched surface, as a journalist put it: "What countless vials of vitriol, revolvers and knives, blood-stained garments, from satin dresses to workmen's blouses and ladies' corsets, have been piled up in this Morgue for things inanimate!"

At 11:45, Judge Robert entered and summoned the twelve jurors one by one, who took their seats in the box. The lawyers for the defense, Félix Decori, representing Eyraud, and Henri Robert, Gabrielle's counsel, strode across the courtroom in their robes and caps. Along with them came the lawyer Albert Danet, known in the halls of justice as "honeyed, persuasive, irresistible," who represented Gouffé's daughters as civil parties in the case.

Appearing for the state was France's renowned chief prosecutor, Jules Quesnay de Beaurepaire, who took on the case not just because of its notoriety but because a forceful closing statement rebutting the unprecedented hypnotism defense required a man of his prominence. Quesnay de Beaurepaire was a fifty-two-year-old legal lion and man of letters who wrote stories of French peasant life. His was a family of high ambitions: His great-grandfather bought the estates of Beaurepaire and Glouvet from the Marquise de Pompadour and adopted the name Beaurepaire for an aura of nobility. Quesnay de Beaurepaire was a devotee of Napoleon III until his downfall; then he switched allegiance to the Third Republic. He moved in elite circles and was known for taking on the toughest cases, most often the ones that posed a threat to the Republic; his latest claim to fame was the prosecution in absentia of Georges Boulanger, the rebellious general and potential leader of a coup d'état who had fled the country a year earlier. Although a bit frail on his feet, Quesnay de Beaurepaire was given to grand theatrical gestures. He had a bony, clean-shaven face and a mocking eye. Adorned in his red robe, he wore his legal cap tilted toward the back of his head in a jaunty, collegiate flourish. A man of unsurpassed eminence in the courtroom, Quesnay de Beaurepaire was one of the chief reasons lawyers in robes fought for a seat on the spectator bench.

Now the stage was set for the entrance of the leading players. There was a stirring as a door in the courtroom wall was opened. Someone cried out: *"Les voici!"* (There they are!) In a scuffling of heels everyone shot to their feet, and those who had their views blocked by ornate female hats cried out: *"Assis! Assis!"* (Sit down! Sit down!)

The first defendant to make an appearance was Michel Eyraud, looking large and powerful in a black frock coat. His thick mustache and short hair were neatly groomed. Holding his hat in his hand, he cast his eyes on the packed courtroom then looked away.

When Gabrielle Bompard stepped into the doorway a melee broke out as spectators fought for a glimpse, sending the bailiffs rushing forward. Judge Robert, seeing his court personnel outmanned, exclaimed: "But we're missing a bailiff here!"

The irony wasn't lost on the crowd—and laughter erupted as someone hollered: "For sure!"

Once order was restored, Gabrielle was led in wearing a black dress with a dotted veil, a winter coat, gloves with four buttons, and a close-fitting round hat with otter trim. She looked out at the courtroom, then lowered her head and was escorted to the dock. Eyraud, who was already there, separated by a wooden partition, threw "a furtive, hateful look her way," according to one report. The judge ordered Gabrielle to lift the veil and keep her face visible at all times.

The proceedings began with a reading of the charges. Michel Eyraud and Gabrielle Bompard were accused of committing voluntary homicide in the death of Toussaint-Augustin Gouffé on July 26, 1889, with premeditation. The homicide also involved acts of ambush and robbery. Although the charges were already fully known, Eyraud made a show of listening attentively, while Gabrielle dabbed a handkerchief to her eyes and was heard to sob.

The theater of the streets had come indoors: The actors knew their roles, though their lines were unscripted. And the setting—this temple of justice where Christ gazed down from a massive wood cross on the paneled wall—promised God's judgment, both solemn and majestic. While the stakes could not have been higher for the accused, the spectators decked out in all their finery settled in to be entertained. "To imagine the Assize," a later court observer wrote, "let us choose a day when a crime célèbre is being tried; on such days, when the Parisian Court session is invaded by the public, the dominant note . . . is gaiety."

Judge Robert, the president of the court, began by laying out the case against the defendants, a proceeding that typically mocks, and even demeans, the accused. "The defendant is immediately put upon his defense," an American legal scholar wrote, describing the difference between U.S. and French legal procedure at the time. "The reasoning is that the defendant having reached the Cour d'Assises must explain why he is in court." The judge uses the opening examination to set the tone for the trial, exposing to the jury the facts in the dossier; it was a presentation known to be "usually long, involved, minute . . . one-sided" and "highly prejudicial." Americans took a withering view of French judicial procedures, which were an affront to the honored premise in the United States that a defendant was innocent until proven guilty. Writing in 1891, *The Washington Post* noted that the French "president of the court, instead of being . . . prepared to hold the scales of justice impartially between the prisoner and the state, has informed himself of the charges in advance, and with his mind apparently made up that the prisoner is guilty, proceeds to get the jury into a similar frame of mind. He virtually acts as coadjutor in the prosecution."

Judge Robert chose to present evidence against Eyraud first; so Gabrielle, who was not invited to witness it, was escorted out of the courtroom. The judge began with a review of Eyraud's past, painting it in the harshest possible light. He enumerated the defendant's shady business and private dealings: the distillery in Sèvres, the theft of funds from Fribourg & Cie, his failure to pay a Paris jeweler for a ring and earrings, his violent streak.

"All this pales next to the crime I'm blamed for," Eyraud commented sensibly.

A murmuring throughout the courtroom suggested that the spectators agreed with him, and the judge was wasting his time on trivialities.

"I bring it up," the judge retorted, "to show what kind of man you are and how you graduated to murder."

To demonstrate the depth of Eyraud's brutality, Judge Robert asked if he wasn't violent even toward his own mother, and then he described his attempt to extort money from her on the pretext of saving the family vineyard.

"That's slander!" Eyraud cried.

The accused acknowledged that he'd had a hand in a crime, and he was prepared to accept the consequences. But, he demanded, "I don't want anyone discussing my past."

"That's a very arrogant position," the judge warned him.

Although Eyraud was reviled as a brutal strangler, most important to him was protecting scraps of his imagined reputation. "I will defend my past," he asserted.

Judge Robert charged that Eyraud had corrupted Gabrielle, an allegation more rhetorical than factual; the subtleties of truth were dismissed as the judge sought to fashion a thoroughly reprehensible image of Eyraud for the jury. In a French trial, the judge, defendants, and witnesses were all permitted to speak more freely than they were in an American court; attorneys, however, had no recourse to correct erroneous or misleading statements either through objections or cross-examinations, the result being an imperfect, messy journey toward justice.

Drawing on the dossier, the judge asserted that Gabrielle had met Eyraud when she went to his office at Fribourg & Cie looking for work.

"No, I met her on the boulevard," Eyraud countered, implying that she was a woman of loose morals offering herself on the street. He added: "I will prove it." Here was the con man at work. He would say anything, float any proposition, in the hope that it would stick— that it would influence the jury.

"It's a minor point," the judge said dismissively. What was important, he continued, was that she became Eyraud's mistress and that he introduced her to his degenerate lifestyle; he took her to disreputable places and even turned her into a prostitute to collect the cash. "You robbed her of her morals to the point where this girl, who still had a certain discretion, who still was chaste enough in her language, began to express herself in such obscene terms that some women, even those who were not themselves virtuous, completely broke off with her."

"That's false."

The judge retorted that Gabrielle entertained numerous lovers for pay and that Eyraud lived off the proceeds.

"That's slander!" Eyraud charged.

Amid these exchanges, a juror suddenly fell ill, causing a small commotion in the jurors' box and forcing the judge to declare a brief recess.

When court resumed just before 3:00 p.m., Judge Robert reminded the jury that by June 1889, Eyraud had fled in disgrace from Fribourg & Cie and no longer had any means of income, ill-gotten or not.

"Didn't you often have the intention of killing someone to procure money for yourself?" he prodded.

"Never."

"Who had the idea of extortion, blackmail, and murder?"

"That's Gabrielle Bompard."

Eyraud told the court that at first Gabrielle devised a robbery plot. She had her sights set on a very rich gentleman she knew, a jeweler reputed always to have a fat wallet on him and pockets full of jewels. "I was shocked," Eyraud said. "But she insisted. One night we had a violent discussion and I had no choice except to hit her to make her stop talking." But she wouldn't drop it, Eyraud insisted; she talked incessantly about finding someone rich to rob so Eyraud could pay off his debts and the couple could flee to Argentina and live a tranquil life. "She said it so much I finally agreed," he explained.

Although they hadn't yet decided on a victim, they plotted their method of attack. "She spoke to me of a rope that we would pass through a pulley," Eyraud said. "I would only have to pull on it." He described the trip to London, shopping for fabric for a sack, the purchase of a *cordelière,* then, back in Paris, renting the apartment at 3, rue Tronson du Coudray. "One night, Gabrielle said to me, 'Your friend Gouffé is rich. He has a lot of money. He gives lots of money to women!'" Eyraud claimed that he didn't know Gouffé was rich but he asked around and discovered that the bailiff was indeed quite wealthy. On July 26, Eyraud nailed the pulley into the ceiling crossbeam. "Then Gabrielle set out to trap Gouffé. She encountered him on the boulevard and set a rendezvous for that night at eight." Eyraud left out his role in the entrapment. Gabrielle had explained her version to Dopffer, that Eyraud's strategy was to purposely bump into Gouffé and tell him he'd ended things with Gabrielle and urge him to see her, and then to position Gabrielle on the boulevard so she, too, would bump into Gouffé moments later to confirm the breakup and invite him to the apartment that evening.

At eight fifteen Gouffé entered the apartment and, according to Eyraud, told Gabrielle, "You have a very pretty little nest."

The judge wanted to know if Gabrielle then sat on Gouffé's lap.

"Yes. He kissed her."

"And he fondled her more or less?"

The judge's high-pitched voice posing a salacious question like that in a solemn setting like this was too much for the crowd. There was an outburst of laughter, which caused the judge to flare with anger. "In a case of this gravity," he scolded the courtroom in his soprano pitch, "I do not understand the attitude of the public. If this reaction occurs again," he warned, his voice undermining his authority, "I will have the room evacuated." Then he went right back to his bawdy line of inquiry: "He fondled her?"

"Yes," Eyraud said. "He kissed her on the face."

"And then?" the judge asked.

"No, sir, just on the face."

The judge wouldn't let it go: "He at least began to open her dressing gown?"

"Yes, Mr. President," Eyraud acknowledged.

The plan, the suspect maintained, was just to frighten Gouffé: toss the *cordelière* over his head and give a tug on the rope to ensure he knew they meant business. The killers intended only to hide him in the apartment while his family delivered money to a location Gouffé was to designate in a letter. But as the plot moved forward, it swung out of control. The *cordelière* was on Gouffé's neck and Eyraud pulled down on the rope. "I looked through the curtain," he said, "and unfortunately the accident had happened. I found I was in the presence of an inanimate body. I slapped his hands. I blew on his face. Nothing there. No one there. I was shattered. I cried."

But, the judge reminded him, his anguish didn't prevent him

from running off to Gouffé's office and rummaging in the dark with lighted matches on a blind hunt for cash. "Perhaps you had planned on extortion," he said. "But then you changed your mind and decided to murder him and then rob his office."

"Not at all," Eyraud pushed back. "I was very agitated. I went back to rue Tronson du Coudray and I said to Gabrielle, 'We're lost!' I wanted to blow my brains out. I drank a bottle of cognac. But I wasn't tipsy enough. So I drank a bottle of champagne." Eyraud failed to mention that Gabrielle claimed he raped her that night. Instead, he said of his drinking binge, "I needed to give myself courage. I had never touched a dead person in my life."

The judge asked about the diamond-and-sapphire ring Eyraud stripped from the victim's pinkie. "What did you do with the diamonds?"

"Gabrielle had them made into a pair of earrings."

"What happened to the earrings?"

"They were left in San Francisco," the accused said, "in a pawnshop, as I recall."

The judge then pointed out other evidence indicating not accidental murder but premeditation: the existence of the oilcloth that went over the corpse's head, the giant sack the size of a man sewn by Gabrielle, and the trunk. He asked cynically if these materials were bought in anticipation of an accident.

"In preparation for a possible accident, yes," Eyraud replied. "But I was convinced I wouldn't make use of them."

"So, all was ready in preparation for a murder," the judge concluded.

Jurors had a look at photographs of the murder scene at rue Tronson du Coudray. Then Judge Robert took the red *cordelière* from the evidence table—it was not the sash used in the killing but a similar one purchased in London at the same store as the original. The judge instructed Eyraud to show the jury how he transformed it for use in the killing. The defendant obliged willingly, with foolish pride—his thick fingers working coolly and swiftly, turning the silk cord into a noose.

Watching Eyraud in court Jaume couldn't help being impressed by his performance. "He is energetic, lucid and crafty," the inspector wrote. "Eyraud is no longer abject. But he is not yet sympathetic.

He could not be. He has no physical beauty, no youth." In Jaume's estimation, Eyraud lacked an important poetic quality, something that Gabrielle possessed. He was all too real, his degenerate brutality was an ugly fact, while Gabrielle was chimera-like, impossible to fully behold; she was seen through a gauze of mystery like a heroine in a novel. Eyraud was easy to hate. Gabrielle, by contrast, was an object of wonder.

Chapter 43

The judge declared: "Bring back Gabrielle Bompard."

The door in the wall opened and there stood the little demon in her simple black dress. There was a murmuring, an alertness, from the press on the benches in front all the way to the riffraff standing in back as she was led across the floor and seated in the dock.

Judge Robert agreed with the conclusions of the dossier: Gabrielle was guilty of the murder, her responsibility was as absolute as Eyraud's, and there was no reason to impose extenuating circumstances because of the influence of hypnotism or mental instability. The judge's examination of Gabrielle took the shape of a prolonged accusation intended to convey his position to the jury. He recited the facts of her life, her birth in Lille in 1868, her father's wealth, her mother's death, her boarding with her uncle in Belgium, her residence in a variety of convents.

"Everywhere it was observed that you had a rare intelligence but at the same time you were very vicious. Is this true?"

Gabrielle ignored the question, or perhaps wasn't listening. She seemed a million miles away, barely engaged in these proceedings which held her life in the balance.

"Answer," the judge demanded. "You know very well how to speak when you want."

She maintained a surly silence and looked bored. Her stubbornness would not play well with the jury. In a French court, a defendant had to show an effort to defend herself or risk appearing all the more guilty. If Eyraud lost sympathy because of his hostility, Gabrielle sank in the eyes of the jury because of her sullenness, her unwillingness to fight for herself.

The judge prodded her again: "Your conduct was such that your father had to send you to a convent for delinquent girls. Your vicious behavior was commented upon there as it was everywhere. Is this true?"

Finally she spoke in a soft, reluctant voice: "Yes, Mr. President."

"You returned to your father's home and he wanted to put you to work. But the work bored you and you passed your time reading novels."

"I was never happy at my father's home," she replied. "I do not want to talk about that chapter of my life."

The judge moved on to her departure from home, her arrival in Paris, her rapid squandering of her money, and her appearance before Eyraud at Fribourg & Cie in search of a job.

"Almost immediately you became his mistress."

"Yes, sir."

"How could you have stayed with him, a man of forty-nine and you—you were only twenty?"

"Misery makes you do many things."

"You know Eyraud claims he encountered you on the boulevard."

"That's false."

Eyraud shouted from the dock: "The dossier contains convincing proof the Bompard girl does not speak the truth."

Ignoring the interruption, the judge mentioned Gabrielle's beatings by Eyraud. "If he beat you, why didn't you leave him?"

"I don't know," she answered. "I couldn't."

"Eyraud claims it's he who couldn't separate from you."

This seemed preposterous to Gabrielle. "What influence could I have had on him?"

The judge offered his jaundiced view: "You wouldn't be the first woman who had the power to exert an influence."

"What would you have liked me to do?" Gabrielle asked. "Take up with another man?"

To which the judge replied, "That wouldn't have bothered you much."

The interrogation jumped to the murderers' activities in London: the purchase of the trunk, the *cordelière,* the rope, the large pieces of fabric.

"He had me make a sack without telling me what it was for," Gabrielle said.

"How could you—who are so intelligent—how could you make this large sack destined to contain a man who is five feet nine inches tall without asking what this could be used for?"

Gabrielle replied with stony indifference: "I didn't ask him why it was made and he didn't tell me."

"You don't habitually make sacks," the judge pressed. "Eyraud doesn't usually use them, and you didn't ask for any explanation?"

"I would have been beaten," she explained.

Judge Robert didn't understand how Gabrielle could have rented the apartment on rue Tronson du Coudray if she and Eyraud were pressed for money. She ignored the financial question and merely suggested she was sleepwalking at the time.

"I had only to obey," she said. "Eyraud wanted it."

"But this does not explain it," the judge reasoned. "This was a man who did not have money."

"I could only obey," Gabrielle repeated. "He would have killed me if I had questioned him."

"When did you first become aware of this planned crime?"

She knew nothing until the day it took place: Friday. "He told me: 'If Gouffé doesn't give me money, I'm going to hang him.' That made me laugh a lot. I found it very funny. I couldn't believe he was serious."

"When Gouffé arrived, what did he say to you?"

"He said, 'Hello, little demon!'"

"Wasn't that the moment to tell him he was in great danger? You knew that Eyraud wanted to hang him."

Alerting Gouffé was impossible, for Eyraud was within earshot behind the curtain. "If I said a word, he would have come out. I didn't dare."

"There was a chaise longue," the judge said, urging her to go on.

But suddenly, as she approached the moment of the killing, Gabrielle seemed to have drifted away. "Ah, yes," she said.

"He lay down?"

Her mind was somewhere else. "I think he sat down."

"You were very close to him or far from him?"

She was lost now. "I don't know."

"You were not sitting on his lap?"

"No."

"He didn't kiss you?"

"No."

"You didn't have a *cordelière* around your body?"

The judge might have asked her anything—her answer would have been the same.

"No," she said.

"What did you say to him?"

"I don't know." After several moments, she said, "I'm lost in all this." Her voice was aloof, her eyes had gone blank, she was unreachable.

Was this a calculated act? Was she performing for the jury? Or was she losing touch with reality? Was her mind melting?

Judge Robert again asked about her actions just prior to the murder, when she was entertaining Gouffé. But she ignored the questions and skipped to the final moment.

"Gouffé found himself face-to-face with Eyraud," she said, then added with coolness: "It's at this moment he strangled him."

"What did you do?"

"When Eyraud seized Gouffé, I let out a cry."

"You were only a witness, you didn't play any part."

"None."

The judge contradicted her: "That's really unlikely or very implausible. If things happened like this, Gouffé would have had time to cry out. He could have been heard. He could have thrown himself against the window and called for help. Things could not have happened the way you say. The passersby would have heard."

"Passersby on a deserted street?"

"People taking in the cool air in their doorways. We are in the month of July. It was very hot."

"I cannot tell you anything but what I know," Gabrielle replied. "Wasn't I the one who first told you the story of the pulley? And you told me that I was mad."

"Not at all," the judge said. "No one said that to you."

"Oh yes, the investigating judge told me I'd read all this in a novel. He even cited the page to me."

"The truth," Judge Robert asserted, "is that it was you who organized everything. You prepared the crime."

"How? Do you think that if I'd been free, I'd have stayed there?"

An odd laugh fluttered out of her, and she said, as if responding to something in her head: "No, not that!"

"Gouffé dies," the judge went on. "What happens then?"

"He undressed him, tied him up, put him in the sack, pushing him into it as if putting on a glove."

"Eyraud claims you helped him in this job."

"In that?" Again, she shuddered and gave an odd laugh.

"He also remembers this: Gouffé seemed to have opened his eyes in the midst of all this. And you said, 'Take care—he'll recognize us. Finish him!'"

"Me?" Gabrielle scoffed. "That's something I'd have said? It's the first I ever heard of it."

"What's the point? Why would he say it if it's not true?"

"Because I betrayed him," she said angrily. Then, with indifference: "It doesn't matter. It's all the same to me."

"Really? When the guillotine is waiting?"

"Oh, I assure you. Yes, it's all the same to me."

The judge pressed Gabrielle on why she stayed with the cadaver after Eyraud departed for the night. If she were innocent, as she claimed, she could have fled. "You could have placed yourself under the protection of the police."

"I could not."

"Why?"

"I don't know. I couldn't." Was she implying she had lost the will to act on her own? "If there had been a whole regiment there, I could not have been able to run away."

The judged changed direction. "You're vague about Eyraud's role. How did he throw the *cordelière* over Gouffé's head?"

"I don't know."

"How'd he do it?"

"Gouffé turned around," she said. "He recognized him. So Eyraud strangled him."

"And Gouffé didn't say one word?"

"No, not one."

"But, still, how did Eyraud throw the *cordelière* over him?"

"I told you everything I know. To me, Gouffé was not hanged. He was strangled."

Surprisingly, Eyraud kept silent.

Judge Robert called a twenty-minute recess, then questioned Eyraud again, keeping Gabrielle in the courtroom this time. The judge went through the disposal of the body, the sojourn in Marseille with Eyraud's brother Jean-Baptiste, the return to Paris, and the defendants' departure from France. He moved on to their introduction to Georges Garanger in Vancouver.

"You had the idea of exploiting Mr. Garanger?" the judge said.

"Never."

"What did you do in San Francisco?"

Eyraud, still the con man, rattled off a series of lies. "I wanted to start a business," he told the courtroom, though everyone already knew the fraudulent nature of that ambition. "Garanger followed me everywhere. He told me, 'I am a gentleman. Have confidence in me. I've just made a trip to Indochina to guarantee French interests there.' That's when he asked me for Gabrielle's hand in marriage. I wanted to say to him that she is not my daughter but my mistress."

"Stop there," the judge instructed Eyraud. Turning to Gabrielle, he said, "Recount the facts for us as you remember them."

Gabrielle described their hasty retreat from France, her dressing as a boy with her hair cut short, their meeting Garanger in Vancouver and his arrival in San Francisco. "He was with us almost every day," she told the judge. "And then Eyraud said to me, 'I don't have any more money. Garanger has ten thousand francs on him. I'm going to lure him outside of San Francisco and kill him.' I was absolutely opposed to this and I told him, 'Rob him if you want, but I don't want you to kill him.' I was afraid he was going to do something."

So she followed them everywhere; she didn't want Garanger to be alone with Eyraud. And once, when Gabrielle and Eyraud were alone, he became enraged. "Now you're going to have your turn," Gabrielle said he told her. "He tried to force a bottle of chloroform into my mouth but I got away from him."

She described leaving with Garanger and being free of Eyraud. "I laughed a lot. I was so happy to escape him finally." And in Paris she went to the prefect of police.

"What did you tell the prefect?" the judge asked.

"I don't remember. All I know is that my story was not completely true."

"If only all of it wasn't true!" the judge offered dramatically.

"It's all so tangled," she said simply.

"Eyraud," the judge said, "you've heard all this. What do you have to say?"

"I never intended to murder Garanger."

For the jury's benefit, the judge then had Eyraud recount his life alone on the run from San Francisco to Mexico to Havana and then his capture. By the time Eyraud ended his tale the courtroom was darkening.

The judge recapped, turning to Eyraud: "So, according to you, the crime was inspired by Gabrielle Bompard."

"Yes, sir."

"At first you resisted, then you yielded, and the two of you participated together."

"Yes, Mr. President."

"The woman Bompard," the judge said, turning toward Gabrielle, "do you have any further explanation?"

"No, Mr. President."

Judge Robert closed the session at 5:45 p.m., and the crowd, sated on the spectacle, filed out into the subfreezing evening.

Chapter 44

The deep chill eased a little overnight, but a wicked hailstorm in the morning sent the crowd outside the courthouse dashing for cover. When the doors finally opened, ticket holders bolted inside, pushing and shoving to claim their seats.

The scheduled witnesses were mostly bit players, except for Georges Garanger, who was to reveal his own role in the sordid affair. The gossipmongers wondered how Eyraud—and Gabrielle—would react to the sight of the dignified gentleman. Did Eyraud still harbor a murderous vengeance for him? Was Gabrielle still in love with him and might she swoon, or collapse in a hysterical attack?

She looked very pale as she made her entrance.

The witness parade began with Louis-Marie Landry, who recounted the disappearance of his brother-in-law. Georges Fribourg, the thirty-two-year-old son of the owner of Fribourg & Cie, denounced Eyraud for appropriating company funds for his private use; he produced a letter in which Eyraud threatened the elder Fribourg: "I am ready to prove to you that I can mete out my own kind of justice." An eighteen-year-old locksmith named Edmond Gentil from a shop on rue Saint-Jean said he repaired the trunk on July 26, 1889, the day of the crime. "I put metal bands under the bottom of it to strengthen it," he told the court.

Judge Robert taunted Eyraud: "This was in case of what you have called an accident?"

"Yes," Eyraud replied. "The bottom was weak."

After a half-hour recess, Nicolas Demange, the fifty-nine-year-old husband of the concierge at 3, rue Tronson du Coudray, took the stand in place of his wife, who handled most of the duties at the site but was ill. As Demange settled in, it was apparent to everyone that he was a clumsy, witless oaf, and before the judge could ask him anything he blurted out: "I know absolutely nothing." When Judge Robert stated the obvious—"We know that"—the courtroom burst into laughter. Under questioning, Demange flubbed up the layout of the apartment, prompting Gabrielle to jump in: "It's not like that. I think you should have a look." His idiocy brought a rare moment of agreement between the two accomplices, with Eyraud defending Gabrielle: "I believe Gabrielle Bompard is right on this point."

Denis Coffy, the road mender in Millery, described finding the corpse at the foot of an acacia bush: "I nearly suffocated at that moment." And Alphonse Richard, a thirty-six-year-old day farmer, declared proudly: "It is I who found the trunk."

At last, the adventurer-businessman Georges Garanger, who had managed to keep out of the limelight throughout the investigation, strode toward the witness stand. He was a handsome forty-six-year-old with a strong neck, cheerful face, and red beard trimmed to a point, although one newspaper commented that "his peregrinations around the world have left him prematurely fatigued." He had a wealthy, well-fed look, a roundness of the body. Gabrielle glanced at him, then covered her face with a handkerchief.

Garanger spoke in a monotone, his sober voice drained of any emotion as he recounted meeting Eyraud and Gabrielle and believing that they were E. B. Vanaerd and his daughter Berthe. He spoke of signing a business contract with Vanaerd and of learning later that Vanaerd was Eyraud and that the proposed business was a fraud. He said he gave Eyraud five thousand francs before he and Gabrielle set off together for France, money Eyraud swindled from him.

Judge Robert, turning to Eyraud, said, "What do you have to say to this?"

"I absolutely deny having received five thousand francs from Mr. Garanger." Eyraud challenged Garanger to produce a receipt for the money.

"I told him it wasn't necessary," Garanger explained, "because we were in business together."

Eyraud volleyed back: "Mr. Garanger is not a man to give five thousand francs in the first place without getting a receipt."

Garanger sensibly asked, "Can the witness say how he was able to live in San Francisco without my money?"

Eyraud ignored the question and accused Garanger of trying to swindle his brother-in-law in Paris out of the five thousand francs for a bogus repayment.

Gabrielle, unable to watch the confrontation between her lovers, put her head down and chewed on her handkerchief.

The prosecutor Quesnay de Beaurepaire pressed Eyraud: "You did not answer the question the witness posed to you. How did you live in San Francisco, if it was not with his money?"

"I had arrived in San Francisco with three hundred francs," Eyraud said.

Gabrielle suddenly looked up and shouted, "He had fifteen francs in his pocket!"

"When Mr. Garanger says I swindled him of five thousand francs, that's slander," Eyraud cried.

Gabrielle shouted, "We constantly lived on the money from Garanger. He does not want to admit it, but that's the truth."

Garanger interjected that Eyraud only wanted to harm him in every possible way. "Everything he said is a fabric of lies."

"The slander is on your part," Eyraud shot back. "You told the newspapers I wanted to kill you."

"I never said anything to the newspapers."

Eyraud was in a rage, "furious at the witness," *Le Figaro* said, adding wryly: "If he were free, he'd have thrown himself on him to eat his nose."

Judge Robert incited passions further. "Eyraud," he said, "the truth is that you never forgave Mr. Garanger for taking Gabrielle Bompard from you."

At that, Gabrielle shrieked: "He did not take me!" She threw her arms into the air. "It is I who left with—" Whatever she said after that was drowned out by thunderous laughter.

Eyraud, sensing her fragile state, gave her a push. "Mr. Garanger," he said, "would you like to comment on Gabrielle's mental condition?"

"My mental condition!" she cried. "I took a carriage and I went to the prefecture—and voilà!"

After two days in the dock, swinging between frenzy and apathy, Gabrielle now plunged over the cliff. She waved her arms, cried out hoarsely, and stamped her feet until she fell backward and came to rest in a catatonic state on the floor behind the bench. A guard swooped in and lifted the childlike figure in his arms. Pandemonium broke out in the courtroom as spectators climbed on their seats, straining for a look. Suddenly she came alive and cried out hysterically: "Oh Michel! Michel! Don't kill me! Don't kill me!" Doctors rushed to her, one administering ether while another unlaced her clothing, and she was carried from the courtroom.

In America, these theatrics left newspaper readers puzzled. Comparing courtroom conduct in the two nations, the *San Francisco Chronicle* wrote that there were many more opportunities for dramatics in a French proceeding. "One defendant is allowed to contradict the other in court, and even to terrify her into hysterics, and it is all considered as proper and tending to further the ends of justice. It may be that the system is more effectual, but it is revolting to our ideas."

After a half-hour recess, Gabrielle reappeared, without her hat, her hair in disarray. She had a lace wrap around her shoulders. Her face was drawn, her skin pale. The courtroom physician, Dr. Floquet, sat at her side in the dock for the duration of the session.

When court resumed, her lawyer, Henri Robert, had a question for Garanger, playing off her display of hysteria in front of the jury.

"Mr. Garanger," he began, "didn't you often put Gabrielle Bompard to sleep? Wasn't she a very remarkable subject for hypnotism?"

"That's correct," Garanger said.

The lawyer then sought to establish a crucial fact: that Gabrielle was so extraordinarily sensitive to hypnosis that even someone with little experience as a hypnotist could induce a deep trance in her and take possession of her will. He asked the witness, "Do you have expertise in matters of hypnotism?"

Giving the jury something to ponder, Garanger replied, "I don't know anything at all."

Chapter 45

On day three, snowflakes drifted out of a gloomy sky, blocks of ice clogged the Seine, and snow-draped construction sites were shut down. Some twelve thousand masons trudged home, temporarily out of work. It was such a dreary day that Judge Robert ordered the gas lamps in the courtroom to be fully lighted. In the press gallery, journalists hovered over candles in their inkwells. "The line of flickering lights gave the press bench the aura of a small chapel," one scribe wrote.

In the dock Gabrielle sat almost motionless. From time to time she stirred and kneaded her handkerchief in her fingers then resumed her passivity, looking almost lifeless.

The session opened at eleven forty-five, but then Judge Robert immediately halted it when he realized the jury chief was absent. Fifteen minutes later, the missing juror climbed into the box. This was the day for the "princes of science," as they were known: the doctors who investigated Gabrielle's mental state, the medical examiners who studied the corpse, and the Bompard family physician who knew Gabrielle before her slide into crime.

Before the scientists, however, came another parade of ordinary witnesses. In its edition that morning *Le Figaro* had already lamented the previous day's procession: "Thirty witnesses," the paper complained, "one more insipid than the next. This Gouffé case is so worn out that at each new deposition, one wants to cry out: 'Move on then! It's already known.'"

Heedless of the complaint, the court introduced a stream of fresh witnesses, including Léon Darras, a workman who told the court that Eyraud once boasted to him: "If someone bothers me, I'd open his stomach like a dog's." And there was Joseph Taurel, a forty-year-old acquaintance of Eyraud's in America who gave the weary audience a moment of mirth at his own expense. When the judge asked him if Eyraud chased women, Taurel replied, "That I cannot tell you, having never had relations with a woman myself."

A friend of Eyraud's cast doubt on Gabrielle's truthfulness. In a deposition read to the court in his absence, a hypnotist named Risler claimed he regularly put Gabrielle into a trance at the Paris salon of Madame Marmier. "Gabrielle Bompard had some very bad habits," he said in the document. "There was more: she was a liar."

Judge Robert asked Gabrielle: "Did Risler put you to sleep?"

"Yes," she answered.

Then the judge zeroed in on the key question. "Did Eyraud put you to sleep?"

"I don't know," she said.

"Did he try?"

"I don't know."

"During the investigation, you said he tried and he couldn't."

"All right then," she said testily. "No, he was not able to put me to sleep."

Her answer was baffling. Did Gabrielle just purposely shatter her own defense? Did she even realize what she did and, if so, why would she sabotage herself? Had her mind become so weak that she would send herself to the guillotine? During her pretrial interrogation she often admitted to what she thought investigators wanted her to confess just so they'd leave her alone. She may have wanted to put an end to questioning on a subject for which she simply didn't have an answer. It was possible, in fact, that she didn't know whether Eyraud ever succeeded in hypnotizing her. If he did put her into a trance he could have planted a posthypnotic suggestion that wiped out her memory of the experience afterward. So she could truthfully have had no recollection of having been hypnotized even though it might very well have occurred. What seemed a crippling admission was in fact evidence that could save her. Her attorney, Henri Robert, only had to assert that she had participated in the murder in a hypnotic trance but didn't have a clear recollection of it because of a posthypnotic suggestion. This reasoning bolstered the argument that she was unconscious of her actions, that she had surrendered her will to Eyraud and therefore had no responsibility in the commission of the crime.

Dr. Alexandre Lacassagne, the forensic medical expert in Lyon who teased Gouffé's identity out of the rotted cadaver, took the stand. "Dr. Lacassagne," inquired Henri Robert, "did you not observe lesions in the area of the neck? Did they come, in your opinion, from strangulation produced with a rope or with the hand?"

Henri Robert asked that the *cordelière* be placed in Dr. Lacassagne's hands.

"I repeat," said Lacassagne through his bushy mustache, "that these lesions were caused by the act of the pressing of some fingers."

The judge turned to Eyraud. "Did you grab the victim by the throat?"

"No," Eyraud said.

Albert Danet, Gouffé's daughters' attorney, requested that Gabrielle be invited to explain what happened. She repeated what she had said earlier, adding that Eyraud threw Gouffé to the floor and put a knee on his stomach and strangled him.

"Where were you?" Danet asked Gabrielle.

"Right next to the table."

"He grabbed him, you say," the judge asked. "How?"

"I don't know," Gabrielle replied with annoyance. "He threw him down and strangled him. I was terrified!"

Eyraud leaped up. "In another deposition," he asserted, "Gabrielle said I put the cord around Gouffé's neck."

"I never said that," she snapped.

"She said it," Eyraud insisted. "I will indicate the passage for you."

Félix Decori, Eyraud's attorney, thumbed through a stack of papers.

Gabrielle's lawyer, Henri Robert, came to her defense: "A nervous and impressionable woman could not have had the presence of mind to remember all the details from a scene like that."

"I ask the doctor," Eyraud said, turning to Lacassagne, "how long does it take to strangle a man like Gouffé?"

"Sometimes it only takes a very short time," Lacassagne offered. "A simple pressure on the neck, even light and momentary, could be enough."

Decori found the passage from Gabrielle's deposition and read it into the record. His role was to defend Eyraud, but the passage he read damned his client. Gabrielle had testified that Eyraud came out of hiding and put the *cordelière* around Gouffé's neck. But Gouffé was not hanged, she said. "Eyraud gave up hanging Gouffé. He dropped the rope and grabbed him by the neck and strangled him. Monsieur Gouffé neither spoke a word nor uttered a cry. It was done very quickly. It did not last more than two seconds. *I* was in the corner of the room, terrified." No one seemed to notice that this testimony conflicted with other statements Gabrielle had made. She had also said that Eyraud strangled Gouffé after the pulley collapsed and the two men dropped to the floor.

Amid the confusion of the proceedings, spectators welcomed the occasional slide into slapstick. As Paul Bernard, the thirty-one-year-old medical examiner from Lyon, testified, Judge Robert ordered that the sack that once contained Gouffé's decomposed body be put on display for the jury. A courtroom porter went to the evidence table, opened a sealed bag, and pulled out the soiled burlap sack. Immediately, a ghastly stench—the same misery that overwhelmed the small town of Millery—spread throughout the courtroom. Amid the groaning and blatant discomfort, the judge sensibly advised the jurors not to breathe too deeply, causing a burst of laughter. After a few moments, the judge instructed the porter to stuff the murder sack back into the bag and seal it up again. He then invited the poor man to leave the room to wash his hands, and the room again burst into laughter.

Chapter 46

Dr. Paul Brouardel knew more than anybody about the personal life and criminal instincts of Gabrielle Bompard. He and doctors Auguste Motet and Gilbert Ballet had conducted a months-long medical examination to assess her motives, her susceptibility to hypnosis, her criminal responsibility. Brouardel began his presentation to the court by summarizing his conclusions, although they were already well-known to everyone in attendance. The doctor's report, which was never meant to be published, found its way into the newspapers and became the subject of dinner conversation in Paris.

As Brouardel revealed intimate details of her personal life, Gabrielle hid her head in her hands. He reminded the jurors of her birth in Lille, her childhood spent in a series of convents, her early obesity, her slimming down by age seventeen, her tiny stature. He noted that she reached puberty at a very young age: "She became a woman at an age that one almost never is, at eight."

The audience listened in rapt silence.

Brouardel found that Gabrielle had no hereditary predisposition for crime and admitted that she had an extraordinary intelligence but also a tendency toward amoral behavior.

"From another point of view," he explained, "we found that she was incontestably a hysteric."

Now he had crept to the edge of the hypnotism debate. Using Charcot as his guide, Brouardel told the courtroom he had concluded that Gabrielle was not a grand hysteric but rather subject to small attacks of nerves. This was an important distinction. If she were a grand hysteric, along the lines of the women locked up at the Salpêtrière Hospital, she would also be prone to episodes of grand hypnotism—raising the possibility that she could be induced to act in almost any way while in a trance. A diagnosis of grand hysteria would have supported the defense's argument that Gabrielle could have been under a hypnotist's control when she participated in the murder.

Brouardel was firmly on the side of the prosecution; he appeared as an expert witness not to pronounce objectively on Gabrielle's mental condition but to help build the case against her and ensure the failure of the hypnotism defense. He, therefore, needed to demolish the contentions of the Nancy school, so he went after its leader, Dr. Hippolyte Bernheim, telling the jury: "The day after we finished our exam, we read an interview with Dr. Bernheim in the journal *Hypnotism* in which he declared that this young woman, whom he had never seen, had certainly acted under the influence of hypnotism. We were therefore obliged to examine her from this point of view." Brouardel and his associates hypnotized Gabrielle, and the sessions proved to him that she was only a *petite hypnotique.* "She went to sleep and presented some phenomena that were absolutely trivial from the point of view of hypnotism," he testified. Gabrielle was extremely intelligent and she understood the consequences of her actions, he added. Although slightly hysterical, she was in full command of herself. "At no moment was she unconscious of her behavior," Brouardel concluded. "She is therefore responsible for her actions."

Gabrielle's lawyer, Henri Robert, strode forward. He needed to prove that Gabrielle was as hysterical and as prone to deep hypnosis as the women of the Salpêtrière. One symptom of the *grandes hypnotiques* was their intense physical sensitivities in certain parts of their bodies. The newspapers had already reported that Gabrielle had hyperesthesia—abnormal skin sensitivity—a fact Brouardel had left out of his deposition.

"Did you observe some points of exaggerated sensitivity on Gabrielle Bompard?" Henri Robert asked him.

"Yes, there is exaggerated sensitivity in the arms. If one touches her arms she jumps."

"Did you observe that her crises of hysteria were more tragic than in others? That's the word you used in your report."

"I said that in my report," Brouardel admitted. "In her attacks of nerves she indicates a terror of Eyraud. I don't know if this is the same in all of her attacks, but in front of me she was like this. I would say, however, that my use of the word *tragic* was a bit exaggerated."

"Does not one encounter these terrors in grand hysteria?" the law-yer persisted.

"It did not resemble that at all," Brouardel countered. "It's like what a little bronchitis is next to deadly pneumonia."

But, Henri Robert persisted, wouldn't repeated hypnotization, as Gabrielle had experienced through her life, have a profound impact on her? It was understood that the more often a person went into a trance, the more fragile the subject became. Robert was implying that Gabrielle's repeated exposure to hypnosis had turned her into a *grande hypnotique*—and therefore she was capable of a profound state of hypnotism like the grand hysterics at Charcot's Salpêtrière. Henri Robert needed to prove that Gabrielle was a hysteric who could go into a state of hypnosis so deep that she could kill a man against her will. He inquired of Brouardel: "Could not all these experiences have had an unfortunate influence on her nervous state?"

Brouardel conceded: "These experiences are very dangerous in a general way because they develop nervous states."

A juror then posed the fundamental question: Was it possible to coerce someone to act in a criminal way through hypnosis? This was the central question that the two schools, Paris and Nancy, had battled over for years. Gabrielle had challenged the academics to face it in the real world. But there was no simple answer. The resolution to the debate would be revealed in her fate.

To address the question, Brouardel began by distinguishing between two types of behavior under hypnosis. The first was the array of actions a subject would often agree to carry out while in a trance—drinking water and believing it's wine, biting into a potato and believing it's an apple. The second type of behavior consisted of the actions one could be commanded to undertake after coming out of hypnosis in an awake, posthypnotic state. The Salpêtrière school believed—and had conducted experiments proving—that a hypnotized person would indeed perform simple acts both while in a trance and post-hypnotically, such as hugging a person or stabbing someone with a paper knife. But anything beyond these simple, unthreatening actions was impossible. By contrast, the Nancy school believed a hypnotized person—robbed of her free will—could be forced unknowingly to perform all manner of actions. "The school of Nancy," Brouardel told the court, "professes that a person awakened from hypnotic sleep will under the influence of suggestion carry out an act with the same inevitability that a rock falls to the earth." Brouardel dismissed this theory, raising the question of fakery: "How is it possible to know that one is not deceived?"

Motet, who co-authored the report on Gabrielle, followed Brouardel to the witness stand and reiterated that Gabrielle was immoral but not insane and displayed only a minor form of hysteria. "Mild hysteria has never been successfully invoked for a lessening of responsibility in criminal acts," he said. Further, he affirmed, her behavior under hypnosis revealed that she was a *petite hypnotique,* not a *grande hypnotique.*

Ballet, the third contributor to the report, added yet another voice of medical authority for the prosecution. "There was no disagreement among the doctors," he stressed to the court. "The facts were simple and clear." He dismissed the defense's argument. "This idea of possible hypnotism in this case did not move us much," Ballet said. "That's because until now not a single crime has been committed under the influence of hypnotic suggestion. There is not one authentic case. Let me make it clear: We are in the presence of the first of these cases. Suffice it to say that we have seen nothing in Gabrielle Bompard that would make hypnotism accountable for this crime."

Chapter 47

The Bompard family physician, Dr. Sacreste, settled into the witness stand. The forty-one-year-old doctor, who had looked after the family since 1883, recently had taken a position as the chief physician at a hospital in the French colony of Algeria. He recalled for the judge that he hypnotized Gabrielle during a visit to the Bompards' home in Lille around 1887. "She was almost immediately put to sleep, which seemed curious to me since, according to her, she had never been hypnotized," Sacreste told the court. He described the experiments he tried on her: he told her a glass of water was champagne and watched her act drunk after drinking it. He recounted his other visit when he anesthetized her through hypnosis to remove a wart, and she showed no signs of pain whatsoever.

Sometime in 1888, Sacreste said, Pierre Bompard showed up at his home distraught over his daughter's conduct. He was embarrassed by her provocative clothing and her sauciness on the streets, and asked if Sacreste could use hypnotism to alter her behavior. "I placed myself at his disposal, but I did not think one could easily get such a result," Sacreste informed the judge. When Sacreste went to see Gabrielle, he said she announced: "I know why you've come. I don't want you to put me to sleep and you will not put me to sleep." Sacreste managed to hypnotize her but it took much longer than usual. While she was under he suggested to her that she conduct herself better and gave her some advice on how to do so. He tried the same procedures on three occasions. "These were absolutely without result," he said. "However, at the end, she made a veritable confession." Gabrielle told Dr. Sacreste about her lover in Lille and that he repeatedly hypnotized her. Sacreste understood then why his interventions had little effect; he was unable to break through the hypnotic hold of her lover.

What his efforts showed, however, was that Gabrielle was enormously susceptible to suggestion and that she was being made increasingly vulnerable because of her many hypnotic experiences. This heaping of hypnosis was overwhelming her mentally.

Sacreste informed Pierre Bompard in May or June 1888 that his mission to rescue Gabrielle was over. That was barely a month or so before she fled to Paris. In September, Sacreste said, he got a letter from Gabrielle in Paris telling him that she had to leave Lille because of her unhappiness at home. She asked Sacreste to tell her father she needed money. The doctor talked Pierre Bompard into parting with six hundred francs, which were sent to Gabrielle in four installments. She then wrote asking for ten thousand francs to set up a business in America, but this time her father balked. In conclusion, Sacreste told the court he believed Gabrielle was a hysteric—not one with violent attacks but nonetheless a hysteric. In his view, her hysteria suggested an abnormality in the brain that significantly diminished her responsibility for the crime. "As to the intervention of hypnotism," Sacreste continued, "I do not think that one can cause a person to commit a crime through hypnotism. To test for that, a decisive experiment is necessary. Unfortunately," he paused with a laugh, "or fortunately, that is not possible."

But he did believe that a kind of coercion could occur—whether it was by actual hypnosis or by suggestion didn't really matter. Without naming Eyraud, he blamed him. "I am convinced," he concluded, "that by repeated suggestion one can bit by bit habituate a subject to the idea of a crime and lead them there insensibly."

Returning to the question of hypnosis, Judge Robert reminded the witness of Gabrielle's own testimony. "Gabrielle Bompard herself," he said to the doctor, "recollects that Eyraud was never able to put her to sleep."

"That's extraordinary," exclaimed Sacreste. His own experience had shown that Gabrielle was a magnificently easy subject for hypnosis. That Eyraud was the only one who couldn't hypnotize her seemed impossible. Sacreste then offered his explanation for why Gabrielle would say such a thing: She had been programmed to say it. "I would think then there had been a posthypnotic suggestion," he asserted.

The judge invited Dr. Brouardel to comment on Dr. Sacreste's testimony.

"I cannot admit that her criminal experiences were forced under the influence of suggestion," Brouardel said.

Henri Robert sought a conclusion from the family physician. "Dr. Sacreste knows the character of Gabrielle Bompard. Does he think her capable of such a crime?"

"I was very shocked," Sacreste recalled. "She was very reserved."

Henri Robert then pursued Sacreste's explanation that if Gabrielle were not hypnotized to commit the crime, she might very well have been encouraged by suggestion to do it. "Dr. Sacreste," he posed, "do you think that one can suggest actions without putting the person to sleep?"

"The theory of the Nancy school seems right to me," he replied. "Without putting a person to sleep, one can suggest actions."

"Can you cite a case to support your opinion?" the judge asked.

"I don't have any at present but they are cited in the works on hypnotism," replied Sacreste.

Henri Robert returned to another key issue: the question of post-hypnotic memory. "If one had forbidden a person to remember that she had been put to sleep, would she remember?" he asked Dr. Sacreste.

"Certainly not."

The next witness, Dr. Jules Voisin—the doctor at the Dépôt prison—refused to be sworn in. "Before I take the oath," he said, "I have to state that I cannot speak."

Henri Robert quickly interjected: "Gabrielle Bompard could be facing capital punishment," he reminded the judge. "Dr. Voisin has spent several months at Gabrielle's side."

The judge informed Henri Robert that he understood the seriousness of the case but he also recognized Voisin's reticence. He told the doctor he would be free to say as much or as little as he pleased, but he must first take the oath.

"Make your statement," the judge instructed.

"I can say nothing," Voisin persisted. "Professional confidentiality prohibits it."

Henri Robert interjected again: "Over the past eleven months, Dr. Voisin performed many hypnotic experiments on Gabrielle Bompard. There is perfect reason—"

"I think he made a big mistake," prosecutor Quesnay de Beaurepaire interrupted, unhappy that Voisin had taken such a liberty with Gabrielle.

"And I as well!" chimed in the judge.

"Whether he was right or wrong," Henri Robert continued, "it does not lessen the fact of the experiments. He received some very important confidences."

Henri Robert reminded the judge and prosecutor that he had requested permission to have Jules Liégeois, his expert witness on hypnotism and crime, interview Gabrielle. It was only fair, since the state had conducted its own exhaustive examination of Gabrielle, which included hypnotizing her. Shouldn't the defense have a similar opportunity? "This authorization was refused," Henri Robert said. He had called Dr. Voisin as a witness hoping for some enlightenment into Gabrielle's mental state. "But now we are in a situation where Liégeois cannot see Gabrielle and Voisin cannot speak." He insisted that the question of confidentiality be ruled upon by the court.

The judge asked Henri Robert how he would resolve the matter.

"Gabrielle Bompard could release Dr. Voisin from his professional confidentiality," Robert proposed.

The courtroom, tantalized by the prospect of hearing Voisin's secrets about Gabrielle, broke into chatter. Quesnay de Beaurepaire stepped to the front, explaining that Liégeois had no standing to visit with Gabrielle. In a condescending tone, he pointed out that Liégeois was not a doctor and that three doctors, one of them the head of the medical faculty at the University of Paris, had already spent months studying the mental condition of the accused. What could Liégeois possibly offer that the distinguished medical men could not? "They do not have to be checked by a professor of law." The prosecutor demanded that Voisin's testimony remain private. "Dr. Voisin was there to care for the illnesses of the prisoners and not to stand as an expert on other matters," he said. "The doctor should adhere to the sanctity of his profession."

The judge had heard enough and indicated his agreement.

But before he could rule, Henri Robert tried to speak again: "Just a word—"

"The matter is closed," the judge decreed.

But Henri Robert wouldn't let it go, pleading with the judge: "Would you permit me to respond?"

To which the judge roared: "I permit you nothing at all!"

Henri Robert approached the bench and there commenced a prolonged, angry exchange that the spectators strained to hear. Although the words were unintelligible, the gestures and facial expressions attested to the incivility on both sides. Suddenly, breaking from the heated colloquy, the judge cried out: "Guards! Clear the room! Everyone goes! The trial is suspended."

But the crowd refused to go: A furor broke out. The guards tried to sweep the room but the protestors dug in. "Tumult. Uproar," observed Inspector Jaume. "Some applaud. Others yell. The audience is divided into two camps: there are the Eyraudistes and the Bompardeurs. The atmosphere becomes bizarre. One will say that a wind of madness blew through the courtroom." The elite spectators managed to brush off the police and stay in their seats, while the riffraff, more vulnerable on their back benches, were bullied out of the courtroom for the recess.

In the dock, Gabrielle watched the hullabaloo, laughing. Every so often, she threw her head back and brought a small bottle to her lips, tipping into her mouth a sedative called syrup of ether that a doctor had supplied. For his part, Eyraud sat motionless, dark-eyed and smoldering.

Chapter 48

Some twenty minutes later, after the spectators had filed back to their seats, the judge resumed the session. Henri Robert had lost his battle. Dr. Voisin was allowed to keep Gabrielle's secrets to himself and the defense was not allowed to hypnotize her. The last hope of the defense was the final witness of the day, Jules Liégeois, the world's leading expert on the link between hypnotism and crime. His appearance was historic: No expert had ever argued in court that a murder defendant had killed under hypnosis, without free will and therefore without responsibility. Gabrielle's fate was in Liégeois's hands. Only he could save her from the guillotine.

Henri Robert asked the law professor for his thoughts on the medical report by the three experts for the prosecution.

"They do not think that hypnotism plays a role in this trial," Liégeois said, adding: "My explanation will be long." He was a fifty-seven-year-old professor of administrative law at the University of Nancy. His testimony would require a detailed explanation of hypnotism and crime for the jury. "And I do not want to be interrupted," he told the judge in a dry, professional voice. He cited article 319-s-2 of the criminal code, which allowed a witness to deliver his deposition without interruption.

"I don't understand what you are insinuating," Judge Robert countered. "You will be free to testify. How much time do you think you'll need?"

"One and a half to two hours."

Noting the late hour, the judge said, "It will be better to do your deposition tomorrow. You could say a few words today."

"But then Professor Liégeois would be interrupted," Henri Robert pointed out.

"In that case," the judge said, turning to Liégeois, "we'll hear from you tomorrow."

He adjourned the session at five forty-five.

Writing in *Le Figaro,* the court reporter Albert Bataille set the stage for the following day's performance. "We haven't finished with hypnotism?" he mused. "We will attend this interesting spectacle of a law professor from Nancy discussing criminal suggestion in the case of a woman he has never seen."

On Friday, December 19, 1890, the fourth day of the trial, the snow began to melt as the temperature climbed to forty-three degrees. Jules Liégeois returned to the packed courtroom as the man of the hour and an unlikely celebrity. He was widely respected but also something of an oddity, an obsessive and stodgy defender of his land-mark research linking hypnosis and crime. At eleven forty-five, he began speaking in a tone that was so dull that the anticipation lead-ing up to this moment instantly withered and the air seemed to drain from the courtroom. Unhappy ticket holders girded themselves for a painstaking presentation. An extraordinary subject was suddenly rendered mundane. From the dock Eyraud watched stony-eyed and Gabrielle, seated next to Dr. Floquet, had drifted miles away.

"I didn't seek the perilous honor of addressing you," Liégeois told the court, explaining that he was appearing in place of Dr. Hippolyte Bernheim, who had broken his leg and was unable to travel to Paris. Though Liégeois was the recognized expert on the question at hand, Bernheim was by far the more compelling speaker, and his absence was felt all the keener as the rumpled professor droned on. "I consider it a matter of honor and conscience to come here to present to you the doctrines of the Nancy school."

Mercifully Liégeois refrained from dragging his listeners back to the eighteenth century and the discoveries of Mesmer, but he did reminisce about the past two decades, declaring: "The idea that I had developed in my report in 1884 was the following: The subject in a hypnotic state loses all spontaneity. It is as if the free will is abolished." His many experiments, he said, proved his point. Among them was a hypnotized woman who fired a revolver at a man Liégeois introduced to her as a judge. "A friend verified that the gun was not loaded," the professor said, with a laugh. The woman popped off a round, and the man dropped to the floor. The woman said she saw the victim lying there dying in a puddle of blood. She felt no remorse—she had been ordered to shoot and she did. There was another woman, Liégeois continued, who fired a pistol at her own mother. When Liégeois blew on her eyes and woke her from her trance, the woman was confronted by her mother who asked, "How could you fire at me?" And the woman replied, "Because you are there." On yet another occasion, Liégeois gave a man some sugar and told him it was arsenic, then ordered him to poison his nephew, which he did willingly. The experiment was carried out realistically and the boy's aunt was so frightened she refused to bring her nephew back to the laboratory ever again.

Laughter rippled through the courtroom.

But what did such laboratory experiments tell us about the commission of a real crime under hypnosis? The answer, Liégeois said, required an understanding of what he called the second state. "The second state, and I am, I think, the first who perceived it, is the special state in which crimes could be committed by hypnotic suggestion or by a suggestion made to someone in a waking state," he explained. The second state was not a normal condition. He likened it to the state of an insane person who gets an idea in her head and allows it to grow bit by bit until all checks on it have been eliminated. Several published cases had shown the influence of the second state. There was a man who stole a watch while in a second state after a hypnotist placed the idea in his mind. Liégeois noted the similarity between the second state and intense religious experiences in which congregants were whipped into action.

Turning to the trial, he complained that he had been prohibited from seeing Gabrielle. "Perhaps that's legal," he said. "I do not know if it is just." He attacked Quesnay de Beaurepaire for ridiculing his credentials. Doctors—and only doctors—should examine the accused? "Monsieur prosecutor contests my competence. If I were incompetent, what danger would there be in letting me see Gabrielle Bompard? If I am competent, isn't it an outrage against morality and justice in preventing a full defense for the accused? What a situation I'm in! The experts had three hundred days to examine Gabrielle Bompard. Me, not a minute!"

With that the judge called a recess. It was one forty-five. Liégeois had already filled two hours.

"I arrive now at the basis of the trial," Liégeois said when he resumed his testimony at two twenty. "What is my opinion on the possibility that Gabrielle Bompard executed acts by virtue of a suggestion? It seems to me it is possible that Gabrielle received some criminal suggestions and that she realized them in a second state."

He addressed the charges that Gabrielle was fundamentally immoral and that she lied. What explained her different stories about the crime? Why did she appear indifferent to the brutality? Why did she seem more like a witness than a participant in the murder? Liégeois provided a simple explanation, one that absolved her. "She forgot all that had happened to her," he said. "She forgot things that had been done to her. There was a complete rupture of memory. If this is true, then all that has seemed inexplicable about her attitude and her testimony finds a complete and luminous explanation." When she was in a waking state, he continued, she remembered nothing. In her second state, she would remember everything. Therefore, he declared, "it would be necessary to put her back into a second state so that she could tell all." He complained again about not being permitted, adding that if Dr. Voisin had discovered anything about her during his unauthorized hypnotic sessions, the jury ought to hear about it. It was true, Liégeois acknowledged, that Gabrielle had been a difficult suspect; she was not forthcoming; she changed her story; at times she had been confused. But, he said, there was a reason for all that. "If someone had made a suggestion to her while she was in a second state that she should forget everything on reawakening, it is not surprising that she doesn't remember any of the acts in which she participated."

Next he addressed the key question: Did Eyraud even hypnotize Gabrielle? The claim that Eyraud never accomplished it seemed absurd. "All those who wanted to put her to sleep succeeded," he pointed out. "And only Eyraud could not do it?" Look at Gabrielle's behavior. "How then do we explain this undeniable link between him and this young woman who with her appeal certainly didn't have to worry about loneliness? She was tied to him like a dog to its master. Is there anything that can explain it? Nothing outside of suggestion."

The judge interrupted. "It wasn't only Eyraud who said he couldn't hypnotize her. Monsieur Risler said he saw Eyraud fail."

That was easily explained, Liégeois said: What if Eyraud purposely failed for the sake of an alibi? Suppose Eyraud knew it was to his advantage for someone to believe he couldn't hypnotize Gabrielle. What would he do? Eyraud certainly knew the power of suggestion. He could announce that he wanted to put her to sleep but, knowing how suggestible she was, he could say in her presence, directly to her, that she was difficult to hypnotize. He planted the idea that he wouldn't be able to do it. He would provide a negative suggestion rather than a positive one—and that would be enough to ensure that she would be impossible to hypnotize at that time. If the question ever came up that he controlled her through hypnosis, he would have his alibi, and he would have a witness to support him.

Liégeois then attacked the doctors Brouardel, Motet, and Ballet for the way they handled Gabrielle when they hypnotized her. What happened? She had a hysterical crisis. "She had terrifying hallucinations," Liégeois reminded the court. "As soon as she was put to sleep, she found the memory she had forgotten in the waking state." After her crisis—and still in her hypnotic state—she could have been questioned about the crime. But the doctors chose not to seek the truth from her. Instead of using hypnosis to fully explore her role in the crime, they simply concluded that she was an immoral person and responsible for her actions. To his amazement, Liégeois said, their report asserted that hypnotism was of no use in investigating a criminal case.

"That's not quite what we said," objected Dr. Motet.

Liégeois stood his ground. "I say you had a duty to interrogate her in that state."

It was curious, Liégeois went on, that Eyraud had demanded to see Gabrielle again after she was taken from him by Georges Garanger. In one of his menacing letters, he told Garanger he wanted to see her just for five or six minutes. He repeated this request several times in the letter. Liégeois wondered what Eyraud was hoping to accomplish. Eyraud was worried that Garanger would hypnotize Gabrielle and that she would reveal the truth. Eyraud would then find himself portrayed as the murderer he was. He wanted his five or six minutes with her to renew his posthypnotic suggestion eliminating her memory of the crime.

Now Liégeois turned his displeasure with the prosecutor, Quesnay de Beaurepaire, who had ridiculed him for his opinions. Quesnay de Beaurepaire had argued that if the justice system accepted Liégeois's argument that criminals are not responsible for their actions, there would be no more criminals. Liégeois refused to allow his reasoning to be denigrated in this way, saying that was not his thesis at all. If an ordinary person commits a crime, of course they are responsible. But if a person commits a crime in a state of hypnosis, they cannot be judged responsible. "Am I alone in this opinion?" Absolutely not, he declared. He invoked his Nancy supporters: Dr. Hippolyte Bernheim and Dr. Ambroise Auguste Liébeault.

Having spoken now for another two hours, Liégeois brought his deposition to a close with a fervent declaration: "I would rather chop off my hands than sign a verdict of condemnation of Gabrielle Bompard."

In the dock, Gabrielle had her head on Dr. Floquet's shoulder and was sound asleep.

Chapter 49

Judge Robert asked if the lawyers had any questions for Liégeois.

Prosecutor Quesnay de Beaurepaire took the floor on his unsteady feet. The squint of his eye and the tilt of his head conveyed an air of skepticism. Was it really possible, he asked as if the question itself was ludicrous, that a hypnotic suggestion planted in a subject's head could persist over several weeks?

"Perfectly," Liégeois replied.

The question was meant to cast doubt not only on Liégeois's defense of Gabrielle but on the nature of Liégeois's work. Posthypnotic suggestion was related to Liégeois's contention about the existence of a second state—the condition in which he contended Gabrielle committed the crime.

Dr. Brouardel stepped forward in support of Quesnay de Beaurepaire's misgivings, raising doubts about how long a suggestion could remain with a subject. To both men, it was all far-fetched nonsense, and they meant to demolish this vital element of the defense. If Liégeois had constructed a preposterous theory of a second state based on questionable research into posthypnotic suggestion, the men implied, why should the jury believe any of his testimony related to hypnosis in this case? Their attack was not limited to Liégeois alone. They were dismissing a large portion of the work of the entire Nancy school, for Liégeois, Bernheim, and another adherent, H. E. Beaunis, the chair of physiology at the University of Nancy, had all conducted experiments in long-term posthypnotic suggestions.

The school's experiments were startling. Bernheim had a subject take a specific action 63 days after hypnosis, Beaunis after 172 days—and Liégeois a full 365 days. In this one-year experiment, begun on October 12, 1885, Liégeois told a hypnotized eye patient of Bernheim's that he would return to the doctor's office exactly a year later to thank him for his treatment. Liégeois directed the patient to embrace both Bernheim and Liégeois on seeing them and then hallucinate a series of events: He would see a monkey and a dog in the office, and the monkey would be carrying the dog and they would romp and make faces. Five minutes later the patient would see a bohemian-type man enter followed by a tamed grizzly bear from America. The bohemian would be happy to find his dog and monkey, which he thought he'd lost, and then he would make the bear dance. As the bohemian was about to leave, the patient would ask Liégeois for six centimes and would hand the money over as a donation for the performance. After this elaborate scenario was planted in his head, the patient was brought out of his trance and sent on his way. According to Liégeois's report, the patient returned exactly a year later, on October 12, 1886, at 10:10 a.m. Everything went off just as it was ordered, except that the patient didn't embrace Bernheim and Liégeois and he said nothing about a bear. Liégeois hypnotized the patient and asked him why he saw the monkey and dog, and the patient replied that it was because Liégeois had given him the suggestion on October 12, 1885. But why didn't he embrace the experimenters or see the bear? That was simple, the patient said; the dog and monkey suggestions were made three times, while the others were made only once. When the patient was awakened, he had no memory of any of his actions. Writing about the case in the *Revue de l'hypnotisme*, Liégeois said the experiment was an example of a subject carrying out deeds in a second state, the condition in which he contended that Gabrielle had carried out her deeds. "All scientific precautions were taken to ensure the validity of the experiment," Liégeois wrote in the journal.

To Brouardel, none of it was legitimate. How do you prove that a subject isn't just saying what the experimenter wants to hear? In a harmless case with monkeys and dogs, the only damage from actions in a supposed second state was to one's scientific credibility. In a murder case like Gabrielle's the consequences were far more serious. If an implausible argument such as this held sway in the courtroom, the nation risked an unacceptable miscarriage of justice. Brouardel wondered if Gabrielle wasn't just following the lead of her lawyer and witnesses like Liégeois simply to save her neck. How does the court weigh whether her defense isn't a fiction based on faulty hypnosis research? "What guarantee do we have of the sincerity of the subject?" Brouardel asked the jury.

He then denigrated Liégeois's laboratory procedures. Did the law professor use proper scientific controls? Brouardel measured Liégeois's work against that of eminent scientists such as Jean-Martin Charcot and Louis Pasteur. "Would they have proceeded in a similar manner?" he asked rhetorically. Next he circled back to Liégeois's demand to examine Gabrielle under hypnosis. Out of the question, Brouardel asserted: It was not appropriate to wheedle a confession out of Gabrielle while she was under hypnosis. "That is a thing I would never do," he declared, "and I am sure that my honorable confrères are of the same opinion."

And what of Gabrielle's actions prior to the murder: going to London, returning to Paris, renting an apartment, sewing the sack, helping Eyraud prepare the scene? "Do you seriously think that during all this time she was in a second state?" How could Eyraud have kept her from remembering everything? "I do not know of a case in which a person had put another to sleep and then as a last command barred him from remembering all previous hypnotizations," Brouardel said.

What was the real source of Eyraud's influence over Gabrielle? It was all very natural, Brouardel explained. When people are together, one exerts an influence over the other. "This is what we see every day and it is not necessary to see anything extraordinary in it," he said. "It's like three schoolboys who make a stupid mistake. Each father will say, 'My son was dragged into it.'" Brouardel laughed and the courtroom laughed with him.

Fighting back, Henri Robert invited Dr. Sacreste to share his view. Did the doctor agree with the testimony put forth by Liégeois? Sacreste allowed for Gabrielle's acquittal, or at least a mitigation of her sentence. "I consider Gabrielle Bompard not responsible," he replied, "or at the very least that her responsibility is diminished."

The judge asked Dr. Motet, Brouardel's partner in the report on Gabrielle, if he wished to offer his observations. Motet said that if Gabrielle had been under hypnosis at the time of the crime, it was true she would have had no memory of what took place. However, she gave complete and precise testimony. She re-created for investigators and the court large portions of the crime and described her and Eyraud's actions before and after the killing. "Thus, she was not hypnotized," he said. "We would have been very satisfied to have found such an interesting case." But, he said, this was not it.

Henri Robert got to his feet. His defense needed a dramatic surprise. "If it pleases the court," he said to the judge, "order Messieurs Brouardel, Liégeois, Voisin, or whichever expert it pleases you to designate, to examine Gabrielle Bompard here in public. I make this plea in the name of truth. All of us here have a passion for truth. We are here at trial for facts not theories." He turned and addressed the jury. "You need facts, messieurs of the jury, and not a discussion of schools. You need facts and conclusions, so your expertise as a jury could be put to work." Entreating the jury, he continued: "Put Gabrielle Bompard to sleep, interrogate her on the crime. I do not fear her revelations."

"Monsieur Robert," the judge interrupted, "it's to the court and not the jury that you should address yourself. It is only the court that has the duty to decide on your plea."

"That's true," Henri Robert said. "But the gentlemen of the jury can request this experiment. In a case as grave as this, if there is a way to discover the truth, no method should be refused."

Quesnay de Beaurepaire stood up and thundered: "This has the air of a courtroom spectacle!" It didn't promise any revelations but rather it was a last-minute wish to create a sensation in the courtroom. "What you're asking for is a séance of magnetism! What purpose would this serve? What would be the value of any declarations Gabrielle Bompard makes during hypnotic sleep? She is a known liar. I ask the court to reject the plea."

The judge had heard enough. He called a recess and retired to his chambers to deliberate on the request. If the trial weren't already a sensation, this defense maneuver promised to turn it into a carnival. To hypnotize a young murderess in court would enthrall the world but also invite ridicule. If the judge ruled in favor of the defense's request, he knew his decision would dance in headlines everywhere. But how was he to weigh the uproar against the search for truth?

His contemplation of the question didn't take long.

On his return to the courtroom, Judge Robert came right to the point. He explained that the discussion of hypnotism had already been so thorough that the jury was in possession of enough information to reach a decision with complete knowledge of the issue. "Considering that the experiments demanded in the name of Gabrielle Bompard are not necessary to the discovery of the truth," he continued, "the request is denied." And with that, he called another ten-minute recess.

When the session resumed, Albert Danet, the lawyer for Gouffé's daughters, pleaded the civil case against Eyraud and Gabrielle. He spoke of the hardworking Gouffé who suffered the sad loss of his wife in 1882 and raised his young daughters on his own. To accentuate Gouffé's saintliness he demonized Eyraud in every way possible. Then in conclusion he told the jury: "Voilà, gentlemen, my last word. Do not forget to think a bit of these orphans on whom I call your merciful attention."

The judge adjourned for the day at five forty-five. The trial, which was supposed to last only four days, needed a fifth. On Saturday, the prosecution and the defense would deliver their final arguments. Then the jury would retire to consider its verdict.

Across the Atlantic, American newspapers played the case in large headlines. "Hypnotic Mysteries" declared the *Daily Inter Ocean* in Chicago. "Interest of Many Scientific Men Drawn to French Murder Trial." The paper was of the opinion that "the chances are that the head of the pretty strangler will not drop in the bloody basket from the guillotine." It described Gabrielle as a modern Jekyll and Hyde: "Scientific men will prove that she is a very impressionable subject, and unconsciously possessed of a double nature, and that in the hands of an unscrupulous man she was actually unable to resist, her mind being completely in his power."

The *San Francisco Chronicle* wondered about the potential impact of the case on future courtroom dramas. An acquittal for Gabrielle meant defense lawyers would have a new potent weapon in their arsenal. "If Gabrielle Bompard succeeds in saving her life it is probable that hypnotism will come into general use as a defense in murder cases, rivaling the present popularity of emotional insanity, and even dividing honors with self-defense."

In Paris, the defendants' guilt was not in question. The conversation on the streets focused on sentencing: How severe a punishment? Would the men of the jury send both killers to the guillotine? Few Parisians had qualms about executing a strangler as vicious as Eyraud. But Gabrielle was another matter. Some French murderesses had lost their heads to the blade, but squeamishness over female beheadings existed—especially if, as in Gabrielle's case, there was any possibility she had been an unconscious pawn of Eyraud.

The courtroom drama was playing to tremendous reviews. Parisians were delighted to have the show extended another day. *Le Figaro* declared that the scenes in the Cour d'Assises were more fascinating than anything in the Parisian theater. "The theater, that's fiction," the paper explained. "In the Cour d'Assises, that's life."

Chapter 50

Warmer weather—forty-four degrees—and radiant sunshine brought out the largest crowd yet to mill about the courthouse. There was festive anticipation on the streets as the trial headed toward its climax. Inside, the prosecutor, Jules Quesnay de Beaurepaire, took the floor. "I come to conclude in the interest of justice," he told the jurors. "My task seems arduous because we have heard so many far-fetched stories. Forget all that has been said and all that has been written and form an opinion based on what will unfold before you now." He sought to turn the jury away from consideration of a certain factor in the case that in his eyes was so outrageous it didn't even merit serious discussion. But he had to address it nonetheless: It had distorted the trial and inspired the defense. "It is," he said, "the love of the fantastic. This love of the otherworldly arises from the dramatic circumstances of this crime. Instead of it being seen for what it was—just a vulgar act—it has played on the imagination. We have seen something extraordinary in it." He said the young heroine in this tale was regarded by some as pretty and engaging but she was also bizarre. "We are asked," Quesnay de Beaurepaire continued, "to believe she committed this crime without her free will. But to believe that, one must venture back several centuries and see her as a veritable subject of possession."

He addressed the crucial question: "Did she commit the crime in a state of suggestion, yes or no?" His answer sought to strike terror into the soul. "If hypnotism explains the crime, if it is a way to deny free will, then we must recognize there is no such thing as human freedom. There will be no conscious choice between good and evil. No criminal will be accountable for the blood he spills. And the book of eternal justice will be closed."

Science, the prosecutor insisted, rejected this hypothesis. He stressed that while the free will was confiscated during hypnosis, it was not abolished. "Monsieur Charcot told me that very often it's been suggested to people to steal under hypnosis. They protest: 'Me steal? But I am not a robber.' If the hypnotist insists, they have an attack of nerves."

As far back as 1780, Quesnay de Beaurepaire told the court, the Marquis de Puységur proved that the power of hypnosis was limited. When Puységur asked a hypnotized woman to do something that offended her modesty, he met with invincible resistance. "Do not then say," the prosecutor thundered, "that one can throw the hypnotic toward the crime like a dog after a scent!"

So how did Michel Eyraud coerce Gabrielle Bompard into joining him in this crime? Was it suggestion? Hypnotism? Not at all, Quesnay de Beaurepaire insisted. Liégeois would have people believe that his theory provided a new understanding of subjugation. "Such theories amaze me," the prosecutor scoffed. It was simply brutal male domination. "The stronger being always imposes his will on the weaker being," the prosecutor explained. "This is not something new. This has been happening for six thousand years. The audacious one has always petrified the pusillanimous with his look. This is not the history of hypnotism. This is the history of the world."

Quesnay de Beaurepaire now came to his most important duty: to persuade the jury to send Eyraud and Gabrielle to the guillotine. Since 1832, juries were empowered to recognize extenuating circumstances in their sentencing decisions—a legal right aimed at offsetting excessively harsh rulings by judges in earlier years. There was a wide range of possible reasons for easing a sentence. The jury was to determine, as one commentator put it, whether "the individual has committed a crime under such conditions as to mitigate the enormity of the offense." Which was exactly the argument of Gabrielle's defense. So Quesnay de Beaurepaire sought to deny Gabrielle any protection and portray the murder in the most heinous light. This crime, he said, was worse than most. Some people commit terrible acts because of a sudden, unexpected temptation. "This was an atrocious ambush planned well in advance," he reminded the jury. "I ask you, what becomes of public security if you do not deliver a punishment in proportion to the crime?" Few people were likely to oppose the death penalty for Eyraud. But what about Gabrielle? Should the jury answer in the same way?

"I feel a profound emotion in coming to ask you to render a sentence of capital punishment on a girl twenty-two years old," he said. "As guilty as she is, as intelligent as she is, as responsible as she is, I have waited for a sign of repentance from her that might have tipped the balance. You must decide what your conscience suggests to you. But I cannot demand for her any special attenuated circumstances. My last word: Jurors, you must be faithful to the oath you took at the start of this trial. You must render a verdict without weakness."

After Quesnay de Beaurepaire's summation the court went into a two-hour recess. Most spectators stayed in the courtroom guarding their seats. But as the delay dragged on they grew impatient, then agitated; some stood up on the benches. Finally, at two thirty, Gabrielle and Eyraud were led back to the dock. She was paler than ever but maintained an air of indifference. Dr. Floquet escorted her to her seat and took up his position directly behind her.

Eyraud's lawyer, Félix Decori, had an impossible task: to win leniency for the strangler. With his Mephistopheles mien, he seemed perfectly cast to try to rescue the devil from the executioner. As he stepped forward, the obvious question hung over the court: How in the world would Decori frame a plausible defense for one as irredeemable as Eyraud? "Gentlemen of the court, gentlemen of the jury, this man comes before you loathed by everyone," he began, attacking the issue head-on. "People everywhere say he committed an abominable crime and only death should be his penance. The public prosecutor asked you in the name of justice to raise the scaffold and allow his head to fall. Everywhere a gigantic clamor of death rises up, and this elegant mob comes here as to a spectacle and awaits impatiently for this pleasure. But the law demands that at this very moment a voice rises up amid the clamor to speak for moderation and pity. Such is my responsibility, large as it is, and I undertake it without faintness. I will carry out my task to the end." He asked the jury to overlook the cries of vengeance and to weigh the question of Eyraud's sentence without passion and with a strong conscience. He then sought to soften the portrait of Eyraud as a pillaging, gun-toting outlaw who sank to the bloody depths of murder. "I hasten to destroy this legend of Eyraud," Decori said. "I would like to show him to you from his childhood through his difficult, adventurous life."

He ran through the events of Eyraud's youth: his birth to an industrialist father, education at a boarding school at age ten, then with the Marists, a Roman Catholic order, from age twelve to sixteen. Eyraud's troubles began, Decori said, when his wanderlust led him into the army at age seventeen and later he became a deserter. "He commits a grave error and, if he deserts," Decori explained, "it is not fear of death or cowardice that leads him away." The Spanish-speaking Eyraud was sent on a special mission to a farm, where he met a young woman and became her lover. When she invited him back to the farm for Christmas dinner, Eyraud longed to join her. "He asks for permission and it is refused," Decori said. But Eyraud slipped out of camp anyway and spent the night at the farm—and for his disobedience he faced a military tribunal. So he ran. "He is only twenty years old," Decori impressed upon the jury. "This first error was inspired by love. Love would inspire him again in another error."

That error was murder, a crime Eyraud committed only out of blind love for Gabrielle. "He had a violent passion: It's a passion for the woman," Decori said. "He had an inextinguishable need for that woman, for her caresses, for her presence. Before her, he is a child, seduced by her charms, by the softness of her voice. Luck put him in a relationship with a grasping woman lacking in all morality. She would command him, dominate him, and he would obey her. This is what Gabrielle Bompard did to him."

Decori described how Gabrielle laid the plans for the murder and directed its execution. Here was the crux of Eyraud's defense: Gabrielle was to blame for the crime. She was, in Decori's telling, reprehensible in every way. She led Eyraud into evil by her charms. "Without doubt," the lawyer told the jury, "this opinion will surprise you. But you must ask your conscience because you are the judges."

As Decori resumed his seat, applause erupted from all corners. By crafty storytelling, heavy on the heartstrings, Mephistopheles had aroused sympathy for the devil.

Chapter 51

As he stepped forward to begin his final plea on behalf of Gabrielle, Henri Robert approached one of the thorniest legal challenges of the belle époque. His extraordinary mission was to convince a jury to convict hypnotism rather than his client for a murder she indisputably had a hand in. He needed to show that Gabrielle's quixotic behavior, poor judgment, and callous actions were none of her own doing but rather the convincing proof of a young woman in a posthypnotic trance. No legal defender had ever tried to absolve a killer of responsibility for her crime by shifting the blame to a manipulative hypnotist. Failure to sway the jury carried fateful consequences—potentially a visit to the Monsieur de Paris.

"I am neither philosopher, nor fool, nor scientist, and I come modestly to present to you the defense of Gabrielle Bompard," Robert began. He walked the jury through the many allegations against her, the charges from Michel Eyraud that she inspired the crime, advocated for it, participated in its preparations, even attached the *cordelière* to the rope, and then helped with the cadaver and finally fled with him to America. "I have only one true adversary here," Robert said. "It is not Michel Eyraud. His lies are easily discredited. My adversary is public opinion."

Who is Gabrielle Bompard really? Robert asked, and set about trying to build sympathy for her because of what she had suffered at the hands of her father. "I do not exaggerate anything," he promised the jury. He said that Gabrielle never once denounced her father, adding: "I am not constrained by the same formality." And he vilified the prosperous Lille businessman as an "abominable" father who abandoned his daughter to the streets of Paris, where she had to fend for herself without a scrap of help from him. After she had been in

Paris for nearly a year she wrote to her father several times to beg him to take her back. He didn't reply. "So she asked one of her friends to write to him," Robert said. " 'If you are not one of *my* friends,' Monsieur Bompard replied, 'stay out of my affairs.' Monsieur Bompard only had to make some sign of affection to save his daughter. But he did not make it. This man, whose daughter's life plays out before you, has not had a word of pity for her." His callousness began many years earlier. When Gabrielle was five she watched her mother die, and her father installed his mistress as his housekeeper-governess before the coffin had even left the house. "Who then taught this unfortunate child the difference between good and bad?" Robert asked. "No one, ever, since no one was ever occupied with her. What examples did she find in the paternal home? Some detestable examples. What kind of life did she lead there? An infernal life. This father was the murderer of his daughter's soul." Those who had rushed to judgment on Gabrielle, Robert wondered, "Do they all know this—those who call for the supreme punishment?"

From the father's iniquities Robert moved on to Eyraud's barbarity. Since false statements weren't formally challenged or scratched from the record in the French court, attorneys only had the chance to set the record straight in their summations. So Robert now sought to extinguish Eyraud's charges against Gabrielle. His task was made easier by Eyraud's long life of deceit and crime. "I only want you to remember three facts that characterize him accurately," he said. "He stole at school, he deserted from the army, and he killed at rue Tronson du Coudray. Child—he steals. Young man—he deserts. Old man—he murders." But what of Eyraud's allegation that Gabrielle was the dominant figure in their relationship? Did she take the lead in planning and executing the crime, as Eyraud insisted, and was it *she* who drove *him* "like a lapdog," as he testified? Eyraud had tried to persuade the court that if it weren't for the perverse Gabrielle, he would still be an exemplary father and loving husband. "Is this possible?" Robert asked. "Is this serious? Was it Gabrielle Bompard who pushed him in 1884 to abandon his wife and daughter? Was it Gabrielle Bompard who pushed him ten years ago when he left for America, taking his wife's dowry with him?"

The story of their liaison was very simple, Robert explained. "Why did this young, intelligent, pretty girl live with this old man? She gave him a kiss for a morsel of bread. Then she stayed under the influence of misery and violence. When you hear that here is a woman who was beaten and broken down by his blows, can you seriously pretend that it was she who was the dominant one?" Eyraud controlled the young woman not just by his brutality, Robert said, creeping toward the cornerstone of his defense. As soon as Eyraud discovered she was easily hypnotized, he took her to the home of Madame Marmier, where it quickly became apparent that she was a remarkable subject for hypnosis. Gabrielle was hypnotized repeatedly at Madame Marmier's salon and that only intensified her susceptibility.

And the stage was set for murder under hypnosis.

At this time Eyraud's world was collapsing. At Fribourg & Cie his stealing was discovered and his cash flow dried up. He needed money. Worse, Fribourg threatened to have him arrested. "Eyraud had no choice," Robert said. Either he could go to prison or commit a crime and flee. "He preferred the crime." So Eyraud hypnotized Gabrielle and gave her her instructions. "Gabrielle Bompard wanted to carry out the order she had been given," Robert said. "She had the *cordelière* in her hands. She moved toward the bailiff with it but she could not realize the criminal act." Robert argued that like other hypnotized subjects who recoil from performing an act that offends their moral judgment, Gabrielle resisted. "At that moment," he continued, "she had an attack of nerves, and then Eyraud threw himself on Gouffé and strangled him."

Robert knew all this because Dr. Voisin told him. Voisin was the doctor at the Dépôt who had hypnotized Gabrielle and then refused to testify because of what he claimed was professional confidentiality. But he was not so tight-lipped outside of the courtroom. "Monsieur Voisin told the story to anyone who would listen," Robert said. "I know at least three or four people to whom he confided." Voisin had placed Gabrielle in a hypnotic state and had her re-create the chilling moment of the murder. "He obtained from her a confession of everything that happened," Robert explained. "Gabrielle mimed the act of murder in front of him. What I have told you is the truth."

Robert's argument that Gabrielle backed away from murder because of her moral strength undercut Liégeois's testimony that a hypnotized individual goes toward her goal like an unstoppable automaton. By discounting Liégeois's theory, Robert gave credence to the doctrines of the Salpêtrière school. But at the same time he counteracted the prosecution's contention that Gabrielle was an amoral creature. Robert was seeking to convey something that was more subtle than the blunt arguments from either side for or against murder under hypnosis. His purpose was not to prove or negate any academic proposition but rather to save the life of his client. A vigorous hypnotism defense based on Liégeois's argument was simply impossible to support. His line of reasoning was too murky. Hypnosis was too mysterious, its influence too elusive, to deliver a definitive verdict in a court of law. The judge, the prosecutor, the doctors had all reflected the skepticism that widely greeted the defense's position. To exonerate Gabrielle on a hypnotism plea seemed to Robert simply unimaginable. Robert understood that she was destined for conviction, but did she have to die? Instead of trying to prove that hypnosis had the remarkable power to direct a murder, Robert retreated from his historic moment and pursued a different goal. He sought to win the jury's sympathy for her fragile mental state.

"According to the doctors, Gabrielle Bompard is a broken being," Robert began. "If she is a broken person, then she should be sent to a hospital for her mental health. But no, to the prosecution doctors she is a broken woman but still responsible. I do not understand this at all." He reminded the jurors of Gabrielle's unhappy childhood, her abandonment by her father, the brutality of Eyraud—this unconscionable treatment throughout her life left her mentally unstable. "If you have a case of a disturbed person like Gabrielle Bompard, is it possible to pronounce the verdict that is asked of you? Here is the truth. Gabrielle Bompard is sick. You take care of the sick. You cure them, if you can. You do not send them to prison or to the guillotine. Men, you must act in accordance with your heart and your conscience. Let your hearts be touched."

Robert strode back to his seat amid the embrace of warm applause.

The judge asked if Eyraud or Gabrielle had anything to add in their own defense. They declined. He then reminded the jurors of the charges: voluntary homicide with premeditation involving ambush and robbery. He instructed the jurors in their duty and dismissed them so they could begin their deliberation. It was 6:50 p.m.

Eyraud and Gabrielle were escorted from the courtroom, he looking tense and feral, she sagging. The audience stayed put. No one expected the jury to be out very long; there would be no haggling over the defendants' guilt or innocence. The only matter for debate was the question of extenuating circumstances. And yet time ticked by. Amateur experts in the courtroom weighed the performances, the young Henri Robert against the aging Jules Quesnay de Beaurepaire, nodding their head in favor of Gabrielle or shaking a fist at Eyraud. Some wondered whether a gruesome public spectacle was coming: a pair of early-morning executions by guillotine, his and hers. In his tiny waiting room Eyraud paced like a wild animal. Outside in the street, a festive crowd formed to await the verdict.

Chapter 52

Nearly two hours after they began deliberations, the jurors returned. Outside, the darkness was complete. Inside the courtroom, spectators shuffled back to their seats in the subdued light of the gas lamps. As Gabrielle made her way toward the dock she was pallid behind her black veil. Struggling to see her, women stood up with a rustling of skirts. There was some pushing and a few shrill cries that caused the judge to call the women to order.

The denouement finally was at hand for a case that very nearly never came to trial. That the body of Toussaint-Augustin Gouffé was positively identified was an achievement of police persistence and modern medical science. Without the brilliance of Marie-François Goron and Alexandre Lacassagne, each striving in his own way, justice might never have been served. Had the putrescent body never been linked to Paris and never whispered its name, Gabrielle and Eyraud might never have stood in the Cour d'Assises.

After months of spectacle and impassioned debate, the jury was ready to speak. The foreman, a wine merchant named Jean-Baptiste Gagnier, delivered the verdict at 8:45 p.m. His first pronouncement came as little surprise: Eyraud, guilty on all counts. No mitigating circumstances. The decision couldn't have been worse for Eyraud. To the hushed courtroom Gagnier announced the second verdict: Gabrielle, guilty on all counts, with extenuating circumstances. No explanation was given but none was necessary. The jury had accepted Henri Robert's plea for compassion. Both defendants were also found guilty in the civil case and each was assessed a token one franc in damages.

Judge Robert asked if either of the convicted criminals had anything to say and both replied in strong voices: No.

The judge then retired to his chambers to consider the sentences and in a notably short time was back in the courtroom. In a high-pitched voice that clashed with the severity of his words, he condemned Michel Eyraud to death. A stillness fell over the courtroom as the judge announced Gabrielle's fate: twenty years of hard labor. She was spared. Eventually she would settle into a cloistered routine in a women's prison. For Eyraud the future also was clear—and short. As was customary, he was to be marched before the executioner in La Roquette square in full view of the public in about forty days.

Of his fate, Eyraud muttered to a guard: "I was waiting for that."

Gabrielle was visibly relieved, sighing: "At last, it's over."

As the convicts were led from the courtroom, some spectators jumped up for a better view, prompting others behind them to cry out: *"Assis! Assis!"* (Sit down! Sit down!) As the crowd made its way toward the exits like theatergoers after a show, some women were heard muttering their dismay over the final scene. They despised Gabrielle and all she represented: She was a curse on home and hearth, country, and God. The jury's leniency toward her outraged them. They had been deprived the pleasure of her execution.

In the wagon on the trip back to the Dépôt, Eyraud was as garrulous as ever, even as his death loomed. "Do you think these people imagine I put Gabrielle Bompard to sleep?" he asked. "If I had that power I'd put you to sleep right now and break out." He wasn't surprised by the verdict, he said, but he complained bitterly about the lighter sentence for Gabrielle. "She did as much as me," he insisted. "These jurors didn't understand anything about this case."

Already, his lawyer, Félix Decori, was working on an appeal of the death sentence. Of the twelve jurors, five had voted for extenuating circumstances. Decori set out to change the minds of the others in hopes of a favorable appeal hearing.

The Paris newspapers had their editions ready to hit the streets while the jurors deliberated; all that was missing was the verdict. So as soon as the sentences were handed down the presses roared to life and the papers were on the streets before the murderers were back in their cells at the Dépôt. Newsboys on the street corners cried: *"Le verdict de l'affaire Eyraud!"* Parisians swarmed the kiosks, and latecomers found the special editions had quickly sold out, and they had to read over a shoulder.

In her cell that evening, Gabrielle ate only a little soup, leaving the bread on the corner of her bowl. She wrote a letter to Henri Robert, praising him for his eloquence and thanking him for saving her life. Two nuns stayed by her side throughout the night. In the morning she was to be transferred to Saint-Lazare, a prison in the tenth arrondissement.

Eyraud's night was rougher. By tradition, a condemned man was forced into a straitjacket for his own protection, but Eyraud wanted nothing of it. At the Dépôt, he insisted he had no desire to kill himself; he was perfectly calm, he told his guards, and promised to cause no trouble. His powers of persuasion were still formidable: He spent the night free of the straitjacket.

He ate his dinner in his cell with a hearty appetite but soon came down with a vicious bout of diarrhea, stirring rumors that someone had tried to poison him. No such skullduggery had taken place, however; the culprit was Eyraud's teapot, which was sent to Dr. Paul Brouardel for toxicological study and found to have been improperly cleaned.

At eight the next morning, Eyraud climbed into a closed black wagon for the journey to La Roquette Prison, a grim stone citadel for convicts awaiting death. On his arrival, he was given a haircut and a shave under the watchful eye of the prison governor, Monsieur Beauquesne. Without his beard and mustache the killer looked small and vulnerable. He was then dressed in the prison garb of beige wool pants, a wool cap, and boots without laces, and was installed in cell number 1, the most spacious of the three reserved for killers awaiting execution. He was watched day and night and was allowed to smoke and play cards with his guards.

By lunchtime, Eyraud was hungry, his raging stomach of the previous night having calmed. Beauquesne sent for some bread, sausage, and wine from the canteen, and the condemned murderer enjoyed a light meal.

Chapter 53

Félix Decori worked on Eyraud's clemency appeal through the end of the year—a thankless, impossible task. Few figures were as reviled as the remorseless Eyraud. To save his neck, Decori needed to convince all twelve jurors to accept a condition of extenuating circumstances. With diligence, he approached each juror, and one by one he was able to get all twelve to sign on to the appeal. On January 6, he submitted the request for clemency and a court date was set for January 15.

Although Eyraud had been horrid to his wife, Louise-Laure nonetheless favored leniency and was ready to do what she could to save him from the guillotine. If the appeal was rejected, she intended to beg Madame Carnot, the wife of the French president, to intercede on her husband's behalf. By then Eyraud's last hope would be a commutation by the president. But in all of Paris, the faithful Louise-Laure was virtually a lone voice speaking up for the killer. Describing her husband to a reporter, she said: "He is not the ferocious criminal" that was portrayed in the press. "This intelligent, shrewd, absolutely immoral woman threw him into this crime." Louise-Laure insisted he was a good man before all this, adding "I only suffered from his infidelities." She blamed the newspapers for her husband's situation. Reporters, she said, used their excessive imagination to sensationalize the case, and she called on them to help her win a reprieve. "Since part of this misfortune was caused by the press, monsieur," she scolded the reporter, "it's in your power to have the press aid me in obtaining a pardon."

But even Louise-Laure's sympathy had its limits. She was willing to campaign against her husband's execution for murder, but she drew the line at his adultery. On December 30, she divorced him, citing his relationship with Gabrielle; she dispensed with her married name and reverted to her pre-Eyraud identity of Louise-Laure Bourgeois.

While Eyraud awaited his hearing, new questions arose over his murky past. The suspicions centered on the disappearance of a Frenchman in America some years before the Gouffé murder. Émile Breuil was a wine merchant who left France for the United States in 1881 and was never heard from again—that is, until Eyraud used his name as an alias in Lyon after murdering Gouffé. Having learned of this alias, Émile's brother Auguste asked the public prosecutor to investigate, arguing that Émile may have encountered Eyraud in America when the killer visited the country years earlier. Auguste suspected Eyraud murdered his brother and snatched his identification papers for one of his many aliases. The suspicion was taken seriously enough that a guard at La Roquette casually raised the matter in conversation with Eyraud in his cell. "Why did you change your name so frequently when you traveled—even before the Gouffé case?" the guard asked him. Creditors, Eyraud said, were always after him, so he had to protect himself by adopting new names. "But where the devil did you find all the names you invented?" the guard persisted. "Why did you call yourself Vanaerd when you were with Monsieur Garanger? Why did you pass yourself off as Émile Breuil in Lyon?" The name Émile Breuil caused Eyraud to blanch, and he hesitated before replying.

"By pure chance," he said. "Breuil, like Vanaerd, were names of people I met here and there." He paused. "What's your interest in this? What does it have to do with anything?"

"It's just a question many people have," the guard replied. "People are curious what your motive was for taking one name or another."

"I repeat: Chance alone guided me."

"Don't you know what's happened recently?" the guard said. "Monsieur Émile Breuil has a brother. The other day he was reading about your trial and was struck by a coincidence." The guard told Eyraud what people were saying: that Émile may have been in America at the same time as Eyraud and, strangely, Émile disappeared while there, and even more strangely, Eyraud used his name as an alias in Lyon.

"I knew someone named Breuil but I don't remember where I met him," Eyraud allowed. Then, as if suddenly remembering, he added:

"It was while I was in Paris that we met. Pure chance that I took his name. Perhaps when I arrived in Lyon I found a letter or card from him in my papers."

"Too bad you can't remember the exact circumstances," the guard said pointedly, "because his brother accuses you of having a hand in his disappearance. He says you encountered Émile Breuil in America, and he wants an inquest into the matter."

Eyraud was annoyed. "What do you want me to do? I'm sure nothing will be found out against me. My conscience is quite clear on this." He then refused to say another word.

On January 15, Eyraud's clemency hearing finally arrived. The court of appeals convened and with brutal dispatch rejected the request. Unless President Carnot intervened, Eyraud was to face the executioner in about twenty days. The exact date was not given. The condemned were never informed when precisely they would die; they would know the time had come when early one morning they were awakened in their cell by a parade of officials in top hats and overcoats.

About ten days before the execution Decori personally handed President Carnot the clemency appeal signed by the twelve jurors. The president now had little more than a week to make up his mind. For her part, Madame Carnot refused to see Eyraud's wife and daughter.

As decision day approached, the French seemed to soften toward Eyraud. "Strange thing!" declared *Le Figaro*. "A change of heart occurred in public opinion. Those who called the most strongly for a condemnation to death before the trial now found it acceptable, and even just, to commute the penalty."

If Eyraud rode a wave of sympathy, Gabrielle was vilified. The public seemed to agree that she had exerted a vixen's influence over the weak-willed, middle-aged Eyraud, who was little more than clay in her young, sexy hands. "When one saw Gabrielle condemned only to twenty years," the paper said, "one took relative pity on he who alone had to pay the communal debt."

On Tuesday, February 3, 1891, Eyraud was sitting in his cell on the edge of his bed at 6:45 a.m., waiting. Someone had whispered to him that this was the day: On this chilly morning the men were coming. And so they came: A procession of officials in black frocks and top hats filed into his cell, led by prison governor Monsieur Beauquesne.

The chief of the Sûreté, Marie-François Goron, was there, with his secretary, Soulière. So, too, was the prefect of police, Henri-Auguste Loze, and Father Faure, the prison priest. Others crowded into the cell: Monsieur Hamon, the chief of the municipal police; Monsieur Horoch, a clerk from the court of appeals; and Judge Louiche, a judicial representative.

Keeping with tradition, Governor Beauquesne delivered the news to Eyraud: President Sadi Carnot had rejected his petition for clemency.

"Very well," Eyraud replied.

Judge Louiche asked if the condemned had any statement to make before being escorted to the guillotine. Eyraud declined. When he stood up to begin the march, he bore none of the glamour and romanticism that the press had attached to him: He was bowlegged, bull-necked, and broad-shouldered; his large hands were white and pudgy; and his eyes were small. There was a lump on the left side of his forehead.

Beauquesne handed Eyraud the black dress pants he had worn at his trial, and the murderer changed out of his wool prison pants. He pulled off his dark socks and put on a pair of white ones that had been passed to him.

Father Faure offered to convey a message to Eyraud's wife and daughter.

"Tell them that I bid them adieu and hope they'll be happy."

When the priest offered Eyraud a traditional last glass of cognac the convict pushed it aside, mumbling, "No, that will do me no good."

The entourage led Eyraud from his cell to the dressing room, where the executioner awaited him. Louis Deibler was a stout sixty-year-old with a graying tuft on his chin. By custom he slept at the prison the night before an execution. He'd already been out in the square at 4:30 a.m. with two assistants to meet the wagon delivering the guillotine. By then barricades were up around the perimeter, and two divisions of police were in place. There were also two detachments of Republican Guards: a hundred on foot and another fifty on horseback, all fighting the cold. The activity had alerted the carousers in the cafés and hotels around the square, and word had filtered out: An execution was at hand. By early morning the drunks lifted their voices in song, their bloodlust drifting over the square: *"C'est Eyraud qu'il nous faut. C'est sa tête qu'il nous faut."* (It's Eyraud we must have. It's his head we must have.) A throng had wandered toward the barricades but there was nothing to see. Just a few men with lanterns ablaze clustered at a spot marked by five stone slabs. The night was extremely cold and there was a drizzling rain, but still the curious lingered. At 5:00 a.m. a wagon had pulled into the square, and a cheer rose from the crowd: The guillotine had arrived.

Deibler and his assistants had assembled the device, working in a damp fog, their lanterns casting a dull light on the red uprights. With one hand Deibler fidgeted with the bolts and fussed over the cords and pulleys, while with his other hand he held an umbrella over his head. At 5:45 a.m., he tested the instrument, sending the almost ninety-pound blade shrieking downward in its grooves at lightning speed, completing its descent in three-quarters of a second. Deibler, a fastidious man, ran the blade back up into place and let it go again, and then he tested it one more time. It was his duty—indeed, his obsession—to carry the bloody ceremony off without a hitch.

Now, inside the dressing room, Deibler sliced off Eyraud's shirt collar to expose his neck. He pinioned the murderer's arms behind his body to prevent any last-minute flailing. Eyraud asked Governor Beauquesne to ensure that his body would not go to the medical school. Goron had promised it to the school to be carved up by students. "Your body will be given to your family," Father Faure assured Eyraud. When the priest then offered to embrace Eyraud's wife and daughter for him, Eyraud didn't react, and when the priest repeated himself Eyraud again was silent. Then suddenly he erupted. Looking around wildly, the condemned man cried: "Constans has won his case! Now his prize!" Ernest Constans was the minister of the interior and head of the nation's police and security. As though possessed, Eyraud shouted: "He will be with Gabrielle tonight!" And he jerked away as Deibler was pinioning his wrists, causing the executioner to pinch him. "You're hurting my fingers!" Eyraud cried. To calm him down, Father Faure again offered him a glass of cognac, and Eyraud shook his head: "I told you no."

The time had arrived for the march to the *bois de justice,* the wood of justice. When Father Faure began to pray, Eyraud growled and demanded silence. Tradition called for the priest to bestow a final kiss upon the condemned before the procession moved into the square, and the condemned by convention was to return the gesture. But when Father Faure leaned toward him, Eyraud dodged his lips.

At 7:20 a.m., the men left the dressing room and entered the square, passing through a stone arched gate. As he approached the block, Eyraud scanned the crowd looking right and left, then fixed his eyes on the guillotine. Suddenly he swung his body to one side, attempting to break away, and shouted angrily toward the mob: "Constans is a murderer. He is more of a murderer than I am!" It was a mystery what inspired his rage at the minister of the interior. In his twisted mind Eyraud had reason to hate the country's top police and security official. When arrested, he had complained that Constans had captured him to settle a political score: Eyraud had idolized the dashing General Georges Boulanger, who had posed a coup d'état threat that Constans was instrumental in eliminating. But Eyraud's reasoning had no basis in reality. "What a bizarre manifestation!" Jaume exclaimed in his diary. "What a singular way to express your last thoughts. Up to the threshold of death, Eyraud remained an incomplete being, his head full of gaps."

With Eyraud raging, Deibler had no time for reflection; he had to prevent the execution from spiraling out of control. But he also knew he faced a danger if he acted too precipitously. In 1829, an executioner's assistant lost three fingers when he had to force an unruly murderer's head onto the lunette. To a critic who once chided Deibler for taking too long to release the blade, the executioner said, "I'd like to see you there. I have no desire to have two or three fingers eaten by the blade."

Now he acted quickly. He and his assistants seized the thrashing murderer as he shouted "Constans is—" and threw him against the inclined plank and locked his head in the lunette. An execution at times became a rough ballet and Deibler had been criticized for manhandling the condemned. "On one or two occasions Deibler has been taken to task by the Parisian journals, who have accused him of unnecessary roughness," the *London Globe* wrote a few years before Eyraud's execution. However, the paper came to Deibler's defense: "His looks hardly bear out such a charge, for there is nothing of the bully about him, and those who meet him of a Sunday afternoon, when he takes his wife out for a walk with him along the boulevards, would take him to be an ordinary workingman bent on enjoyment."

Eyraud had no chance to finish his outburst. With a swift motion, Deibler pressed the knob that released the blade suspended over the murderer's neck. The knife whistled downward and in less than a second sliced through Eyraud's fourth vertebra and his head separated from his body, dropping onto a tin pan filled with straw at the bottom of a basket.

In a surge of bloodlust the mob pushed forward but was driven back by soldiers on horseback.

News of the execution quickly hopped across the world. American newspapers were ablaze with the headlines. "Eyraud's Head Fell Off" cried the *Milwaukee Journal*. "His Head in the Basket" proclaimed Chicago's *Daily Inter Ocean*.

After the execution, the body was snatched from the scaffold, placed in a coffin, with the head between the feet, and the wagon drove off at a full gallop toward the cemetery, escorted by mounted gendarmes. Deibler cleaned up the site and disassembled the guillotine. He packed the large, bright blades into their leather cases, to be kept out of sight under lock and key at his home until called upon again. With his task accomplished and the uprights safely back in the wagon, Louis Deibler, the executioner of Paris, turned his thoughts toward a cup of coffee, a rolled cigarette, and his traditional post-execution *petit verre*—a small glass of wine.

Epilogue

In August 1893, Jean-Martin Charcot set off on a tour of the Morvan region, a quiet expanse of meadows and lakes and pine trees in Burgundy. His traveling companions were two former students and Louis Pasteur's son-in-law, Pierre Vallery-Radot. Were there portents of doom? Vallery-Radot would recall certain remarks made by the great neurologist that in retrospect seemed ominous. Did Charcot have an inkling he might not return from this journey? On the party's departure from Gare de Lyon, Charcot offered a bit of somber advice to Vallery-Radot: "When saying good-bye, one must avoid the expression of sentimental feelings as much as possible." Charcot was not religious. By some accounts, he was even hostile to the Catholic church. But on a visit to a cemetery while on this holiday, he commented to Vallery-Radot: "Ill will to him who has no faith." In an earlier conversation he had offered: "For me there is a God, but distant and vague."

Four days into the trip, on August 15, the group spent the night at a rural inn called L'Auberge du Lac des Settons after a day of considerable activity. Early in the evening Charcot excused himself from his companions and went to his room. That night, in a letter to his wife he confided that he didn't feel well. After midnight on August 16, Charcot's condition turned desperate; the innkeeper was summoned. By 3:00 a.m., Charcot's fellow travelers, roused from their sleep, were ushered into his room. The great man was sitting in an armchair, perspiring and pale, his breaths short and noisy, his lungs sounding moist. His medical companions diagnosed pulmonary edema. Gradually Charcot's breathing improved, he felt better, he rested awhile. But then suddenly he took a turn for the worse.

Before dawn, Charcot was dead.

Several days later the Salpêtrière's incurable patients—humbly dressed, some on crutches—filed by his coffin in the hospital's chapel, side by side with luminaries in medicine, literature, and government. At Charcot's request, the funeral was simple. His coffin was draped in black cloth woven with the letter *C.* Mourners heard Beethoven's "Funeral March" and selections by soloists from the Paris Opera.

More than seventy eulogies were published around the world. In Sigmund Freud's words, "the 'school of the Salpêtrière' was, of course, Charcot himself." Freud praised his teacher for his voluminous contribution to the understanding of neuropathology. The Charcot method fascinated Freud. "He was not much given to cogitation, was not of the reflective type," Freud wrote, "but he had an artistically gifted temperament—as he said himself, he was a *visuel,* a seer. He himself told us the following about his method of working: he was accustomed to look again and again at things that were incomprehensible to him, to deepen his impression of them day by day, until suddenly understanding of them dawned upon him . . . He was heard to say that the greatest satisfaction man can experience is to see something new, that is, to recognize it as new."

Freud praised Charcot for giving legitimacy to hypnotism. Charcot's experiments allowed advances to be made in understanding the "hitherto neglected and despised" phenomena of hypnotism. None of it would have been possible without the weight of Charcot's reputation—he "put an end once and for all to doubts of the reality of hypnotic manifestations." But Charcot's research into hypnotism and hysteria, Freud reminded his readers, met with "violent opposition." Charcot was denounced for his unyielding belief in the stages of a hysteric attack and for insisting that only hysterics could be hypnotized. Charcot denied the broad psychological foundation of hypnosis—to his detriment, Freud said.

Apparently Charcot himself recognized some of his failings near the end of his life. Evidence emerged later that he was close to reworking his beliefs before death intervened. Georges Guinon, Charcot's last private secretary, recalled conversations he had shortly before Charcot took off on his final journey to Morvan. "He told me that his concept of hysteria had become decadent and his entire chapter on the pathology of the nervous system must be revised," Guinon wrote. Charcot, speaking with his secretary in his library, indicated a stack of papers on the desk. Guinon recalled that Charcot then told him "he had already begun to collect the essential elements for the accomplishment of this task." The revisions to a lifetime's work were to begin soon.

With Charcot's death, the doctrines of the Salpêtrière school floundered. Alan Gauld, author of the massive and authoritative *A History of Hypnotism,* noted that the process in fact had begun several years earlier. "From 1887 onwards, it became increasingly apparent that the Salpêtrière was rapidly losing ground in its disputes with Nancy," he wrote. The Salpêtrière faithful were defecting, and the Salpêtrière viewpoint was looking increasingly absurd in light of the results at Nancy. "No effective answer was found to [the Nancy school's] arguments," Gauld explained, "and the somewhat numerous foreign and other visitors to the Salpêtrière could hardly have been impressed by the demonstrations."

By the time of Charcot's death, Freud had come to accept the Nancy teachings of Ambroise-Auguste Liébeault and Hippolyte Bernheim, which stressed the influence of suggestion and the capacity for hypnotism to heal the afflicted. Freud did not spare his mentor: "Only the opponents of hypnotism who content themselves with hiding their own lack of experience behind some recognized authority still cling to Charcot's pronouncements, and like to quote an expression uttered in his last years denying that hypnosis has any therapeutic efficacy whatever."

Charcot's notions on hypnotism and hysteria had become antiquated. In his eulogy Freud sought to place Charcot in an appropriate historical light. "The progress our science has made in additions to its knowledge will inevitably diminish the value of much that Charcot has taught us," he concluded, "but neither the passing of time nor the changing of ideas will diminish the glory of the man whom we—in France and elsewhere—are mourning today."

After Charcot's death, scientists at the Salpêtrière turned away from the study of hypnosis and returned to pure neurology. In his absence the famed three stages of hypnosis disappeared, lending credence to accusations that the performances of the women were, if not staged, less than honest. But how could such fakery have occurred on such a grand scale? Years later Charcot still had his defenders. In 1910, Joseph Babinski, one of his leading disciples, insisted that a massive deception was impossible because it required a kind of collusion among the hysterics that could not have been maintained: The truth would inevitably have leaked out. Charcot may have been complicit not so much in willful fakery but in fostering an atmosphere of mimicry, coaching, and imitation. His students, who often hypnotized his star patients, were eager to please their master, and the women themselves wanted nothing more than to put on a good show for him. This desire to please fed a willingness to perform in a style that supported the established doctrines. The students encouraged it and the women acquiesced. Once the plotline had been written—catalepsy, lethargy, and somnambulism—the stage was set for grand theatrics.

Jeanne Richepin, who would grow up to become the famous Moulin Rouge dancer Jane Avril, spent some time in Charcot's hysterics ward as a young girl. She revealed years later that the women competed with each other to put on a good show for the doctors. Those who best satisfied the demands of the research got the best treatment in the hospital wards. "In my tiny brain, I was astonished every time to see how such eminent savants could be duped . . . when I, as insignificant as I was, saw through the farces," Avril wrote in her memoir. "I have said to myself since that the great Charcot was aware of what was happening."

One woman who held the answer to the question of simulation was Blanche Wittman, the queen of the hysterics. She continued to live at the Salpêtrière but her displays of grand hypnotism abruptly ceased after Charcot's death. "Like all hysterics of the Belle Époque," wrote A. Baudoin, an intern under Charcot's successor, "she seemed to deny her past and, when asked about the smallest detail of that phase of her life, she angrily refused to answer." Wittman took on a new task, working as a technician in the photography lab. She then moved into the emerging science of radiology, and her handling of radium without proper protection ultimately killed her. Before Wittman's death Baudoin pressed her to speak on her performances as queen of the hysterics. He said to her, "They claim all these attacks were faked, that the patients pretended to be asleep and that the whole thing was a joke on the doctors. What's the truth in all that?" She replied, "None of it is true. It's all lies. If we fell asleep, if we had attacks, it was because we were helpless to do otherwise. What's more, it was very unpleasant." An eccentric full of contradictions to the end, she then added: "Fakery! Do you think it would have been easy to fool Charcot? Yes, there were tricksters who tried. He used to glance at them and say: 'Be still.'"

———

Georges Gilles de la Tourette endured some agonizing years after Charcot's death. The year 1893 was particularly rough: Gilles de la Tourette lost not only his master but also his own son Jean, to meningitis. Then, toward the end of the year, on the evening of December 6, he returned home after visiting a patient to find a respectable-looking woman named Rose Kamper waiting for him. The widow followed him into his consulting room, where she produced a sheet of paper with the names of three doctors from the Salpêtrière, including Charcot. She claimed these doctors had ruined her life, and now she needed fifty francs. Gilles de la Tourette politely declined to give her money but offered to admit her to the Salpêtrière under his care: It was clear to him that this distraught woman had lost her mind.

When she didn't respond to his suggestion, the neurologist turned his back to walk out of the consulting room as three gunshot blasts shattered the silence. Gilles de la Tourette stopped cold—he was hit. He felt a stinging sensation in the back of his head. A surgeon was summoned and removed a bullet that had lodged under the skin. Gilles de la Tourette would make a full recovery. Right after the shooting, Rose went out into the hall and sat down in a chair. "I know what I have just done is wrong," she said, "but it is necessary and now I am satisfied. At least one of them has paid for the others." Her behavior was mysterious and raised the question: Was she acting under a posthypnotic suggestion? Dr. Paul Brouardel, the medical forensic specialist, was called in to examine Rose after her arrest and declared that hypnosis played no role. He concluded that she suffered from what one day would be known in medical circles as paranoid schizophrenia. "Within me, there are actually two different people," Rose told investigators, "one physical and one intellectual. My thoughts no longer belong only to me but also to those who possess me. During the day my intellect allows me to resist the power which enters me without my knowledge but at night I am overpowered. It is to defend myself against these impulses that I bought a revolver."

Rose wound up in the Institute for the Insane until she tried to kill a nurse with a fork; she was sent to a sanatorium and put under restrictive confinement.

Gilles de la Tourette moved away from neurology and associated himself more closely with Brouardel, finally earning an appointment as a professor of forensic medicine in 1894. He was an unpleasant personality, but his behavior was possibly aggravated by the symptoms of syphilis. In these days before penicillin, he could only ride out the ravages of his disease, although he tried to disguise his condition as a severe case of melancholia. By 1899, he was in the late stages, and his deterioration came rapidly. He became delusional; he stole menus from a hotel restaurant and eventually wound up in a mental hospital. His behavior was so bizarre that he was locked away in a cell, where he suffered from megalomania and stared at visitors through eyes whose pupils had frozen. He eventually lost control of his bodily movements, spoke incoherently, suffered convulsions, and died at age forty-six in 1904.

———

Although the hypnotism defense expounded by the Nancy school did not prevail at Gabrielle Bompard's trial, the school's belief in the primacy of suggestion gained substantial scientific and public acceptance in the following years. The leader of the Nancy school, Hippolyte Bernheim, refined his own views and even moved away from an emphasis on hypnotism in favor of the power of suggestion. It was not necessary, Bernheim believed, to put a patient into a hypnotic sleep to achieve positive therapeutic results. Only suggestion was required. He believed that all the phenomena of hypnosis could be achieved in a waking state through suggestion. And he produced dramatic therapeutic outcomes in the absence of hypnosis—that is, without inducing sleep.

The severity of Bernheim's break with earlier conceptions of hypnotism was evident at the International Congress of Medicine in Moscow in 1897 when he created a stir by asserting: *"Il n'y a pas d'hypnotisme."* (There is no such thing as hypnotism.) By this time, after Charcot's death and the fragmenting of the Nancy school, hypnotism was losing its popularity and status as a fad. In 1917, shortly before his death, Bernheim framed his belief on hypnosis like this:

"One could have discovered these phenomena directly in the waking state, without passing through the unnecessary intermediary of induced sleep; and then the word hypnotism would not have been invented. The idea of a special induced magnetic or hypnotic state provoked by special maneuvers would not have been attached to these phenomena. Suggestion has been born of the old hypnotism, as chemistry was born of alchemy." But by now the world was as uninterested in Bernheim's ideas as it was in hypnotism. He died in Paris in 1919, largely forgotten by his contemporaries.

———

Although renowned for his clever sleuthing, Marie-François Goron was dismissed from the Sûreté in July 1894 after nearly seven years at the helm. He became the victim of a wide-ranging political and financial scandal centered on the building of the Panama Canal, a massive project under the leadership of the French and guided by the engineering genius of Gustave Eiffel. When the firm building the canal went belly-up and its bond price plummeted, bringing financial devastation to a wide swath of the population, including many bondholding members of the National Assembly, the Panama affair became, as one historian put it, "the scandal of scandals in contemporary French history." The scandal singed Goron for the sin of not having chased after the wrongdoers strenuously enough.

Goron had an earlier brush with dismissal in 1887 due to an incident far more bizarre than the Panama Canal scandal. As deputy chief of the Sûreté, he had helped reel in a charming murderer named Henri Pranzini, who was convicted of a sensational triple killing. After Pranzini's execution, Goron asked one of his detectives to get him a souvenir of the case. Keepsakes were fairly common at the time—Gustave-Placide Macé, who had been the Sûreté chief until 1884, had collected enough artifacts to create a criminal museum. But the efforts of Goron's detective overstepped the bounds of propriety and forced Goron to launch a charm offensive to save his job. As Goron explained it, the detective thought that "the souvenir which I should value above all others would be what the murderer valued above all else in the world—namely, his own skin." Goron and the Sûreté chief, Hippolyte Ernest Auguste Taylor, were presented with business-card cases that, to the unsuspecting eye, appeared to be covered in white leather. But the material for the casing was, in fact, skin taken from the body of the murderer. Goron tossed the souvenir into his desk drawer and forgot about it until *La Lanterne* created a storm by revealing its existence. Goron, caught off-guard, quipped that *La Lanterne* showed "a respect for the dead bodies of assassins which I had been very far from suspecting had ever been the case."

To fend off calls for his and Taylor's resignations, Goron accepted full responsibility, telling an examining magistrate who was appointed to investigate: "If in this unfortunate affair anyone is guilty I am that man." He admitted that he should never have accepted the card cases. But something more dramatic was needed. So the guilty parties— Goron, Taylor, the detective, and the head of the mortuary that supplied the skin—were assembled in front of a judge. A fire was then lighted and the cases were thrown into the flames. Thus the matter was resolved without harm to the participants, except for the lowly assistant at the mortuary who helped remove the skin—he lost his job. Goron noted how unfair this was, because gruesome uses of body parts was a vibrant tradition, particularly among medical students who made tobacco pouches from the bodies they studied and placed bones on their mantelpieces.

Despite the clouds that darkened his tenure, Goron has occupied an honored place in the annals of criminal history, thanks in no small measure to his successes in the Gouffé case. He solved other high-profile mysteries and is remembered for his doggedness, insight, and organizational skills. Some of his unabashed admirers have exaggerated his talents, among them Philip A. Wilkins, who translated and edited some of Goron's memoirs and who opined that the sleuth "might perhaps be described as a real-life police official worthy to take his place with Sherlock Holmes, the Poirots, and the Inspector Hornleighs of fiction."

Goron was rightly praised for his humanitarian streak—he fervently opposed capital punishment and abhorred being present at an execution—"he was as the French say, *sympathique*," Wilkins wrote, "a strange quality you will think for a man so much of whose life had been devoted to the apprehension of criminals."

Goron expanded the ranks of the Sûreté and improved its professionalism by hiring agents of a high caliber; he replaced untrustworthy former criminals of earlier days who knew the haunts and habits of the underworld with married men, fathers, and others with strong morals who, the historian Clive Emsley has said, had the "rectitude to avoid the temptations with which they were faced daily." In his memoir, Goron praised his men for their selflessness and disregard for their own safety; these detectives, he said, were motivated by self-esteem. "It isn't personal interest that guides them, and they are of such high professional standards that you will never see one of them accepting a large sum of cash in exchange for not arresting a guilty party."

On his departure from the Sûreté, Goron established the first international private investigators' company in Europe and wrote easy-to-read—and somewhat sensational—tales of his real-life detective adventures for a widening popular audience that craved a good crime story.

His sidekick, Pierre-Fortune Jaume, wrote an engaging memoir in his own idiosyncratic style. Years later, *The Washington Post* described Jaume as a man who followed his own "peculiar science . . . called individualist criminology." Writing in September 1915, six months after Jaume's death at age sixty-nine, the paper described the inspector as a true original in his manner of sleuthing. He donned disguises with such ease and expertise that "his only boast . . . was that he never had been mistaken for a detective." He never carried a gun; his only weapon was a bit of cord to use as handcuffs. He was so averse to being known on the streets that, it was said, only two photographs were ever taken of him, both of those in his youth.

Goron long outlived his friend, dying in February 1933 at age eighty-five. The newspaper *L'Intransigeant* announced the news on February 4 with an exclamation—"M. Goron is dead!"—and, after describing his adventures stalking criminals, ended with: "Curious detail: he loved all kind of birds, and was a member, vice president, or president of a large number of bird-watching societies."

———

In her early days in prison Gabrielle Bompard was still a celebrity, her accommodations, diet, and clothing—indeed, her life in jail—matters of intense public interest. Before her transfer to Clermont women's prison she stayed briefly at the jail at Nanterre where, it was dutifully reported, she was housed in cell number 1 on the second floor along with a total population of one hundred and sixty women and a hundred and eighty men who were all afforded one bath a month. The fashion-crazy Gabrielle was now garbed in a gray wool camisole, a white bonnet and shawl, and clogs. She ate the institution's greasy meals and was employed sewing shirts for infants whose mothers were in prison. Her behavior was said to be good "but her gaiety [was] disappearing under the influence of perpetual solitude."

After her transfer to Clermont in January 1891, she began to show up less frequently in the press and had to work hard to get some ink. In the summer of her first year, it was falsely reported that she had contracted typhoid fever and later that she had died. She was still drawing attention to herself with dramatic, even hysterical, behavior: In 1894, she complained to a guard that she feared her life would end in prison. "If only I were sure of not dying here. Ah!" she cried. "If only I could keep the promise I made to God and make up for my faults and rehabilitate myself to my poor father whom I dishonored!" It was a dramatic speech during which, *La Presse* reported, "Gabrielle Bompard fell ill and doctors gave up on her."

She survived, of course, suffering only from a sudden bout of theatrics, and began a long campaign for a reduction in her sentence. But six years later, she had little to show for it. As *Le Journal des Débats* said of her, "she is neither resigned nor repentant and seems to be completely unaware of what resignation and repentance are." Other journalists, however, reported that she was a changed woman. That same year, *Le Figaro* called her "a model of gentility and resignation" and indicated that she was hard at work as the bookkeeper for the prison's corset-making operation. By 1901, Gabrielle had convinced her keepers that she had reformed, prompting *Le Journal des Débats,* which had earlier condemned her behavior, to declare she "had the most exemplary conduct" and that she demonstrated wisdom and gentleness and that her crime had "perhaps been unconsciously committed."

With her lawyer Henri Robert working diligently on her behalf, Gabrielle finally won her release from prison on June 8, 1903, having served just twelve years of her twenty-year sentence. She was nearly thirty-five and largely forgotten, but her craving for the spotlight was as strong as ever. She needed a sensational spectacle to mark her return to the national eye. Outside the prison, on a beautiful spring morning, she met with a reporter who noted how small and cheerful she was and that her "face, pale and round, was lit up by big eyes." She had an "opulent mass of chestnut hair" and "one could hardly discover any hardness in the outline of her thin lips." She said that being free felt very natural to her. "My release," she told the reporter, "didn't make me emotional at all. I didn't cry. I didn't faint."

She boarded a train at the Clermont-de-l'Oise station and rode the fifty miles to Paris for a publicity-generating lunch. At the fashionable Pavillon d'Armenonville restaurant in the Bois de Boulogne she joined the table of the attention-seeking aeronaut Alberto Santos-Dumont, with whom she had corresponded during her incarceration. While in prison she also had written to the well-known newspaper editor Jacques Dhur "so he'd be interested in me," she said. Santos-Dumont was a Brazilian eccentric, a darling of the Paris press, who was in competition with the Wright brothers to become the first to pilot an airplane. He was often pictured in the newspapers floating over Paris in a lighter-than-air flying machine; one of his favorite stunts was to drop in at a café or a friend's apartment in the cigar-shaped airship, tying it up to a lamppost while he visited inside.

Of her afternoon at the Pavillon d'Armenonville with Santos-Dumont and other celebrated characters, Gabrielle said, dreamily, "Oh! A good lunch, a bottle of wine, the crowd—it's nice, it's gay."

One observer, however, was disgusted by the sight of "the petite strangler nibbling her dessert in this elegant milieu . . . the memory of her crime not seeming to bother her much." Gabrielle was a little plumper than she had been in her early twenties at the height of her notoriety, but still attractive and well-mannered in a black silk bolero and tight gray skirt pleated in the back. She was a mix of sugar and vitriol, of presumed virtue and real vice, this critic asserted; there was about her a stench of rotting cadaver, fouling the springtime arboreal scent of the Bois de Boulogne.

When news of her release reached San Francisco, the *Chronicle* rebuked celebrities like Santos-Dumont and Dhur for entertaining "the confessed strangler and woman of shame." The paper noted that cartoons in the press showed society people telephoning one another, saying: "Do come to my five o'clock tea. Gabrielle Bompard will be there. She is too sweet for anything." Indeed, the *Chronicle* concluded, Gabrielle was having "the gayest time of all her wicked life."

Several days after her Santos-Dumont lunch, she traveled to Nancy, where she stayed with her brother and visited with one of her staunchest defenders, Jules Liégeois of the University of Nancy. The law professor who had begged the court—in vain—for permission to hypnotize Gabrielle now had his chance, with her willing consent. Only in this way, Liégeois believed, could he get at the indisputable truth of the crime. Only in a hypnotic state would Gabrielle be free to reveal what really happened.

The professor grasped her wrists, looked into her eyes, and said, "You must fall into a deep sleep and act out the crime again." She was still an easy subject after twelve years in prison, and she fell quickly into a trance. "There you are," Liégeois urged, "it is the moment before the murder. Go on."

Acting out the scene, an anguished Gabrielle sank to her knees and refused to assist Michel Eyraud in the murder. She mimed a horrific quarrel in which her lover went for her throat with his powerful hands. Writhing, she cried, "He's strangling me!" He kept at it while she begged him to stop until finally she promised to do his bidding: She agreed to lure the victim to the apartment and seduce him so Eyraud could rob and murder him. Moving into the next phase of the crime, Gabrielle got to her feet and acted it out: She conducted an imaginary person to the corner of the room and removed a sash from around her waist. Then she froze, unable to take the next step, and went into convulsions, falling to the floor. After several minutes of hysterics Gabrielle got back onto her feet shrieking, "Murderer! Murderer!" and calling out the name of Eyraud. When Liégeois pressed her to describe what Eyraud had done, Gabrielle took several steps forward and closed her fingers around the professor's throat.

It was a dramatic and revealing demonstration, one that Liégeois believed should have been delivered in court. If jurors had seen Gabrielle in the throes of the crime, the outcome of the trial might have been quite different.

Believing it was important to bring his discovery to the public, Liégeois invited the press to witness the demonstration. In both Nancy and Paris the professor and Gabrielle repeated her hypnotic portrayal of the crime. As she performed the reenactment, reporters busily jotted down her cries and writhings while photographers captured still images of the emotional scene. But there was little interest in rectifying a potential wrong in this old case. It was a "very weird spectacle," one reporter wrote, adding "many terrible things are done in France in the name of science." He described Gabrielle's "mental torture" and "the severe ordeal she'd been through" during the crime, but he was unmoved. "It was a horrible exhibition," the reporter concluded, "and it is difficult to see any justification for it."

Undeterred, Gabrielle sought to force herself on the public. She published a brief memoir in a new journal created by her admirer Jacques Dhur. To promote her life story, Dhur circulated autographed postcards on the streets bearing Gabrielle's photograph in a ball gown with a high collar. "Curious about my life?" the murderess wrote across the card. "Read my confession." The editor inscribed a note intended to excite the public: "She recounts the death as if she had simply been an accidental spectator of the crime." This caused one cynic to sneer: "She is a star upon which the Barnums could count to make themselves rich."

Indeed, there were riches to be had, or so Liégeois and Gabrielle believed. They rehearsed their hypnotic exhibition and prepared to take it on the road as a traveling show. It would serve two purposes: to prove that she was unjustly convicted of the crime; and to attract a paying audience in large entertainment halls. But Parisian moralists were appalled: "As Christians we must observe the law of forgiveness but this does not extend to glorifying rogues," one critic wrote. "Let's not confuse a mother who steals bread to feed her children with a seductress who lures a client home so her lover can rob and strangle him." These keepers of French virtue scorned the press for playing along, for "deprecating the public," for providing a "new job opportunity for a romantic female criminal." Critics worried that Gabrielle's return would be a scourge on French honor. "We are in an age of rehabilitations," lamented *La Presse*, voicing a complaint that echoes oddly into our day.

Before their bizarre tour began, however, Gabrielle and Liégeois had a falling-out, and the professor was suddenly out of the picture. In his stead came a dentist named Gaston Cardos, who fancied himself an impresario and hypnotist and who recognized this rare and promising opportunity. But in Paris sentiment was strongly opposed to the return of the little demon—the public had lost its fascination with her—and an audience could not be found. Another venue was needed, so the pair turned their sights on America. Gabrielle and Cardos set sail, traveling in second class aboard the luxury steamer *Lucania,* and arrived at the port of New York on January 17, 1904.

Immigration officials, alerted by cable, awaited the steamer at the Cunard pier. Chief Inspector Jackson came aboard, confirmed Gabrielle's identity, interviewed the couple, and learned the purpose of the trip. Although the pair vigorously pleaded their case, Jackson denied them entry to America on the grounds that Gabrielle was a convicted criminal and Cardos was an undesirable immigrant; they were taken to Ellis Island to await deportation. Gabrielle was described as calm throughout the ordeal, while Cardos became enraged and demanded their release, declaring he would appeal the matter to the highest levels in Washington. Gabrielle's appeal was quickly denied, and when the *Lucania* left New York a week later on its return trip, it stopped near Ellis Island to pick her up. She was on her way back to Europe on her own while her companion was marooned on Ellis Island, awaiting the resolution of his own appeal.

The traveling show was Gabrielle's last chance at redemption and celebrity, and after its collapse, she drifted into obscurity. Her glamour had faded; no one was interested in her hysterics or in the hypnotism defense. Liégeois, too, had never fully recovered from his botched performance in court. After the trial he dropped out of sight for a while under a barrage of ridicule. A Nancy newspaper had mocked his disappearance, noting that his former students jokingly wondered whether he hadn't become the victim of a new Eyraud and his diabolical hypnosis skills. Even his colleague Hippolyte Bernheim disparaged him. Writing to another Nancy scholar, Bernheim was dismayed by Liégeois's clumsy handling of the case. Instead of establishing the predominance of the Nancy school, Bernheim lamented, Liégeois had exposed the school's doctrines to ridicule.

Many in the legal community were relieved that the hypnotism defense had failed. After the trial, *The New York Times* spoke for many in an article headlined "Hypnotism and Murder." "What the world has principally to be thankful for," the paper said, "is that the theory of hypnotic influence was not admitted by the court to be a legitimate defense, and that no precedent for such a defense in murder trials was established." A different result would have had repercussions around the world. Had the defense prevailed, the paper continued, it "would have been a sad blow to the cause of justice at the hands of the French court." Had Gabrielle's lawyers "succeeded in establishing this defense, a wider door would have been opened for the escape of criminals than that thrown open by the first successful plea of insanity in a murder case. The number of 'hypnotized' murderers would have increased alarmingly, and hypnotism would have more crimes to answer for than insanity itself."

Afterward, the hypnosis defense was tried rarely and to poor effect. Excitement over the Gouffé case in America prompted an accused murderer in Fargo, North Dakota, to consider claiming in 1891 that he was under the hypnotic command of a Minneapolis woman when he killed a grain elevator agent during a robbery. Misled by the news reports on the Bompard trial, the murderer, Joseph Remington, believed Gabrielle got off more lightly than Eyraud because of the effectiveness of her hypnotism plea. The newspapers, reporting that Remington was susceptible to hypnotic influence, noted that "should this line of defense be adopted, it will probably be the first one of its kind in the United States." In the end, Remington pleaded guilty and was sentenced to life. In the 1950s, two Dutch criminals robbed a bank and shot two bank officials; one of the culprits claimed he was under the complete hypnotic control of the other. The court sent the dominant criminal to prison and the other to an insane asylum. In 1981, a Ms. Phillips said she killed two federal marshals under the hypnotic command of her husband. The jury found her guilty.

Although Gabrielle did not influence the course of legal history, she nonetheless brought to the forefront French anxieties in the belle époque. She symbolized the gaiety and darkness of the era, its freedom and recklessness, its cleverness and uncertainty. Her decadent life reflected the desires and fears of the French in a changing world on the precipice of the twentieth century.

She also set the stage for future criminal stars and gave the world a taste of what was to come—the tabloid excess, the public fascination with famous murderers, the exploitation of brutal crimes as popular entertainment. She laid down the historical lineage for the twentieth century's most notorious defendants in sensational murder cases, from Leopold and Loeb to O. J. Simpson to Casey Anthony.

But as the new century wore on, Gabrielle was a celebrity without an audience. She eventually dropped from view, popping up only occasionally in the press. In 1912, the International News Service reported that she was living on boulevard Saint-Denis in Asnières. She "is a middle-aged woman now, but there are traces still of her beauty," the agency reported. "She lives quietly and respectably by her needle, and has a pretty gift for embroidery."

She lived on through the First World War. By then she had virtually vanished from the public's consciousness, and her death on December 9, 1920, caused scarcely a ripple. *Le Figaro* noted that she had taken refuge in Hirson on the Belgian border and died there "in misery." So obscure had the sensational hypnotic murderess become that *La Presse* titled its obituary: "An Unnoticed Departure."

Acknowledgments

The making of a book is a story itself driven by its own characters and plotline. This one got started about eight years ago when I happened upon an academic article titled "Murder Under Hypnosis" by the scholar Ruth Harris. The article recounted Gabrielle Bompard's case, with an emphasis on its role in the courtroom of the belle époque. The piece was irresistible. I read it again and again until I finally understood it—and was hooked on this mesmerizing moment in Parisian history. I wanted to know everything I could about Gabrielle, hypnosis, the murder, and the belle époque.

I began researching the case and the era and discovered a trove of material in French archives and libraries and in French journals, newspapers, and books. I'd lived in Paris for four years and must admit with considerable shame that my French language skills are an embarrassment. Here is where the leading character in these acknowledgments enters the story. My wife, Suzanne Allard Levingston, who studied French as a student and had the benefit of a French-Canadian father, stunned me with her aplomb and proficiency when we first moved to Paris—and then again when she began translating mountains of nineteenth-century French-language documents. I did my little part—I was far better at reading French than speaking it, and with a digital dictionary at hand delved into Chief Marie-François Goron's easy-reading memoirs. Meanwhile, Suzanne sat patiently translating for hours on end. Her work fills two file cabinets and several fat, three-ring binders. Her skills as a researcher were equally remarkable. With a phone call here or a few taps on the computer there, speaking and writing in French, she tracked down vital details from Paris, Lille, Nancy, and Lyon. Her scouring of libraries and databases is responsible for the book's evocative photographs and illustrations, and her composure in wrestling down footnote citations helped temper my own mania. Our creation of this book was a partnership in the truest sense, though any errors, omissions, or misperceptions are my fault alone.

This book has been written and rewritten, and even sold and resold. In its first formulation, it was longer, more academic, and a slower read. It found a publisher in 2007 but before it could be released, the American economy began to self-immolate—and my book was tossed onto the flames. In a panic the publisher canceled the contract. Abandonment was a blessing, however, and it allowed the book to evolve in important ways. I was left with a manuscript I didn't particularly like and the time to reimagine Gabrielle's story from beginning to end. First I wanted to know Gabrielle better: Who was this tiny woman who caused so much sensation in her day? To probe her inner being, I wrote a one-woman play in which she recounts her life and turmoil. It was produced in the D.C. area and gave me fresh enthusiasm to tackle her tale again in book form. Realizing I'm not an academic but a journalist, I began rewriting Gabrielle's story with a mind toward producing a popular history—something that would highlight both the wonderful and the bizarre contained in this story and engage a general audience, even one unfamiliar with the period. The making of this book has been filled with elation, exhaustion, frustration, and deep satisfaction, and Suzanne has been right by my side, enjoying and suffering through it all, with unfailing patience, depths of insight and intelligence, and always ready with the net to catch me every time I plummeted in spirit.

The research required a trip to Paris so I could walk the same streets that were once home to Eyraud and Gabrielle and Goron and Gouffé, and dive into archives and libraries and other institutions. I visited the scene of the crime at 3, rue Tronson du Coudray; Gouffé's home at 13, rue Rougemont; his office at 148, rue Montmartre; the site of the defunct Café Véron on the boulevard Montmartre, where Gouffé had his final aperitif; and other locations along the *grands boulevards.* I walked through the mansion at 217, boulevard Saint-Germain that once belonged to Jean-Martin Charcot, and strolled the grounds of the Salpêtrière Hospital where the famed neurologist reigned. I stood at the site where executions by guillotine used to be held in an area once known as place de la Roquette, just outside the gates of the long-demolished La Roquette Prison.

I am grateful to Gregory Auda and his colleagues Malik Ben-Miloud and Alain Rozenblum at the Archives of the Prefecture of Police for supplying stacks of original French newspaper clippings of the crime and its aftermath. Véronique La Roux-Hugon kindly endured my awful French and pointed me to valuable information on Charcot at the Charcot Library on the campus of the Salpêtrière Hospital. Florence Greffe graciously showed me through the magnificent Academy of Sciences and sent a chill down my spine when she led me into the very room where Charcot defended hypnotism as a valid discipline of science. I am indebted to many others who have helped me understand French science, law, culture, and politics in the nineteenth century, among them Jérôme Sgard at the Institut d'Études Politiques de Paris, commonly known as Sciences Po; Ghislaine Dangé and Thierry Caillier at the Bibliothèque Municipale de Lille; Gérald Andres at the Bibliothèque Municipale de Lyon; Christian Fonnet at the Association pour l'Histoire des Chemins de Fer; and Jean-Claude Farcy.

Linda Hervieux, a tremendous researcher, pored over documents at the Archives de la Seine, digging up crucial police reports, letters, interviews, and testimony. Her careful indexing and translations helped smooth the process, and she cheerfully went back again and again to chase down specific requests.

While this is a work of popular history, I have endeavored to depict historical themes and characters with as much verisimilitude as possible. As a result I have asked several academics to put their eye to my manuscript. I am deeply grateful to Katrin Schultheiss, for her insights overall and on Charcot in particular; to Alexandre Klein, for his thoughts on Jules Liégeois and my usage of certain French phrases; to Brady Brower, for applying his sharp historian's eye to the manuscript; to Heather Cox Richardson, for her writerly wisdom and astute analysis of the text.

I want to give a special shout-out to my friend Ron Soriano, an American whose fluency in French was astounding, and whose humor and kindness were in abundant supply as he provided eloquent translations for me even while suffering from the undiagnosed early stages of a rare, debilitating brain disease known as Pick's. His translations in this book will stand as a lasting testament to a man of formidable brain power.

I'd also like to thank Del Wilber, my colleague at *The Washington Post* and a fierce reporter and stylish writer, who combed over the manuscript offering key suggestions and was a welcome e-mail pal on matters literary early in the morning and late at night and on weekends. I'm also grateful to Dennis Drabelle for his superb last-minute editing.

The folks at Doubleday, the publisher who bought my reimagined book, couldn't have been more kind and helpful. I'm thrilled by publicity manager Todd Doughty's enthusiasm from the earliest stages, and in awe of Gerry Howard's fine editing touch—not to mention the humorous and encouraging asides about the characters and storyline he jotted in the margins of the manuscript. His assistants, Hannah Wood, Nathaniel Sufrin, and Jeremy Medina, have helped smooth the production process. Copy editor Karla Eoff made this a much better book than it was before she put her hand to it. My agent, Dan Lazar, has been a steadfast advocate for this project from its first glimmers through all the turmoil to its happy conclusion. I am forever grateful to him for sticking by it and for his steady professionalism.

Which brings me back to my family. I'm saddened that my father, my biggest fan, was only able to read early chapters of the book and didn't live to see its completion. My mother also passed away during the writing, even as she was eagerly preparing to have me entertain at her book club. It took me so long to finish this book that my kids, Katie and Ben, grew into young adults over the eight years. Katie even headed off to college before its completion. But with her own French proficiency, she will be studying at the Sorbonne in Paris this year and will have the chance, if she so wishes, to track down the steps of the characters who for so long obsessed her father. Thank you, Katie and Ben, for your patience. Though Gabrielle seemed like a delinquent third child in the family, she's not in the way anymore, and I'm back.

Finally, it's a cliché but some clichés are borne out by fact: This book could not have been written without my wife, Suzanne, and maybe, just maybe, another trip to Paris will start me on the way toward repayment for all she's done.

Notes

PROLOGUE

2   "**Look at me**": Bernheim, *Hypnosis & Suggestion in Psychotherapy*, 2.

3   "**It was not a time**": Tuchman, *The Proud Tower*, xi.

3   "**half-Dante, half-Napoleon**": Goetz et al., *Charcot—Constructing Neurology*, 272.

4   "**the plaything of a fixed idea**": Gauld, *A History of Hypnotism*, 497.

4   "**All conscience**": Forrest, *Hypnotism: A History*, 244.

5   "**subject to brusque**": "Michel Eyraud et Gabrielle Bompard," 79.

5   "**all the symptoms**": Lacassagne, *L'Affaire Gouffé*, 105.

6   "**You have a temperament**": Ibid., 85.

6   "**clay in the hands of a potter**": Laurence and Perry, *Hypnosis, Will, and Memory*, 182.

CHAPTER 1

10   **Toussaint-Augustin Gouffé:** Gouffé has been variously cited as Toussaint-Augustin Gouffé, Augustin-Toussaint Gouffé, and Alexandre Toussaint Gouffé.

10   "**bedlam of noise**": Skinner, *Elegant Wits and Grand Horizontals*, 1.

11   "**Paris is the only corner**": Rearick, *Pleasures of the Belle Époque*, 41.

11   "**It is we**": Ibid., 40.

11   "**People must make merry**": Ibid., 208.

11   "**the bomb that cleanses**": Rudorff, *Belle Époque*, 158.

12   "**Our dear France**": Harriss, *The Tallest Tower*, 112.

13   "**the dead speak**": Ibid., 129.

13   "*concert gigantesque*": Rearick, 127.

13   "**At a height of 350 feet**": Harriss, 102.

14   **rue Tronson du Coudray:** The street on which the murder occurred appears in documents as Tronson Ducoudray and Tronson-du-Coudray, and on street signs in today's Paris as Tronson du Coudray.

14   "**So is it true**": Goron, *L'Amour Criminel*, 272.

14   "**Everyone is heading for**": Harriss, 125.

CHAPTER 2

18   "**You did not have**": Bouchardon, *La Malle Mystérieuse*, 14.

18   "**He was easy prey**": Ibid., 18.

CHAPTER 3

19   "Would you like to see": Goron, *L'Amour Criminel*, 308.
20   "This man": Ibid., 152.
20   "You're nice": Ibid., 151.
21   "He could do what he wanted": Ibid., 152.
21   "Women are like cutlets": Weber, *France*, 86.
21   "Don't be afraid": Goron, 166.
21   "From: Paris 1231": Ibid., 200, and Bouchardon, *La Malle Mystérieuse*, 81.
22   "What do you want": *Le Figaro*, Nov. 13, 1889.

CHAPTER 4

23   "tawny-colored": Wilkins, *Behind the French C.I.D.*, 11.
23   "Many people momentarily disappear": Goron, *L'Amour Criminel*, 172.
24   "I didn't have the power": Goron, *Les Mémoires de M. Goron,* 33.
25   "Little by little": Ibid., 51–52.
25   "I penetrated behind the scenes": Ibid., 53–54.
25   "I must confess": Wilkins, 12.
25   "a look as sharp as a needle": Ibid., 11.
26   "veritable museum": Moriarity, *The Paris Law Courts*, 241.
27   "Patriotic and conscientious": Ibid., 252.
27   "The judge of instruction": Ibid., 244.
27   "lacking in all psychological": Jaume, *La Vérité sur l'Affaire Gouffé*, 6.

CHAPTER 5

29   "Her father gave her": "Michel Eyraud et Gabrielle Bompard," 81.
30   "a grand tendency": *Le Matin*, Nov. 29, 1890.
30   "If one knew": *Le Petit Journal*, late edition, Jan. 4, 1890.
31   "Bah!": Bouchardon, *La Malle Mystérieuse*, 186.

CHAPTER 6

33   "Whoever has not undressed": Skinner, *Elegant Wits and Grand Horizontals*, 22.
33   "There was first the problem": Ibid., 63.
34   "whose skin": Baldick, *Lives and Letters*, 293.
34   "glorious frenzy": Ibid., 322.
34   "where one finds practically": Schwartz, *Spectacular Realities*, 23.
34   "I myself don't have any complaints": Jaume, *La Vérité sur l'Affaire Gouffé*, 8.
35   "air of an ancient cavalry officer": *L'Écho de Paris*, Nov. 11, 1889.
35   "The investigation so far": Ibid., Aug. 4, 1889.
37   "Like everyone else": Thompson, "The Thief-Takers of Paris," 456.

CHAPTER 7

38   "could wheel and deal": *Le Figaro*, Feb. 3, 1890.
38   "Oh, this one here": *Le Matin*, Dec. 18, 1890.
39   "indefinable as Marseille itself": Fisher, *Two Towns in Provence: A Considerable Town*, 5, 6.
39   "ferocious jealousy": *Le Petit Journal*, Jan. 31, 1890.
41   "A point is clarified for me": Jaume, *La Vérité sur l'Affaire Gouffé*, 58.

CHAPTER 8
42   "My dear Goron": Goron, *Les Mémoires de M. Goron*, 159.
42   "A little shudder": Ibid.
42   "freedom of the press law": Schwartz, *Spectacular Realities*, 29.
43   "golden age of the press": Ibid., 27.
43   "This was well reciprocated": Goron, 194.
43   "must have rejoiced": *Le Temps*, Nov. 13, 1887.
43   "I laughed with the professional": Goron, 164–65.
44   "The landau for a wedding": Ibid., 168.
44   "I had a pang": Ibid., 170.
44   "After nightfall": Ibid., 169.
45   "I had not known an impression": Ibid., 174.
45   *"Au revoir"*: Ibid., 175.
45   "this butchery without grandeur": Ibid., 177–78.
45   "contempt for human life": Ibid., 179, 184.
45   "I understood quickly": Ibid., 196.
46   "How many times": Ibid., 203.
46   "The press has a tremendous skill": Ibid., 204.
46   "M. Goron . . . marches": *Le Gil Blas*, Aug. 21, 1889.
47   *"Rien, rien"*: *L'Écho de Paris*, Aug. 7, 1889.

CHAPTER 9
49   "Imagine . . . every kind": Weiner, *The Citizen-Patient in Revolutionary and Imperial Paris*, 22.
51   "ugly as a louse": Krämer and Daniels, "Pioneers of Movement Disorders," 695.
51   "perilous task": Bérillon, *Premier Congrès International de l'Hypnotisme Expérimental et Thérapeutique*, 245.
52   "In this case": Ibid.
52   "experimental crimes": Ibid., 246.
52   "I am convinced": Ibid., 249.
53   "I had never heard": Delboeuf, *Magnétiseurs et Médecins*, 31.
53   "You cannot look at someone": Bérillon, 266.
54   *"À l'Élysée!"*: Harding, *The Astonishing Adventure of General Boulanger*, 189.
55   "It was the noisiest occasion": Delboeuf, 31.
55   "Back in 1887": Bérillon, 267.
55   "And so": Delboeuf, 32.
56   "Would you want me to bring": Ibid.
56   "Me! Me!": Ibid.

CHAPTER 10
57   "I'll find what stupidity": Bouchardon, *La Malle Mystérieuse*, 62.
59   "I think that the victim": Lacassagne, *L'Affaire Gouffé*, 23.

CHAPTER 11
63   "Faith is indispensable": Goron, *L'Amour Criminel*, 193–94.
64   "If you are in a sinister place": Ibid.
64   "It is at present established": *L'Éclair*, Aug. 27, 1889.

CHAPTER 12

66   "One can understand": Lacassagne, *L'Affaire Gouffé*, 69.
67   "they lived riotously": *The Morning Call*, May 22, 1890.
67   "Vanaerd was a hail fellow": *The Salt Lake Herald*, Feb. 13, 1890.
68   "blue eyes of incomparable softness": *L'Écho de Paris*, Jan. 30, 1890.
68   "one of those men": *Le Figaro*, Jan. 28, 1890.

CHAPTER 13

70   "You tell anyone": Bouchardon, *La Malle Mystérieuse*, 79.
70   "with bad grace": Thorwald, *The Century of the Detective*, 120.
71   "I do not like money": *Le Gaulois*, Mar. 21, 1890, in Darmon, *La Malle à Gouffé*, 49.
72   "You are incapable": *La Presse*, Jan. 26, 1890.
72   "It is well-proven": Ibid.
72   "going from one person": Darmon, 50.
73   "There is a man who disappeared": Goron, *L'Amour Criminel*, 207–8.

CHAPTER 14

74   "Could it be one": Jaume, *La Vérité sur l'Affaire Gouffé*, 17.
75   "You can't accuse him": Darmon, *La Malle à Gouffé*, 54.
76   "One sees that it's not necessary": *La Jeune République*, Sept. 1, 1889.
76   "I tell you frankly": *L'Éclair*, Sept. 3, 1889.
76   "In learning of the discovery": Jaume, 11.
76   "What do you want": *L'Éclair*, Sept. 3, 1889.
76   "The more the newspapers": Ibid.
77   "Opinion continues": *Le Figaro*, Sept. 4, 1889.
77   "I see . . . that Goron's mustache": Jaume, 9–10.

CHAPTER 15

78   "Where does the Gouffé case stand": *Le Figaro*, Sept. 20, 1889.
78   "All right": Bouchardon, *La Malle Mystérieuse*, 78.
78   He then turned his attention: Ticket details can be found in Goron, *L'Amour Criminel*, 200, 226; and Bouchardon, 81.
80   "Was he mistaken": *Le Gil Blas*, Nov. 10, 1889.
80   "Now search inside": Bouchardon, 118.
80   "Listen, my friend": Goron, 219.
80   "a good man": Ibid.
80   "From this moment on": Ibid., 220.
80   "Monsieur Goron's cookshops": Thorwald, *The Century of the Detective*, 46.
81   "What do you want": Goron, 221.
81   "If I was able to give": Bouchardon, 119.
81   "So I thought": Ibid., 221.
81   "I hoped that as a reward": Bouchardon, 119.
81   "It seemed to me": Ibid.
81   "The entire inquiry": *Le Passe-Temps*, Nov. 24, 1889.
81   "an attitude": Ibid.
82   "It's since the beginning of July": Goron, 224.
82   "M. Cornély came": Ibid., 224.

82   "No doubt is possible": Ibid.
83   "I had the excellent idea": Ibid., 215.
83   "I asked for a bit": Ibid.
83   "He recognized immediately": Ibid.
84   "naturally mistaken": Jaume, *La Vérité sur l'Affaire Gouffé*, 29.
84   "Decidedly, luck returned": Goron, 222.
84   "At the moment of the burial": Ibid., 222–23.
84   "Without this hat": *Le Passe-Temps*, Nov. 24, 1889.
85   "This modest one": Goron, 223.

CHAPTER 16
87   "If it pleases Providence": *The Allahabad Pioneer*, Nov. 30, 1889, cited in
      Barker, *More San Francisco Memoirs 1852–1899*, 274, 275.
87   "San Francisco is a mad city": Ibid., 271.
87   "I am certainly grateful": Goron, *L'Amour Criminel*, 302.
88   "He is a regular brandy sharp": *The Washington Post*, Mar. 16, 1890.
88   "He was way ahead": Ibid.

CHAPTER 17
90   "strong, rhythmic step": Starr, *The Killer of Little Shepherds*, 17.
91   "One must know": Thorwald, *The Century of the Detective*, 128.
91   "a mixture of every repulsive odor": Starr, 20.
91   "I had such eagerness": Goron, *L'Amour Criminel*, 227.
92   "A bungled autopsy": Thorwald, 128.
94   "Gentlemen, I herewith": Ibid., 131.

CHAPTER 18
95   "Light is shed": *Le Petit Journal*, Nov. 14, 1889.
95   "We were given": *L'Écho de Paris*, Nov. 16, 1889.
95   "the very skilled": *Le Figaro*, Nov. 11, 1889.
95   "Yes, there cannot be": *L'Écho de Paris*, Nov. 18, 1889.
96   "I assigned some workers": Goron, *L'Amour Criminel*, 232.
96   "The police search": *L'Écho de Paris*, Nov. 18, 1889.
96   "a petite, attractive brunette": *Le Petit Journal*, Nov. 12, 1889.
96   "a ravishing brunette": *L'Écho de Paris*, Nov. 15, 1889.
96   "Eyraud presented himself": Ibid.
97   "She was adored there": *Le Petit Journal*, Nov. 13, 1889.
97   "How could Eyraud": Jaume, *La Vérité sur l'Affaire Gouffé*, 33.
97   "He was so good": *Le Figaro*, Nov. 13, 1889.
98   "The investigation advances": *L'Écho de Paris*, Nov. 23, 1889.
98   "Suffice it to say": Freud, *The Letters of Sigmund Freud*, 187.
98   "a little cocaine": Ibid., 192.
98   "All day long a multitude": Schwartz, *Spectacular Realities*, 64.
99   "It is nothing but": Ibid., 59.
99   "I don't think": Freud, 187–88.
99   "Cré Dieu!": Pessis and Crépineau, *The Moulin Rouge*, 11.
100   "I have an elastic anus": Nohain and Caradec, *Le Pétomane*, 8–10.
100   "supersalacious entertainment": Knapp and Chipman, *That Was Yvette*, 70.

100   "the overcrowded, overheated": Ibid., 71.
101   "It was necessary": Goron, 232.
101   "Many women were very pale": *Le Petit Journal*, Nov. 24, 1889.
101   "This trunk transported": Goron, 233–34.
102   "There was last night": *L'Écho de Paris*, Nov. 24, 1889.
102   "a veritable traffic jam": *Le Gil Blas*, Nov. 24, 1889.
102   "Amid the innumerable curious": *Le Petit Journal*, Nov. 24, 1889.
102   "It took an interrogation": Goron, 234–36.
102   "Illuminated by a reddish light": *Le Petit Journal*, Nov. 28, 1889.

CHAPTER 19
104   "They are people given to": Freud, *The Letters of Sigmund Freud*, 188.
104   "as common mortals": *L'Écho de Paris*, Nov. 28, 1889.
104   "You look unhappy": *Le Petit Journal*, Nov. 27, 1889.
105   "That he has abandoned us": *Le Figaro*, Nov. 28, 1889.
106   "The magistrates": Jaume, *La Vérité sur l'Affaire Gouffé*, 39.
106   "I am nearly certain": Bouchardon, *La Malle Mystérieuse*, 134.
107   "He is capable of anything": Ibid., 137.
107   "I can still see it": Ibid., 135.
108   "The reporting rises": Jaume, 39.
108   "That's the one": *Le Figaro*, Dec. 7, 1889.
109   *"Oui, monsieur":* Ibid., Dec. 8, 1889.
109   "This is not a big thing": Jaume, 42.

CHAPTER 20
112   "Chenest is going": Jaume, *La Vérité sur l'Affaire Gouffé*, 43.
112   "I was very sick": Goron, *L'Amour Criminel*, 240.
112   "Brr!": Jaume, 44.
112   "burlesque incident": Goron, 240.
113   "May God be of aid": Ibid., 241.
113   "Do you know where": Jaume, 47–48.
114   "Oh, we'll have plenty": Goron, 243,
114   "Come. All is ready": *Le Petit Journal*, Dec. 24, 1889.
115   "From then on": Goron, 243.
115   "dreadful expression": Jaume, 48.
115   "I'm living the most": Ibid., 45.

CHAPTER 21
118   "an intelligent, honest": Jaume, *La Vérité sur l'Affaire Gouffé*, 68.
118   "I am not aware": Lacassagne, *L'Affaire Gouffé*, 75.
118   "My dear Berthe": Letter from Eyraud, Dec. 29, 1889, Archives de la Seine.
118   "You do not have": Letter from Eyraud, Dec. 31, 1889, Archives de la Seine.
119   "Murderer!": *La Presse*, Jan. 27, 1890.

CHAPTER 22
120   "Without doubt I would have lost my sight": Goron, *L'Amour Criminel*, 262.
120   "family considerations": *L'Écho de Paris*, Jan. 8, 1890.
121   "I thought I had": Goron, 245.

121   "To think that I murdered him": Ibid., 247.
121   "Ah! Monsieur, how I suffer": Ibid., 246.
121   "I cried like a baby": Ibid., 252.
121   "I am lost": Bouchardon, *La Malle Mystérieuse*, 147.
122   "I have deserted my home": Ibid., 150.
122   "I never saw that trunk again": Ibid., 146.
122   "She burst into laughter": Goron, 252.
122   "Did they find": Bouchardon, 148.
123   "We have not seen each other again": Ibid., 149.
123   "I wrote more than twenty letters": Goron, 256.
123   "Ah! Ah! I am dead": Ibid., 256–57.
123   "Her hair is now cut": Bouchardon, 150.
123   "The sadness of this creature": Goron, 257.
123   "I am not guilty": Ibid., 253.
123   "It was possible that Eyraud": Ibid., 246.
123   "His Gabrielle was taken": Ibid.

CHAPTER 23
126   "In her mind": Goron, *L'Amour Criminel*, 305.
126   "Do you have a letter": Ibid., 263–64.
126   "The prefect's bailiff": Ibid., 264.
126   "But I need to see": Ibid., 265.
127   "He is sick": Jaume, *La Vérité sur l'Affaire Gouffé*, 49–50.
127   "Tell me, Jaume": Ibid., 50.
127   "How can you be sure": Ibid.
127   "who the devil": Ibid., 51.

CHAPTER 24
128   "was a *coup de théâtre*": *Le Petit Journal*, Jan. 24, 1890.
128   "We find that": Lombroso and Ferrero, *Criminal Woman, the Prostitute, and the Normal Woman*, 191.
128   "all the characteristics": Ibid., 140.
129   "Her biggest concern": *Le Petit Journal*, Jan. 26, 1890.
129   "No one said a word": Jaume, *La Vérité sur l'Affaire Gouffé*, 51.
129   "Flowers for your madame": Ibid.
129   "Voilà": Ibid.
129   "pretty ladies": Ibid., 53.
130   "La belle Gabrielle": Ibid., 54.
130   "the least cry": *Le Petit Journal*, Jan. 26, 1890.
132   "I look spiffy": Goron, *L'Amour Criminel*, 275.
133   "One thus avoids": *Le Petit Journal*, Oct. 19, 1890.
133   "The emotion was great": Ibid., Jan. 24, 1890.
133   "It is thus now permitted": *Le Gil Blas*, Jan. 24, 1890.
133   "A man who should be": *Le Petit Journal*, Jan. 24, 1890.

CHAPTER 25
134   "We were right yesterday": *Le Gil Blas*, Jan. 24, 1889.
135   "A beautiful hat": Goron, 273.

135 **"So, little demon"**: The name *petit démon* appears in several places: *Le Gil Blas* mentions *petit démon* in an analysis of the Gouffé case on Jan. 28, 1890; the Jan. 29, 1890, *L'Écho de Paris* uses *petit démon* as the term Gouffé calls Bompard when encountering her on the street; Beaujoint calls her the pretty petite demon (in *La Malle Sanglante*, 8); Jaume also uses *petit démon* (in *La Vérité sur l'Affaire Gouffé*, 59). Goron calls chapter 15 of *L'Amour Criminel*, in which Bompard turns herself in to the prefect, "The Appearance of the Petit Démon."

136 **"Are you afraid of me?"**: Goron, 274.

136 **"What a nice necktie"**: Ibid., 345.

137 *"C'est fait"*: Ibid., 274.

137 **"a disconcerting aplomb"**: Jaume, 57.

138 **"She shows the need"**: *Le Petit Journal*, Jan. 28, 1890.

138 **"She is a suitable heroine"**: Ibid., Jan. 26, 1890.

138 **"I am especially very happy"**: Jaume, 55.

138 **"proved in the Gouffé case"**: *L'Écho de Paris*, Jan. 30, 1890.

138 **"certainly right"**: *La Presse*, Jan. 24, 1890.

CHAPTER 26

139 **"Here a cook"**: Moriarty, *The Paris Law Courts*, 246.

140 **"his role in this affair"**: *Le Gil Blas*, Jan. 24, 1890.

140 **"Eyraud had the real intention"**: Georges Garanger, police statement, Jan. 22, 1890, Archives de la Seine, 17.

141 **"voyage companion"**: Ibid., 15.

141 **"Ah, they are all like this"**: *Le Figaro*, Jan. 29, 1890.

141 **"The rascal knows men"**: Jaume, *La Vérité sur l'Affaire Gouffé*, 62.

141 **"The interest he shows"**: Ibid., 70.

141 **"a vulgar prostitute"**: Ibid.

142 **"My child!"**: *L'Écho de Paris*, Jan. 30, 1890.

142 **"The play-acting"**: Jaume, 62.

CHAPTER 27

143 **"A Criminal Heroine"**: *San Francisco Chronicle*, Feb. 7, 1890.

143 **"He Can Tell Good Brandy"**: *The Washington Post*, Mar. 16, 1890.

143 **"Ah, there's something here"**: *La Presse*, Jan. 27, 1890.

143 **"I do not hide"**: Jaume, *La Vérité sur l'Affaire Gouffé*, 74.

143 **"We have seen her in black"**: *L'Écho de Paris*, Feb. 6, 1890.

144 *"côtelette de mouton"*: *Le Figaro*, Jan. 28, 1890.

144 **"La belle Gabrielle"**: Goron, *L'Amour Criminel*, 292.

144 **"I would have never thought"**: *Le Figaro*, Jan. 30, 1890.

145 **"Gabrielle tells stories"**: Jaume, 58.

145 **"tied up Gouffé"**: Ibid., 71.

145 **"This woman is a nervous person"**: *Le Gil Blas*, Jan. 24, 1890.

145 **"offers attentive observers"**: *La Presse*, Jan. 27, 1890.

146 **"Like a globule of mercury"**: Veith, *Hysteria*, 1.

146 **"acridity in [women's] sexual organs"**: Didi-Huberman, *Invention of Hysteria*, 72.

146 **"the most unnerving impudence"**: *L'Écho de Paris*, Jan. 28, 1890.

146 "Each time I see Gabrielle": Jaume, 75.
146 "I allow that Gabrielle": Ibid., 71.
147 "Monsieur Garanger does not believe": *Le Petit Journal*, Jan. 28, 1890.
147 "She is, he says": Ibid., Jan. 26, 1890.
147 "Gabrielle submitted": *La Presse*, Jan. 27, 1890.
148 "For this reason": *The New York Times*, Feb. 22, 1903.
149 "It's a new theory": *Le Figaro*, Jan. 26, 1890.
149 "For the first time": *Le Petit Journal*, Jan. 28, 1890.
149 "These stories of hypnotism": Jaume, 77.

CHAPTER 28
150 "described how wonderful": Freud, *The Collected Papers: Vol. 1*, 11.
151 "Here, the assiduous student": Goetz et al., *Charcot—Constructing Neurology*, 12.
151 "The entire page": Ibid., 25.
152 "grand asylum": Guillain, *J. M. Charcot 1825–1893*, 35.
152 "causes presumed": Didi-Huberman, *Invention of Hysteria*, 15.
152 "Behind those walls": Ibid.
152 "museum of living pathology": Guillain, 10.
152 "While unquestionably": Ibid.
155 "What do you want": Bourneville and Regnard, *Iconographie Photographique de la Salpêtrière*, 140.
157 "For Charcot, a neurologist": Janet, *Psychological Healing*, 166.
157 "prudent and conservative": Guillain, 167.
158 "The arch of the mouth": Goetz, 272.
158 "frowning eyebrows": Guillain, 17.
158 "imperious masked face": Goetz, 268–69.
158 "Just like plays": Didi-Huberman, 243.
159 "furnished in perfect taste": *L'Écho de Paris*, Jan. 28, 1890.

CHAPTER 29
163 "Grévin must be": Schwartz, *Spectacular Realities*, 102.
163 "O glorious transitory": Ibid., 110.
164 "famous trunk": *Le Gil Blas*, Feb. 4, 1890.
164 "I was beginning to go moldy here": Jaume, *La Vérité sur l'Affaire Gouffé*, 73.
164 "Her fame is immense": Ibid.
164 "There will be a lot of people": *Le Figaro*, Feb. 7, 1890.
165 "Had they only known": Jaume, 77.
165 "They would have wanted": *Le Petit Journal*, Feb. 8, 1890.
165 "I pity Wahlen and Robert": Jaume, 76.
165 "She burst out laughing": *Le Petit Journal*, Feb. 8, 1890.
166 "Only Napoleon's entrance": Jaume, 78.
166 "So many people!": Ibid.
166 "Ah, I've had a success!": *L'Écho de Paris*, Feb. 9, 1890.
166 "There's not even a mirror": Ibid., Feb. 10, 1890.

CHAPTER 30

168   "Only . . . you were brunette": *Le Petit Journal*, Feb. 9, 1890.
168   "He threw it like one": *Le Figaro*, Feb. 9, 1890.
168   "Well, you are more gallant": Jaume, *La Vérité sur l'Affaire Gouffé*, 83.
169   "Coachman, to the palace!": *L'Express de Lyon*, Feb. 11, 1890.
169   "I didn't do anything": *Le Nouvelliste de Lyon*, Feb. 12, 1890.
169   "he had rarely seen": *Le Progrès de Lyon*, Feb. 11, 1890.
170   "We have come": *L'Express de Lyon*, Feb. 11, 1890.
170   "Should one laugh": Jaume, 83.
170   "I am enchanted": *Le Lyon Républicain*, Feb. 11, 1890.
170   "There is an unconsciousness so profound": Ibid.
170   "I did everything": Ibid., Feb. 12, 1890.
170   "I never loved him": *L'Express de Lyon*, Feb. 12, 1890.
171   "I didn't do anything": *Le Figaro*, Feb. 13, 1890.
171   "Very skillful": Jaume, 75.
171   "this sad heroine": *Le Lyon Républicain*, Feb. 11, 1890.

CHAPTER 31

172   "I was gravely ill": Goron, *L'Amour Criminel*, 261.
172   "The truth is": *Le Gil Blas*, Feb. 14, 1890.
173   "Yesterday, rumors circulated": *Le Figaro*, Feb. 13, 1890.
173   "They advertised their errand": *The New York Times*, Feb. 13, 1890.
174   "The journalists here": Letter from Soudais and Houlier, February 17, 1890, Archives de la Seine, 1583, 10.
174   "We do not yet have": Ibid., 2.
174   "At night he was heard pacing": *The New York Sun*, June 23, 1890.
174   "Except for his eyes": Interview with Florence Stout, July 5, 1890, Archives de la Seine, 1855, 2.
175   "My god!": Darmon, *La Malle à Gouffé*, 163.
175   "I will kill myself": *The New York Sun*, June 23, 1890.
175   "I have plenty of money": Interview with Florence Stout, 14.
175   "Here are dresses that cost": Ibid.
175   "I never saw such": *The New York Sun*, June 23, 1890.
176   "I shall make the story": Ibid.

CHAPTER 32

177   "This man finds himself": *L'Écho de Paris*, Mar. 8, 1890.
177   "had in his life": *Le Matin*, July 3, 1890.
178   "With a top-flight address": *L'Écho de Paris*, Mar. 8, 1890.
178   "I will buy it from you": Ibid.
179   "We have determined": Letter from Soudais and Houlier, Feb. 20, 1890, Archives de la Seine, 1585, 10.
179   "There is no less than": Letter from Soudais and Houlier, Mar. 4, 1890, Archives de la Seine, 1600, 2.
179   "Decidedly, Eyraud has": *Le Figaro*, May 2, 1890.
180   "They learned many things": Jaume, *La Vérité sur l'Affaire Gouffé*, 89.
180   "Houlier and Soudais had toured": Goron, *L'Amour Criminel*, 314.
180   "If these facts are true": *Le Gil Blas*, Apr. 18, 1890.

180   "Once more has luck": Ibid., Apr. 3, 1890.
181   "The simple expedient": *Le Radical*, Apr. 15, 1890.
181   "This man exerts such": *Le Figaro*, Mar. 9, 1890.

CHAPTER 33
182   "for these men": Harris, *Murders and Madness*, 95.
183   "He hit me": Lacassagne, *L'Affaire Gouffé*, 75.
184   "Woman is rarely wicked": Lombroso and Ferrero, *Criminal Woman, the Prostitute, and the Normal Woman*, 182.
184   "One can easily understand": Lacassagne, 69.
184   "the bright look": Ibid., 68.
185   "these acts were exactly": Ibid., 80.
185   "If a hypnotized person": *Affaire Gouffé*, 249.
185   "It did not enter": Lacassagne, 81.
186   "Gabrielle Bompard is not": Ibid., 83.

CHAPTER 34
187   "He knew by a series": *Le Figaro*, Feb. 27, 1890.
189   "All the newspapers": Transfer of Eyraud in Havana, Archives de la Seine, 1653–1654, 15.
190   "Look, the portrait of Eyraud": Ibid., 16.

CHAPTER 35
192   "Gautier, I saw you earlier": Transfer of Eyraud in Havana, Archives de la Seine, 1653–1654, 19.
193   "Again, it was this satyr's": Goron, *L'Amour Criminel*, 332.
194   "*Buenas noches*": Transfer of Eyraud in Havana, Archives de la Seine, 1653–1654, 29.
195   "Yes, monsieur": Ibid., 33.

CHAPTER 36
196   "Arrestation d'Eyraud": *Le Petit Journal*, May 23, 1890; the story of Eyraud's capture was in *The New York Herald*, May 27, 1890.
196   "This time it's not a lie": *L'Écho de Paris*, May 24, 1890.
196   "The news is very official": *Le Petit Journal*, May 23, 1890.
196   "Ah good news": *L'Écho de Paris*, May 27, 1890.
196   "Don't leave me alone": Ibid.
197   "Another sentiment": Jaume, *La Vérité sur l'Affaire Gouffé*, 92.
198   "Yes. Two thousand miles away": *The New York Herald*, June 13, 1890.
198   "Farewell, Cuba": Ibid., June 17, 1890.
198   "The world thinks": Ibid.
198   "My greatest punishment": Transfer of Eyraud in Havana, Archives de la Seine, 1653–1654, 6.
199   "The first time": *The New York Herald*, June 17, 1890.
199   "This very wise and proper": Ibid., June 30, 1890.
199   "He has nothing": Ibid., June 17, 1890.
200   "the *Lafayette*'s bugaboo": Ibid., June 30, 1890.

CHAPTER 37

201   "My trial": *The New York Herald*, June 30, 1890.
201   "Thank God": Ibid.
201   "is utterly incapable": Ibid.
202   "He presents a very pitiful": Ibid.
203   "*Le voilà!*": *Le Petit Journal*, July 1, 1890.

CHAPTER 38

205   "*Je suis cuit*": *Le Petit Journal*, July 2, 1890.
206   "Whatever one says": *Le Matin*, July 3, 1890.
207   "Permit us to remark": Ibid., July 4, 1890.
207   "If we had been captured together": Ibid.
207   "It is said that I terrorized her": Ibid., July 5, 1890.
207   "*Moi?*": Ibid.
208   "The newspapers say": *Le Petit Journal*, July 5, 1890.

CHAPTER 39

209   "She detested him": Goron, *L'Amour Criminel*, 314.
209   "It was necessary": Ibid., 310.
210   "I am reborn": Jaume, *La Vérité sur l'Affaire Gouffé*, 99.
210   "The heart of a man": Ibid.
211   "Eyraud seemed emotional": Ibid.
211   "Poor animals": *Le Matin*, July 9, 1890.
212   "I can't see this man": Jaume, 99.
212   "Some enormous contradictions exist": *Le Matin*, July 9, 1890.
212   "I did not strangle Gouffé": Jaume, 99–100.
212   "You lie, monsieur!": *Le Matin*, July 9, 1890.
213   "Eyraud strangled him": Goron, 345–46.
214   "That's true": *Le Matin*, July 9, 1889.
214   "What nerve he has!": Jaume, 100.
214   "Oh! What cheek!": Goron, 345.
214   "Gabrielle seems to have taken": *Le Matin*, July 9, 1980.
214   "How my heart beats": Ibid., July 10, 1890.
214   "He's a liar!": Ibid., July 9, 1890
215   "Do you think": Ibid., July 10, 1890.

CHAPTER 40

216   "It is true to say": *Le Petit Journal*, July 13, 1890.
216   "The Reconstruction of the Crime": complete version in Goron, *L'Amour Criminel*, 348.
216   "useless experience": *Le Matin*, July 9, 1890.
217   "Some political men": Goron, 347.
217   she begged her keepers: Jaume, *La Vérité sur l'Affaire Gouffé*, 100.
217   "Since I am suffering": *Le Matin*, July 15, 1890.
219   "Nos bons jurés": *Le Matin,* Nov. 25, 1890.
219   "Everyone has had enough": *Le Petit Journal*, Dec. 9, 1890.
220   "make Gabrielle not responsible": Jaume, 88.

CHAPTER 41

222 "The president of the Court": Moriarity, *The Paris Law Courts*, 185.

223 "veritable passion for hypnotism": *Le Petit Journal*, Dec. 12, 1890.

223 "The public waits": *Le Figaro*, Dec. 16, 1890.

223 "What a spectacle!": Jaume, *La Vérité sur l'Affaire Gouffé*, 106.

223 "They must laugh abroad": *Le Matin*, Dec. 17, 1890.

224 "Few people of real refinement": *The Royal Gazette*, Dec. 25, 1890.

224 "What countless vials": Moriarty, 181.

225 "honeyed, persuasive": Ibid., 194.

225 *"Les voici!"*: *Le Figaro*, Dec. 17, 1890.

225 *"Assis!"*: *Le Matin*, Dec. 17, 1890.

CHAPTER 42

226 "But we're missing": *Le Petit Journal*, Dec. 17, 1890.

226 "For sure!": Ibid.

226 "a furtive, hateful": *Le Matin*, Dec. 17, 1890.

226 reading of the charges: *Affaire Gouffé*, 16.

227 "To imagine the Assize": Harris, *Murders and Madness*, 212.

227 "The defendant is immediately": Ferrari, "The Procedure in the Cour d'Assises of Paris," 45–46.

227 "president of the court": *The Washington Post*, Jan. 4, 1891.

227 "All this pales": Judge Robert's examination of Eyraud can be found in *Affaire Gouffé*, 18–27.

231 "He is energetic": Jaume, *La Vérité sur l'Affaire Gouffé*, 107.

CHAPTER 43

233 "Bring back": Judge Robert's examination of Bompard and other details of the proceedings can be found in *Affaire Gouffé*, 28–40, and Locard, *La Malle Sanglante de Millery*, 8.

CHAPTER 44

240 "I am ready to prove": Details of the trial, except where otherwise noted, are from *Affaire Gouffé*, 40–73.

241 "his peregrinations": *Le Figaro*, Dec. 18, 1890.

242 "furious at the witness": Ibid.

243 "Oh Michel!": *Le Petit Journal*, Dec. 18, 1890.

243 "One defendant": *San Francisco Chronicle*, Dec. 20, 1890.

CHAPTER 45

244 "The line of flickering lights": *Le Figaro*, Dec. 19, 1890.

244 "princes of science": Ibid.

244 "Thirty witnesses": Ibid., Dec. 18, 1890.

244 "If someone bothers me": Details of the trial are from *Affaire Gouffé*, 77–90.

CHAPTER 46

248 "She became a woman": Details of the trial are from *Affaire Gouffé*, 96–101.

CHAPTER 47
252 "She was almost immediately": Details of the trial, unless otherwise noted, are from *Affaire Gouffé*, 105–10.
256 "Guards! Clear the room!": *Le Matin*, Dec. 19, 1890.
256 "Tumult. Uproar": Jaume, *La Vérité sur l'Affaire Gouffé*, 113.

CHAPTER 48
257 "They do not think": Details of the trial, unless otherwise noted, are from *Affaire Gouffé*, 110–25.
258 "We haven't finished": *Le Figaro*, Dec. 19, 1890.

CHAPTER 49
263 "Perfectly": Details of the trial, unless otherwise noted, are from *Affaire Gouffé*, 127–45.
264 "All scientific precautions": Liégeois, "Suggestion à 365 Jours D'Intervalle," 148.
267 "Hypnotic Mysteries": *Daily Inter Ocean*, Dec. 19, 1890.
267 "If Gabrielle Bompard succeeds": *San Francisco Chronicle*, Dec. 20, 1890.
268 "The theater, that's fiction": *Le Figaro*, Dec. 21, 1890.

CHAPTER 50
269 "I come to conclude": Details of the trial, unless otherwise noted, come from *Affaire Gouffé*, 146–71.
270 "the individual has committed": Ferrari, "Procedure in the Cour d'Assises of Paris," 55.

CHAPTER 51
273 "I am neither philosopher": Details of the trial are from *Affaire Gouffé*, 172–80.

CHAPTER 52
279 "Assis!": *Le Matin*, Dec. 21, 1890.
279 "Do you think": Ibid.
279 Already, his lawyer: Other posttrial information from *Le Petit Journal*, Dec. 22, 1890; *Le Matin*, Dec. 22, 1890; and *Le Petit Journal*, Dec. 23, 1890.

CHAPTER 53
281 "He is not the ferocious criminal": *Le Matin*, Dec. 31, 1890; *Le Matin* quoted Madame Eyraud's interview from *Le Gaulois*.
282 "Why did you change": *Le Matin*, Jan. 9, 1891.
283 "Strange thing!": *Le Figaro*, Feb. 4, 1891.
284 "Very well": *The Washington Post*, Feb. 4, 1891.
284 "Tell them": *Le Figaro*, Feb. 4, 1891.
284 "*C'est Eyraud qu'il nous faut*": Darmon, *La Malle à Gouffé*, 238.
285 "Your body": *Le Figaro*, Feb. 4, 1891.
285 "Constans has won his case!": *The Washington Post*, Feb. 4, 1891.
285 "I told you no": *Le Figaro*, Feb. 4, 1891.

286   "Constans is a murderer": Jaume, *La Vérité sur l'Affaire Gouffé*, 115.
286   "What a bizarre manifestation": Ibid.
286   "I'd like to see you there": Gerould, *Guillotine*, 67.
286   "On one or two occasions": Story from the *London Globe*, published in *The Washington Post*, May 6, 1883.

EPILOGUE
289   "When saying good-bye": The account of Charcot's final days is from Goetz et al., *Charcot—Constructing Neurology*, 312.
289   "For me there is a God": Ibid., 278.
290   "the 'school of the Salpêtrière'": Freud, *The Collected Papers, Vol. 1*, 14.
290   "He was not much given": Ibid., 10.
290   "hitherto neglected": Ibid., 23.
290   "He told me that his concept": Guillain, *J. M. Charcot 1825–1893*, 176.
291   "From 1887 onwards": Gauld, *A History of Hypnotism*, 336.
291   "Only the opponents": Freud, 23.
292   "In my tiny brain": Bonduelle and Gelfand, "Hysteria Behind the Scenes: Jane Avril at the Salpêtrière," 37.
292   "Like all hysterics": Hustvedt, *Medical Muses*, 138.
292   "They claim all these attacks": Bonduelle and Gelfand, 40.
293   "I know what I have just done": Krämer, *Georges Gilles de la Tourette*, 696.
293   "Within me": Ibid., 697.
294   "*Il n'y a pas d'hypnotisme*": Gauld, 562.
295   "One could have discovered": Ibid., 354.
295   "the scandal of scandals": Harriss, *The Tallest Tower*, 155.
295   "the souvenir which I": Wilkins, *Behind the French C.I.D.*, 105.
296   "a respect for": Ibid., 106.
296   "If in this unfortunate affair": Ibid., 107.
296   "might perhaps be described": Ibid., 7.
296   "he was as the French say": Ibid., 12.
297   "rectitude to avoid": Emsley, "From Ex-Con to Expert," 72.
297   "It isn't personal interest": Goron, *Les Mémoires de M. Goron*, 215.
297   "peculiar science": *The Washington Post*, Sept. 19, 1915.
298   "but her gaiety": *La Presse*, Jan. 14, 1891.
298   "If only I were sure": Ibid., June 2, 1894.
298   "she is neither resigned": *Le Journal des Débats*, Aug. 14, 1897.
298   "a model of gentility": *Le Figaro*, Oct. 30, 1897.
298   "had the most exemplary conduct": *Le Journal des Débats*, Jan. 18, 1901.
299   "face, pale and round": *Le Temps*, June 9, 1903.
299   "so he'd be interested": Ibid.
299   "Oh! A good lunch": Ibid.
299   "the petite strangler": *La Presse*, June 11, 1903.
299   "the confessed strangler": *San Francisco Chronicle*, June 29, 1903.
300   "You must fall": *Sydney Morning Herald*, Jan. 15, 1904.
301   "very weird spectacle": *The Mercury* (Hobart, Tasmania), Jan. 20, 1904.
301   "Curious about my life": *La Presse*, Dec. 17, 1903.
301   "As Christians": Ibid.

302   "What the world": *The New York Times*, Dec. 22, 1890.

303   "should this line of defense": *The Washington Post*, Apr. 3, 1891.

304   "is a middle-aged woman": *Oakland Tribune*, Jan. 7, 1912.

304   "in misery": *Le Figaro*, Dec. 10, 1920.

304   "An Unnoticed Departure": *La Presse*, Dec. 11, 1920.

Bibliography

ARCHIVES AND LIBRARIES
Archives de l'Académie des Sciences; Archives de la Préfecture de Police; Archives de la Seine; Association pour l'Histoire des Chemins de Fer; Bibliothèque Inter-universitaire de Santé; Bibliothèque Municipale de Lille; Bibliothèque Municipale de Lyon; Bibliothèque Nationale de France—Gallica, Association pour la con-servation et la reproduction photographique de la presse; Library of Congress; National Library of Medicine

NEWSPAPERS AND JOURNALS
Foreign-language: *Le Journal des Débats, Le Journal la Liberté, La Croix, La Jeune République, La Lanterne, La Petite République Française, La Presse, L'Authorité, L'Écho de Paris, L'Éclair, Le Figaro, Le Gaulois, Le Gil Blas, Le Lyon Républicain, Le Matin, Le Nouvelliste de Lyon, Le Passe-Temps, Le Petit Journal, Le Radical, Le Soleil, Le Temps, Le Voltaire, L'Express de Lyon, L'Humanité, L'Intransigeant, Le Progrès de Lyon*

English-language: *Anaconda Standard* (Montana), *Arizona Republic, Daily Inter Ocean* (Chicago), *The Evening World, Fort Worth Daily Gazette, The Mercury* (Hobart, Tasmania), *The Morning Call* (San Francisco), *The New York Her-ald, The New York Sun, The New York Times, New York Tribune, Oakland Tri-bune, Omaha Sunday Bee, Pittsburgh Dispatch, The Royal Gazette, Sacramento Daily Record-Union, St. Paul Daily Globe, The Salt Lake Herald, Sydney Morn-ing Herald, The Washington Post, The Washington Times, The Wichita Daily Eagle*

BOOKS
Affaire Gouffé: Procès Eyraud-Bompard, tiré du compte-rendu in extenso de la Gazette des tribunaux. Paris: J. Strauss, 1890.

Baldick, Robert, ed. and trans. *Lives and Letters: Pages from the Goncourt Journal.* Middlesex: Penguin Books, 1984.

Barker, Malcolm, ed. *More San Francisco Memoirs 1852–1899: The Ripening Years.* San Francisco: Londonborn Publications, 1996.

Beard, George M. *The Study of Trance, Muscle-Reading and Allied Nervous Phenom-ena in Europe and America, with a letter on the moral character of trance subjects, and a defence of Dr. Charcot.* New York: 1882.

Beaujoint, Jules (de Grandpré). *La Malle Sanglante: assassinat de l'huissier Gouffé, affaire Eyraud et Gabrielle Bompard*. Paris: A. Fayard, éditeur, 1890. Available at http://gallica.bnf.fr/ark:/12148/bpt6k5791861x.

Bérillon, Edgar, ed. *Premier Congrès International de l'Hypnotisme Expérimental et Thérapeutique: Comptes rendus*. Paris: Octave Dion, 1889.

Bernheim, Hippolyte. *Hypnosis & Suggestion in Psychotherapy: A Treatise on the Nature and Uses of Hypnotism*. Translated by Christian A. Herter. 2nd rev. ed. New York: University Books, 1965.

———. *L'Hypnotisme et la Suggestion Dans Leurs Rapports Avec la Médecine Légale*. Paris: Octave Dion, 1897.

Binet, Alfred, and Charles Féré. *Animal Magnetism*. London: Kegan Paul, Trench & Co., 1887.

Blaze De Bury, Yetta. *French Literature of To-day: Study of the Principal Romancers and Essayists*. London: Archibald & Constable, 1898.

Blum, J. L. "La Vie d'Hippolyte Bernheim." In *IIIe Colloque de la Société International d'Histoire de la Psychiatrie et de la Psychanalyse*. Caen, France: Frénésie Éditions, 1985.

Bouchardon, Pierre. *La Malle Mystérieuse*. Paris: Albin Michel, Éditeur, 1933.

Bourneville, (D. M.), and P. Regnard. *Iconographie Photographique de la Salpêtrière*. Paris: Progrès médical–A. Delahaye, 1878.

Bramwell, J. Milne. "What Is Hypnotism." In *Proceedings of the Society for Psychical Research*. Vol. 12. London: Kegan Paul, Trench, Trubner & Co., 1896.

Cambor, Kate. *Gilded Youth: Three Lives in France's Belle Époque*. New York: Farrar, Straus and Giroux, 2009.

Capildeo, Rudy. "Charcot in the 80s." *Historical Aspects of the Neurosciences*. Edited by F. Clifford Rose and W. F. Bynum. New York: Raven Press, 1981.

Carrer, Laurent. *Ambroise-Auguste Liébeault: The Hypnological Legacy of a Secular Saint*. College Station, TX: Virtualbookworm.com Publishing, 2002.

Cauquetoux, Anne. *Paris Autrefois Aujourd'hui*. Paris: Sélection du Reader's Digest, 2001.

Charcot, J. M. *Lectures on the Diseases of the Nervous System*. Translated and edited by George Sigerson. New York: New York Academy of Medicine, 1962.

Chertok, Léon, and Raymond de Saussure. *The Therapeutic Revolution: From Mesmer to Freud*. Translated by R. H. Ahrenfeldt. New York: Brunner/Mazel, 1979.

Congrès International de l'Hypnotisme 1889. Paris: Imprimerie de la Faculté de Médecine, 1889.

Corbin, Alain. *The Foul and the Fragrant: Odor and the French Social Imagination*. Cambridge, MA: Harvard University Press, 1986.

Crosland, Maurice. *Science Under Control: The French Academy of Sciences 1795–1914*. Cambridge: Cambridge University Press, 1992.

Darmon, Pierre. *La Malle à Gouffé: Le guet-apens de la Madeleine*. Paris: Éditions Denoël, 1988.

Daudet, Alphonse. *Artists' Wives.* Translated by Laura Ensor. New York: Turtle Point Press, Helen Marx Books, 2009.

———. *In the Land of Pain.* Translated and edited by Julian Barnes. New York: Alfred A. Knopf. 2002.

Daudet, Léon, and Ernest Daudet. *Memoirs of Alphonse Daudet.* Translated by Charles de Kay. Boston: Little Brown, 1898.

Delboeuf, J. *Magnétiseurs et Médecins.* Paris: Ancienne Librairie Germer Baillière, 1890.

Didi-Huberman, Georges. *Invention of Hysteria: Charcot and the Photographic Iconography of the Salpêtrière.* Translated by Alisa Hartz. Cambridge, MA: The MIT Press, 2003.

Donato, Professor. *Cours Pratique de Magie.* Macon: Alain Labussière, 1998.

Dorsey, Hebe. *Age of Opulence: The Belle Époque in the Paris Herald 1890–1914.* New York: Harry N. Abrams, 1986.

Ellenberger, Henri F. *The Discovery of the Unconscious: The History and Evolution of Dynamic Psychiatry.* New York: Basic Books, 1970.

Emsley, Clive. "From Ex-Con to Expert: The Police Detective in Nineteenth-Century France." In *Police Detectives in History: 1750–1950.* Edited by Clive Emsley and Haia Shpayer-Makov. Aldershot: Ashgate Publishing, 2006.

Evans, Colin. *The Casebook of Forensic Detection: How Science Solved 100 of the World's Most Baffling Crimes.* New York: Berkley Books, 2007.

Fisher, M. F. K. *Two Towns in Provence.* New York: Vintage Books, 1983.

Forrest, Derek. *Hypnotism: A History.* London: Penguin Books, 1999.

Forster, Robert, and Orest Ranum, eds. *Deviants and the Abandoned in French Society.* Translated by Elborg Forster and Patricia M. Ranum. Vol. IV of *Selections from the Annales: Économies, Sociétés, Civilisations.* Baltimore, MD: Johns Hopkins University Press, 1978.

Foucault, Michel. *Psychiatric Power: Lectures at the Collège de France, 1973–1974.* Translated by Graham Burchell. New York: Palgrave MacMillan, 2006.

Freud, Sigmund. *The Collected Papers: Vol. 1.* Edited by Joan Rivère, London: Hogarth Press, 1950.

———. *The Collected Papers: Vol. 5, Miscellaneous Papers 1888–1938.* Edited by James Strachey. New York: Basic Books, 1959.

———. *The Letters of Sigmund Freud.* Edited by Ernst L. Freud, translated by Tania and James Stern. New York: Basic Books, 1975.

Gauld, Alan. *A History of Hypnotism.* Cambridge: Cambridge University Press, 1995.

Gelfand, Elissa D. *Imagination in Confinement: Women's Writings from French Prisons.* Ithaca, NY: Cornell University Press, 1983.

Gerould, Daniel. *Guillotine: Its Legend and Lore.* New York: Blast Books, 1992.

Gildea, Robert. *Children of the Revolution: The French, 1799–1914.* London: Allen Lane, 2008.

Gill, Merton M., and Margaret Brenman. *Hypnosis and Related States: Psychoanalytic Studies in Regression.* New York: International Universities Press, 1961.

Gilles de la Tourette, Georges. *L'Hypnotisme et les États Analogues*. Paris: Librarie Plon, 1889.

Goetz, Christopher G., Michel Bonduelle, and Toby Gelfand. *Charcot—Constructing Neurology*. New York: Oxford University Press, 1995.

Goron, Marie-François. *L'Amour Criminel*. Paris: Ernest Flammarion, 1899.

———. *Les Mémoires de M. Goron: Ancien Chef de la Sûreté: De l'Invasion à l'Anarchie*. Paris: Ernest Flammarion, 1897.

———. *The Truth About the Case: The Experiences of M. F. Goron, Ex-Chief of the Paris Detective Police*. Edited by Albert Keyzer. Philadelphia: J. B. Lippincott, 1907.

Gribble, Leonard R. *Famous Feats of Detection and Deduction*. New York: Garden City Publishing, 1938.

Guilbert, Yvette. *The Song of My Life*. London: George G. Harrap, 1929.

Guillain, Georges. *J. M. Charcot 1825–1893: His Life—His Work*. Edited and translated by Pearce Bailey. New York: Hoeber, 1959.

Harding, James. *The Astonishing Adventure of General Boulanger*. New York: Charles Scriber's Sons, 1971.

Harrington, Anne. "Hysteria, Hypnosis, and the Lure of the Invisible: The Rise of Neo-Mesmerism in Fin-de-siècle French Psychiatry." In *The Anatomy of Madness: Essays in the History of Psychiatry*. Vol. 3. Edited by William F. Bynum, Roy Porter, and Michael Shepherd. New York, London: Routledge, 1988.

Harris, Ruth. *Dreyfus: Politics, Emotion, and the Scandal of the Century*. New York: Metropolitan Books, 2010.

———. *Murders and Madness: Medicine, Law, and Society in the Fin de Siècle*. Oxford: Clarendon Press, 1991.

———. "Murder Under Hypnosis in the Case of Gabrielle Bompard: Psychiatry in the Courtroom of Belle Époque Paris." In *The Anatomy of Madness: Essays in the History of Psychiatry*. Vol. 2. Edited by William F. Bynum, Roy Porter, and Michael Shepherd. New York, London: Routledge, 1985.

Harriss, Joseph. *The Tallest Tower: Eiffel and the Belle Epoque*. Washington, DC: Regnery Gateway, 1975.

Hilgard, Ernest R. *Hypnotic Susceptibility*. New York: Harcourt Brace Jovanovich, 1965.

Hilgard, Josephine R. *Personality and Hypnosis: A Study of Imaginative Involvement*. Second Edition. Chicago: University of Chicago Press, 1979.

Hoffman, Paul. *Wings of Madness: Alberto Santos-Dumont and the Invention of Flight*. New York: Theia, 2003.

Houdré, Bénédicte. *Petit Voyage: Lille*. Paris: Lonely Planet, 2007.

Hussey, Andrew. *Paris: The Secret History*. New York: Bloomsbury, 2006.

Hustvedt, Asti. *Medical Muses: Hysteria in Nineteenth-Century Paris*. New York: W. W. Norton, 2011.

Institut de France. *Index Biographique de L'Académie des Sciences 1665–1978*. Paris: Gauthier-Villars, 1979.

Janet, Pierre. *Psychological Healing: A Historical and Clinical Study.* Translated by Eden and Cedar Paul. London: Allen & Unwin, 1925.

Jaume, Pierre-Fortune. *La Vérité sur l'Affaire Gouffé.* Paris: Librairie Ollendorf, 1909.

Johnston, Roy. *Parisian Architecture of the Belle Époque.* Chichester, West Sussex: Wiley-Academy, 2007.

Jonnes, Jill. *Eiffel's Tower.* New York: Viking, 2009.

Jordan, David P. *Transforming Paris: The Life and Labors of Baron Haussmann.* New York: The Free Press, 1995.

Knapp, Bettina, and Myra Chipman. *That Was Yvette: The Biography of Yvette Guilbert, the Great Diseuse.* New York: Holt, Rinehart and Winston, 1964.

Krämer, Hermann. *Georges Gilles de la Tourette: Life and Work.* Translated by Christine Daniels. Accessed May 8, 2013, at www.tourette.org.au/biographydrtourette .pdf.

Lacassagne, Alexandre. *L'Affaire Gouffé: Acte d'accusation, Rapports de MM. les Drs. Paul Bernard, Lacassagne, Brouardel, Mottet et Ballet—Documents divers.* Paris: G. Masson, 1891.

La Leçon de Charcot: Voyage Dans Une Toile. Paris: Musée de l'Assistance Publique de Paris, 1986.

L'Aulnaye, Rémy de. *Les Confessions Secrètes de Gabrielle Bompard.* Lille: Librarie Populaire Hayard, 1890. Courtesy of Bibliothèque Municipale de Lille.

Laurence, Jean-Roch, and Campbell Perry. *Hypnosis, Will, and Memory: A Psycho-Legal History.* New York: Guilford Press, 1988.

Liégeois, Jules. *De la Suggestion et du Somnambulisme: Dans leurs rapports avec la jurisprudence et la médecine légale.* Paris: Octave Doin, 1889.

Liston, Robert. *Great Detectives: Famous Real-life Sleuths and Their Most Baffling Cases.* New York: Platt & Munk, 1966.

Locard, E. *La Malle Sanglante de Millery.* Paris: Gallimard, 1934.

Lombroso, Cesare, and Guglielmo Ferrero. *Criminal Woman, the Prostitute, and the Normal Woman.* Translated by Nicole Hahn Rafter and Mary Gibson. Durham, NC: Duke University Press, 2004.

Martin, Benjamin F. *The Hypocrisy of Justice in the Belle Epoque.* Baton Rouge: Louisiana State University, 1984.

Maurier, George du. *Trilby.* New York: Oxford University Press, 1995.

McAuliffe, Mary. *Dawn of the Belle Epoque.* Lanham, MD: Rowman & Littlefield, 2011.

Merz, John Theodore. *A History of European Scientific Thought in the Nineteenth Century.* Vol. I. New York: Dover Publications, 1965.

Micale, Mark S. *Approaching Hysteria: Disease and Its Interpretations.* Princeton, NJ: Princeton University Press, 1995.

"Michel Eyraud et Gabrielle Bompard." In *Revue des Grands Procès Contemporains.* Vol. IX. Edited by Gaston Lèbre. Paris: Chevalier-Marescq, 1891.

Moll, Albert. *Hypnotism.* New York: Scribner and Welford, 1890.

Morain, Alfred. *The Underworld of Paris: Secrets of the Sûreté*. New York: Blue Ribbon Books, 1931.

Moriarty, Gerald P., ed. and trans. *The Paris Law Courts: Sketches of Men and Manners*. New York: Charles Scribner's Sons, 1894.

Morton, James. *The First Detective: The Life and Revolutionary Times of Eugene Vidocq: Criminal, Spy, and Private Eye*. New York: Overlook Press, 2004.

Motte, Dean de la, and Jeannene M. Przyblyski, eds. *Making the News: Modernity & the Mass Press in Nineteenth-Century France*. Amherst: University of Massachusetts Press, 1999.

Munthe, Axel. *The Story of San Michele*. New York: E. P. Dutton & Co., 1929.

Néaumet, Jean-Émile. *Un flic à la Belle Époque: Anarchistes, assassins mondains, et scandales politiques*. Paris: Editions Albin Michel SA, 1998.

Nicolas, Serge. *L'Hypnose: Charcot face à Bernheim*. Paris: L'Harmattan, 2004.

Nohain, Jean, and F. Caradec. *Le Pétomane*. Los Angeles: Sherbourne Press, 1967.

Nye, Mary Jo. *Science in the Provinces: Scientific Communities and Provincial Leadership in France, 1860–1930*. Berkeley: University of California Press, 1986.

Owen, A. R. G. *Hysteria, Hypnosis and Healing: The Work of J.-M. Charcot*. New York: Garrett Publications, 1971.

Pessis, Jacques, and Jacques Crépineau. *The Moulin Rouge*. Edited by Andrew Lamb. New York: St. Martin's Press, 1989.

Poirier, René. *The Fifteen Wonders of the World*. Translated by Margaret Crosland. New York: Random House, 1961.

Read, Piers Paul. *The Dreyfus Affair: The Scandal That Tore France in Two*. New York: Bloomsbury Press, 2012.

Rearick, Charles. *Paris Dreams, Paris Memories: The City and Its Mystique*. Stanford, CA: Stanford University Press, 2011.

———. *Pleasures of the Belle Époque: Entertainment & Festivity in Turn-of-the-Century France*. New Haven, CT: Yale University Press, 1985.

Richardson, Joanna. *The Bohemians: La Vie de Bohème in Paris 1830–1914*. South Brunswick, NJ: A. S. Barnes and Company, 1971.

Riese, Walther. *The Legacy of Philippe Pinel*. New York: Springer Publishing Company, 1969.

Robb, Graham. *Parisians: An Adventure History of Paris*. New York: W. W. Norton & Company, 2010.

Rudorff, Raymond. *Belle Époque: Paris in the Nineties*. London: Hamish Hamilton, 1972.

Saint-Germain, Comte C de. *Practical Hypnotism: Theories and Experiments*. (Originally published in 1901.) Whitefish, MT: Kessinger Publishing Reprints, 2007.

Schwartz, Vanessa R. *Spectacular Realities: Early Mass Culture in Fin-de-Siècle Paris*. Berkeley: University of California Press, 1999.

Seigel, Jerrold. *Bohemian Paris: Culture, Politics, and the Boundaries of Bourgeois Life, 1830–1930*. Baltimore, MD: Johns Hopkins University Press, 1986.

Shapiro, Ann-Louise. *Breaking the Codes: Female Criminality in Fin-de-Siècle Paris*. Stanford, CA: Stanford University Press, 1996.

Shattuck, Roger. *The Banquet Years: The Origins of the Avant-Garde in France 1885 to World War I*. New York: Vintage Books, 1968.

Shercliff, Jose. *Jane Avril of the Moulin Rouge*. London: Jarrolds Publishers, 1952.

Skinner, Cornelia Otis. *Elegant Wits and Grand Horizontals*. Cambridge, MA: The Riverside Press, 1962.

Starr, Douglas. *The Killer of Little Shepherds: A True Crime Story and the Birth of Forensic Science*. New York: Alfred A. Knopf, 2010.

Stead, Philip John. *The Police of Paris*. London: Staples Press Ltd, 1957.

Sweetman, David. *Explosive Acts: Toulouse-Lautrec, Oscar Wilde, Félix Fénéon, and the Art & Anarchy of the Fin de Siècle*. New York: Simon & Schuster, 1999.

Taylor, Katherine Fischer. *In the Theater of Criminal Justice: The Palais de Justice in Second Empire Paris*. Princeton, NJ: Princeton University Press, 1993.

Thorwald, Jürgen. *The Century of the Detective*. New York: Harcourt, Brace & World, 1965.

Tuchman, Barbara W. *The Proud Tower: A Portrait of the World Before the War, 1890–1914*. New York: Ballantine Books, 1994.

Vallery-Radot, René. *The Life of Pasteur*. Translated by R. L. Devonshire. Garden City, NY: Doubleday Page, 1923.

Veith, Ilza. *Hysteria: The History of a Disease*. Chicago: University of Chicago Press, 1965.

Vizetelly, Ernest Alfred. *Paris and Her People Under the Third Republic*. London: Chatto & Windus, 1919.

Walmsley, D. M. *Anton Mesmer*. London: Hall Press, 1967.

Waterfield, Robin. *Hidden Depths: The Story of Hypnosis*. New York: Brunner-Routledge, 2003.

Weber, Eugen. *France: Fin de Siècle*. Cambridge, MA: Belknap Press of Harvard University Press, 1986.

Weiner, Dora B. *The Citizen-Patient in Revolutionary and Imperial Paris*. Baltimore, MD: Johns Hopkins University Press, 1993.

Weiner, William J., and Christopher G. Goetz, eds. *Neurology for the Non-Neurologist*. 2nd ed. Philadelphia: J. B. Lippincott, 1989.

Wilkins, Philip A., ed. and trans. *Behind the French C.I.D.: Leaves from the Memoirs of Goron, Former Detective Chief*. London: Hutchinson, 1941.

Willms, Johannes. *Paris, Capital of Europe: From the Revolution to the Belle Époque*. New York: Holmes & Meier, 1997.

Wolfe, H. Ashton, and Edmond Locard. *The Invisible Web: Strange Tales of the French Sûreté*. Tiptree, Essex: Hurst and Blackett, 1929.

Wright, Gordon. *Notable or Notorious: A Gallery of Parisians*. Cambridge, MA: Harvard University Press, 1991.

JOURNALS

Aguayo, Joseph Richard. "Freud and His Mentors: The Clinical Construction of Hysteria 1885–1905." PhD dissertation, University of California, Los Angeles, 1995.

Bonduelle, Michel. "Charcot Intime." *Revue Neurologique* 150, 8–9 (1994): 524–28.

———. "Léon Daudet, mémorialiste de Charcot." *La Revue du Practicien 49* (1999): 804–7.

Bonduelle, Michel, and Toby Gelfand. "Hysteria Behind the Scenes: Jane Avril at the Salpêtrière." *Journal of the History of the Neurosciences* 7, 1 (1998): 35–42.

Bramwell, J. Milne. "What Is Hypnotism." *Proceedings of the Incorporated Society for Psychical Research* XXX, XII (June 1896): 234–41.

Charcot, Jean-Martin. "Accidents hystériques graves survenus chez une femme à la suite d'hypnotisations." *Revue de l'Hypnotisme* (1889–1890): 3–13.

Chertok, Léon. "Freud in Paris: A Crucial Stage." *The International Journal of Psycho-Analysis* 51 (1970): 511–20.

———. "Theory of Hypnosis Since the First International Congress, 1889." *American Journal of Psychotherapy* XXI, 1 (January 1967): 62–73.

Daudet, Alphonse. "At the Salpêtrière—A Reminiscence by a Medical Student." *Journal of Balneology and Climatology* ix (1905): 241–47.

Ferrari, Robert. "The Procedure in the Cour d'Assises of Paris." *Columbia Law Review* 18, 1 (1918): 43–62.

Gelfand, Toby. "Charcot and Freud Revisited." *XXXI Congresso Internazionale di Storia della Medicina* (September 4, 1988): 459–65.

———. "Charcot's Brains." *Brain and Language* 69 (1999): 31–55.

———. "Neurologist or Psychiatrist? The Public and Private Domains of Jean-Martin Charcot." *Journal of the History of the Behavioral Sciences* 36, 3 (Summer 2000): 215–29.

Gilles de la Tourette, Georges. "L'Affaire Gouffé: XII L'Epilogue d'un procès célèbre." *Archives d'Anthropologie Criminelle* 6 (1891): 179–205.

———. "Sociétés Savantes: Société de Médecine Légale, Séance de 10 décembre." *Revue de l'Hypnotisme* (1888–1889): 219–21.

Goetz, Christopher G. "Charcot in Contemporary Literature." *Journal of the History of the Neurosciences* 15 (2006): 22–30.

———. "Shakespeare in Charcot's Neurologic Teaching." *Archives of Neurology* 45, 8 (Aug. 1988): 920–21.

Harrington, Anne. "Metals and magnets in medicine: hysteria, hypnosis and medical culture in fin-de-siècle Paris." *Psychological Medicine* 18 (1988): 21–38.

Harris, James C. "A Clinical Lesson at the Salpêtrière." *Archives of General Psychiatry* 62 (May 2005): 470–72.

Hillman, Robert C. "A Scientific Study of Mystery: The Role of the Medical and Popular Press in the Nancy-Salpêtrière Controversy on Hypnotism." *Bulletin of the History of Medicine* 39 (1965): 163–82.

Iragui, Vincente J. "History of Neurology: The Charcot-Bouchard Controversy." *Archives of Neurology* 43 (March 1986): 290–95.

Krämer, H. "Pioneers of Movement Disorders: Georges Gilles de la Tourette." Translated by C. Daniels. *Journal of Neural Transmission* 111 (March 19, 2004): 691–701.

Lanska, Douglas J., and James M. Edmonson. "The Suspension Therapy for Tabes Dorsalis: A Case History of a Therapeutic Fad." *Archives of Neurology* 47 (June 1990): 701–4.

Laurent, Émile. "Les Suggestions Criminelles." *Archives d'Anthropologie Criminelle* 5 (1890): 596–641.

Leblanc, André. "Thirteen Days: Joseph Delboeuf Versus Pierre Janet on the Nature of Hypnotic Suggestion." *Journal of the History of the Behavioral Sciences* 40, 2 (Spring 2004): 123–47.

Liégeois, Jules. "Des expertises médico-legales en matière hypnotisme recherche de l'auteur d'une suggestion criminelle." *Revue de l'Hypnotisme et de la Psychologie Physiologique* (1887–1888): 3–8.

———. "Hypnotisme Téléphonique—Suggestions à Grande Distance." *Revue de l'Hypnotisme: Expérimental et Thérapeutique* 1 (July 1, 1886): 19–24.

———. "Suggestion à 365 Jours D'Intervalle." *Revue de l'Hynotisme: Expérimental et Thérapeutique* 1 (November 1, 1886): 148–50.

Micale, Mark S. "The Salpêtrière in the Age of Charcot: An Institutional Perspective on Medical History in the Late Nineteenth Century." *Journal of Contemporary History* 20 (1985): 703–31.

Nicolas, Serge. "L'école de Nancy et l'école de la Salpêtrière en 1890 à l'occasion du procès Eyraud-Bompard suivi de: Hippolyte Bernheim 'Hypnotisme et suggestion: doctrine de la Salpêtrière et doctrine de Nancy' 1891." *Bulletin de Psychologie* 55, 4 (July–August 2002): 409–19.

Plas, Régine. "Hysteria, Hypnosis, and Moral Sense in French 19th-Century Forensic Psychiatry: The Eyraud-Bompard Case." *International Journal of Law and Psychiatry* 21, 4 (1998): 397–407.

Riskin, Joy Dana, and Fred Frankel. "A History of Medical Hypnosis." *History of Psychiatry* 17, 3 (September 1994): 601–9.

Thompson, Vance. "The Thief-Takers of Paris." *Everybody's Magazine* XV, 4 (October 1906), 456–64.

Illustration Credits